THE STRANGE CAREER OF LEGAL LIBERALISM

THE STRANGE CAREER
OF LEGAL LIBERALISM

LAURA KALMAN

YALE UNIVERSITY PRESS   NEW HAVEN AND LONDON

IN MEMORY OF MELANIE MANN BRONFMAN

AND WESTLAKE SCHOOL

PUBLISHED WITH ASSISTANCE FROM THE MARY CADY TEW MEMORIAL FUND.

DESIGNED BY SONIA L. SCANLON
SET IN SABON WITH COPPERPLATE DISPLAY TYPE BY RAINSFORD
TYPE, DANBURY, CONNECTICUT.
PRINTED IN THE UNITED STATES OF AMERICA BY
BOOKCRAFTERS, INC., CHELSEA, MICHIGAN.

LIBRARY OF CONGRESS CATALOGING-IN-PUBLICATION DATA
KALMAN, LAURA, 1955–
THE STRANGE CAREER OF LEGAL LIBERALISM / LAURA KALMAN.
P. CM.
INCLUDES BIBLIOGRAPHICAL REFERENCES AND INDEX.
ISBN 0-300-06369-5 (ALK. PAPER)
1. UNITED STATES—CONSTITUTIONAL LAW—PHILOSOPHY.
2. UNITED STATES—CONSTITUTIONAL LAW—INTERPRETATION AND
CONSTRUCTION. 3. LIBERALISM—UNITED STATES—HISTORY—20TH
CENTURY. 4. LAW—UNITED STATES—METHODOLOGY—
HISTORY. I. TITLE.
KF4552.K35 1996
342.73'001—DC20
[347.30201] 95-47297
CIP

A CATALOGUE RECORD FOR THIS BOOK IS AVAILABLE FROM THE BRITISH LIBRARY.

THE PAPER IN THIS BOOK MEETS THE GUIDELINES FOR PERMANENCE
AND DURABILITY OF THE COMMITTEE ON PRODUCTION GUIDELINES
FOR BOOK LONGEVITY OF THE COUNCIL ON LIBRARY RESOURCES.

10 9 8 7 6 5 4 3 2 1

CONTENTS

ACKNOWLEDGMENTS

Many people have helped me with this book, though none should be blamed for its errors or polemics. I thank Joyce Appleby, Robert Gordon, Hendrik Hartog, Linda Kerber, Martha Minow, and Avi Soifer for commenting on portions of it. I am grateful to Gregory Alexander, Bernard Bailyn, J. M. Balkin, John Blum, Rena Fraden, Jon Glickstein, Morton Horwitz, Sanford Levinson, Frank Michelman, William E. Nelson, David M. Rabban, Jack Rakove, John Reid, John Henry Schlegel, Mark Tushnet, G. Edward White, Joan Williams, and Rosemarie Zagarri for reading the entire manuscript and making many helpful suggestions. I am also obliged to colleagues and friends: Ahkil Amar, Patricia Bagley, Mia Bay, W. Elliot Brownlee, Wallace Chafe, Bill Felstiner, Hope Firestone, Jamie Gracer, Susan Hunt, Leslie Jacobs, the late Robert Kelley, W. Davies King, Alan Liu, David Marshall, Ken McCann, Sears McGee, Marianne Mithun, Harry Scheiber, John Schweizer, Judy Shanks, Cybelle Shattuck, Linny Kammer Smith, Ray Solomon, Clyde Spillenger, Meg Taradash, and Candace Waid. Then there is my family: Celeste

Garr, Lee Kalman, and Newton Kalman. Most of all, I thank W. Randall Garr.

I benefited from opportunities to present this work at the law schools of Harvard University, the University of Texas, and the University of Wisconsin; at the history department of Harvard University; and at Harvard's Charles Warren Center for Studies in American History. I greatly appreciate the financial support provided by the University of California, Santa Barbara, Interdisciplinary Humanities Center, and especially the Warren Center.

I thank my manuscript editor, Ruth Veleta, and, at Yale University Press, I thank Otto Bohlman, Charles Grench, Mary Pasti, and especially Cynthia Wells.

Next to working with John Blum, I most enjoyed learning at Westlake School. Smart, funny, and kind, Melanie Mann Bronfman personified what I remember about the school at its best. To her memory and that of Westlake I dedicate this book.

FAITH OF OUR FATHERS

Faith of our fathers! Living still
In spite of dungeon, fire, and sword:
O how our hearts beat high with joy,
Whene'r we hear that glorious word:
Faith of our fathers, holy faith!
We will be true to thee till death.
Episcopalian Hymnal, no. 558 (1982)

This book grew out of my insomnia. For years I staved off wakefulness by reading law reviews. One article in the middle of the night seemed the best soporific. Law review articles no longer serve my purpose: they have become too interesting.

Why? Law professors, who have long ignored the work of historians as important as Charles Beard and Richard Hofstadter, now seem fascinated by them. The debate between Gordon Wood and J. G. A. Pocock is refought in the law reviews. Even more important, legal scholars have enlisted history, as they have drafted other disciplines, in their battle on behalf of legal liberalism.

I use the term *legal liberalism* to refer to trust in the potential of courts, particularly the Supreme Court, to bring about "those specific social reforms that affect large groups of people such as blacks, or workers, or women, or partisans of a particular persuasion; in other words, *policy change with nationwide impact*." Because of the nation's experience with the Warren Court, legal liberalism has been linked to political liberalism since midcentury.[1] The Warren Court established its reputation as liberal bastion in 1954, when it declared school segregation unconstitutional in *Brown* v. *Board of Education*. "I suppose that realistically the reason this case is here was that action couldn't be obtained from Congress," Justice Jackson observed during oral argument of *Brown*. "[W]e must always remember that it was the Court, not Congress or the President, that put an end to official segregation in this country," one federal appellate judge stressed forty years later. "It was the Court, not any other branch of government that for the first time gave meaning to the phrase 'with liberty and justice for all.' " Or, as one law school dean put it, *Brown* "created a societal commitment, launching a value that was before in every meaningful sense unreal." Those who appreciated it believed that *Brown* placed "the quest for racial justice . . . historically, socially, and politically at the center of the quest for constitutional meaning."[2]

For law professors and other liberals, *Brown* was the "paradigmatic event." *Brown* represented "*the* turning point in terms of people's conception of what the law could do," A. E. Dick Howard emphasized. "Where medieval societies had morality plays, we had *Brown*." To a generation of lawyers, *Brown* served as "a sign that law (and therefore we) could play a part in building a better society." The historian C. Vann Woodward later described the reaction to the *Brown* decision in the South as one of "incredulity . . . the Supreme Court was demanding the impossible." But at the time Woodward thought the Court had made the inconceivable attainable. "A unanimous decision, it has all the moral and legal authority of the Supreme Court behind it, and it is unthinkable that it can be indefinitely evaded," he proclaimed in *The Strange Career of Jim Crow*. As the Court reached other, more difficult decisions over the next fifteen years, liberal law professors' and social reformers' faith in the transformative power of the Warren Court grew even stronger.[3]

In 1991, Professor Owen Fiss provided a classic description of the Warren Court's accomplishments:

In the 1950's, America was not a pretty sight. Blacks were systematically disenfranchised and excluded from juries. State-fostered religious practices, like school prayers, were pervasive. Legislatures were grossly gerrymandered and malapportioned. McCarthyism stifled radical dissent, and the jurisdiction of the censor over matters considered obscene or libelous had no constitutional limits. The heavy hand of the law threatened those who publicly provided information and advice concerning contraceptives, thereby imperiling those most intimate of human relationships. The states virtually had a free hand in the administration of justice. Trials often proceeded without counsel or jury. Convictions were allowed to stand even though they turned on illegally seized evidence or on statements extracted from the accused under coercive circumstances. There were no rules limiting the imposition of the death penalty. These practices victimized the poor and disadvantaged, as did the welfare system, which was administered in an arbitrary and oppressive manner. The capacity of the poor to participate in civic activities was also limited by the imposition of poll taxes, court filing fees, and the like.

These were the challenges that the Warren Court took up and spoke to in a forceful manner. The result was *a program of constitutional reform almost revolutionary in its aspiration and, now and then, in its achievements.* Of course the Court did not act in a political or social vacuum. It drew on broad-based social formations like the civil rights and welfare rights movement. At critical junctures, the Court looked to the executive and legislative branches for support. . . . Yet the truth of the matter is that it was the Warren Court that spurred the great changes to follow, and inspired and protected those who sought to implement them.[4]

The same year Fiss wrote, a political scientist was publishing different conclusions. In his 1991 book *The Hollow Hope: Can Courts Bring about Social Change?* Gerald Rosenberg said: "Growing up in the 1960s in a liberal New York City household, I naturally looked to the Supreme Court, identifying it with important liberal decisions." As Rosenberg matured, however, he came to doubt the ability of courts to "produce liberal social change" that would transform society. In *The Hollow Hope,* he presented data to argue that they "almost never" could. Though little empirical evidence had appeared on the Court's role in fostering social reform before he wrote, some readers found Rosenberg's conclusion unsurprising. According to one academic, it is "rather obvious that asking courts to be the engine of fundamental social change in our complex society makes as little sense as using a word processor to cook dinner, or a hair dryer to spray-paint a house: It is simply not the job the machine was designed to do." Rosenberg has suggested such skeptics accompany him on "some of my law school presentations. That old dead horse of judicial efficacy rears up with a vengeance that is sometimes quite frightening."[5]

Many Americans do continue to see the Court as the great engine of social change. True, on the fortieth anniversary of the first decision in *Brown,* one journalist concluded: "For an earlier generation, the Supreme Court's majestic *Brown* decision illuminated a path to equality through the dismantling of segregation. Today, *Brown*'s beacon has dimmed, and in the gloom lurks the fear that no one knows which road now leads to racial reconciliation." Likewise, in 1995, the fortieth anniversary of *Brown II*—the decision ordering the implementation of school desegregation in the South "with all deliberate speed"—it seems obvious there was no speed whatsoever. At least through the Bork battle, however, Americans retained their obsession with the power of the Supreme Court. Why else would they take the Bork nomination so seriously? And most liberal law professors have continued to make *Brown* their lighthouse. Cass Sunstein has observed that they have remained under "the spell of the Warren Court," their faith in it religious and mystical. Their trust in the power of the Court has helped to make constitutional law "the most prestigious field in the legal academy."[6]

In this book, I do not address the question of whether courts can transform society, an issue that has proven of greater interest to political scientists than academic lawyers. Rather, I focus on how law professors have kept the faith in what has been called "the cult of the Court," defined here as confidence in the ability of courts to change society for what judges believe is the better. Legal scholars have remained members of that cult, despite their changing attitude toward the Supreme Court and their anxiety about judicial activism.[7]

Associated with conservative justices who enacted their personal prejudices into law in cases such as *Lochner* v. *New York* (1905), when they struck down regulatory legislation on the grounds it interfered with the "liberty to contract" that the Fourteenth Amendment's due process clause allegedly granted workers, judicial activism initially seemed the child of substantive due process. That doctrine, it was always emphasized, gave judges unusual power. "For the benefit of laymen, Substantive Due Process is the idea that the Court can hold legislation unconstitutional on the ground that the legislature lacked a rational basis for enacting it," one law professor explained in the *New York Times*. Or, as another said, when the Court did "the substantive due process thing," it substituted its judgment for the legislature's. Although substantive due process faded for a time after the constitutional crisis of the 1930s, which culminated in Roosevelt's 1937 attempt to pack the Supreme Court, judicial activism did not. Once the legal realists had questioned the existence of principled decision making, academic lawyers spent the rest of the twentieth century searching for criteria that would enable them to identify objectivity in judicial decisions. "By objectivity I mean that quality of a rule of law which enables it to be applied to similar situations with similar results regardless of the identity of the judges who apply it," one student of the realists explained. That seemingly simple attribute had come to seem elusive, because both the realists and the constitutional crisis had raised the possibility that all judicial opinions, not just those that favored the rich through invocation of neutral-sounding terms such as "liberty to contract" or "substantive due process," were inherently idiosyncratic.[8]

As they struggled to identify how objective judicial decisions should be reached, liberal law professors faced a new obstacle, the Warren Court. In retrospect, the Warren Court came at a bad time for liberal law professors. Though they revered the Warren Court as much as they had reviled the *Lochner* Court, and though many of their students celebrated Warren Court activism, the mission they had set themselves by the time Earl Warren arrived in Washington forced an older generation of law professors to try to prove the decisions of his Court were based on objective foundations of justice. While *Brown* became the seminal decision for a new generation of legal scholars coming to maturity, the task of their elders, who remembered 1937, became difficult during the Warren years. *Brown* spurred the development of both liberal judicial activism and contemporary constitutional theory. For the legal liberals who loved the Warren Court's results, if not its reasoning, and who dominated the law professorate between the New Deal and the Vietnam War, the Warren Court starkly posed "the counter-majoritarian difficulty," the dilemma of legitimating an appointed judiciary in a democracy.[9]

Even after the Warren Court passed into history in 1969, law professors continued to rely on the Court. Abortion rights, for one example, had no better chance of success in the legislatures than school desegregation. Despite widespread sympathy for pregnant women who had consumed thalidomide or contracted German measles, and who sought abortions because they feared birth defects, the reformers working to legalize therapeutic abortions had been successful in only three states by 1967. Even those victories were largely Pyrrhic because the new reform laws proved restrictive, and hospitals and doctors conservative in implementing them. As David Garrow saw in his history of *Roe* v. *Wade,* "more and more signs began to appear that the passage of reform bills might actually serve to illuminate the inadequacy of therapeutic reform and the preferability of the seemingly far more radical step of repeal." Repeal bills rarely survived the legislative process, although in 1970 legislatures finally repealed abortion laws in Hawaii, New York, and Alaska, and a popular referendum on abortion repeal succeeded in Washington. Consequently, the emphasis shifted from "lobbying for reform to litigating for repeal." By 1969, Garrow found, "federal litigation was where almost all of the activists believed the real breakthroughs would come." The first abortion case was filed in federal court in 1969, and soon over twenty cases were on their way to the Supreme Court. *Roe* v. *Wade,* the 1973 case in which Justice Harry Blackmun struck down every abortion law in the country, declaring that during the first trimester of pregnancy, abortion was a fundamental right, "whether it be founded in the Fourteenth Amendment's concept of personal liberty and restrictions upon state action, as we feel it is, or as the District Court determined, in the Ninth Amendment's reservation of rights to the people," was just one of them.[10]

For a new generation of academic lawyers, and for some of their elders, too, *Roe* became a defining case. Professor Pamela Karlan, a 1984 law school graduate, stressed that "*Roe* v. *Wade* has served as a lightning rod for modern constitutional law; it is the *Brown* v. *Board of Education* of our generation."[11] The reappearance of substantive due process as a tool of judicial authority in 1973, at a time when liberal legal scholars were struggling to rationalize the Warren Court while guarding against conservative judicial activism, seemed to threaten the legitimacy of the Warren Court. Though they appreciated the legalization of abortion, many law professors despised the Court's appeal to substantive due process in *Roe* and argued that the Court had dodged its duty to ground the right in the Constitution. In a comment rushed to print in the 1973 *Yale Law Journal,* John Hart Ely, one of the Warren Court's staunchest defenders, attacked *Roe* not because it was "bad constitutional law" but because it was "*not* constitutional law and gives almost no sense of an obligation to try to be":

> What is frightening about *Roe* is that this super-protected right is not inferable from the language of the Constitution, the framers' thinking respecting the specific problem in any issue, any general value derivable from the provisions they included, or the nation's governable structure. Nor is it explainable in terms of the unusual political impotence of the group judicially protected vis-à-vis the interest that legislatively prevailed over it. And that, I believe— the predictable early reaction to *Roe* notwithstanding ("more of the same Warren-type activism")—is a charge that can responsibly be leveled at no other decision of the past twenty years. At times the inferences the Court has drawn from the values the Constitution marks for special protection have been controversial, even shaky, but never before has its sense of an obligation to draw one been so obviously lacking.[12]

At least Ely liked the results in *Roe*. "Were I a legislator," he conceded, "I would vote for a statute very much like the one the Court ended up drafting." As the years passed, and the Court became more conservative, law professors from various generations found its results as dissatisfying as its reasoning. While Americans increasingly came to see the Court as arbiter of divisive cultural issues, academic lawyers became more distant from the Court and openly hostile to it. This shift was apparent on the right, where, for example, Stephen Presser lamented that the Supreme Court had "lost its way" and condemned it as "the institution that led us into our present wilderness of the spirit." The negative mood was especially evident left of center, where Yale Law School dean Guido Calabresi (now a federal appellate court judge) used the op-ed page of the *New York Times* to declare in 1991: "I despise the current Supreme Court and find its aggressive, willful, statist behavior disgusting."[13]

Yet Calabresi, Ely, and other legal liberals of all ages operate in a twilight zone where Earl Warren receives artificial life support. A recent law review article began: "Earl Warren is dead. A generation of liberal legal scholars continues, nevertheless, to act as if the man and his Court preside over the present." Meanwhile new political perspectives and insights borrowed from other disciplines have led young law professors to question the future of legal liberalism.[14]

Recently, some liberal law professors have reacted to what they perceive as a crisis of legal liberalism by turning to other disciplines themselves. Some have embraced history. The discovery by liberal legal scholars of an eighteenth-century republicanism they can attribute to the Founders responds to the exaltation by conservatives of "original intent." Ironically, and despite the promise it holds out of a virtuous citizenry pursuing communitarian goals, the republican revival in the hands of some law professors attempts to recapture an improved version of the legal and political liberalism that characterized the law school world of the 1960s.

Who are the republican revivalists? "After almost two hundred years, Thomas Jefferson has been proven right: We are all republicans now," one law professor announced in 1995. In fact, not all law professors subscribe to the republican revival. Law professors differ over the identities of republican revivalists, beyond ascribing to them a political location left of center, as much as they disagree about those of the legal realists. Though I would not classify all on it as republican revivalists, my own list of people whose work has been deeply influenced by the republican revival and whose work has significantly affected the way the legal academy understands the republican revival includes Bruce Ackerman, Ahkil Amar, and Owen Fiss of Yale; Sanford Levinson of Texas;

Frank Michelman of Harvard; Suzanna Sherry of Minnesota; Cass Sunstein of Chicago; at times, Gregory Alexander of Cornell; and two legal historians, Morton Horwitz of Harvard and Mark Tushnet of Georgetown.[15]

The republican revivalists' turn to history holds both promise and peril. Soon after the Court handed down decisions that may signal an effort to return the federal government and the interpretation of the Commerce clause to their contours before the New Deal, Linda Greenhouse wrote that conservatives on the Court who are "[b]lowing the dust off the Constitution that was" hope to turn back the clock. History, one of the weapons used by conservatives, can be turned against them. The reorientation toward history holds peril because when law professors colonize other disciplines, they leave themselves open to being judged by different methodological standards. Liberal legal scholars who "abuse" history undermine their credibility. Though this book is one legal liberal's intellectual history of legal liberalism, it does contain an explicitly normative element. I suggest that historians inside and outside the law schools have something to say to academic lawyers, and that both lawyers and historians would benefit from the interchange. I also argue that historians should recognize that the historic turn represents a sensible strategy for legal liberals and that law professors, who yearn for validation from the rest of the academy, should not curry favor with historians by abandoning the attempt to discern original meanings of the Constitution.[16]

Thus my epigraph is relevant in two respects. The "faith of our fathers" is the trust generations of law professors placed in legal liberalism. Further, just as the hymn "Faith of Our Fathers" was written by nineteenth-century Anglo-Catholics working to erase the Reformation by creating a "Catholic" past for the Church of England, so originalism may prove a useful fiction.[17]

My perspective is that of a scholar educated as both lawyer and historian, who identifies with historians, but whose dual training and career in a history department makes her something of an outsider to both disciplines. My outsider's perspective is reflected in my notation style, in which I have combined the aspects of law professors' and historians' citation practices I like best. Part I provides an intellectual history of legal liberalism. In chapter 1, I examine how legal realism, the constitutional crisis of 1937, and legal and political liberalism affected the way law professors wrote about the Supreme Court from the 1930s until the 1970s. In chapter 2, I show how law professors in the 1970s harnessed other disciplines to their efforts to legitimate legal liberalism. Nevertheless, new political perspectives within the legal academy and demographic changes threatened legal liberalism. As I demonstrate in chapter 3, the threat was not that great. Chapter 4 is a description of how interdisciplinary scholarship challenged both legal liberalism and the search for principled decision making in the early 1980s. The ensuing intellectual and political polarization in the law schools is placed within the context of parallel developments in other disciplines. In chapter 5, I explain how the search for solutions by legal scholars to the crisis of legal liberalism led some of them to history. In Part II, I use law professors' turn to history and historians' reactions to it to investigate how lawyers and historians do their work. Chapter 6 is a report on how "the republican revival" became an "academic cottage industry." I also examine the debates between historians and law professors over republicanism and method arising from historians' attraction to historicism, context, change, and explanation and from lawyers' affinity for originalism, text, continuity, and prescription. In chapter 7, I suggest that history will remain an important form of constitutional argument and explore how lawyers, law professors, and historians can work together as activists toward shared objectives, including the defense of causes that legal liberals cherish.[18]

Such a strategy has pitfalls of its own. "Mandarin legal history," it focuses on what professors in elite institutions have thought about law. In reality, only a few law professors may have actually experienced the crisis of legal liberalism according to the terms described in my narrative. Nor have all those who suffered it tried to solve it by turning to other disciplines and to history. I submit, however, that those who have experienced it are sufficiently important to legal thought, the sense of crisis sufficiently widespread, and the turn to history sufficiently significant to warrant this book.

PART I

THE SPELL OF THE WARREN COURT

CHAPTER 1

TIMES TO REMEMBER

Although legal and political liberalism have been longtime allies, and legal realism affected both, they have had different careers. Unlike liberalism in politics and other disciplines, however, liberalism in law emerged from the 1960s intact. Only the question of rationalizing legal liberalism remained.

JOINED AT THE HIP: POLITICAL LIBERALISM AND LEGAL REALISM

When law professors write history, they mark legal realism as the jurisprudential divide between the old order and modernity. Adopting a "generous" definition of legal realism, William Fisher, Morton Horwitz, and Thomas Reed recently described the "heart" of the movement as "an effort to define and discredit classical legal theory and practice and to offer in their place a more philosophically and politically enlightened jurisprudence. All of the lawyers, judges, and legal scholars who contributed to that project should, in our view, be considered realists." By this view, Oliver Wendell Holmes marked himself as a realist when he declared that the life of the law was "not logic but experience," that the

Fourteenth Amendment did not "enact Mr. Herbert Spencer's Social Statics," and when he condemned classical legal thinker Christopher Columbus Langdell as the world's greatest living "legal theologian," whose "ideal in law, the end of all his striving, is the elegantia juris, or logical integrity of the system as system." The realists included not only such legal thinkers as Holmes and Felix Frankfurter but also Roscoe Pound, Benjamin Cardozo, and Louis Brandeis, along with law professors in the 1920s and 1930s who might have labeled themselves realists. Seen this way, Fisher, Horwitz, and Reed maintain, legal realism "set the agenda" for legal and, later, constitutional theory, by calling into question "three related ideals cherished by most Americans: the notion that, in the United States, the people (not unelected judges) select the rules by which they are governed; the conviction that the institution of judicial review reinforces rather than undermines representative democracy; and the faith that ours is a government of laws, not men."[1]

We might complain with John Schlegel, a historian of the realist movement, that this "big-tent" conception of realism and the realists conflates realism with an antiformalism that treats law as autonomous from society, and we might observe that most realists wrote almost nothing about public law. Yet the Fisher-Horwitz-Reed definition of realism I largely adopt in this book does illuminate one story that today's law professors, whatever their politics, tell about realism. And surely one reason the realists wrote so little about constitutional law was that they subscribed so fully to the antiformalist critique.[2]

Certainly the New Deal, which coexisted with legal realism, served as a political divide. Despite Herbert Hoover's best attempts to claim that he epitomized the liberal tradition, it was Franklin Roosevelt who gave "liberalism" popular meaning. "For the great majority of Americans, the word 'liberal' was literally born in the early New Deal." Instead of freedom from government, in the style of classical laissez-faire liberalism, Roosevelt spoke of liberalism in terms of freedom through government. Instead of "rights as freedoms" to be discovered, he thought in terms of "rights as claims" to be created.[3]

Alan Brinkley has chronicled the two stages of New Deal liberalism. During the Depression, liberals were concerned with the "critique of modern capitalism," especially "issues involving the structure of the industrial economy and the distribution of wealth and power within it."

Though practice did not always match rhetoric, the New Dealers defined social issues "almost entirely in terms of economics and class," maintaining that the "best hope for aiding oppressed minorities was economic reform." During World War II, this "reform liberalism" yielded to contemporary "consumption-oriented" and "rights-based liberalism," grounded on "a belief in the capacity of American abundance to smooth over questions of class and power by creating a nation of consumers" and dedicated to "increasing the rights and freedoms of individuals and social groups." Confident "that their new consumer-oriented approach to political economy had freed them at last from the need to reform capitalist institutions and from the pressure to redistribute wealth and economic power," liberals reconceived the role of government in the political economy. Relying on countercyclical spending to promote consumption and employment, the federal government would "create a compensatory welfare system (what later generations would call a 'safety net') for those whom capitalism had failed" and intervene more aggressively to protect individual and civil rights.[4]

Superficially, the New Dealers' faith in progress clashed with the legal realists' critical vision. Consider a staple of the realist corpus in the 1920s, "Legal Theory and Real Property Mortgages." In it Wesley Sturges examined three theories of mortgage law that logically led to different results. He showed that judges generally followed the three different paths to the same conclusion. Then Sturges analyzed the opinions of a randomly selected state court and proved that North Carolina's judges had not adhered to any one theory. State law was incoherent. "The point of the study was to demonstrate that the North Carolina law of mortgages made no sense and could most charitably be described as a species of collective insanity on the march," Sturges's student, Grant Gilmore, remembered later. Many of the realists agreed with Sturges that traditional and abstract legal categories or concepts, which isolated law from society, did not enable lawyers to predict the course of law.[5]

More generally, realists argued that classical legal thought ignored the indeterminacy of law and the role of idiosyncrasy in explaining judicial decisions. Their scholarship was in some respects traditional: it was doctrinal work, explicating the internal logic of legal rules and institutions and their relationship to other rules and institutions. Yet the realists saw that for each legal rule that led to one result, at least one more rule pointed toward another result. One realist said that legal rules and principles were "in the habit of hunting in pairs." Whenever judges confronted a doubtful situation, they would find that "in the past conflicting interest and conflicting social policies have each received recognition from the courts to some extent, and that these results have been rationalized in terms of 'conflicting' principles (or rules), each of which can easily and without departing from any prior decisions, be 'construed' as 'applicable' to the new case." By the realists' accounts, the doctrinal scholarship of traditionalists erred in treating law as a system of neutral rules that judges mechanically applied to reach the one legally "correct" decision. By pretending law was not socially constructed, classicists had imbued the rule of law with a false integrity.[6]

The realists debunked the rule of law as part of an effort to improve it. In undermining the predictive force of age-old legal rules, for example, realists often spoke of laying the groundwork for new ones. Their improved legal rules would utilize the insights of the social sciences and increase lawyers' proficiency at predicting the course of law. In using such rhetoric, realists sought to justify the place of the law school within the modern university, where Thorstein Veblen had declared that it no more belonged "than a school of fencing or dancing." Asked about his tenure as dean of Yale Law School, the center of legal realism after 1928, Robert Maynard Hutchins admitted to promoting realism because of his sense that a professional school's relationship to a university " 'had to' amount to more than simply 'sharing the same heating plant.' " Where traditional law professors exalted legal doctrine, realists spoke of "integrating" law with political science, economics, anthropology, sociology, and linguistics.[7]

The realists advocated a two-step program. They would expose both legal indeterminacy and judicial idiosyncrasy. While older legal scholars analyzed legal doctrine to demonstrate consistency, the realists' dissection of judicial decisions proved cases inconsistent and indeterminate. Having done that, the realists freed themselves to treat law as a tool of social policy and to look to the social sciences to define good policy.

Why the realists expected so much help from the social sciences was unclear. It may be, as some legal scholars now say, that the positivism, objectivism, and ethical neutrality of the social sciences at the time led realists to subordinate "political and moral passion to social science expertise." Perhaps, as some claim, the second step suppressed the radicalism of the first.[8] Further, though the realists made "law and social science" their mantra, they never got very far in their attempts to integrate the two. Nevertheless, they were the first generation of law professors to grapple with other disciplines and to demonstrate their importance to legal scholarship.

In part the realists did not advance their interdisciplinary agenda further because politics distracted them. However advanced their thought may have been and though realism predated the New Deal, most realists considered themselves political liberals. According to one of them, Jerome Frank, the realists made New Deal liberalism possible. They staffed the New Deal agencies that promoted reform and recovery. Legal realism proved the jurisprudential analogue of reform liberalism, and the realists became midwives to the birth of the contemporary constitutional order. Like the New Dealers, they tended to subordinate process to results. Both realists and New Dealers believed that human choice lay at the core of much private and public law. They characterized the distinction in classical liberalism between private and public law as arbitrary, demonstrating that all private transactions involved the state and that all law was, in an important sense, public law. They put their faith in the utility of social sciences. They employed an imaginative, modern, experimental approach to problem solving and to expanding the role of the welfare state.[9]

The realists also became devoted to the regulatory state, converting administrative law into "a vehicle for partisan objectives; for liberal partisanship." New Dealers were unimpressed by James Harrington's declaration that "a commonwealth comes to be an empire of laws and not of men." James Landis, a New Dealer who subscribed to much of legal realism, retorted that "good men can make poor laws workable," while "poor men will wreak havoc with good laws." By bringing the brightest to Washington to join regulatory commissions, New Dealers and realists hoped to ensure that a politically liberal, meritocratically selected elite would resolve disputes relating to the public good and advance the public interest.[10]

While their scholarship illuminated the judicial process, reflecting both their obsession with judging and the extent to which they identified with judges, realist law professors of the 1930s had little affinity for judicial activism as it was then practiced. "Indeed the rise of modern regulatory agencies was largely a product of a belief that the judiciary lacked the will, the means, and the democratic pedigree to bring about social reform on its own." Judicial activism had meant laissez-faire constitutionalism since the 1890s. The realists and New Dealers came of age in an era when the Court's decisions "seemed to be a road block to legislative developments . . . thought to be necessary for the decent humanization of American capitalism." Their hostility to the late nineteenth- and early twentieth-century Court far exceeded that of earlier modern American reformers. For realists and New Dealers, the paradigmatic case was *Lochner* v. *New York,* in which they believed Supreme Court members had gone out of their way to insist the rule of law "forced" them to reject social welfare legislation. For example, in declaring that law compelled them to strike down a centerpiece of the New Deal recovery program in *United States* v. *Butler* (1936), Justice Roberts pledged himself to textualism, expounding his infamous "T-square rule" of decision making: "When an act of Congress is appropriately challenged in the courts as not conforming to the constitutional mandate, the judicial branch of the Government has only one duty,—to lay the article of the Constitution which is invoked beside the statute which is challenged and to decide whether the latter squares with the former." The rhetoric intimated the majority believed itself constrained, but in fact, as Justice Harlan Fiske Stone charged in dissent, Roberts had "tortured" the Constitution to make it hostile to the New Deal. Others accused the justices of acting as "a superlegislature."[11]

With "the nine old men" of the Supreme Court seemingly on the verge of holding the entire New Deal unconstitutional, law professors who sympathized with Roosevelt's program acted. Harvard Law School professors Henry Hart and Felix Frankfurter, for example, attacked the Court in the law reviews. Following up on Frankfurter's suggestion, Hart also wrote a series of unsigned editorials in the *New Republic* alleging that Supreme Court justices such as Roberts couched reactionary results in neutral rhetoric. When Hart's exhortations against treating the Constitution as "the straitjacket for the status quo" proved unavailing, and Roosevelt proposed "packing" the Supreme Court by adding up to an additional six justices, Hart came out against Harvard University President James Bryant Conant with an argument for Roosevelt's Court packing plan. "If an evil exists, what solutions are possible other than President Roosevelt's proposal?" Hart asked. The majority of the Court was dissipating its prestige and influence by substituting its will for that of the lawfully elected representatives of the people. "Responsible men have earnestly to ask themselves whether the increasing popular dissatisfaction with the Court may not so undermine respect for the Court, and for all courts, as to threaten damage far exceeding anything which, by any calm view, may be anticipated from President Roosevelt's suggestion."[12]

In this showdown between the executive and judiciary, the Court blinked. Shifting course in 1937, it began upholding FDR's legislative program. The result of the 1937 showdown, according to political scientist Edward Corwin, was that the Court "discarded the idea that the laissez-faire, noninterventionist conception of governmental function offers a feasible approach to the problem of adapting the Constitution to the needs of the Twentieth Century" and began permitting the national government "to employ any and all of its powers to forward any and all of the objectives of good government." In the process, as Robert McCloskey said later, "many of the ancient myths which had long served as justifications for the Court's activities" were bruised. "Thereafter it was no longer possible for the judges and their supporters to take refuge from reasoned criticism behind the old incantations—the idea that the Court was merely the passive mouthpiece of an unambiguous constitution; the idea that the nature and range of the Court's power to intervene was settled once and for all by the Constitution itself or by unmistakable inferences from the Constitution." That was one lesson of 1937, although the realists had learned it long ago.[13]

Like their descendants, the realists did not all derive the same moral from 1937.[14] For members of the emerging legal process school, such as Hart, who remained a law professor, and Frankfurter, who was appointed to the Court in 1939, the moral was that the Court should take more seriously Justice Brandeis's admonition to use its power sparingly. Distinguishing between legislation and adjudication, they argued that the Court should respect the choices of the people's democratically elected representatives. It should show greater restraint, refraining from "imposing its own view of what the Country's good is." They did not believe, as Frankfurter said, that the Court they had claimed was a "superlegislature" when conservatives controlled it "should become a 'superlegislature' for 'our crowd.'" Legal process theory sought to explain "how respect for procedure and principled decision making might lead judges to outcomes that conform to institutional and democratic norms . . . develop a process explanation of law and adjudication that would achieve social purposes through the institutional settlement of disputes . . . [and defend] the view that right answers in legal decision making could be developed from a conceptual understanding of the institutional functions and competency of different governmental agencies of the legal system." For others, including some aging realists, the lesson was that the old Court had engaged in the wrong kind of activism. Instead of protecting property, they believed, the Court should focus on individual rights, which surged to the forefront of the liberal agenda during World War II. That obligation the Court seemed willing to contemplate undertaking, when in footnote 4 of *United States* v. *Carolene Products* (1938), Justice Stone proposed the Court uphold all reasonable economic legislation, while subjecting to stricter scrutiny legislation involving civil liberties and civil rights, which was particularly vulnerable "to perversions by the majoritarian process." Stone, who would soon become chief justice, now seized "the high ground of democratic theory" from advocates of judicial restraint by claiming that the defects of the majoritarian process created the need for judicial review. In claiming that judicial review furthered democracy by reconciling minority rights with majority rule, he set the Court in a new direction as activist as its old one.[15]

Footnote 4, then, did not make judicial review less idiosyncratic. By the time it was written, as George Braden said in a 1948 article entitled "The Search for Objectivity in Constitutional Law," Roosevelt's effort to pack the court and legal realism had helped change judicial parlance. "To talk, as Justice Roberts did, of simply laying a statute alongside an article of the Constitution to see if the former squares with the latter, now seems like dredging up an antiquity." Judges must have always known "that the judicial process is not that simple, that in the constitutional field the process is primarily political, not judicial; but it is only recently that they have admitted as much and have begun to discuss publicly their methods of deciding cases." Braden's readings of constitutional decisions convinced him that in the era after *Carolene Products*, the typical Supreme Court justice seemed to be saying: " 'I admit that Justice Roberts' mechanical method of squaring the statute and the Constitution was nonsense. Of course, we wield power. But this is potentially dangerous. Therefore, we must create a rule which is sufficiently objective to circumscribe us and our successors in our exercise of political power.' Thus the Supreme Court goes galloping off in search of objectivity." But to Braden, neither Stone nor any other justice had succeeded in finding it. For one example, Stone's thesis in footnote 4 appears to be something like this:

> "I am first of all a man of reason. I believe in reason and its power in the market place of discourse. I am also a democrat. I believe that our governments are to be run by the governed. Therefore I shall use my great power as a Supreme Court justice sparingly, but I shall use it when it is necessary to preserve the democratic process or to protect those injured by unreason under circumstances where political processes, cannot be relied on to protect them. . . ."
>
> This is not an objective theory of judicial review. The Chief Justice never claimed that it was. . . . It is perhaps unfair to set forth his thesis as an example of the effort to catch the will-o'-the-wisp of objectivity, but it does seem appropriate to present it as an early attempt to do the next best thing—i.e., to make an open declaration of personal beliefs.[16]

"To make an open declaration of personal beliefs"—was that the most realists would demand of judges? So the realists' critics believed. And because "the internal goods of constitutional adjudication" had been "respect for text and prior decisions, logical coherence and adherence to the norms of ordinary legal argument, freedom from partisan politics" since John Marshall's death in 1836, not everyone agreed with Braden that judicial candor was "the next best thing" to objectivity. In the context of the debate about relativism sparked by World War II, many antagonists read realists to say that idiosyncrasy swamped the rule of law altogether. More orthodox law professors ridiculed them for espousing a "gastronomic jurisprudence," which explained judicial decisions on the basis of what judges ate for breakfast. At the very least, opponents warned, the realists' focus on the subjectivity of the decisional process "gave even the most offensive Nazi edict the sanction of true law." Traditionalists branded the realists as nihilists and excoriated them for preaching Holmes, Hobbes, and Hitler. Where the realists espoused ethical pluralism, their antagonists saw ethical relativism.[17]

PLURALISM, PROCESS, AND THE "COUNTER-MAJORITARIAN DIFFICULTY"

Amid the revulsion against dictatorship in the aftermath of the war, an emphasis on democratic process, sometimes in a transparently political "apolitical" fashion, spread across the American intellectual landscape. In 1939, Clyde Kluckhohn had characterized cultural relativism as "probably the most meaningful contribution which anthropological studies have made to general knowledge." In the 1950s, anthropologists Alfred Redfield and A. L. Kroeber found universal values. "They suggested not only that there are general standards of judgment that transcend cultural boundaries, but that the moral standing of primitive societies is below that of civilizations like the United States," which exalted free speech. So, too, abstract expressionism in the postwar era "was full enough of alienation and anxiety, and expressive enough of violent fragmentation and creative destruction (all of which were surely appropriate to the nuclear age) to be used as a marvellous exemplar of US commitment to liberty of expression, rugged individualism and creative freedom. No matter that McCarthyite repression was dominant, the challenging canvas of Jackson Pollock proved that the United States was a bastion of liberal ideas in a world threatened by communist totalitarianism."[18]

Literature reinforced that message. Just as the realists were reproached for gastronomic jurisprudence, so Cleanth Brooks complained that "almost every English professor is diligently devoting himself to discovering 'what porridge had John Keats.' This is our typical research: the backgrounds of English literature." Brooks and others who subscribed to the New Criticism shifted the focus to structure, irony, tension and ambiguity. "Reading poetry in the New Critical Way," Terry Eagleton said later, "drove you less to oppose McCarthyism or further civil rights than to experience such pressures as merely partial, no doubt harmoniously balanced somewhere else in the world by their complementary opposites." By decontextualizing literature, the New Critics promoted a "benign pluralism" suited to the new crop of university students of all classes who lacked the common values their prewar counterparts learned in prep schools.[19]

At a time when America perceived itself at danger from without, historians and political scientists made that benign pluralism characteristic of their nation in past and present. "While only a few years earlier, the relativity of value threatened to disarm democracy, the same relativism now became the theoretical foundation for free government." In a world where ethical values always changed, ensuring that interest groups fought them out through a fair process became more important than guaranteeing specific outcomes.[20]

In the early twentieth century, Progressive historians such as Charles Beard had concentrated on presenting America's history as a battle between the classes and the masses. At a time when decisions such as *Lochner* enraged reformers, the Constitution came in for an especially hard time; Beard claimed that instead of "working merely under the guidance of abstract principles of political science," the Founders labored for "distinct groups whose economic interests they understood and felt in concrete, definite form through their own personal experience with identical property rights." According to him, "protection of property rights lay at the basis of the new system," and the "crowning counterweight to 'an interested and over-bearing majority,' as Madison phrased it, was secured in the peculiar position assigned to the judiciary, and the use of the sanctity and mystery of the law as a foil to democratic attacks." The Constitution represented a counterrevolution. His contemporaries had hailed Beard "for undermining the patriotic banalities of nineteenth century historiography." Beard, however, was no longer blessed. For the historians, sociologists, and political scientists of the 1950s who sought to displace the Beardian, or Progressive, paradigm, the salient point was the consensus, rather than the conflict, between Americans.[21]

Indeed consensus allegedly made the United States unique. In explaining the absence of socialism in the United States and the reason for "American exceptionalism," Louis Hartz painted a picture of an America born free, rich, and modern. There individualism, pluralism, economic self-interest, capitalism, and natural rights had long predominated. "Here is a Lockian doctrine which in the West as a whole is the symbol of rationalism, yet in America the devotion to it has been so irrational that it has not even been recognized for what it is: liberalism," Hartz wrote in *The Liberal Tradition in America,* his reinterpretation of American thought. "There has never been a 'liberal movement' or a real 'liberal party' in America: we have had the American Way of Life, a nationalist articulation of Locke which usually does not know that Locke himself is involved." Locke's preeminence explained "the unusual power of the Supreme Court and the cult of constitution worship on which it rests. Federal factors apart, judicial review as it has worked in America would be inconceivable without the national acceptance of the Lockian creed, ultimately enshrined in the Constitution, since the removal of high policy to the realm of adjudication implies a prior recognition of the principles to be legally interpreted." The "fixed" and "dogmatic" philosophical, or classical, liberalism which accounted for America's "moral unanimity" did not bar political liberalism. "Indeed, as the New Deal shows, when you simply 'solve problems' on the basis of a submerged and absolute liberal faith, you can depart from Locke with a kind of inventive freedom that European liberal reformers and even European socialists, dominated by ideological systems, cannot duplicate."[22]

Though a poignant tone suffused Hartz's presentation of Locke as proto-Babbitt, his contemporaries in the mid-1950s celebrated the Constitution, continuity, and consensus as interdependent. Hailing the American Revolution as a "Revolution without dogma . . . a prudential decision taken by men of principle rather than the affirmation of a theory," and stressing the "continuity of American political thought," Daniel Boorstin jubilantly explained why Americans lacked enthusiasm for Fascism, Nazism, or Communism. "We have actually made a society without a plan. Or more precisely, why should *we* make a five-year plan for ourselves when God seems to have had a thousand-year plan ready-made for us?" Daniel Bell applauded "the end of ideology." For Bell, the word *ideology,* which he defined as "a hardening of commitment, a freezing of opinion," and "the conversion of ideas into social levers," reeked of the left. He insisted that the old ideologies, "particularly Marxism," had become "exhausted" in the West by midcentury. Once dangerous mobs were blamed for having led their countries down the road to totalitarianism, scholarly enthusiasm for "the people" disappeared.

As Robert Wiebe said, the citizen became "democracy's weak link," the "public psyche" a thing of horror. The goal was to keep government out of the hands of citizens. For those writing articles with titles such as "In Defence of Apathy," declining voter turnouts were good news; they freed the elites to safeguard democracy. Political scientists such as David Truman pointed to the role of interest groups with overlapping memberships in serving "as a balance wheel" in the United States. Truman emphasized that despite "polite fictions," pressure group politics affected the judiciary, "inevitably a part of the political process," as well. The Constitution and Founding Fathers became fashionable again. Seymour Lipset's *The First New Nation* made the Constitution the key to "stable democracy"; Reinhold Niebuhr declared it the Founders' purpose to preserve "democratic stability." To Niebuhr and Lipset, democracy *was* stability.[23]

Potitical scientist Robert Dahl tried to steer a middle road between Madison and the people. He stopped just short of placing Madison "in the camp of great antidemocratic theorists," and he challenged the notion the Constitution was important to "democratic theory," which Dahl defined as the "processes by which ordinary citizens exert a relatively high degree of control over leaders." Dahl was no more positive, however, about populism, which he thought focused on the goals of "political equality and popular sovereignty" to the exclusion of all else. Elections rarely indicated majority predilections, he said. Many people did not vote, and those who did were not necessarily endorsing their candidates' policies: "the essence of all competitive politics is bribery of the electorate by politicians." Elections did, however, "vastly increase the size, number, and variety of minorities, whose preferences must be taken into account by leaders in making policy choices." And it was "this characteristic of elections—not minority rule but minorities rule" which distinguished democracies from dictatorships. Where the fear of majority tyranny led Madison to constitutional checks and balances, Dahl acclaimed "minorities rule" as the answer. "If majority rule is mostly a myth, then majority tyranny is mostly a myth too. For if the majority cannot rule, surely it cannot be tyrannical." Dahl's "American hybrid" of "polyarchal" democracy concentrated on the "social" checks and balances pluralism provided. Its key feature, government by minorities, might cause "frustration as minorities thwarted each other," but at least it foreclosed dictatorship and ensured balance and stability. In this system, the Supreme Court functioned as "policy-maker and legislator in its own right." Hardly "the *deus ex machina* that regularly saves American democracy from itself," the Court generally followed election returns, though sometimes it took its time about doing so. As they had operated in the past and would continue to function, constitutional rules had not guaranteed "government by majorities or . . . liberty from majority tyranny. . . . Constitutional rules are mainly significant because they help to determine what particular groups are to be given advantages or handicaps in the political struggle." In America, as nowhere else in the world, and "to an extent that would have pleased Madison enormously," governmental decision making was "the steady appeasement of small groups. . . . Decisions are made by endless bargaining." The American political system was a "strange hybrid," Dahl concluded, but it proved "a relatively efficient system for reinforcing agreement, encouraging moderation, and maintaining social peace." Pluralism became an end in itself, polyarchy the best way of achieving it. Where the New Dealers envisioned pluralism serving liberalism and social justice, Dahl saw only pluralism.[24]

Even John F. Kennedy got into the act. At his Yale University commencement speech in 1962, he proclaimed that Americans had entered an era of "more subtle and less simple" domestic problems. "They do not relate to basic clashes of philosophy and ideology, but to ways and means of reaching common goals—to research for sophisticated solutions to complex and obstinate issues." The age demanded the technocrat.[25]

Harvard Law School's Mark DeWolfe Howe hinted in 1953 that a Supreme Court decision holding segregation unconstitutional would mesh nicely with the pluralist vision of balancing interest groups. Yet pluralism's emphasis on the importance of interest-group jostling only underscored the belief of some legal scholars, particularly Howe's colleagues at Harvard, that the Supreme Court should serve a different and purer function. Horse trading might happen in the legislature or executive, but they saw little place for it in the judiciary. They viewed the notion of "judicial politics" as normatively oxymoronic. In the words of later legal scholars, legal process theorists thought the Court should be "the forum of principle," a place where the goal of "maximizing the total satisfaction of human wants" was pursued, as in popularly elected governmental branches, but where process and precedent were taken seriously, legal craft coveted, and cases decided according to law, regardless of who got what, when, and how. The popularity of the legal process idea in the postwar era reflected not only a reaction against legal realism, but also law professors' determination to prevent the pragmatism of pluralism from infecting the judiciary. As Neil Duxbury said, process theorists viewed jurisprudence "as quality control. . . . Different organs have different tasks to perform within the legal process; and it is for students and scholars not only to identify those tasks but also to ascertain whether or not they are being performed properly."[26]

Brown v. *Board of Education* tested such inspectors. It was fuzzy. Beyond declaring school segregation unconstitutional, what exactly did the opinion do? Did it put an end to segregation or require integration? Further, the opinion seemed self-consciously realist: devoid of constitutional analysis, it relied in part on sociological data and did not attempt to demonstrate that the Fourteenth Amendment's framers intended to outlaw school segregation. Nor did the Court actually say it was overruling the key precedent standing in the way of *Brown*—*Plessy* v. *Ferguson* (1896). That decision, legitimating segregation in railway cars, had found the doctrine of "separate but equal" consistent with the Fourteenth Amendment's equal protection clause and said that segregation did not stamp African Americans with a "badge of inferiority." While *Brown* left the sense *Plessy* was no longer good law, Chief Justice Warren evaded the question of whether *Plessy* was correct at the time it was decided and implicitly distinguished *Plessy,* hinting that since *Plessy* involved intrastate travel, it was not really germane. In addressing segregation in the schools, the Court could not "turn the clock back to 1868 when the Amendment was adopted, or even to 1896 when *Plessy* v. *Ferguson* was written," he insisted. Because of changed circumstances, the Court had to address public education "in light of its . . . present place in American life throughout the Nation." Observing that "[t]oday, education is perhaps the most important function of state and local governments," Warren noted that it was "the very foundation of good citizenship." The state had decided to provide education, and it must make that opportunity "available to all on equal terms." Regardless of whether the separate facilities were "equal" to those afforded whites, segregation of children in public schools on the basis of race deprived "the children of the minority group of equal educational opportunities." Contrary to "psychological knowledge" at the time of *Plessy*, contemporary social science showed that school segregation did make African Americans feel inferior. "Any language in *Plessy* v. *Ferguson* contrary to this finding is rejected." The Court concluded that "in the field of public education the doctrine of 'separate but equal' had no place. Separate educational facilities are inherently unequal." *Plessy* was "inapplicable to public education." A remedy came later: the following year, in *Brown II*, the Court simply required that desegregation take place with "all deliberate speed."[27]

We still cannot be certain of how the Court went about deciding *Brown*. Influenced by the imprint Frankfurter had left on the archives and on his clerks, those who first reconstructed the case tended to present Frankfurter as its hero: he had stalled a decision until unanimity was possible, he had ensured unanimity by separating the decision segregation was unconstitutional in *Brown I* from the decree indicating when segregation had to end in *Brown II*, and he had devised the gradualist desegregation formula in *Brown II*. A quarter-century after *Brown*, one law professor wrote: "In some sense, all of constitutional theory for the past twenty-five years has revolved around trying to justify the judicial role in *Brown* while trying simultaneously to show that such a course will not lead to another *Lochner* era." That certainly set out the challenge as Frankfurter wanted others to believe he had articulated it.[28]

But as Frankfurter's star dropped in the law school world after the late 1960s, other histories of the case appeared. They suggested that the only justice in *Brown* deeply bothered by the specter of 1937 was Frankfurter and that he ensured unanimity only in the sense that he devised a formula that would enable him to go along with his brethren. Frankfurter apparently believed that by proceeding slowly with school desegregation, and remaining silent about segregation outside the schools—above all, about the sensitive southern miscegenation laws preventing intermarriage between the races—the Court would win the compliance of "respectable" southerners. If these histories are correct, he was a poor prophet. Southerners rejected *Brown*, and Frankfurter's inconsistency may have only made them less likely to comply with it. Further, as Mark Tushnet said, Frankfurter's "innovation, 'all deliberate speed,' when coupled with southern resistance, transformed constitutional law" by disconnecting the right abridged from the remedy. By this account, justices Black and Douglas had prescribed a traditional remedy—requiring "immediate desegregation, in the sense that every child who applied to attend a desegregated school with room for him or her would have to be admitted, knowing full well that where resistance was likely to be strongest, few parents would subject their children to the inevitable ordeal." Frankfurter resisted, and ironically, the gradualist formula the Court ultimately adopted "made the Constitution a mere instrument to accomplish socially valuable ends, not a commitment to the immediate vindication of fundamental—present and personal—rights. Moreover, it encouraged the federal courts to see themselves as managers of social transformation," legitimating "the very activism" Frankfurter had feared.[29]

Frankfurter also made *Brown* a tough case for some of his followers. In the words of Gerald Gunther, "Frankfurter, despite his general avowal of a restrained position on judicial review . . . was given to expediency, discretion, and manipulation in the interests of prudence and avoiding political attacks on the Court." Of Frankfurter's protégés, only his former clerks, Alexander Bickel and Harry Wellington, both of whom became professors at Yale, seemed to understand and share their mentor's prudentialism, which would have restricted the Court's intervention in controversial political issues to vital occasions. "No good society can be unprincipled; and no viable society can be principle-ridden," Bickel contended. "[W]ould it have been wise at a time when the Court had just pronounced its new integration principle, when it was subject to scurrilous attack by men who predicted that integration of the schools would lead directly to 'mongrelization of the race' and that this was the result the Court had really willed, would it have been wise just then . . . on an issue that the Negro community as a whole can hardly be said to be pressing hard at the moment, to declare that the states may not prohibit racial intermarriage?" he asked publicly regarding the miscegenation issue. As Gerald Gunther observed, the young Alexander Bickel stood for "100% insistence on principle, 20% of the time." Bickel, who declared it judges' duty to extract fundamental principles and values "from the evolving morality of our tradition," later admitted he had never dealt successfully with one criticism of his work—that "the whole thing boils down to a disagreement about results and a certain personal distrust you have for these judges, the only additional thing being, perhaps, that you don't think they have been very skillful in expressing themselves." Taking Frankfurter's pose more seriously, other members of the legal process school—a group that included Henry Hart and Albert Sacks of Harvard, Herbert Wechsler of Columbia, Philip Kurland of Chicago, and Judge Learned Hand—treated Frankfurter as the symbol of judicial restraint and the integrity of the legal process he pretended to be. Like Bickel, most process theorists had been trained at Harvard, and as Bickel complained to Frankfurter, those who stayed on in Cambridge to teach often sounded "a little priestly." Process theory attracted both theologians and prudentialists, the apostles of consistency and those willing to accept inconsistency.[30]

Some scholars have maintained that *Brown* "produced a sharply critical reaction among elite legal thinkers, for it challenged at the deepest levels their effort to re-establish a neutral, value-free system of constitutional doctrine." Gary Peller placed the process theorists of the 1950s within the mainstream of the benign pluralist consensus of that decade. Acknowledging that they were "by and large liberal reformist in their political outlook," he alleged that with respect to questions of public law, they placed their faith in a "procedural freedom symbolized by free speech and open inquiry" and refused "to take a stand on substantive social issues."[31]

That indictment seems harsh. Process theorists were, of course, obsessed with procedural issues, with limiting the role of the federal courts, with ensuring courts found and followed statutory purpose, and with developing "the boundaries for the institutional competence of the judiciary when acting in the special role of judicial review," what Hart called "the morality of function." Though Hart and Sacks never published their casebook on the legal process, Hart and Wechsler's *The Federal Courts and the Federal System* (1953), dedicated to Felix Frankfurter, is "probably the most important and influential casebook ever written." It is also true that process theorists, such as Hart, Sacks, and Wechsler, never successfully integrated *Brown* or other key Warren Court decisions with either their vision of the legal process or their narrow and intricate conception of federal jurisdiction. In one of his own more theological moods, Frankfurter once sent Hart a cartoon of a boy standing at the blackboard telling his teacher: "O.k., o.k.! So two and two equals four—let's not make a Federal case out of it!" Treating the "Court as protector of human rights," Frankfurter grumbled in an accompanying note, meant "Ter Hell with jurisdiction!" Appropriately, the Warren Court opinion that apparently alienated Hart most was *Baker* v. *Carr,* the jurisdiction case Warren considered his most significant, and which may have given Frankfurter a stroke.[32]

Yet for *Brown* what stands out is the lengths to which process theorists went to justify it or to set out broader and more consistent grounds on which it could have rested. Though no one knew for sure what constitutional principles underlay the opinion, from the beginning, "[a]cceptance of *Brown*" by law professors operated as an "admission ticket for entry into mainstream constitutional dialogue." A student who heard Hart hold forth against *Baker* v. *Carr* told him: "You easily (I might say hurriedly) distinguish *Brown* v. *Board* whenever it is brought up as precedent." In his Supreme Court "Foreword" for the 1953 *Harvard Law Review,* Sacks, a former clerk for Frankfurter, said of *Brown:* "The outstanding feature of the decision lies in the triumph of a principle—a principle which the Court must have found to be so fundamental, so insistent, that it could be neither denied nor compromised. The principle can be easily stated: the Constitution requires equal treatment, regardless of race." Separating the declaration that segregation was unconstitutional from the decree setting out the remedy did not trouble Sacks: that, he said, was an act of "judicial statesmanship." Nor was he bothered by the fact that southerners might dislike the opinion. "It seems fair to reply that even in those states, there exists an inner, unexpressed sense that segregation and equality are like oil and water, even though it is accompanied by an equally strong feeling that segregation is nevertheless essential." Perhaps that inner sense might not win out in the electoral process, but it was "relevant to the problem before the Court, a politically sheltered institution whose function it is to seek to reflect the sober second thought of the community." Sacks queried the Court's extension of *Brown* to strike down segregation outside the schools in a series of summary per curiam opinions without explanation. (He did so with good reason. As one scholar wrote some forty years later: "*Never* did the Court get around to informing the nation of the legal basis for desegregating the South, outside the context of education," and it was not until 1963 that the Court "finally announced that a State may not constitutionally require segregation of public facilities.") Yet Sacks raised his question in the most tentative manner. More confidently, he stressed "the need for fuller statements" of the views of the Court in his discussion of per curiams in general. "At stake is the value which the Court handled so carefully and so well in the *Segregation Cases,* the acceptability of the Court's decisions to the lower courts and to the Bar as a whole." Sacks thus tried to remove *Brown* from the arena of responsible criticism of the Court.[33]

For his pains, Sacks received a letter from his former boss. Quoting Sacks, Frankfurter wrote: " 'The principle can be easily stated; the Constitution requires equal treatment regardless of race.' Really!? Are you overruling the Civil Rights cases [of 1893, which prevented Congress from taking affirmative steps to combat racial discrimination and from outlawing private discrimination]? Is all this bother about F.E.P.C. [Fair Employment Practices Commission] redundant and wasteful in that the Constitution itself already contains a F.E.P.C.?" Had Sacks become so entrenched in the academy that he had forgotten that "a summary disposition may be indicated in cases where there might be easy agreement about the result but not by the roads for reaching it, in short, where there is difficulty about the very statement you want"?[34]

Chagrined, Sacks replied that he "had no intention of suggesting that the Fourteenth Amendment goes beyond state action," a position still too broad for Frankfurter, and insisted that hiding disagreement did little to help the Court as an institution. "The explanation of per curiams in terms of differences among the justices may seem quite natural to the justices, but I don't think it can fully satisfy the outsider. It affords virtually complete immunity to criticism for failure to explain. . . . I have had letters from two lawyers both of whom won their cases this past Term on per curiam opinions, both of whom felt that the Court was not justified in being so cryptic." On receiving this letter, Frankfurter immediately "risk[ed] being deemed academic"—a charge to which the onetime Harvard professor unashamedly" pled guilty—by circulating his correspondence with Sacks to his colleagues on the Court. "Sacks' comments are worthy of consideration because, unlike much that is written even by law professors regarding the Court's work, Sacks' reflections are highly informed and sophisticated." The episode was typical of Frankfurter, who routinely used his law professors' letters and articles as conduits through which to exhort his brethren on the bench to produce better-reasoned decisions.[35]

In *Brown,* however, Frankfurter's efforts misfired. He regarded *Brown* as a special case in which the Court's action had been appropriate. Behaving pragmatically, he tried to circumscribe the impact of the case among those disinclined to support action. In 1955 and 1956, he twice persuaded the Court to dismiss *Naim* v. *Naim,* which would have raised the constitutionality of state laws against miscegenation, on "a make-weight excuse." In doing so, he ran the risk of consuming *Brown* with some of the fires he had helped set. At a time when Frankfurter was trying desperately to shore up the legitimacy of the Court, he alienated the theologians who would otherwise have supported *Brown* and its progeny on the very grounds he himself so often publicly and privately criticized other Warren Court opinions—inconsistent reasoning. Gunther's biography of Learned Hand, for example, demonstrates that Hand injected criticism of *Brown* into his 1958 Holmes Lectures at the last minute and that he would have accepted *Brown* had he been allowed to interpret it broadly. Obsessed with the desire to win over the South, however, Frankfurter convinced Hand that "the somewhat opaque *Brown* opinion . . . was an education case and that the permissibility of racial discrimination in other areas had to be decided by context-specific, case-by-case balancing analysis." To Hand, if *Brown* applied just to education, it was a substantive due process case. Under Frankfurter's hammering, Hand concluded that the Court "had not meant to propound an absolute rule against racial inequality but instead engaged in its own reappraisal of legislative judgments." Therefore, and though he spoke at the time of the Little Rock crisis—"the greatest crisis over school desegregation since *Brown* was decided"—at a time when the Warren Court's "efforts at dismantling the widespread institutionalization of attacks on civil liberties during the McCarthy era" were also under attack, and at a time when, for the first time since the Civil War, Congress was threatening to reduce the Court's appellate jurisdiction, Hand not only queried the legitimacy of judicial review, but also rejected judicial activism on behalf of all "preferred freedoms" except the First

Amendment, and specifically criticized *Brown* as judicial legislation. Ironically, Hand's original interpretation of *Brown* may have correctly stated what the justices had in mind and might have made clear, but for Frankfurter's intervention in the opinion-writing process.[36]

The following year, another veteran of the "early decades of this century, [when] judicial activism had meant 'anti-progressivism,' " Herbert Wechsler, used his Holmes Lectures to criticize the reasoning in *Brown,* "an opinion which is often read with less fidelity by those who praise it than by those by whom it is condemned. The Court did not declare, as many wish it had, that the Fourteenth Amendment forbids all racial lines in legislation." He maintained that its opinion simply subordinated one constitutional value, freedom of association of whites facing integration, to another, freedom of association of African Americans suffering segregation. Wechsler added that he took "no pride" in saying the procedural grounds on which the Court had dismissed *Naim* were "wholly without basis in law." He later explained: "My point was that a judge is obliged, insofar as he deals with the extrapolation of a particular constitutionally protected value, to give it an even-handed development."[37]

Wechsler's article was reprinted in the same issue of the *Harvard Law Review* as Henry Hart's "Time Chart of the Justices," which criticized the Court "as essentially a voice of authority settling by virtue of its own ipse dixit the questions that duly come before it. This conception unhappily seems to underlie some of the Court's own actions, as when it decides opinions which do not explain, or decides important questions without any opinion whatever." Hart called on the Court to leave more time for "the maturing of collective thought," concluding "the time must come when it is understood again, inside the profession as well as outside, that reason is the life of the law and not just votes for your side." When Wellington wrote Hart "that a judicial position which is unable to embrace and approve the Supreme Court's action in *Naim* v. *Naim* . . . is not a fully matured philosophy" and that any decision of the merits in *Naim* "would have seriously undercut the effectiveness of the Supreme Court's segregation decision" and "might seriously have threatened the Court as an institution," Hart was unimpressed. The "question is whether a court is ever justified in giving a false reason in order to avoid facing up to an embarrassing issue," Hart replied. "This view may seem to you excessively unworldly. But I am able to persuade myself that worldly as well as unworldly considerations support it. Segregation is ultimately a moral issue, and the moral authority of the Court is one of the principal instruments we have for getting rid of it. I do not think that it makes good sense to let that sharp edge of the instrument get blunted."[38]

Such declarations left little doubt about where Hart's heart lay. Like Hand's correspondence with Frankfurter, they were private, but, with the exception of Hand, scholarly commentators were generally publicly sympathetic to *Brown*. Process theorists joined other, more activist law professors, such as Charles Black, who asked, "How long must we keep a straight face" when "we are solemnly told that segregation is not intended to harm the segregated race, or to stamp it with the mark of inferiority?" Together, the two groups made *Brown* sacred. In the lead article of the 1955 *Harvard Law Review,* Bickel argued that "the direct and noble march to the Court's conclusion in the Segregation Cases" was not precluded by the original understanding of the Fourteenth Amendment. The historical record, "properly understood, left the way open to, *in fact invited,* a decision based on the moral and material state of the nation in 1954, not 1866." In 1956, Charles Fairman used the increasingly prestigious annual "Foreword" to the *Harvard Law Review*'s discussion of the previous Supreme Court term to evaluate "the principal criticisms" of *Brown,* all of which he found wanting. He concluded: "It is futile to make war 'to keep the past upon its throne.'" Even those who were skeptical of the opinion's reliance on sociological data, such as Edmond Cahn, saw *Brown* as a victory for "the whole American people." Further, law professors' reaction to Hand underlined the extent of their pro-*Brown* sympathies. Privately, Hart raged at Hand's "obtuseness," complaining "What he . . . seemed to me to be saying in his lectures . . . is that at bottom law and the social order reflect nothing but a struggle among contending classes. The most striking thing in this analysis is the total failure to recognize the existence of any principles of social order which are independent of the appetites and wills of the contending groups." Responding to Hand publicly, Wechsler vowed his allegiance to *Brown* as the decision with "the best chance of making an enduring contribution to the quality of society of any that I know in recent years" and defended judicial review. Gunther observed that "the rare praise" Hand received for the Holmes Lectures "came from the South." Otherwise, "the reception of Hand's message proved almost universally negative. . . . The academics' response was equally predictable. Most of them were supporters of the Warren Court; even those who had doubts tended to suppress them in the face of the more obvious evil of assisting the reactionary critics during a time of political crisis."[39]

Other decisions of the Warren Court were not off limits, however. Process theorists did seek to "integrate a tamed realism back into the mainstream of legal thought" by emphasizing "institutional competence," calling for "reasoned elaboration of judicial decisions," and attempting to separate law from politics, process from substance, fact from values. Even its defenders would admit that except in the case of *Brown,* process theorists generally did favor the status quo, employing a "thin theory of democracy," which subordinated substance to procedure and did not make "substantive fairness . . . a primary element of political legitimacy." The prototypical process theory charge that the Court's sloppy craftsmanship, subjectivity, and activism threatened its future was prominently featured in the 1957 *Harvard Law Review.* In an attack on Douglas's majority opinion in the recent *Lincoln Mills Case* and a hymn to Frankfurter's dissent there and craft skills in general, Bickel and Wellington declared that scholars' duty was to "defend the Court against ill-intentioned nonsense which comes decked out in legal trappings," but added that could not mean a moratorium on responsible criticism of the Court. They continued: "The Court's product has shown an increasing incidence of the sweeping dogmatic statement, of the formulation of results accompanied by little or no effort to support them in reason, in sum, of opinions that do not opine and of per curiam orders that quite frankly fail to build the bridge between the authorities they cite and the results they decree." Quoting this critique, Hart's 1959 "Foreword" warned "that these failures are threatening to undermine the professional respect of first-rate lawyers for the incumbent Justices of the Court, and this at the very time when the Court as an institution and the Justices who sit on it are especially in need of the bar's confidence and support." Wechsler likewise called on the Court to reach "principled" decisions resting on reasons "that in their neutrality and generality" transcend "the immediate result that is achieved."[40]

Wechsler later explained that he was not developing "a formula to guide or produce the decision of hard cases, but rather . . . a negative test, which would force the judge to ask himself, 'Would I reach the same result if the substantive interests were otherwise?' ' His contemporaries misunderstood him. They thought he had advanced a positive test, somehow injecting neutral principles with substance. As he admitted, they perceived him to have denounced realism.[41]

Writing in 1963, Bickel, "the most influential scholar of his generation in the field of constitutional law," made no bones about expressing his opposition to activist judicial review and realism. After eight years of the Warren Court, Bickel was pessimistic about judicial power. The Founding Fathers had "invited" judicial review, he conceded in *The Least Dangerous Branch*. They had "specifically, if tacitly, expected" the Court to review the constitutionality of other branches of government, both federal and state, and Chief Justice John Marshall had followed their wishes when he justified judicial review in *Marbury* v. *Madison* with the lame explanation that "the *writtenness* of the Constitution and . . . its supremacy in cases of clear conflict with ordinary law" gave the Court "what is nowhere made explicit in the Constitution— the ultimate power to apply the Constitution, acts of Congress to the contrary notwithstanding." Bickel noted that no one would disagree with Marshall's proposition that a court could not allow a legislative "act repugnant to the Constitution" to stand when that act conflicted with the Constitution. "But Marshall knew (and, indeed, it was true in this very case) that a statute's repugnancy to the Constitution is in most instances not self-evident; it is, rather, an issue of policy that someone must decide. The problem is who." Marshall's opinion "begged the question-in-chief." Bickel demolished the "props" for judicial review Marshall had provided, demonstrating that they were both "frail" and "too strong. . . . Literal reliance on *Marbury* v. *Madison* may lead to a rampant activism that takes pride in not 'ducking' anything." Had Bickel been a historian, his inquiry might have ended with some observations about motivation. Since Bickel was a law professor, however, and unashamedly viewed the enterprise of scholarship as more normative than explanatory, he argued with the Founders about their wisdom.[42]

"The root difficulty" with judicial review, Bickel proclaimed, is that it "is a counter-majoritarian force in our system." Bickel had little use for the Founders' effort to make popular sovereignty meaningful. When Alexander Hamilton claimed in *Federalist 78* that judicial power was not superior to legislative power, reasoning "that the power of the people is superior to both; and that where the will of the legislature, declared in its statutes, stands in opposition to that of the people, declared in the Constitution, the judges ought to be governed by the latter rather than the former," Hamilton, according to Bickel, had been using the word *people* as "an abstraction. Not necessarily a meaningless or a pernicious one by any means; always charged with emotion, but nonrepresentational—an abstraction obscuring the reality that when the Supreme Court declares unconstitutional a legislative act or the action of an elected executive, it thwarts the will of representatives of the actual people of the here and now; it exercises control, not in behalf of the prevailing majority, but against it." For that reason, "the charge can be made that judicial review is undemocratic." With these words, Bickel assured the revival of the "majoritarian paradigm" in constitutional theory.[43]

Though Bickel had worked to isolate pluralism from the judiciary, he now went further, seeming to reject pluralism itself. For he not only quarreled with the Founders, but also queried the political theorists of his generation. Oddly, at a time when they were exalting the Constitution for stabilizing democracy, dismissing the individual citizen, and proclaiming the impossibility of majority rule, Bickel apparently equated democracy with majoritarianism. Democracy meant "a representative majority" had the power to make and reverse decisions, he emphasized. Nothing political scientists said could "alter the essential reality that judicial review is a deviant institution in the American democracy." Even assuming Dahl had correctly identified "minorities rule" as the alternative to majority rule, "it remains true nevertheless that only those minorities rule which can command the votes of a majority of individuals in the legislature who can command the votes of a majority of individuals in the electorate." Somehow or other, in elections and the legislative process, "the minorities must coalesce into a majority." Nor was Bickel swayed by political theorists, such as David Truman, who pointed to the impact of interest groups on the judiciary. Such writers had shown that the electoral process was not the only way of ensuring responsiveness of government to the governed, and that by extrapolation, "judicial review, although not responsible, may have ways of being responsive." Yet the ultimate responsiveness of the Court to public opinion was not sufficient to justify judicial review. "[N]othing can finally depreciate the central function that is assigned in democratic theory and practice to the electoral process; nor can it be denied that the policy-making power of representative institutions, born of the electoral process, is the distinguishing characteristic of the system. Judicial review works counter to that characteristic."[44]

Bickel's concept of democracy was both populist and simplistic. "For me," he explained to Eugene Rostow, judicial review was "not democratic, unless we so play with that word as to drain it of all content." Without any evidence, Bickel assumed that the legislature pursued a majoritarian perspective, reflective of the popular will. His legislature, like that of other process theorists, rationally and pragmatically pursued the public interest. Without any evidence, he assumed that the public could identify well-reasoned opinions, and that they would bolster popular faith in the rule of law. Further, in focusing on *Marbury,* Bickel had chosen an easy target. He glossed over important cases in the development of judicial review, such as *McCulloch* v. *Maryland,* which used judicial review as a means toward the goal of achieving federal supremacy over the states, and in which, Bickel himself admitted in passing, Marshall had gone "beneath the bland proposition advanced in *Marbury* v. *Madison.*" As the subject matter of *McCulloch* would suggest, Bickel also downplayed the role of federalism in necessitating judicial review. While many instances of judicial review involved separation of powers and the Supreme Court against Congress, or individual rights against government, surely national supremacy was also important to the Founders. As Holmes put it, "the United States would not come to an end if we the Supreme Court lost our power to declare an Act of Congress void," but it might "if we could not make that declaration as to the laws of the several States." The Founders apparently foresaw judicial review could assist in establishing the relationship of the national government to the states, as well as strengthen the authority of state courts against popular majorities. As it developed, judicial review did help to resolve conflicts between federal and state government before and after the Civil War. "And," as the historian Jack Rakove emphasized, "this in turn should have mitigated the countermajoritarian dilemma, to some degree, especially as it would or should have been perceived in the wake of *Brown*," when the authority of the national government was challenged throughout the South. Nevertheless, Bickel had spoken, and suddenly democracy "became a central legitimating concept in American constitutional law," and "democratic legitimacy" a concept threatened by judicial review.[45]

As Bickel knew, inside the law school world little he said was new. Law professors and judges had been mocking *Marbury* and worrying about the undemocratic nature of judicial review since the time of Thayer and Holmes. Still, Bruce Ackerman and Michael Klarman rightly credited Bickel with the "classic statement" of the problem. The words he used to sum it up, "the counter-majoritarian difficulty," were epigrammatic.[46]

Ironically, within pages of introducing that epigram, Bickel came around to the pluralist view that judicial review *was* democratic. Instead of following Marshall or the *Federalist,* however, he justified judicial review by proclaiming it the Court's role to pronounce and guard public values in principled fashion and to build consensus around them. On some occasions, such as *Brown,* whose specter haunted *The Least Dangerous Branch* and epitomized "all that I have tried to say about the role of the Supreme Court in American government," he emphasized, the Court did need to inject "itself decisively into the political process." Such occasions were "relatively few," the Court must bank its prestige for them, and having acted, it must "foster assent, and compliance through consent." Bickel applauded *Brown II* and the "all deliberate speed" formula precisely because it represented such an attempt. For even on the rare occasions the Court appropriately intervened in the political process, its law could not ultimately prevail "if it ran counter to deeply felt popular needs or convictions, or even if it was opposed by a determined and substantial minority and received with indifference by the rest of the country. This, in the end, is how and why judicial review is consistent with the theory and practice of political democracy." Readers paid less attention to that language, however, than they did to Bickel's explication of "the charge" that judicial review was undemocratic. To them, Bickel seemed to be heralding a return to the bad old days before 1937 when judicial review and democracy were antagonists.

Yet while he questioned the partnership between judicial review and democracy that Stone had tried to establish in *Carolene Products,* Bickel made judicial review and democracy only potential, rather than actual, antagonists. That was still quite an accomplishment: henceforward, the hypothesis that constitutionalism was antithetical to both justice and democracy haunted constitutional law.[47]

At the same time, Bickel reviled legal realism as a "cry of nihilism," claiming it constituted "cynicism pure and simple." According to him, the realists contended there was no such thing as a principled decision. Therefore legal realism provided no criteria for identifying how to reach a decision and no basis for justifying the power of the Court in a democracy. Bickel was unfair, for realism did not necessarily lead to the wholesale judicial activism he condemned. Sometimes it did; at others, it did not. The whole point of realism was that the person wielding the theory was more important to how matters turned out than the theory itself. As Bickel himself acknowledged ever less uneasily as he grew older, the realist tradition had produced his own prudentialism, as it had spawned the other "scholastic mandarins" who rapped the legal reasoning by which Warren Court opinions justified decisions. The criteria process theorists applied in evaluating the Court's success—"instrumental effectiveness, institutional self-regard, and public acceptance"—themselves reflected realism's imprint. Sometimes, one critic said, process theorists almost seemed to exalt an "image of a Supreme Court holding aloft a collective moistened finger to test the drift of popular preference."[48]

What united process theorists such as Wechsler, Bickel, Kurland, Sacks, and Hart was the belief judges had too fatalistically accepted judicial (in)discretion. Haunted by the memories of the conservative Court in the early twentieth century and threatened by Stalinism, such legal scholars sought to domesticate realism, constrain judges, and separate law from politics. Stressing that limits to judicial discretion did exist, they concentrated on the methods by which judges did and should reach decisions. Judges, Hart said, should recognize their duty to articulate and develop "impersonal and durable principles." They could leave the horse-trading to legislators. The job of judges was to promote respect for the rule of law.[49]

Process theory, which in part represented an attempt to indict the

Warren Court's more lamely articulated decisions, urged judges to spot-light the reasoning and craft techniques of the legal profession in their opinions. In so exhorting, process jurisprudents searched for a consti-tutional theory that would reinforce the integrity of the legal process, enable judicial decisions to transcend results, justify the negotiated doc-ument the Court had produced in *Brown,* and reduce worry about the counter-majoritarian difficulty. They never found it.[50]

In fact, frequently neutral principles and process theory led to a pe-culiar sort of doctrinal scholarship. It was easy to parody student notes of the era. All one need include, the editors of the *Harvard Law Review* said in another context later, was "a takeoff on lines such as these: ' . . . Thus, it appears that traditional bright line rules should no longer serve as guides for adjudication in this area. Rather courts should base their determinations on a functional balancing of the relevant interests.' " So the doctrinal work of process theory's patron saint, Justice Frankfurter, and the scholarship of the law professors allied with him could be mocked. Even Bickel acknowledged judges had to choose among "en-during values." Yet the very act of balancing might leave "far too much to the individual judge's predilection." Neutral principles were all well and good, but they did not guarantee neutral attitudes toward the prin-ciples. Balancing simply underlined the extent to which those who sub-scribed to process theory accepted realism's revelation of the role of idiosyncrasy in the decisional process. Meanwhile Frankfurter's retire-ment in 1962 enabled the Warren Court fully to embrace judicial activ-ism.[51]

GLORY DAYS

It was the Warren Court of 1962–69 that became "a cultural phe-nomenon." That was the Warren Court which "came into its own as an independent political actor." During that period, Lyndon Johnson and Earl Warren reintroduced and expanded on the New Dealers' vision of political liberalism, linking it to legal liberalism. "To be a liberal . . . meant favoring a stronger role for the state in the economy, moderate redistribution of income, state action to improve the lot of the disad-vantaged, legal protection for the accused and mentally ill, and legal bans on racial discrimination," law professor David Trubek explained.

To be legalist meant maintaining the "faith in law as an instrument of progressive social change." Legalists, such as Johnson and Warren, assumed that "most of the 'flaws' in American society could and would be corrected through legal means. They had faith in the immanent liberalism of legal institutions and equated 'law' with 'freedom' and 'equality.' " There was a foreign policy dimension to their program as well, which entailed "exporting democratic capitalism." Johnson's Great Society entailed social and economic reform at home and globalism abroad to preserve capitalism and to fight poverty and injustice.[52]

In its heyday between 1962 and 1969, the Warren Court adopted Johnson's politics. Mark Tushnet rightly labeled the Warren Court an element of Johnson's Great Society coalition. The Court's legal liberalism consisted of political liberalism and judicial activism in equal parts. The Warren Court "gave us reason to believe that state activism was a constitutional duty," Owen Fiss recalled. In the words of the journalist Anthony Lewis, the Warren Court's record confirmed "an implausible idea, temperamentally and historically . . . a revolution made by judges." Its decisions reflected an insistence on what Hannah Arendt called "a right to have rights." Opinions emphasized "the importance of individual dignity, the significant role of the modern state in creating and maintaining the good society, and the importance of shaping the relationship between the modern welfare state and the individual so that the state's powers are not imprudently diminished, and individual dignity is preserved." The Court expanded civil liberties and civil rights, while assiduously avoiding a decision on the constitutionality of the Vietnam War and invalidating some of the most eloquent protest against it.[53]

The Court made liberals happy for it dodged the tension between liberty and equality. Justices did so by using liberalism's language of individual rights and freedom to help children, the disenfranchised, non-Christians, suspected criminals, minorities, and the poor. Sub silentio, they took "the group perspective on the victim." Horwitz later described the Warren Court as "the first Court in American history that really identified with those who are down and out—the people who received the raw deal, those who are the outsiders, the marginal, the stigmatized." Expanding equal protection analysis beyond race, Warren Court justices declared a number of rights "fundamental." (In one notorious instance, they even made the right to interstate travel a fundamental right, while

refusing "to ascribe the source of this right . . . to a particular constitutional provision.") The Court also revamped the relationship between
state and federal courts by opening up federal courts to those likely to
be mistreated in state courts. "Barriers to the federal courts came tum-
bling down . . . to provide a sympathetic forum for the enforcement of
rights that genuinely *ought* to be enforced against majoritarian power."
And the Court tried to promote social justice throughout the states by
nationalizing the Bill of Rights.[54]

To its detractors, of course, what the Warren Court called "constitutional interpretation" was "legislation from the bench." "Perhaps
some of you may detect, as I think I do, a return to the philosophy of
St. Thomas Aquinas in the new jurisprudence," Justice Brennan told an
audience during a 1965 speech on the role of the Court. "Call it a resurgence, if you will of concepts of natural law—but no matter." One
commentator responded: "But no matter?!?!?!" Though Anthony Lewis
might celebrate Warren as "the closest thing the United States has had
to a Platonic Guardian, dispensing law from a throne without any sensed
limits of power except what was seen as the good of society" and relish
the feeling of being "present at a second American Constitutional Convention" on the day the Court announced its one person–one vote rule
and demanded reapportionment of state legislatures, other observers
wondered who would guard the guardian. They agreed with Justice Harlan, who warned that decisions such as one person–one vote "give
support to a current mistaken view of the Constitution and the constitutional function of this Court. This view, in a nutshell, is that every
major social ill in this country can find its cure in some constitutional
'principle,' and that this Court should 'take the lead' in promoting reform when other branches of government fail to act." Critics griped that
the Warren Court was "a continuing constitutional convention and a
joint session of Congress rolled into one." As Fred Graham said, "the
gusto" with which Warren Court justices went about changing the law
"struck some people as being unseemly."[55]

Since some of the Warren Court's most enthusiastic activists had been
legal realists, judicial activism now became associated with legal realism.
To skeptics among law professors, no one on the Court exemplified the
realist-gone-amok more than William O. Douglas. In the 1965 case of
Griswold v. *Connecticut,* for example, Douglas cobbled together a con-

stitutionally protected right to marital privacy, though the Constitution never mentioned privacy. The rights enumerated in the First, Third, Fourth, Fifth, and Ninth Amendments and applied to the states through the Fourteenth Amendment, he reasoned, had "penumbras, formed by emanations from those guarantees that help give them life and substance." *Griswold* could have rested on other grounds. Justice Harlan's concurrence developed an alternative rationale for a constitutional right to privacy, based on substantive due process, arguing that "the Fourteenth Amendment's due process clause protection of 'liberty' represented a substantial limitation on state action wholly independent of the specific constitutional guarantees spelled out in Amendments One through Eight." As one who had come of age during the constitutional crisis of 1937, however, Douglas would have none of that because he thought it represented a return to *Lochner*.[56]

To Warren's clerk John Hart Ely, both Harlan's reliance on substantive due process and Douglas's implication of a right to privacy in *Griswold* constituted dangerous judicial activism. "Instead, Ely suggested, the Chief Justice should look at *Griswold* and how the [1879] Connecticut statute [which criminalized the use or prescription of contraceptives by women and their doctors] prevented the operation of birth control clinics for the poor, but not the provision of similar services to better-off patients of private physicians, in the light of an eighty-year-old equal protection decision, *Yick Wo v. Hopkins*." In that case, the Court had announced, "Though the law itself be fair on its face and impartial in appearance, yet, if it is applied and administered by public authority with an evil eye and an unequal hand, so as practically to make unjust and illegal discriminations between persons in similar circumstances, material to their rights, the denial of equal justice is still within the prohibition of the Constitution." Unlike federal courts and other state courts, which had read a "medical exception" into laws such as Connecticut's outlawing contraceptives (permitting physicians to prescribe contraceptives for married women), the Connecticut supreme court had ruled in 1940 that the statute included no implied medical exception. The statute posed no problem for married women who could afford private medical care, because physicians violated it with impunity. But after the Connecticut supreme court's ruling, all birth control clinics in Connecticut had promptly shut down for twenty-five years. Warren ignored Ely's advice, and the equal protection clause analysis was buried in an individual concurrence.[57]

Griswold, a due process case in right to privacy clothing, did not represent the Warren Court's usual approach toward decision making. Nor was Douglas the first member of the Court to ply "penumbras" or the last to resort to "penumbral reasoning." Nevertheless, to legal scholars at the time, *Griswold* seemed typical of Warren Court reasoning, and some groused that no matter what the opinion said, it really represented a return to *Lochner.* The term "unprincipled penumbralist" became synonymous with "realist," "liberal," and "judicial lawlessness."[58]

Some Warren Court opinions did make no pretense of suggesting law and legal theory compelled the justices to reach their decision. In fact, Mark Tushnet thought that "constitutional theory played a rather small role during the height of liberal activism." He pointed out: "Earl Warren had humane instincts, not a systematic philosophy." "Yes, Counsel, but is it fair?" Warren reputedly asked the lawyers who argued before the Court. One popular quip described the apparent thought of the Warren Court majority: "With five votes, we can do anything."[59]

Consider the case of Justice Abe Fortas. A legal realist and New Dealer in the 1930s, he became Douglas's ally and a Great Society liberal in the 1960s. Fortas sometimes wrote draft opinions without legal citations in them, then ordered his law clerks to "decorate" them with the appropriate legalese. That did not mean that Fortas knew the supporting law was there. It meant that he considered law indeterminate and did not care about it much at all. In his hands, realism licensed crude instrumentalism. As one of Fortas's biographers, I found his cavalier attitude toward the rule of law surprising. Since I usually liked the results he reached and since historians explain more than they diagnose, however, his approach and the Warren Court's activism posed no political or professional problems for me.[60]

But the subjectivity of Fortas's opinions and those of his Warren Court colleagues led more principled scholars, particularly the law professors who persisted in doctrinal research and who made their living by analyzing the Court's output, to ask why the Court should possess so much power in a democracy. At Harvard Law School in the 1960s, Morton Horwitz remembered, "it was common to mock Warren for often asking from the bench whether a particular legal position was 'just.' Sophisticated legal scholars did not speak that way."[61]

"Sophisticated legal scholars" believed they must show that legal and constitutional doctrine underlay judicial opinions. Otherwise, they would be doomed to spend their professional lives presenting the opinions as smoke screens for judges' economic, social, personal, and political preferences. That task could be left "to a notable school of historians and political scientists who decline to see the legal process as anything more than a chintz cover for the thrust of sheer power and will." If they did not take judicial opinions seriously, academic lawyers feared they would undermine the integrity of the rule of law. Herbert Wechsler never lost his wonder at those who thought that "the credibility, authority, and power of the federal judiciary is an asset that can be extended to the moon without any loss anywhere." Some law professors worried that respect for the legal process would disappear if the public came to believe America's was a government of men, not law.[62]

The process theory critique, which grew out of legal realism, hurt the legal realism associated with the Warren Court, not legal liberalism. It did not demonstrate dissatisfaction with the Warren Court's results, for almost all law professors at the time were liberal in their politics. "Perhaps the most striking feature of the commentary of the 1950s and 1960s was that the participants battled so fiercely about whether the Court could or should act, while agreeing so fundamentally on the substantive goodness of what the Court was doing or would do if not restrained by its own modesty." Wechsler picked the cases he criticized in his Holmes Lecture because he admired their outcomes. "It seemed more powerful, more persuasive, and morally preferable to exhibit the tension between results and bases, in terms of situations where I liked the result, but felt a moral obligation to question the grounds than to take the easy cases where I disliked the result and undertook to question the grounds," he said. "Indeed, one of the elements of rhetorical effectiveness in the piece was precisely that I persuaded people that I liked the results and still felt it important to question the grounds." Similarly, Bickel, who had a soft spot for the Warren Court's criminal justice decisions, wrote Frankfurter about the opinion preventing state courts from admitting evidence obtained in violation of the Fourth Amendment: "I can't help liking the results (I don't *want* to be reasonable) but what a messy process."[63]

In the 1960s, then, two groups of law professors bickered, but theirs was a family quarrel between Warren Court activists and process theorists, two wings of the realist tradition. Old realists suggested that in their "illusive . . . quest for legal certainty," process theorists were creating "a false faith in judicial objectivity," which would "cripple the exercise of creativity and reinforce the status quo." Arnold claimed process theorists would be satisfied when Supreme Court justices came only from the ranks of those trained by the "dialecticians" at Harvard Law School. Others influenced by realism, such as Charles Black and Eugene Rostow, more tactfully suggested that judicial review protected and enhanced democracy. Echoing Stone, they insisted that judicial review was necessary to protect oppressed minorities from majority tyranny. Black, a "judicial activist proudly self-confessed," imaginatively focused on the "structures and relationships created by the constitution in all its parts or in some principal part," maintaining that "the status of citizenship" alone legitimated the Court's civil rights and First Amendment decisions, and stressing that it "would be wrong not to see in the work of the Warren Court as a matter of net thrust, an affirmation—the strongest, by a very long interval, in our whole history—of the positive content and worth of American citizenship." Still other legal scholars gave themselves to the Court, writing elaborate apologias explaining why the Court had to act as it did. For members of this group, comprised largely but not exclusively of the young, the counter-majoritarian difficulty did not pose a problem when a Court so obviously hoped to further democracy and social justice. Their interest was in how the Court should act. Another group, made up mainly of individuals who remembered the conservative Court before the constitutional crisis of 1937, tempered praise for Warren Court consequences with concerns over whether the Court should act and fears that sloppiness, when the Court did act, hurt judicial legitimacy.[64]

Like Kurland, the Court's most vociferous critic, Bickel did become more doubtful about political and legal liberalism as the decade progressed. But in 1968, Bickel gave himself "heart and mind" to Robert Kennedy, describing him as "our best hope" and suggesting that "his fine and passionate instincts were leading him back to the older, enduring strains in the American liberal tradition—strains that for me are identified with Brandeis." In the summer of 1969, Bickel was still writing favorably of the Warren Court in the *New Republic*.[65] "Compared to the references to the breakdown of American civilization that are strewn through his later works, Kurland's criticisms of the Warren Court [as late as 1970] are small jabs indeed." Mostly united in favor of the social change the Warren Court sought to make, law professors disagreed over the means it used.[66]

The Warren Court made the 1960s a good time for the law schools. All aspects of society—even corporate law firms—seemed viable candidates for reform. Law professors "moved easily between the practical and academic worlds." Through their students and scholarship, they could even believe they ran the world. Some legal scholars became involved in the law and society movement. Their empirical studies reflected their hope for "a union of objectivist knowledge and progressive politics." Such work reflected the faith in scientific models as objective foundations for progress that marked the postwar era. It drew on the social sciences to identify gaps between legal rules and realities and to advance "the liberal legal agenda of the day." Under what circumstances was the impact of legal doctrine "defeated, diverted, or distorted by social forces in need of reform"? Other professors stuck with analyzing the Court's opinions. Their doctrinal scholarship made a difference, they believed. "The growing incidence of law review material cited in Supreme Court opinions is testimony of the extent to which legal writers have influence upon the Justices," one legal liberal wrote in 1965. Still other law professors, such as Thomas Emerson, fought the good fight in the courtrooms. Such individuals had impact: Harry Kalven noted that the Warren Court's opinion expanding First Amendment rights in *New York Times* v. *Sullivan* echoed Weschler's brief on behalf of the newspaper. Charles Reich could dazzle liberals and transform the law by making a broad policy argument for expanding property rights to include entitlement to benefits distributed by the welfare state, in an article that would win the most citations in the history of the *Yale Law Journal* and help to propel the Court's procedural due process revolution.[67]

If Warren Court decisions contributed to the decline and destruction of the Great Society, just as Great Society legislation itself did, so much the better. The right's demonization of Warren for his Court's expansion of individual and civil rights only helped matters. "People are afraid of saying anything that can be misused by the Faubuses and Byrds," who supported segregation, Bickel said privately of law professors in 1958. In the 1960s, the Warren Court attracted even more fire, becoming an issue in the 1964 and 1968 elections. Congress even attempted to overrule some of the Court's criminal decisions by enacting the Omnibus Crime Control and Safe Streets Act in 1968. Because of the intensity of the reaction against it, the Warren Court continued to foster solidarity among academics who joined in support of it. Annoyed that his law professors were not saying the Warren Court at high tide "made the Nine Old Men look by comparison like a collection of juristic angels," Frankfurter once told Bickel that "you law professors really should sharpen your pens so that there is no mistaking as to what the trouble is and where the blame lies." They were generally not as harsh as Frankfurter would have liked. For all Bickel's insistence in personal correspondence that he "generally functioned without regard to the question of aid and comfort" to enemies of the Warren Court and that he could not "bring myself to call a moratorium on criticism of the judicial process, whenever I think, as I most often currently do, that the results are agreeable to me," he vigorously defended the Court and its members in the *New Republic* whenever they were attacked in Congress. Philip Kurland recognized that the Court had "been most fortunate in the enemies that it has made, for it is difficult not to help to resist attack from racists, from the John Birch Society, and from religious zealots who insist that the Court adhere to the truth as they know it." He saw that "the 'passivists' who condemn the Court for its activist role are always in the vanguard of those who rush to the defense of the Court when it is attacked for its activism."[68]

For all Harvard's mockery of Earl Warren's way of asking questions, members of a new generation who went to law school during the Warren years and entered law teaching at Harvard and elsewhere during the 1960s—a group including Jesse Choper, Bruce Ackerman, Ronald Dworkin, John Hart Ely, Owen Fiss, Frank Michelman, and Lawrence Tribe—were not haunted by memories of the old Court and viewed judicial activism even more tolerantly than did their teachers. True, the editors of the *Harvard Law Review* might sarcastically say that "[a]t least a few of the current law school generation, some readers may be surprised to hear, have not in their approval of the Warren Court's reforms entirely forgotten a lesson of the judicial crisis of the 1930's: the warning that a judiciary acting like a Council of Revision in favor of either right or left poses great institutional dangers." Yet those very editors also criticized the form process theory had taken. "Emphasis on principled, restrained adjudication is commonly associated with a great tradition of scholars and judges often connected in some way with the Harvard Law School," they observed, noting that Frankfurter, Hart, and Bickel, among others, had all studied law at Harvard and served on its law review:

> Even to those of us who share their concern for principle, there has sometimes seemed to be too much emphasis on durability and not enough on development. The compelling logic of the Frankfurter-Hart school has often appeared to impose a deadening hand; one has felt impelled to choose between rejecting progressive judicial positions for lack of coherent, principled rationales and abandoning the commitment to principle in frank undisguised result-orientedness.[69]

Most Harvard students chose progressivism. They worried, for example, that Hart did not notice "the air of jubilation among many law students this morning, caused by the Supreme Court decision in *Baker v. Carr.*" One student wrote Hart: "With all respect, I am completely confident that Baker v. Carr is right—and you are wrong." In 1969, the editors of the *Harvard Law Review* dedicated an issue to "Chief Justice Earl Warren who with courage and passion led a reform of the law while the other branches of government delayed." Their counterparts at the law school's student newspaper called on lawyers "to refuse to advance the interests of those things which worsen rather than alleviate the problems of our society," and described the 1960s as "a unique and wonderful age of judicial activism, where the courts have often been ahead of other governmental agencies in attempting to solve the pervasive problems of our society." Fiss, a Harvard law student in the 1960s who went on to clerk for Justice Brennan, insisted that "even in those days it was understood that Harvard did not speak for the profession as a whole, and even less so for the young, who looked to the Court as an inspiration, the very reason to enter the profession."[70]

Among students at other law schools, there were few signs of ambivalence about the Warren Court. Law schools capitalized on the Warren Court. "Glossy admissions brochures entice some students into law school with promises that lawyers of the future, riding white chargers, will crusade against social problems," one student wrote. As a law student working with prisoners at Leavenworth, another future academic learned "that the federal courts are special. They are the most splendid institutions for the maintenance of governmental order and individual liberty that humankind has ever conceived." To the children of the Warren Court, "the law seemed like a romance." The editors of the *Yale Law Journal* said Earl Warren "made us all proud to be lawyers." Alexander Bickel, who deplored the "vision of courts and of the law as instruments for millenarian social change" that brought so many to law school, might remind students that "federal judges were not inevitably 'little Earl Warrens in black robes,' " but he did not produce many "little Alexander Bickels in blue jeans." A red diaper baby who attended Yale in the 1960s, such as Mark Tushnet, would be aware of the many voices claiming that "the experience of the Warren Court and its interaction with the civil rights movement convinced us that, notwithstanding the skeptical determinism associated with Marxist social theory, it was possible for law to become an autonomous force for progressive social change." As one of his contemporaries emphasized: "We did not notice that there were many more clouds in that promising sky than we realized." The president of the *Stanford Law Review* spoke hopefully of infusing the "law, long dominated by traditional motives of security and avarice" with "altruism and self-sacrifice." Judge Skelly Wright concluded "that one of the greatest legacies of the Warren Court has been its revolutionary influence on the thinking of law students. . . . [F]or them, the Supreme Court *was* the Warren Court. For them, there was no theoretical gulf between the law and morality; and, for them, the Court was the one institution in the society that seemed to be speaking most consistently the language of idealism which we all recited in grade school."[71]

A "small but articulate minority of law students" and an occasional professor on the left might claim the Court's lack of position on the Vietnam War meant "our judges are neither bold nor courageous when evil comes full-blown." They might also grumble that for all its expansion of civil liberties, the Warren Court supported the state's power to police dissent in cases involving protest against the war. Like other political and legal liberals, Warren Court members saw a dichotomy between the state and the individual, and they did not always side with the individual. A few outsiders may have seen, too, that the Court's expansion of individual rights and national government did little to foster the left's ideal of community.[72]

But complaints were rare, and generally less forceful than the critiques of Warren Court liberalism for providing "half a loaf," which originated from outside the law schools. No law professor on the left in the 1960s produced as biting a critique of Warren Court liberalism as that written by historian Howard Zinn. Even his critique of the Warren Court paled next to the left's critique of political liberalism and Lyndon Johnson in the 1960s. In launching one of the early salvos against "the myth of rights," political scientist Stuart Scheingold nevertheless stressed that the "civil rights experience provides the clearest demonstration that legal tactics . . . can release energies capable of initiating and nurturing a political movement." As late as 1979, one scholar wrote in *Telos:* "Contemporary left-wing critics of American institutions either ignore the Supreme Court, or accept the liberal view of it. That view, particularly as applied to the Court during Warren's Chief Justiceship (1953–1969), is that the Court was benign, that it acted as a counterweight to oppressive measures of the 'political' branches, that it did not participate in 'cold war' policies, that its major decisions had nothing to do with economic developments, and that its influence has been highly 'progressive.' "[73]

The law schools remained apart from the revolution—in large part because their inhabitants perceived law to be in the vanguard of the revolution. Further, one law professor said, "There were very few elementary or secondary students in the S.D.S., on the one hand, and even fewer law students, Supreme Court clerks, or junior faculty [at law schools], on the other hand." Another law professor acknowledged that the "student revolts that have rocked campuses across the country have left the law schools relatively untouched."[74]

Certainly, the key word was "relatively." Yale Law School briefly housed a "commune" in its courtyard, but when ten thousand people converged on New Haven for the Black Panther trials in 1970, Yale law students focused on opposing "any attempt to stop the trial of the New

Haven Panthers by extralegal or coercive means" and on ensuring their right "to receive a fair trial." Bickel remarked thankfully that "training still tells a little." After Martin Luther King's assassination, *Harvard Law Review* editors likewise intoned that King's "militant nonviolence . . . has left lawyers and public officials with a precious opportunity: to channel the action and passion of our time into legal change now, before the processes of the legal system for orderly resolution of social disputes become largely irrelevant." For the editors of the *Columbia Law Review,* King's death made it even "more important" that "all [lawyers] admit a professional as well as civic obligation to find specific ways" lawyers could help solve "society's problems." Though law students at Harvard struck in 1969, class attendance increased during the strike, and the dean noticed that "law students did not seem to be preoccupied by ROTC, expansion or the other issues debated in the university." Instead they pointed to problems other law school deans liked to think worst at Harvard. The *Harvard Law Record* noted that at an all-night law library study-in, "a suggestion that the study-in discuss the eight demands of the Harvard College strikers was hooted down in favor of a free-flowing give-and-take session on grading, evaluation and alienation at Harvard Law." These issues seemed tame in an era when students in other parts of the university were claiming "with great sonority . . . that the university is an employer, a landlord, a lender, and is thus as prone to exploiting the disadvantaged as is any profit-making enterprise; that the alleged mutualities of knowledge do not exist in the ordinary classroom, where things-to-be-learned are authoritatively superimposed on passive, sullen, and unwilling learners, nor do they exist in the library and the laboratory, where research is in service to the status quo; that professionalism is not at odds with the urge to self-advantage, but a sophisticated method of indulging it, through guild controls and restrictive licenses; that academic freedom is a shibboleth, first because it is not practiced, as the preponderance of safe opinions among scholars testifies, and second because it is not practicable, since the involvements of the university with society are so *ex parte* that the very call for institutional neutrality is itself a disingenuous form of partisanship." Liberalism fared better in law than it did in other fields.[75]

Elsewhere, the compromises of liberalism, the breakdown of "law and order," and the war in Vietnam tarnished the concept by decade's end and led to disciplinary change. Radical sociology grew out of dissatisfaction with the sociologists who supported the war. Rejecting the theory that society was grounded on consensus, one graduate student wrote an essay "entitled, as I recall, 'Karl, Come Home, All is Forgiven,' which expressed my discovery of the power and basic truth of Marxian analysis." In linguistics, the generative semanticist James McCawley, who sometimes adopted the pseudonym Quang Phuc Dong, founded "the *Fuck Lyndon Johnson* school of example construction." In literature, accusations of "political complicity or irrelevance" toppled the New Criticism. "In the 1968 charge on the Modern Language Association convention, one could all but hear echoing from the marbled halls of the old Hotel Americana a version of Wordsworth's cry to Milton: 'England has need of thee, / She is a fen of stagnant waters.' "[76]

Radical historians read their disenchantment with liberalism back into the past. Some turned their backs on the consensus school and intellectual and political history, discovering social history. "If undergraduates could have voted in a binding referendum on the war, peace would have arrived the day after," Paul Buhle reasoned. "Beyond teach-ins, demonstrations, educational agitation, and downright riots, what remained?" The emergence of women's history, black history, and labor history represented, in part, "a search for allies" in America's past. Historian David Hackett Fischer would condemn presentism as "the mistaken idea that the proper way to do history is to prune away the dead branches of the past, and to preserve the green buds and twigs which have grown into the dark forest of our contemporary world." Presentism, however, had long characterized some good historical work, and now it led some radical historians to showcase "the struggles of the past in order to enhance prospects for struggles of the present."[77]

While the new social historians were writing history "from the bottom up" and often through the Marxist prism of class, other colleagues kept the spotlight on "elite manipulation." Some historians now claimed that the New Deal had given the disenfranchised a raw deal. William Appleman Williams and his students decried "corporate liberalism." Buhle stressed that those "two words passed overnight into the national vocabulary: they formed an especially suitable description for a Democratic leadership that steered an almost reluctant military establishment toward a land war in Asia. The phrase seemed to explain the hitherto unexplainable; it responded to a need for understanding that was instinctually felt by tens of thousands of dissenters who were unable to place themselves on any standard political map."[78]

Political scientist Theodore Lowi echoed the dissatisfaction with liberalism. In *The End of Liberalism,* he contended that the 1960s exposed the weakness of an "interest-group liberalism" built on the "flawed foundations" of pluralism. According to Lowi, 1960s liberals had wrongly decided to fight poverty. The phenomenon they confronted was "the injustice that has made poverty a nonrandom, nonobjective category." They should have attacked injustice and worked "to change social rules and conduct in order that poverty become and remain a random thing, an objective category. The interest-group-liberal approach—defining the effort as economic, attaching it to the welfare system, and making it almost totally discretionary—was not merely superfluous and redundant; it produced a whole array of unhappy consequences." Liberal governments would never achieve justice. The War on Poverty had only "diverted attention from civil rights" while leaving the old rules intact. In the end, liberalism was *conservative.* Historians John Blum and Richard Hofstadter had made the same point in the 1950s when they described reform as a way of avoiding revolution, but Lowi's words were redolent of a sinister, conspiratorial elite. He had "deliberately" picked the word "conservative," Lowi said, "because it best evokes a sense of the very things to which . . . liberalism claimed to be most antagonistic." Yet though Lowi condemned "liberal jurisprudence," he associated it with the regulatory process, which pitted interest groups against each other, not Warren Court judges.[79]

Through all of this, the Warren Court shone. Law professors, many of whom had clerked at the Court, celebrated the greatness and courageousness of Warren and his colleagues when Earl Warren surrendered the chief justiceship to Warren Earl Burger in 1969. By the time new courses in poverty law appeared, and Nixon's invasion of Cambodia and the disaster at Kent State had made "political authority . . . so suspect and the danger of civil disorder so great" that "the very basis of the American democracy" was imperiled, Warren was gone. In retirement, he seemed wiser than ever. "We have had many crises in prior years, but none within the memory of living Americans which compares with this one," Warren observed.[80]

Years later, one of his faculty hosts recalled Warren's visit to the University of California, San Diego, in the fall of 1970, a year after his retirement as chief justice:

> [A] huge crowd of students, faculty, and San Diegans packed the quadrangle of John Muir College to hear Warren's talk. As he rose to speak, several students unfurled a large banner from a nearby balcony. A hush fell over the throng, most of whom expected the worst in student graffiti, perhaps "F—k the Chief Justice." Our campus and hundreds of others across the nation had been rocked by student strikes in April when President Nixon launched the invasion of Cambodia. At Kent State and Jackson State, national guardsmen and state troopers had gunned down protestors. Earl Warren, former Chief Justice of the United States, represented the Establishment. But instead of an expletive, the banner read, "Right on, Big Earl!" The crowd roared its approval. Warren flashed a broad grin and proceeded to deliver a scathing attack on those who believed the country could have law and order without social justice.[81]

Even after Kent State and Cambodia, the editors of the five-year old *Harvard Civil Rights–Civil Liberties Law Review* reaffirmed their faith in making "law an effective instrument for advancing the personal freedoms and the human dignities of the American people." Similarly, Michael Tigar's critique, in his 1970 *Harvard Law Review* "Foreword," of the small world that Supreme Court justices occupied espoused continuing the Fifth Amendment work the Warren Court had "begun in *Miranda*," and nostalgically invoked "a sense of injustice, informed by past Court decisions." The Warren Court became "judicial Camelot."[82]

Despite Warren's retirement, then, the Warren era continued. As it did, it seemed clear that legal realism had not fared as well as legal liberalism. Legal realism had become too closely associated with the judicial activism that underlay the Warren Court's liberalism. As with pornography, Warren and his colleagues might know justice when they saw it.[83] But to many legal scholars, it seemed that the Warren Court had not produced objective criteria for justice. With a chief justice in power who might not pursue the politics of the Warren Court or law professors, legal realism now seemed dangerously unprincipled.

The politics of the Burger Court were not exactly clear. On the basis of some of its decisions, some commentators suggested that the Warren era lasted until 1974, and at one point Mark Tushnet even suggested renaming the Warren Court the Brennan Court. "The Brennan Court decided all the central cases of the Warren Court except *Brown* v. *Board of Education,* which the Brennan Court enthusiastically endorsed and extended. The Brennan Court went on to decide *Roe* v. *Wade,* and the gender discrimination cases as well."[84]

But by that analysis, the Warren Court's legacy appeared to be the "rootless activism" or "Lochnering" the Burger Court practiced in the 1970s—a constitutional theory of fundamental rights, and decisions, such as *Roe,* the "classic example of judicial usurpation and fiat without reason." Legal scholar Philip Bobbitt attributed "the universal disillusionment with *Roe* v. *Wade* . . . to the unpersuasive opinion in that case." In the five years following *Roe,* Lawrence Tribe of Harvard developed three different justifications for its outcome, none of which had much to do with the majority's reasoning. Many other law professors tried to find another doctrinal home for *Roe* as well: Richard Posner described the case as "the Wandering Jew of constitutional law." Another academic lawyer complained that *Roe* made a moral question "into a pragmatic issue of ad hoc balancing to be settled by five or more justices. Illustrating again its cleverness and result orientation, the Court reported that constitutional doctrine broke down neatly into trimesters." Judged on the criterion of "intellectual honesty," he concluded, "the Burger Court may have marked the low point in the Supreme Court's not always illustrious history." On grounds of craft, he and others believed, it would make law professors nostalgic for the Warren Court.[85]

That it did. Though *Roe* might have turned out all right substantively, who knew what else the Nixon appointees had up their sleeves? Did they see the record of the Warren Court and *Roe* as license to do whatever they wished? How else to explain their behavior in *Gedulig* v. *Aiello,* when a majority of the Burger Court ruled that discrimination against pregnant women did not constitute a sex-based classification? How else to explain the constant "wavering" of the Burger Court?[86]

In short, since so many law professors continued to believe in the power of courts to effect social change of which they approved, the counter-majoritarian difficulty loomed larger than ever. *Roe* plunged constitutional theory into "epistemological crisis," rekindling interest in judicial review and in the alleged conflict between judicial review and democracy. Legal scholars' task, as they saw it, was to demonstrate that though *Brown* had been correctly decided, *Lochner* and *Roe* had not. It was a worthy mission, one which cast legal scholars as "significant constitutional actors" and "minor oracles" whose scholarship was also Supreme Court advocacy. The effort to come to grips with legal realism, which had spurred process theory, the counter-majoritarian difficulty, and academic reactions to the Burger Court, began anew.[87]

CHAPTER 2

"LAW AND"

This time, law professors looked outward to other disciplines. Economist Paul Samuelson observed that though law schools had long been "an alien and unassimilated element in the body politic of the university," they became part of it "for the first time" in the 1970s. Because of the job crisis among academics, individuals who might once have opted to become humanists or social scientists were choosing to join law faculties. Tenured professors in the humanities and social sciences may have earned more and taught less than they did in previous decades. The young were not so fortunate. Earning a doctorate consumed six to ten years and was followed by exile, if one were lucky, to a series of one-year jobs in obscure schools at starvation wages. "At the 1970 meeting of the American Historical Association there were 2,481 applicants for 188 listed positions, and competition was so fierce that security measures had to be introduced to keep those seeking jobs from destroying invitations to interviews addressed to their competitors." The J.D. demanded only three years. After editing the law review and completing the requisite judicial clerkships, a beginning law professor could earn a great deal more than the humanist or social scientist. In all likelihood, a full professorship would follow in five years.[1]

Unlike departments in the humanities and social sciences, law schools had to tenure new faculty members because in the early 1970s business was booming. Ironically, in the aftermath of Watergate, everyone, so it seemed, wanted to go to law school. Over 135,000 Law School Admission Tests were administered in 1973–74, nearly 14,000 more than the previous year and almost twice as many as those given in any year of the 1960s. The more than 125,000 enrolled law students in 1976 paid more than $275 million in tuition.[2]

Like the realists and scholars in the law and society movement, law professors of the 1970s, some of whom were humanists and social scientists manqués, yearned to incorporate other disciplines in their work. Even those who might never have considered going to graduate school grazed in interdisciplinary pastures. Two of the legal scholars who turned to political philosophy in the 1970s, Frank Michelman and Bruce Ackerman, for instance, were products of what Erwin N. Griswold called "the traditional law school mill." That is, they had the same qualifications as the generation of law professors who preceded them—"high grades in law school—very high." They joined many other academic lawyers in writing of the potential that law possessed to interact with other disciplines.[3]

The appearance of Lawrence Tribe's *American Constitutional Law* in 1978, the first treatise to venture "a unified analysis of constitutional law" since Thomas Cooley's *Constitutional Limitations* more than a century earlier, was the exception that proved the rule. A political liberal, Warren Court devotee, and 1966 graduate of Harvard Law School who would never stop arguing cases before the Supreme Court or writing for judges, Tribe pointed out that all judicial decisions "inescapably" involved "taking sides. . . . Judicial authority to determine when to defer to others in constitutional matters is a procedural form of substantive power; judicial restraint is but another form of judicial activism." He advocated "a more candidly creative role than conventional scholarship has accorded the courts," proceeding "on the premise of a relatively large judicial role" and the idea that "federal courts have a special mission in defending substantive personal interests from governmental action that overreaches because of its unduly limited constituency—action that oppresses people because they are outsiders." Making a structural argument reminiscent of Charles Black's, Tribe rejected "the assumptions characteristic of Justices like Felix Frankfurter and scholars like Alexander Bickel: the highest mission of the Supreme Court, in my view, is not to conserve judicial credibility, but in the Constitution's own phrase, 'to form a more perfect Union' between right and rights within that charter's necessarily evolutionary design." Tribe mocked the "antimajoritarian difficulty" and "the usual hand-wringing over issues of judicial capacity and legitimacy." According to him, "Arguments about the legitimacy of judicial review are ultimately metaconstitutional: the relevant considerations are political, philosophical and historical in the broadest sense." That was exactly the point: in the 1970s, scholars were more interested in the reconciliation of judicial review with democracy than the opinions, or raw materials, of constitutional law, and they were more inclined to think of political, philosophical, and historical considerations.[4]

Yale's Arthur Leff remarked that many law professors of the 1970s spoke in terms of "law and." Contemporaries had ridiculed the legal realists' interdisciplinary ventures, and the empiricism of law and society had only appealed to some. The young legal scholars of the 1970s made it *fashionable* for junior and senior law professors to try interdisciplinary perspectives. Richard Posner declared it "no secret that many law professors have lost interest in the traditional undertakings of legal research."[5]

THE SEARCH FOR OBJECTIVE FOUNDATIONS OF JUSTICE

One group of law professors, who shared Tribe's commitment to a rights-based theory of the Constitution, became enamored of political philosophy. John Rawls enthralled them. His 1971 book, *A Theory of Justice,* won the Coif Award, awarded triennially by the Association of American Law Schools for the best book written on law. Rawls's effort there to develop a rights-based constitutionalism grounded on substantive and objective principles of justice promised a way out of legal realism's subjectivism by integrating constitutional decisionmaking with moral philosophy. At a time when Robert Nozick was about to elegize

the "minimal state" in *Anarchy, State, and Utopia,* Rawls promoted political and philosophical liberalism.[6]

Rawls espoused a theory that favored "the right," justice—which was prior to and presumed no concept of "the good." The hypothetical person behind a "veil of ignorance," which left the individual unaware of his or her education, income level, or values and particular vision of "the good," would select this theory of justice, he insisted. Rawls's imaginary individuals chose freely, unaware of personal desires or goals. "They do not know how the various alternatives will affect their own particular case and they are obliged to evaluate principles solely on the basis of general consideration." Rawls maintained they would prefer the right to the subjective good, and would discard a utilitarian theory of justice directed at achieving the greatest good for the greatest number. "Utilitarianism does not take seriously the distinction between persons." Nor would such people argue the ends justified the means. They would opt for "pure procedural justice," or "the Kantian interpretation of justice as fairness."[7]

Here was a theory to which even Earl Warren would have warmed, based as it was on equality and social justice, or, in Rawlsian terms, on maximum individual equality and the "difference principle." That principle provided that "social and economic inequity . . . are just only if they result in compensating benefits for everyone, and in particular for the least advantaged members of society." Yet Rawls gave hope to process theorists by separating law from politics as Kant might have done, though Warren did not. Citing Wechsler's plea for "principled decisions in law," Rawls pledged that his theory of justice would revive the rule of law *and* reconcile the tension between liberty and equality. *"A Theory of Justice* formulates as well as any book to date the principle of justice expressed by the Constitution," one law professor raved.[8]

As part of his continuing effort to bridge constitutional law and theory with political theory and philosophy, Frank Michelman of Harvard briefly yoked Rawls's work to his own. Michelman sought to justify the Court's enforcement of a governmental duty to provide for individuals' "minimum welfare" in order to increase participation in the political process. Unlike his 1960s counterparts, who had less of a need to do so, because the Court appeared headed in that direction, Michelman also used his first *Harvard Law Review* "Foreword" to urge the Court to assume this role.[9]

And during the early years of the Burger Court, it looked as if he might succeed. In fact, it appeared that the Burger Court might even hold wealth a suspect classification, requiring the Court to subject laws harming the poor to strict scrutiny rather than simply to determine whether they were rational, a step the Warren Court had only anticipated in dicta. But when the Supreme Court refused to declare wealth a suspect classification in 1973, some legal liberals became less optimistic. For others, such as Owen Fiss, the Court's 1976 decision in *Washington v. Davis,* requiring that those alleging equal protection clause violations in school segregation cases prove intent to segregate, represented Thermidor.[10]

In the mid-1970s, Fiss said later, law professors become estranged from the Supreme Court. And the Court returned their hostility. Chief Justice Burger lambasted the law schools for lawyer incompetence, and flayed the "young people who go into the law primarily on the theory that they can change the world by litigation in the courts." Justice William Rehnquist attacked the notion of "a living constitution" as "a formula for an end run around popular government." Legal scholars' isolation from what had once been their most important audience made them both more similar and more receptive to academics in other fields. The legal academy retained the fantasy of "maintaining a kind of interlocking directorate between itself and the Court." As the judiciary became less appealing, though, law professors were writing less for judges and more for each other.[11]

The shift in scholarship worried some law professors. For one example, "it would be a shame if the lawyer who does philosophy were to be judged solely by other lawyers," Richard Posner said. Who would separate "the experts" from "the charlatans"? Law review editors?[12]

In a sense, Posner was fretting needlessly, for legal scholarship was not changing all that much. Most academic lawyers were still courting judges. Even most of the scholarship of those who now dotted their articles with references to Rawls was traditional and focused on judicial decision making.[13]

Much of the scholarship was directed at awakening the spirit of the Warren Court. It was not always clear the law professors knew the

Warren era had ended, though some legal liberals were partially shifting their attention from the Supreme Court to lower federal courts, and from federal courts to the state courts. Opportunity of a sort struck in 1977, when the Court invalidated a congressional attempt to bring state employees within federal wage-and-hour standards. Many Court-watchers, including Justice Brennan and the other three dissenters, viewed the majority's decision in *National League of Cities* v. *Usery,* as "a step back to the pre–New Deal era in which the Court routinely found reasons to limit the exercise of Congress' commerce power." It should have been apparent to the legal liberals—and it probably was to the pessimists among them—that they now faced the conservative hegemony on the Court they had feared. Their students could see it: the editors of the *Yale Law Journal* dedicated their symposium on *National League of Cities* to Brennan, noting that "we have entered a new era in the history of the Supreme Court and a new jurisprudence is ascendant." Yet in an ironic and stunning symposium article, which tried to seize victory from the jaws of defeat by pointing to the incoherence of the opinion and providing a gloss on it he himself characterized as "perverse," Michelman claimed "to see at work in the Supreme Court's own *NLC* [*'National League of Cities'*] opinion a premise ascribing special service responsibilities to the states."[14]

Meanwhile Bruce Ackerman's success in the early 1970s provided reason for retaining hope in the federal courts. Vigorous enforcement of housing codes would help the indigent, Ackerman argued. It would not hurt them by increasing rents and reducing the housing supply. Washington, D.C., Circuit Court of Appeals Judge Skelly Wright cited Ackerman's article in his important 1972 decision establishing an implied warranty of habitability. Ackerman's work, Wright said, supported the proposition that "[w]hen code enforcement is seriously pursued, market forces generally prevent landlords from passing on their increased costs through rent increases."[15]

Traditionally, citation by an important court represented a high point for the legal scholar. As one schooled in the realist tradition, however, Ackerman may have wondered how much his work really influenced Wright. Did the citation constitute window dressing? For whatever reason—perhaps growing doubt about the value of doctrinal work, perhaps interdisciplinary currents—Ackerman, like Michelman, was broadening the way he wrote about law.

And Ackerman too was a Rawls enthusiast. In *Social Justice in the Liberal State,* a book that constituted a long, friendly debate with Rawls and included a modified original position, Ackerman attacked "the conflict between self-fulfillment and social justice" by producing a theory of justice based on dialogue and neutral conversations between individuals on how best to share resources. "The hard truth is this: There is no moral meaning hidden in the bowels of the universe," Ackerman claimed. That was no reason to despair. "We may create our own meanings, you and I." Miraculously, neither that process nor accepting liberalism would involve "Big Questions of a highly controversial character." Along with Rawls, Ackerman helped to "popularize the notion that something called Neutrality was at the heart of contemporary liberalism. . . . [A] principle purpose of my book about *The Liberal State* is to convince you that a commitment to Neutrality leads neither to intellectual bankruptcy nor empty formalism, but to an incisive form of liberal political culture."[16]

Still another Rawls convert, Ronald Dworkin, articulated a rights-based jurisprudence designed to constrain judicial discretion, rationalize the Warren Court's record, integrate law with morals, and promote democracy. Where Bickel linked democracy to majority will, Dworkin thought in terms of rights against the majority. For Dworkin, the debate about the propriety of the Warren Court's imposition of its values on the nation obscured "the issue of what moral rights an individual has against the state." Giving the Warren Court a "rights" spin, he announced that rights were "trumps." Dworkin's idealized judge, whom he named Hercules, possessed a particular vision of rights foundationalism, which treated equality as more important than liberty. Hercules believed that the duty of government was to treat people "with equal concern and respect," and that judicial decisions must "enforce existing political rights." As Dworkin put it in *Taking Rights Seriously:*

> Constitutional law can make no genuine advance until it isolates the problem of rights against the state and makes that problem part of its own agenda. That argues for a fusion of constitutional law and moral theory, a connection that, incredibly, has yet to

take place. It is perfectly understandable that lawyers dread contamination with moral philosophy, and particularly with those philosophers who talk about rights, because the spooky overtones of that concept threaten the graveyard of reason. But better philosophy is now available than the lawyers may remember. Professor Rawls of Harvard, for example, has published an abstract and complex book about justice which no constitutional lawyer will be able to ignore.[17]

Yet the search for objective foundations of justice, which underlay both process theory and the reach to Rawls in rights foundationalism, seemed ever more elusive in the 1970s. In the deconstructionist moment of poststructuralist thought, the opposition of subjectivity and objectivity became quintessential expressions of the old metaphysics. Subjectivity and objectivity stood exposed as artificial constructs that proved more deceptive than revealing. In the context of the decade, however, one need not embrace deconstruction (and few law professors did yet) to see that Rawls did not make idiosyncrasy in the decisional process or the counter-majoritarian difficulty go away. "The Fourteenth Amendment, as Holmes has said, does 'not enact Mr. Herbert Spencer's Social Statics,'" Harry Wellington observed. "Nor does it enact Mr. John Rawls' *A Theory of Justice.*" By 1973 Michelman, at least, had come to agree with Wellington about the inadvisability of courts cutting "welfare rights out of the whole cloth of speculative moral theory—not Rawls' theory, at any rate—and foist[ing] them on resistant legislatures." Michelman did, however, hold out the hope "that there will someday appear some speculative moral theory which displays both sufficient incisiveness to contribute toward the solution of testing cases, and sufficiently persuasive and accessible coherence with latent popular morality to deserve judicial recognition."[18]

Refusing "to accept the possibility that morality can be sufficiently objective to play a role in constitutional adjudication," other law professors rejected moral theory in general, and Rawls and Dworkin in particular. Further, philosophers rushed to point out problems with Rawls's theory of justice. In the end, Rawls proved helpful only to legal scholars predisposed toward political liberalism who were looking for a way to justify its continuance. As Ackerman admitted years later, no version of rights foundationalism could produce satisfactory criteria for identifying which rights were fundamental.[19]

FROM HISTORY TO INTERPRETIVISM

Legal scholars who discovered history in the 1970s, at least as it was written for law professors, found new reasons to question an activist Supreme Court. In the 1950s and 1960s, American legal history had been a "Dark Continent." At its best, it seemed arcane. In the 1970s, the field was professionalized. Academic historians now used the pages of the *American Journal of Legal History* to speak with each other instead of with practitioners, and Harvard University Press established a legal history series.[20]

The 1977 publication of *The Transformation of American Law* by Morton Horwitz, one of the few law professors at the time who held both a Ph.D. (in government, but one obtained through study with Louis Hartz in Harvard's historically oriented department) and J.D., signaled the arrival of legal history. The book exposed nineteenth-century judges self-consciously reshaping the law of torts, contracts, and property, as well as commercial law, to aid "men of commerce and industry at the expense of farmers, workers, consumers, and other less powerful groups within the society." For historians outside the law schools, this was old news. "Historians found Horwitz's work entirely congenial—so congenial that they awarded his book their most prestigious professional award, the Bancroft prize—because he told a story with which most historians were familiar," Mark Tushnet remembered. Since *Transformation* seemed to link realism's emphasis on judicial idiosyncrasy to a Marxist perspective, however, "lawyers felt threatened by Horwitz's story, and the reviews by lawyers were much more critical."[21]

Even so, Horwitz's book transformed legal history. It swung the attention of historians from public to private law. Constitutional law, the author announced, "had been overstudied both in terms of its impact on the development of the American economy and in terms of its representative character." Focus on private law would illuminate "the more regular instances in which law, economy and society interacted." Horwitz thus made legal history "hot" among historians by presenting it as a form of the "new" social history. He gave law professors who might

have become historians in another job market a way of holding up their heads among what Horwitz referred to as the "general" historians. Further, his emphasis on the antidemocratic nature of American law in the nineteenth century "gave the study of legal history the kind of excitement and drama it had been sorely lacking" as it was taught. The book's "impieties" made it memorable. *Transformation* ruled "the field of American legal history for more than a decade, as no book had before, or has since."[22]

Whereas legal history became popular among historians inside and outside the law schools in the 1970s, constitutional history enjoyed a resurgence among law professors. Though the drumrolls of original intent had sounded periodically through the years, they had been muffled since Henry Hart savaged W. W. Crosskey's *Politics and the Constitution in the History of the United States.* During the Warren era, academics believed they were "better off . . . being subjected to the whims of willful judges trying to make the Constitution live [than] . . . being bound by the dead hand of the past." Long before he directed Alexander Bickel to examine the legislative history of the Fourteenth Amendment, Frankfurter was saying that "this business of trying to find the scope of the Fourteenth Amendment in this or that pamphlet or this or that individual expression of hope of what was accomplished by the Amendment is . . . no way of dealing with a 'constituent act' like the Fourteenth Amendment." For Frankfurter, Mark Tushnet said, "original intent mattered only to the extent that it might clearly bar the Court from doing what the Justices believed appropriate." Alexander Bickel sounded like a historian himself when he explained to the historian J. R. Pole in 1963: "At our best, we use history in the development of our constitutional law as a liberating rather than a confining body of knowledge." As Bickel told Robert Bork five years later, it was "one thing to charge the judges with being unprincipled. It is another to charge them with having used the wrong principles, unworkable principles, or principles the implications of which they have not examined and would themselves not accept. It is yet another, and it seems to me most difficult to demonstrate, to charge them with having used principles that can be shown to be wrong through the extrapolation of the right ones from the Bill of Rights, the same sources they disingenuously purport to have used." Even supposing "it could really work," Bickel asked, would being bound by "the dead hand of the past" be any better? "No answer is what the wrong question begets, for the excellent reason that the Constitution was not framed to be a catalogue of answers to such questions." Law professors believed that the great judges were those who "most effectively used the fabric of fiction [dressed up as history] to camouflage their creativity." Warren himself observed forthrightly in his farewell address, "We, of course, venerate the past, but our focus is on the problems of the day and the future as far as we can foresee it." The publication of Alfred Kelly's "Clio and the Court" in 1965 and Charles Miller's *The Supreme Court and the Uses of History* in 1969 demonstrated beyond a doubt that the Warren Court had repeatedly misused history.[23]

Law professors had found no occasion for alarm in the Warren Court's concoctions of "inept and perverted history" to give opinions "the trappings of scholarship and seeming roots in the past." By rooting its product in bogus "law office history," the Warren Court sought to cloak its activism. Yet Kelly pointed out that Supreme Court justices had long written law-office history, which entailed "the selection of data favorable to the position being advanced without regard to or concern for contradictory data or proper evaluation of the relevance of the data proffered." In the nineteenth century, for example, the Court's abuse of history had "tended uniformly to one general consequence: The degradation of blacks in slavery, crypto-servitude, and nominal freedom." Neither that nor subsequent misuses of history aroused concern. The outcry that greeted Justice Black's attempted revision of the history of the Fourteenth Amendment to incorporate the Bill of Rights represented an exception that proved the rule. In the 1960s, John Marshall Harlan was the only justice to demonstrate any real concern for the original understanding of the Fourteenth Amendment. "On those sporadic occasions where a Warren Court majority opinion undertook historical exegesis, the elicited conclusions were sufficiently implausible to suggest virtual contempt for the integrity of the historical record."[24]

No one cared. Historian Leonard Levy could declare it a "notorious fact" that like its predecessors, the Warren Court "flunked history," while applauding "Warren's candid and simple valedictory." Vincent Blasi thought it "striking how the most careful constitutional scholars content themselves with flat assertions when it comes time to dismiss the significance of the framers' original understanding." Arthur Miller, a Warren Court admirer, put it this way: "Trying to read the minds of men long dead is not the way to interpret the Constitution, for it is a document always in a state of becoming."[25]

But in the mid-1970s, constitutional law spawned interpretivism and, more generally, a renewed fascination with constitutional theory. Those constitutional theories that had been advanced to that point generally represented variations of process jurisprudence. In a pathbreaking 1975 article, "Do We Have an Unwritten Constitution?" Thomas Grey of Stanford contended that "in the important cases, reference to and analysis of the constitutional text plays a minor role." The observation was hardly original, but it led Grey to "perhaps the most fundamental question we can ask about our fundamental law," next to "the question of the legitimacy of judicial review itself," and one rarely raised recently. "In reviewing laws for constitutionality, should our judges confine themselves to determining whether those laws conflict with norms derived from the written constitution?" Grey answered no. Judges may "also enforce principles of liberty and justice when the normative content of those principles is not to be found within the four corners of our founding document." At a time when the Burger Court bored or bothered most law professors, Grey gave them the terminology to do something other than pick apart its opinions. By his account, interpretivists believed "that the only norms used in constitutional adjudication must be those inferable from the text" of the Constitution. The judge's task was to interpret the Constitution. Noninterpretivists, on the other hand, espoused a "broader view of judicial review," which went beyond the written Constitution. Grey himself justified contemporary noninterpretivism on the grounds that "there was an original understanding, both implicit and textually expressed, that unwritten higher law principles had constitutional status."[26]

Grey hoped to displace the counter-majoritarian difficulty by concentrating on the scope of judicial power. In actuality, Martin Shapiro said, the interpretivism/noninterpretivism controversy proved just "a rather awkward surrogate for the democracy debate. It is essentially a debate over how much law the Supreme Court should make in light of its particular place in the American polity." Take, for example, John Marshall's statement: "[W]e must never forget, that it is a *Constitution* we are expounding." Interpretivists contended that the chief justice meant to bind the Court to the written text, while noninterpretivists argued he had cut the justices loose to adjust to society's changing needs. Grey himself admitted that noninterpretivism created "a role for our courts [that] is more difficult to justify" than that assigned by interpretivism, which "supports judicial review while answering the charge that the practice is undemocratic."[27]

To Grey, noninterpretivism was nevertheless the answer. The fact of an "unwritten constitution" justified the "courts' additional role as the expounder of basic national ideals of individual liberty and fair treatment, even when the content of these ideals is not expressed as a matter of positive law in the written Constitution." By emphasizing the existence of an unwritten constitution, Grey sought to erase "the tendency of our courts—today as throughout our history—to resort to bad legislative history and strained reading of constitutional language to support results that would be better justified by explication of contemporary moral and political ideals not drawn from the constitutional text." By looking to history, specifically to the Founders' world, judges would be liberated from history. They could construct their own contemporary analogue to the Founders' reliance on natural law. At the same time, the process could justify Warren Court decisions protecting fundamental rights, "the modern offspring, in a direct and traceable line of legitimate descent, of the natural-rights tradition that is so deeply embedded in our constitutional origins," the right to privacy, *Roe* v. *Wade,* and the welfare rights Grey hoped to see constitutionalized.[28]

While Grey used historical reasoning to buttress legal liberalism, others did not. With the publication of *Government by Judiciary* in 1977, which alleged the Warren Court had committed the sin to which his title alluded, Raoul Berger, for one, championed interpretivism. His title alluded to the constitutional crisis of the 1930s; in 1932, Leonard Boudin's *Government by Judiciary* had charged that the justices of the Supreme Court had transformed a "government of laws" into a "government by a Few Conservative men." According to Berger, the shoe now belonged on the liberal foot. "Warren converted the Constitution to a scrap of paper," he alleged. "The academicians loved it because there was no other way of satisfying their aspirations." Berger maintained that the Fourteenth Amendment's drafters intended to protect limited rights. By his thesis, the Warren Court's decisions on school segregation and re-apportionment "revised the Fourteenth Amendment to mean exactly the opposite of what its framers designed it to mean." So great was the hold of *Brown* on the legal profession by this time that Berger acknowledged it could not be reversed. "It would . . . be utterly unrealistic and probably impossible to undo the past in the face of the expectations that the segregation decisions, for example, have aroused in our black citizenry—expectations confirmed by every decent instinct," he said in his conclusion. "That is more than the courts should undertake and more, I believe, than the American people would desire. But to accept thus far accomplished ends is not to condone the continued employment of the unlawful means." It was wrong to "convert the 'chains of the Constitution' to ropes of sand." Like the reapportionment decisions, *Brown* and its progeny were historically illegitimate. Though Berger said he was "not insensible to the tremendous question: how would we be rid of segregation if the Court had not acted," he observed that the question itself "posits that revision in a noble cause is justified, that the end justifies the means."[29]

The book reached a wide audience. "Fie on the Fourteenth: Berger barks again," *Time* announced. According to one commentator, Berger's *Government by Judiciary* "crystallized for millions of non-lawyers the fear that the Court has jumped the bounds of legitimate judicial review and is pursuing a course that bears dismaying resemblance to the excesses of the pre-1937 Court—the 'Nine Old Men' who nearly crippled the New Deal of Franklin Roosevelt." The effect on the profession was equally explosive. One scholar credited Berger with forcing "all constitutional theorists to deal with questions regarding proper principles of constitutional interpretation and the proper role of the courts, questions that many theorists, basking in the warm glow of Warren Court decisions on individual rights, felt content to ignore." Political scientist Walter Murphy proved less gracious. "Running through the entire volume is the clearly articulated theme that the principal, indeed the only, criterion for constitutional interpretation is the 'intent' of the framers," he complained. "Original 'intent' forever settles questions of public law and public policy. . . . Carried to its logical conclusion, Berger's reasoning that constitutional interpretation consists almost solely of historical research would argue for creation of a special federal court in the United

States . . . staffed by professional historians rather than lawyers and . . . [having] exclusive jurisdiction over questions—though not necessarily the final disposition of cases—involving the meaning of the Constitution." Could the "intelligent and patriotic" Framers really have wanted that? And even if they did, should their descendants?[30]

The book provoked academic questions about Founders' intent, or original intent, and few liked Berger's answers. Once Berger had been "the darling of liberal scholars." His books on Founders' intent with respect to impeachment and executive privilege were "said to have helped topple Richard Nixon's presidency." Now Berger anticipated being "torn limb from limb by the Warrenites," who would "recoil like a devout Catholic from criticism of the Virgin birth." He rightly predicted he would receive "scant sympathy from the establishment, which is wedded to the result-oriented jurisprudence of the Warren era." As his evidence and use of it were attacked, Berger joyfully turned constitutional history into a battleground.[31]

Were his motives political? One scholar detected "an increasing frustration with modern American liberalism" in Berger's work. Berger denied his politics influenced his jurisprudence, and swore he was "a political 'liberal.' " "As long ago as 1942 I divorced my personal predilections from my evaluation of constitutional mandates, indicating that I liked it no more when Justice Black read my predilections into the Constitution than when the Four Horsemen read theirs," he said. "From that credo I have never wavered." He thought the confusion about his politics stemmed "from a failure to perceive that conservative-liberal are political *labels*. My political choices are poles apart from the conservative camp; e.g. I am against school prayers, 'right to life' anti-abortionists, malapportionment. . . . It is a cardinal mistake to import the conservative-liberal labels into constitutional analysis." The reaction to Berger's book, however, underlined how integral a part of political liberalism legal liberalism had become. As one of his conservative friends said, Berger was now the darling of the conservatives and was universally considered politically conservative, whether or not he liked it: "There's not one darn constitutional scholar in this country who thinks for a moment that Raoul Berger is a non-partisan, olympian scholar who calls the shots as he sees them. The liberal establishment in our law schools believes that you are the enemy."[32]

Certainly Berger's interpretivism jeopardized legal liberalism. Other critics had claimed the Warren Court's decisions bespoke judicial tyranny, but they did not present themselves as historians. Berger was, Paul Brest emphasized, the only critic to rest his case against the Warren Court and rights jurisprudence exclusively on the grounds that they were "not authorized and not guided by the text and original history of the Constitution."[33]

Because political scientists and historians had surrendered constitutional history to the lawyers, and legal historians in the 1970s were not concentrating on constitutional history, Berger had the field mostly to himself. Ironically, in a sense, Berger made modern American legal history possible. His constitutional histories of impeachment and executive privilege, which appeared in the new series on legal history the American Society for Legal History launched, surely helped convince publishers that legal history was an economically viable field. Nevertheless, constitutional history was experiencing "a loss of prestige in the academy," Harry Scheiber said later in a notable understatement. Some scholars even thought "that blocking constitutional law out of legal-historical studies might easily become a touchstone of new legal history—an entry card, as it were, to the club." In the late 1980s, the legal historian William E. Nelson would produce a book on the Fourteenth Amendment that effectively undercut Berger's thesis by demonstrating that the Fourteenth Amendment's framers possessed two goals—"the protection of rights and the preservation of federalism." In the 1970s, however, Nelson was exploring the Americanization of the common law, dispute and conflict resolution in Massachusetts, and the roots of American bureaucracy. Similarly, in the late 1980s and early 1990s, Nelson's colleague John Reid would publish a multivolume constitutional history of the American Revolution. In the 1970s, though, Reid was writing mainly about the relationship between the Anglo-American and Cherokee conceptions of law, the impact of common law ideas on prerevolutionary Americans' approach to parliamentary power, and how Americans who went west on the Overland Trail brought their concept of law with them.[34]

To be sure, Reid and a few others were writing some constitutional history in the 1970s that would become indirectly relevant to a later debate over whether the colonists marched toward the Revolution with law on their side. But as one law professor pointed out twenty years later, these "conclusions . . . usually appeared in the backwaters of legal publications," and they tended to take on Berger indirectly anyway. At the time, Berger's use of history to justify an interpretivism that would constrict judicial discretion was assailed in articles but not undercut by a book that could be waved to refute his position.[35]

Yet despite some notable exceptions, such as Ronald Dworkin, most of Berger's liberal challengers, who were still lighting candles for the Warren Court, did not want to abandon interpretivism. As interpretivism took its place alongside process jurisprudence as one of "the two leading dogmas of modern constitutional theory," nearly everyone wanted to be an interpretivist. True, interpretivism was even narrower than process theory, which Berger thought left too much to judicial discretion. Had Earl Warren still been alive, however, he might have jumped on the interpretivist bandwagon too. Once interpretivism became a buzzword, it was good strategy to say judges should enforce norms stated or implicit in the Constitution; almost all law professors therefore did so. Further, they stressed the importance of honoring the Founders' intent.[36]

Few scholars would side with Michael Perry, who subscribed to Berger's history but argued it was important "to let the framers sleep." Perry pleaded for noninterpretive review in human rights cases on the grounds that it represented "the institutionalization of prophecy," "has served the American polity as an agency of ongoing insistent moral reevaluation and ultimately of moral growth," and could provide "a right to food, clothing, housing, and education; rights to work, leisure, fair wages, decent working conditions, and social security; rights to physical and mental health; protection for the family and for mothers and children; a right to participate in cultural life." Berger commended Perry for being "[v]irtually the first activist apologist to face up unflinchingly to the adverse historical facts." Yet although fellow constitutional theorists admired Perry's approach, they did not adopt it. Rather, most argued for a "less rigid" form of interpretivism than Berger's. For this purpose, they employed historical arguments but used them instrumentally. They cared little about history. In the late 1970s, law professors fought strict interpretivism in constitutional interpretation, rather than interpretivism per se.[37]

And the professors seemed to be winning. In the 1970s, Robert Bork was too busy fabricating the "original intent" of the Sherman Act's drafters to pay much attention to that of the Constitution's framers or ratifiers. "One does not have to be clairvoyant to predict that *Government by Judiciary* will convince only those already convinced and that it will have little or no effect upon the course of constitutional interpretation," Arthur Miller wrongly predicted. Even in the 1970s, however, the reactions to Berger's and to Horwitz's history showed that legal scholars were becoming more self-conscious about the possibility of objectivity and the effect of their politics on their scholarship.[38]

LEGAL LIBERALISM BESIEGED

Meanwhile, the law professorate began to attract individuals with more diverse politics, who challenged the liberal consensus. The 1970s spawned the taxpayers' revolt, the New Right, and cultural conservatism. Initially, these developments did not disturb the legal academy. Of thirty-eight Harvard Law School professors polled in the fall of 1972, for example, thirty-four registered their support for George McGovern over Richard Nixon, and thirty had donated money to McGovern's campaign. When Alan Freeman began teaching at the University of Minnesota in the early 1970s, he remembered later, "[o]ne could not imagine that real right-wingers (e.g., law and economics theorists, since Posner's book hadn't even come out yet) could become dominant on law faculties, nor exist at all in appreciable numbers of the student body (I had my first authentic right-wing student in about 1974, and felt sorry for him in his loneliness and alienation)."[39]

Posner's book did appear, Bork's followed, and law and economics blossomed. As Posner, then a law professor at Chicago, readily acknowledged, law and economics predated his own interest in the topic and was rooted in legal realism. According to him, however, "The promises of the Legal Realists were never redeemed." This mistake he intended to rectify. As the first editor of the *Journal of Legal Studies*, which began appearing in 1972, Posner declared it his purpose "to encourage the application of scientific methods to the study of the legal system. As biology is to living organisms, astronomy to the stars, or economics to the price system, so should legal studies be to the legal system: an endeavor to make precise, objective, and systematic observations of how the legal system operates in fact and to discover and explain the recurrent patterns in the observations—the 'laws' of the system." Posner traced the birth of modern law and economics to the work of Gary Becker, Guido Calabresi, and Ronald Coase in the late 1950s and early 1960s.[40]

It was Posner, however, who symbolized the movement and whose lucid prose and "unstinting confidence" explained so much of its impact on law in the 1970s. In *Economic Analysis of Law* and in articles, he set out his key proposition: "The basis of an economic approach to law is the assumption that the people involved with the legal system act as rational maximizers of their satisfactions." Sure enough, law and economics scholars were finding that "the participants in the legal process indeed behave as if they were rational maximizers"; that, in contradistinction to the legislative process, a judicial concern with maximizing economic efficiency had strongly influenced the development of the common law; that economic analysis could prove "helpful in designing reforms of the legal system"; and that "quantitative study of the legal system is fruitful." Where a political liberal such as Ackerman might base the argument that housing code enforcement would not harm the very poor it aimed to help on "a series of hypothetical slum markets, each of whose relationship to reality is controversial," a Chicago trained lawyer-economist might employ empirical analysis to say that the housing market would prove less manageable than Ackerman had intimated and that enforcement might lead to higher rents and a lower housing supply.[41]

Posner maintained that scholars in law and economics lacked the inveterate normativity of most law professors. By his account, academics in law and economics did not dwell on justice, though they did illuminate it as they made inroads on fields ranging from antitrust (especially antitrust!—or "anti-antitrust") to zoning. For instance, Posner said they could show that Rawls's theory of distributive justice possessed "little operational content" because the philosopher had assumed too high a degree of "risk aversion" in the hypothetical individual hidden behind the veil of ignorance. "Rawlsism" suffered from "indefiniteness" because it depended on "empirical hunches." But "economics cannot tell us how society should be managed," Posner insisted. "Efficiency is a technical term: it means exploiting economic resources in such a way that human satisfaction as measured by aggregate consumer willingness to pay for goods and services is maximized." John Donohue summed up the general thesis of prominent conservatives in law and economics. "The problem is endemic: by showing excessive concern for say, the poor sap who finds himself in a tight spot, one may increase the number of individuals who end up in tight spots." Posner dismissed the criticism that law and economics scholars showed "a strongly conservative political bias." A finding that "legislation designed to protect the consumer frequently ends up hurting him" did not constitute an endorsement of the free market. So, too, law and economics scholars could say only "that capital punishment deters, not that it is a good thing."[42]

This was a distinction without a difference, which underlined the coyness of those in law and economics. Nevertheless, it served a useful purpose, Arthur Leff noted in a 1974 commentary. Why had law and economics become the rage, he asked? Why was the summer session Henry Manne held on the movement "continuously oversubscribed (to such an extent that his little Pareto-in-the-Pines has its own long and distinguished alumni group rivaling that of more conventional 'legal' alma maters)"? Leff explained that the movement's popularity grew out of law professors' quest for objective foundations of justice, which in turn reflected "an attempt to get over, or at least get by, the complexity thrust upon us by the Realists." To state "the current situation as sharply and nastily as possible; there is today no way of 'proving' that napalming babies is bad except by asserting it (in a louder and louder voice), or by defining it as so, early in one's game, and then slipping it through in a whisper, as a conclusion." No one could "tell (or at least . . . tell about) the difference between right and wrong," but everyone wanted "to go on talking. If we could find a way to slip in our normatives in the form of descriptives, within a discipline offering narrow and apparently usable epistemological categories, we would all be pathetically grateful for such a new and more respectable formalism in legal analysis," he said. "Since that is the promise of economic analysis of law, to an increasing (and not wholly delusive or pernicious) extent," many leaped to embrace it.[43]

In the end, Leff predicted, the effort would prove both delusive and pernicious. The "neo-Panglossian move" of law and economics notwithstanding, the normative dimension could never be evaded. "I don't know how one talks about it," Leff concluded,

> but napalming babies *is* bad, and so is letting them or even their culpable parents starve, freeze, or merely suffer plain miserable discomfort while other people, more "valuable" than they are or not, freely choose snowmobiles and whipped cream. Whatever is wrong with all that, it is only partly statistical. People are neither above reproach, nor are they ever just "sunk costs." *And "the law" has always known it; that is the source of its tension and complexity.* If economic efficiency is part of the common law (and it is), so is *fiat justitia ruat coelum*.[44]

When Posner finally did adopt an explicitly ethical criterion for law, it was hardly one of which Leff was likely to approve. In two articles in 1979 and 1980, which he soon expanded into a book, Posner proclaimed his allegiance to "the economic norm known as 'wealth maximization.'" Like Rawls, Posner opposed utilitarianism. He insisted his theory avoided the "moral monstrousness" that might bring the utilitarian to endorse extermination of a despised minority to increase the happiness of society as a whole. It also ducked the "moral squeamishness" that might bring the Kantian to sacrifice the social good to individual rights. The principle of wealth maximization worked because everything had its price. "Only the fanatic refuses to trade off lives for property." At the same time, the wealth-maximization criterion "encourages and rewards the traditional virtues ('Calvinist' or 'Protestant') and capacities associated with economic progress. The capacities (such as intelligence) promote the efficiency with which resources can be employed; the virtues (such as honesty, and altruism in its proper place), by reducing market transaction costs, do the same."[45]

Though the wealth-maximization criterion included "no *public* duty to support the indigent," at least it cut down genocide. "If Nazi Germany wanted to get rid of the Jews, in a system of wealth maximization it would have had to buy them out." And the wealth-maximization principle would increase the number of adoptable infants and available kidneys by expanding the market to include babies and body parts. There was "no immorality in the idea of a baby market, when morality is derived from economic principle itself."[46]

Predictably, Posner's proposals proved controversial. Though the criterion of wealth maximization itself was clear enough, one reviewer lamented, Posner neglected the crucial question of "why a society organized around such principles is ethically or morally superior to all other imaginable societies that are not so organized. The problem, it seems, is that hardly anyone since King Midas has really believed that wealth is an ultimate goal." The wealth-maximization principle depended on "too thin, flat, and sectarian a conception of value." It was also inherently circular: "whether a policy will maximize wealth is a function of the willingness of individuals to pay for the affected goods or services, which is a function of the existing wealth distribution, which is in turn a function at least in part of the society's policies in prior time periods. Thus under a wealth-maximization system, wealth distribution both determines and is determined by the social rules and institutions."[47]

Of course, Posner's was not the only version of law and economics. In New Haven, for example, political liberals were developing a progressive approach to it. It was Posner, however, with his "willingness to write things that conventionally nice people wouldn't write," who got most of the attention. In the 1970s, law and economics had the effect of promoting political conservatism within the academy.[48]

Students articulated and responded to the conservative impulse. By 1978, Federalist Societies were springing up in law schools around the country. Whereas in the 1960s students had established the *Harvard Civil Rights–Civil Liberties Law Review,* in the 1970s they founded the *Harvard Journal of Law and Public Policy* "to provide an alternative forum to the liberal establishment law review perspectives." Defining the "philosophical premises" of conservatism as "judicial restraint, limited government and the rule of law," they promised that the journal's "editorial perspective will be what may broadly be characterized as conservative."[49]

But why promote judicial restraint when law and economics offered no acceptable substitute for courts? In its application of economic theory to political science and constitutional law, law and economics' cousin, public choice, painted a grim picture of a legislative process where the public interest was irrelevant, dominated by special interests and preexisting preferences, and characterized by incoherent outcomes. Public choice treated the legislative process as irrational. At the very least, this suggested that process theorists, such as Hart and Sacks, had possessed a naive and inadequate picture of how legislators operated. More fundamentally, public choice raised the question of why judges—or legal scholars—should assume they could discern the will of the majority in legislatures, or why they would want to honor it if they could. As Michelman said in 1977, the public choice model showed "no good legislators, only shrewd ones; no statesmen, only messengers; no entrusted representatives, only tethered agents." In contrast, he himself liked to think that, at least in his own area of local government law, Supreme Court justices assisted legislatures in assuming "a Rousseauian public-interest conception of politics." Extrapolating, Michelman wondered whether efficiency was ever judges' only lodestar and whether economics would indeed prove "the key to law."[50]

As conservatism's star rose, disenchantment with legal and political liberalism forced some law professors to the left. For example, David Trubek, once a leading light of the law and society movement, now equated the objective empiricism of its "gaps research" with "positivism," contending that the gaps between rules and reality were only legitimated by the finding they existed. Some on the left, including Trubek and others "purged" from Yale Law School in the early 1970s, belatedly became tenured members of law faculties. Many joined Trubek, Horwitz, Mark Tushnet, Duncan Kennedy, and others in founding the Conference on Critical Legal Studies in 1977. To some extent, critical legal studies (cls) was best understood, Tushnet maintained, as "a political location for a group of people on the Left who share in the project of supporting and extending the domain of the Left in the legal academy." It was more than that, though, for as a movement cls possessed intellectual coherence. And where law and economics used Henry Manne's summer institutes to increase its ranks, critical legal scholars indoctrinated novitiates through their annual "summer camp."[51]

In addition to training the next generation, critical legal studies found its own ancestors, deliberately rooting itself in what law professors understood to be the most important jurisprudential movement in recent history, legal realism. One academic claimed that critical legal scholars' themes "reinforce all the challenges to orthodox legal thought originally generated by Legal Realism—the implicit attack on democratic theory,

the delegitimation of the institution of judicial review, and the erosion
of the ideal of the rule of law." True, when realism was broadly defined—though the realists of the 1920s and 1930s might not have recognized themselves in critical legal scholars' characterization of their
work. Straining to present themselves as the realists' descendants, cls
advocates claimed numerous other progenitors as well, including the
critical theory of the Frankfurt school and structuralism.[52]

With this pedigree in place, critical legal scholars contended that "law
varies according to time and place, and that this historical and social
contingency applies to legal reasoning, legal rules, and governmental social institutions." Yet, they insisted, law was forever "manipulable
and indeterminate—principles as always being balanced by counter-
principles, policy arguments as meeting counter-policy arguments, and
so on." As Posner had shown "Rawlsism" indeterminate, so critical legal
scholars, such as Duncan Kennedy of Harvard, delighted in demonstrating that the indeterminacy problem plagued all forms of law and economics. Like their realist forebears, critical legal scholars were branded
nihilists. The judges Kennedy described were likened to Houdini, and
socialist Houdinis at that. Asked how he would decide a case, for example, Mark Tushnet said, "My answer, in brief, is to make an explicitly
political judgment: which result, is in the circumstances now existing,
likely to advance the cause of socialism? Having decided that, I would
write an opinion in some currently favored version of Grand Theory."
Meanwhile the cls teacher who taught "no torts in Torts and no Contracts in Contracts" became "the 'welfare queen' of pedagogy, an imaginary miscreant students love to hate." In fact, those who subscribed to
cls cheerfully admitted that despite its indeterminacy, law might well
prove predictable; one of Kennedy's heroes was Skelly Wright, and Kennedy considered himself "a doctrinal teacher of law."[53]

Opponents tended to ignore critical legal scholars' concessions, however, because of the forcefulness of the indeterminacy rhetoric. "By its
own criteria," critical legal scholars declared, "legal reasoning cannot
resolve questions in an 'objective' manner; nor can it explain how the
legal system works or how judges decide cases." They spoke gleefully of
"trashing," a technique they used to pick apart legal texts: "Take specific
arguments very *seriously* in their own terms; discover they are actually
foolish ([tragi]-*comic*); and then look for some (external observer's) *or-*

der (*not* the germ of truth) in the internal contradictory, incoherent chaos we've exposed."[54]

Thus critical legal scholars emphasized law's incoherence. Just as Lévi-Strauss had shown that binary oppositions suffused human thought, so the critical legal scholar demonstrated they pervaded legal thought and liberalism. In "the most often-cited of all passages on critical legal studies," Kennedy demonstrated the existence of an intense and pervasive "fundamental contradiction" between the individual and the community: "relations with others are both necessary to and incompatible with our freedom." Law functioned as a process "of mediation, or denial" that hid or disguised the fundamental contradiction.[55]

Kennedy's methods here were traditional. Whereas orthodox legal scholars used doctrinal analysis to make law consistent, he employed doctrinal analysis to prove that it was not. The legal realists had done the same, but they had presented no alternatives. Kennedy was delegitimating doctrinal analysis as a genre of scholarship at a time when interdisciplinary movements, such as law and economics, threatened to take its place.[56]

Further, if law functioned as a process of mediation, it followed that law could not be neutral, objective, or apolitical. It was ideological. Like adherents of law and economics, critical legal scholars jeered at the idea that law could be separated from politics in classical liberalism, maintaining instead that "law is politics, all the way down." Critical legal scholars broadcast to the legal academy a realization reached long ago by the "person on the street" (and reaffirmed by the 1979 publication of that best-seller *The Brethren*), political scientists, historians, and first-year constitutional law students. Law was "a mechanism for creating and legitimating configurations of economic and political power. . . . Lawyers, judges and scholars make highly controversial political choices, but use the ideology of legal reasoning to make our institutions appear neutral and our rules appear neutral."[57]

Worse still, law was a wolf in sheep's clothing. Critical legal scholars did not embrace instrumentalism or vulgar Marxism. With the exception of Horwitz, they never claimed that judges' economic backgrounds explained their decisions. Whereas the realists had focused on the subjectivity of the individual decision maker, critical legal scholars exposed the value systems of different groups of legal actors. Liberal legal pluralists, for example, had long celebrated the paradigm of collective bargaining in the postwar era as a triumph for industrial democracy. Critical legal scholars showed how that paradigm actually operated to favor management over unions. Yet, as they also pointed out, the capitalists did not always win. Society only molded law to a certain extent. Internal forces determined law's development too. The legal system could maintain its credibility and apparent universalism only if law operated with some independence, or with "relative autonomy" from economic interests and social classes.[58]

Chiding those in law and economics for their "sophistries" and predicting that "[f]uture legal historians will need to exercise their imaginations to figure out why so many people could have taken most of this stuff so seriously," critical legal scholars also condemned the "hocus-pocus" of rights-based liberalism. According to cls proponents, the Warren Court was part of the problem. Like all those who ranged the political spectrum from far right to center-left, its members had not practiced legal liberalism but "liberal legalism." Critical legal scholars used the word *liberal* to refer to everyone from "Helms to Tsongas, Larry Byrd to Lady Bird." Joan Williams concluded that "CLS's most powerful rhetorical means of imposing and policing its dichotomy between liberals and critical legal scholars are its all-encompassing definitions of 'liberalism' and 'liberal legalism.' Critical legal scholars use the term 'liberalism' to refer to both liberals and conservatives and in fact often cite contemporary conservatives as examples of the liberal position."[59]

Critical legal scholar Karl Klare provided a frequently cited definition of liberal legalism:

> I mean by "liberal legalism" the particular historical incarnation of legalism . . . which characteristically serves as the institutional and philosophical foundation of the legitimacy of the legal order in capitalist societies. Its essential features are the commitment to general "democratically" promulgated rules, the equal treatment of all citizens before the law, and the radical separation of morals, politics and personality from judicial action. Liberal legalism also consists of a complex of social practices and institutions that complement and elaborate on its underlying jurisprudence. . . . Liberal legalist jurisprudence and its institutions are closely related to the

classical liberal political tradition, exemplified in the work of
Hobbes, Locke and Hume. The metaphysical underpinnings of
liberal legalism are supplied by the central themes of that tradition: the notion that values are subjective and derive from personal desire, and that therefore ethical discourse is conducted
profitably only in instrumental terms; the view that society is an
artificial aggregation of autonomous individuals; the separation in
political philosophy between public and private interest, between
state and civil society; and a commitment to a formal or procedural rather than a substantive conception of justice.[60]

Beginning in the late 1970s, critical legal scholars claimed that the
Warren Court's emphasis on individual rights favored procedure over
substance, legitimated power arrangements, and served as a pressure
valve permitting injustice. The Court had directed attention away from
collective action by encouraging individuals to view themselves "as isolated rights-bearers ('I got my rights') rather than as interdependent
members of a community." Duncan Kennedy declared rights discourse
"internally inconsistent, vacuous or circular." According to critical legal
scholars, "[r]ights are indeterminate, rights limit our imaginations, rights
inhibit political and social change." They alleged that the Warren Court
had prevented transformative social change by perpetuating the dichotomy between the individual and the community.[61]

This was more than a critique of the Warren Court. In attacking the
language of rights, cls was "discarding eight hundred years of legal and
moral language." For law professors, critical legal studies placed even
more at risk—their reason for being. "At least since the civil rights movement, the high culture of American politics has been primarily a legalistic
one," a Scottish critical legal scholar noted. Issues such as abortion were
debated in terms of fetal rights against right to privacy. In this context,
in which dreams of a "movement for large-scale social transformation
through law" were possible, becoming a law professor had made abun-
dant sense. Critical legal scholars' declarations that "liberalism . . . has
become a dangerous political anachronism" and that it was time "to get
over . . . [the] nostalgia for law as the good father" had to raise doubts
which the occasional cls genuflections to the Warrens and Wrights did

not dissipate. What if the law faculty of an elite school "really wasn't the ideal place for a smart boy with a social conscience to go"?[62]

Doubt from within accompanied assaults on liberalism from without. Those law professors in the late 1970s who still would have identified themselves as legal liberals were dividing over their mission. Affirmative action may have proven the issue that puzzled them most, for to them, affirmative action made it impossible to ignore the tension between liberty and equality. Some liberals attacked affirmative action programs for favoring group rights over individual rights. Others hailed them as a new chapter in the struggle to expand civil rights and to compensate for past societal discrimination. The debate revolved around the meaning of *Brown:* did it guarantee a color-blind Constitution or educational pluralism, equal opportunity or equality between the races?[63]

Consider the split between the two most liberal members of the California Supreme Court in *Bakke.* In his lone dissent, Justice Matthew Tobriner argued for the constitutionality of "benign" discrimination, intended to correct "two centuries of slavery and racial discrimination [which] have left our nation . . . a largely separated society, in which wealth, educational resources, employment opportunities—indeed all of society's benefits—remain largely the preserve of the white Anglo majority." On the other hand, Justice Stanley Mosk's majority opinion holding that a public university could not make race a factor in determining admissions relied in part on William O. Douglas's blistering dissent in *De Funis* v. *Odegard,* which to Douglas reflected his own lifelong protection of individual rights. "[T]here is no constitutional right for any race to be preferred," Douglas had said. Regardless of his race, every applicant "had a constitutional right to have his application considered on its individual merits in a racially neutral manner."[64]

The disagreement between Tobriner and Mosk mirrored a division on the United States Supreme Court over affirmative action between Justices Douglas and Brennan. Like Tobriner, Brennan claimed the constitutionality of measures designed "to achieve minority participation in previously segregated areas of public life." Whereas some scholars, such as Frank Michelman, argued Brennan's remark was "addressed to fairness to individuals," others disagreed. In the past, focus on individual rights had led Douglas to side with Brennan in support of liberal judicial activism and the protection of people of color. But in the 1970s, it moved Douglas into an improbable alliance with Alexander Bickel and Philip Kurland, protégés of Douglas's great rival on the Supreme Court, Felix Frankfurter. Bickel and Kurland, who by now had turned decidedly to the right, filed the leading amicus brief in *Bakke* opposing affirmative action as immoral.[65]

Like the arguments between Mosk and Tobriner, Douglas and Brennan, the struggle within the Carter administration over the government's *Bakke* brief for the United States Supreme Court splintered liberalism. John Hart Ely might try to defuse the issue of affirmative action by confessing that he had "trouble understanding the place of righteous indignation on either side of this wrenching moral issue." But as one academic lawyer observed, Ely's comment "may well be read by many as the infuriating elitist insouciance of a tenured Harvard professor." Certainly in the 1970s, liberals on both sides of the issue showed enormous amounts of righteous indignation.[66]

As liberals fought among themselves, conservatives grew stronger. In law, as in other expressions of policy, the Reagan years began during the Carter administration. The conservatism associated with Reagan had won over the country by 1978.

Thus by 1980, legal liberalism was feeble. Ronald Reagan was in the White House, but for law professors it was more important that the books of Jesse Choper and John Hart Ely were in the law libraries. In many ways, Choper's *Judicial Review and the National Political Process: A Functional Reconsideration of the Role of the Supreme Court* and Ely's *Democracy and Distrust: A Theory of Judicial Review* were "twins." Born in the 1930s, Choper and Ely had both served as Warren clerks and become prominent scholars bent on enshrining process theory and legal liberalism. In a classic statement of legal liberalism's claim that judicial review enhanced democracy, Choper insisted that "if judicial review were nonexistent for popularly frustrated minorities, the fight already lost in the legislative halls, would have only one remaining battleground—the streets." Because Choper focused on when the Court should abstain from review, so it could preserve its prestige for "the commendable and crucial task of judicial review in cases of individual constitutional liberties," reviewers tended to focus more on Ely's theory of judicial review.[67]

Ely dedicated *Democracy and Distrust* to Warren, whom he had served as clerk, observing that "you don't need many heroes if you choose carefully." *Democracy and Distrust* maintained there was no one useful method of moral philosophy. As Ely pointed out, for every John Rawls who preached expanding the state's role to help the poor, there existed a Robert Nozick who wanted to reduce it. Thus Ely took a dim view of legal scholars' "invitation to judges . . . [to] seek constitutional values in—that is, overrule political officials on the basis of—the writings of good contemporary moral philosophers, in particular the writing of Rawls":

> Rawls's book *is* fine. But how are judges to react to Dworkin's invitation when almost all the commentators on Rawls's work have expressed reservations about his conclusions? The Constitution may follow the flag, but is it really supposed to keep up with the *New York Review of Books?*
>
> One might be tempted to suppose that there will be no systematic bias in the judges' rendition of "correct moral reasoning" aside from whatever derives from the philosophical axioms from which they begin. ("We like Rawls, you like Nozick. We win, 6–3. Statute invalidated.") That would certainly be bad enough, but the actual situation is likely to be somewhat worse. Experience suggests that there will be a systematic bias in judicial choice of fundamental values, unsurprisingly in favor of the values of the upper-middle, professional class, from which most lawyers and judges, and for that matter most moral philosophers, are drawn.[68]

Lacking sympathy for a Court that expounded fundamental values, Ely nevertheless hoped to save his former boss's opinions and to solve the counter-majoritarian difficulty. "Generally speaking," and unlike the Burger Court, which discovered and imposed fundamental values willynilly, "the Warren Court was a *Carolene Products* Court, centrally concerned with assuring broad participation, not simply in the processes of government but in the benefits generated by those processes as well," Ely had claimed in 1978 *Harvard Law Review* "Foreword." In *Democracy and Distrust,* his "participation-oriented, representation-reinforcing approach to judicial review" postulated that the Warren Court had restricted the Supreme Court's role to ensuring participation in the political process. "These were certainly interventionist decisions, but the interventionism was fueled not by a desire on the part of the Court to vindicate particular substantive values it had determined were important or fundamental," Ely contended. Rather, it reflected "a desire to ensure that the political process—which is where such values *are* properly identified, weighed, and accommodated—was open to those of all viewpoints on something approaching an equal basis."[69]

Ely's theory of constitutional adjudication, which he described (with his tongue only partly in his cheek) as "the ultimate interpretivism," may have represented "the apotheosis" of the attempt to combine process theory with political liberalism. For him, the representation-reinforcing model of judicial review provided "a way of approving *Brown* while disapproving *Lochner*." "[O]ne perfectly well *can* be a genuine political liberal and at the same time believe, out of a respect for the democratic process, that the Court should keep its hands off the legislature's value judgments," Ely insisted.[70]

But according to most reviewers, Ely himself had provided no objective and determinate foundations of justice. Ely's way out of the political liberal's dilemma, one critic wrote, involved dressing up Dworkin's "moral notions of equal concern and respect in the trappings of process and participation." Although Ely's effort on Warren's behalf proved herculean, academic lawyers of all ideologies responded with groans (masked by declarations that *Democracy and Distrust* was brilliant but misguided). One of Ely's more sympathetic readers said, "I lack inside knowledge of the desire that motivated the Justices of the Warren era, although I must note three grounds for doubt: the Warren Court launched the 'access to fundamental rights' branch of the strict scrutiny brand of equal protection; four of the five Justices remaining from the Warren era were members of—indeed necessary to—the majority in *Roe v. Wade;* and Justices Douglas and Brennan, who were usually necessary to a Warren majority, seldom shrank from declaring substantive values." Another commentator wrote that while the representation-reinforcing model of review did "comport with the outcome" of many Warren Court decisions, "there is a distinct irony in juxtaposing Professor Ely's theory with the decision-making method of the Warren Court. It may be that no Court has worn its heart on its sleeve more openly than the Warren Court, at least since . . . the 1930's."[71]

Ely had presented process theory at its purest—or, more accurately, at its least adulterated. To critical legal scholars, his book simply confirmed its bankruptcy. Academic lawyers with liberal politics also found *Democracy and Distrust* uncompelling. Because their own versions of process theory had generally possessed a substantive and normative element, rights foundationalism was best viewed as a subset of process theory. In a paper originally entitled "The Flight from Substance," whose name he changed to "The Forum of Principle," Ronald Dworkin charged that, like the interpretivists, Ely did more harm than good. "We have an institution that calls some issues from the battleground of power politics to the forum of principle," Dworkin said of the Supreme Court. "Academic lawyers do no service by trying to disguise the political decisions this balance assigns to judges." The desegregation debate "would not have had the character it did but for the fact and symbolism of the Court's decisions." Judicial review compelled "political debate to include argument over principle, not only when a case comes to the Court but also long before and long after." So, too, Lawrence Tribe pointed to "the stubbornly substantive character of so many of the Constitution's crucial commitments," observed that "to see why process would itself be valuable—intrinsically so—is to see why the Constitution is inevitably substantive," and puzzled over why "thoughtful judges and scholars continue to put forth process-perfecting theories as though theories could banish divisive controversies over substantive values from the realm of constitutional discourse by relegating those controversies to the unruly world of power." Meanwhile Owen Fiss complained that the rise of the representation-reinforcing model of review "does not stem from doubts about the special capacity of courts and their processes to move us closer to a correct understanding of our constitutional values, but from the frail quality of our substantive vision." For Fiss, the purpose of adjudication in great cases, such as *Brown,* was not so much to resolve disputes as to provide "the social process by which judges give meaning to our public values." Alas, he lamented, "[w]e have lost our confidence in the existence of the values that underlie the litigation of the 1960's, or, for that matter, in the existence of any public values. All is preference."[72]

Like Ely and Choper, however, liberals such as Fiss, Dworkin, and Tribe still saw Earl Warren as the emperor, and they still wanted to give him and his Court clothes. Many constitutional scholars continued "living off the remains of the Warren Court" by writing articles that justified it and glorified courts as the great engine of social and political change. Harvard law professor Richard Parker appealed to "my generation . . . 'the generation of the 1960s' " to realize that "further elaboration" of the theories of Ely and Choper "can only lead us into a fog." Their proposals for "marginal reform" only embraced and apologized "for the status quo, further obfuscating its deep injustice. But that need not be our fate. We grew up in an era when it was virtually impossible to feel comfortable with the status quo." It was "open to us, as it was not open to our predecessors" to construct "a new constitutional theory." Nevertheless, at least until the republican revival of the mid 1980s—and some would say, through it to today—liberal constitutional law professors, such as Fiss, simply produced "a proliferation of theories of judicial review" based on the premise judges should articulate public values. Essentially, such legal liberals were serving up boiled-over Bickel. They received little applause: "In the more cynical, conflictual world of the 1970s, the halls of Harvard Law School . . . echoed with faculty announcements that 'legal process is dead.' " It was not. Still, there had been a significant shift. Process theorists had assumed reasonable law professors could disagree while sharing a basic consensus, but what would happen now that so many "unreasonable" people were perceived to be entering the legal academy? Legal liberals were trying to preserve process jurisprudence by reforming it, but their task was becoming ever more difficult.[73]

Surveying legal scholarship at the end of the 1970s, Arthur Leff saw a "growing, and apparently terrifying realization" gripping his colleagues—"that there cannot be any normative system ultimately based on anything except human will." And if there were no objective foundations of justice, justifying broad powers for courts in a democracy was the least of law professors' problems. "As things now stand," Leff concluded, "everything is up for grabs":

Nevertheless:
Napalming babies is bad.

Starving the poor is wicked.
Buying and selling each other is depraved.
Those who stood up to and died resisting
Hitler, Stalin, Amin, and Pol Pot—and General
Custer too—have earned salvation.
Those who acquiesced deserve to be damned.
There is in the world such a thing as evil.
[All together now:] Sez who?
God help us.[74]

CHAPTER 3

INTERLUDE: THINKING ABOUT THINKING

In 1981, Yale Law School sponsored a conference on "Legal Scholarship: Its Nature and Purposes." The very fact of the conference indicated that anxiety had been building for some time, but I date the beginnings of palpable angst among law professors to that gathering. Leon Lipson of Yale suggested the new sensibility among academic lawyers when he joked "anything you can do, I can do 'meta.' " A generation earlier, the notion of scholarship about legal scholarship, a symposium on "meta-law," would have struck law professors as absurd. "[S]ymposia like this one are convened when it seems that something has gone wrong," one participant stressed. Scholars ranging from Richard Posner on the right to Mark Tushnet on the left used the occasion to voice their fears that legal scholarship was "drifting."[1]

Several reasons for law professors' malaise were at work. The arrival of law and economics and critical legal studies shattered the liberal consensus. At some level male academic lawyers may also have felt that the entrance of women and people of color into their ranks challenged their control of the law schools.

There was no rational basis for concern. Even in the "halcyon days of cls," critical legal scholars probably still faced "Halcion nights" as they sought tenure. True, there were some new courses on the books, and the content of some old ones was changing. When Susan Estrich began teaching criminal law at Harvard in 1980, for one example, she taught rape, a subject she had not been taught as a student. Anyone who considered such a development unfortunate, however, might take comfort in the knowledge that the largest number of women who entered the law professorate in a single year during the 1980s was eighty-four. Similarly "racial tokenism" remained the order of the day on law faculties. Nevertheless, the demographic changes and introduction of new political and pedagogic perspectives called the traditional shared assumptions into question.[2]

Further, law professors, who had long touted themselves as generalists, could no longer keep up with work outside their own research fields. As law schools rushed to become part of the university, Paul Samuelson proclaimed that the "cancer of research is beginning to invade the law school" and joked uneasily that legal scholars might soon be "investigating the frequency of masturbation among judges over sixty." Law professors did seem to be publishing more (in part, perhaps, because their cases for tenure were now undergoing scrutiny by university-wide tenure boards on their way to the president's or chancellor's office). The average length of lead articles in the *Harvard Law Review* and *Yale Law Journal* grew from fifteen pages during the 1890s, to thirty-three pages in the 1950s, to sixty pages in the 1980s. In one sense nothing had changed, for the work was as normative as ever, and, at least at Harvard, law review editors had been fretting since the 1960s that "[m]any single pieces might well be bound as books."[3]

In another sense, everything was different. Academic lawyers may have been beginning to sense, as one law professor said later, that mainstream constitutional scholarship was characterized by "an over-confident intellectualism, a stridently critical instinct, an attachment to theory that subordinates the wisdom of experience and the weight of practice, an affinity for the novel and audacious that verges on the fanciful and conspiratorial, and an excessive devotion to independent judicial power." At one time, law professors had seen themselves as constitutional actors who made a difference, but it was no longer clear the judges were listening.[4]

Interdisciplinary research was as troublesome as the possible loss of audience. In some instances, the pursuit of other disciplines involved some departure from doctrinal analysis. In the prestigious *Harvard Law Review* "Forewords" on the Court's work, for instance, decided cases were increasingly being "dragged in by the heels." In that sense, even though law professors might simply be appropriating useful chunks of other disciplines, the resort to those disciplines fragmented legal scholarship, further unsettling academic lawyers' sense of community. The increased interest in interdisciplinary work threatened to cause "problems of internal specialization within the legal community, producing the kind of babel of incomprehensible languages that so troublingly besets the modern university."[5]

Some also worried that interdisciplinary experiments would crowd out doctrinal scholarship altogether. As they said, law and economics and critical legal studies "resemble each other only in looking outside law for its springs and lifeblood. But that is something." The old orthodoxy had been overturned, "and the only apparent route to scholarly influence in the post-doctrinal world was through 'law and' of one sort or another." Such law professors feared that the narrowing of the gap between the law school and the university only broadened the one between the law school and the legal profession.[6]

Actually, doctrinal scholarship may have been on the rise in the 1980s, but it was perceived to be endangered. Yale dean Harry Wellington morosely told a colleague that "everything that the younger people were critical of" in the work of one prospective faculty appointee "could have been said about mine." Though Posner himself had been a cheerleader for law and economics, one of the most significant sources of the interdisciplinary impulse in the legal academy, he used his Yale conference paper to decry "deans at leading law schools" for making the "academic lawyer who makes it his business to be learned in the law and expert in parsing cases and statutes . . . seem a paltry fellow, a Philistine who has shirked the more ambitious and challenging task of mastering political and moral philosophy, economics, history, and other social sciences and humanities so that he can discourse on large questions of policy and social justice." As Posner and some at the conference saw it, the crisis causing law professors to reach out to the humanities and social sciences was one of law.[7]

In fact, the legal scholars' predicament constituted only an aspect of a larger crisis taking place in the social sciences and humanities. In part, this crisis possessed institutional roots: as a new generation of professors joined the academy, those who had dominated it since the late 1950s contemplated retirement. In part, its roots were intellectual. One anthropologist emphasized that "the intellectual programs which the Sputnik generation put on the agenda are now in question."[8]

In disciplines outside law, this sense of an impending paradigm shift created more excitement than unease. Literary theorist Fredric Jameson saw something significant afoot. "A generation ago there was still a technical discourse of professional philosophy—the great systems of Sartre or the phenomonologists, the work of Wittgenstein or analytical or common language philosophy—alongside which one could still distinguish that quite different discourse of the other academic disciplines—of political science, for example, or sociology or literary criticism," he wrote in his important essay on postmodernism. "Today, increasingly we have a kind of writing simply called 'theory' which is all or none of those things at once. This new kind of discourse, generally associated with France and so-called French theory, is becoming widespread." It certainly was. For example, French universities had shunted Michel Foucault and other new theorists to the margins, but many American academics and their students (most of them, outside philosophy departments, to be sure) worshiped him.[9]

Though postmodernism was linked to a variety of trends, including "mediatization" or "spectaclization" of Foucault and other intellectuals, it defied definition. Since it required "recognition that there is no 'outside' from which to 'objectively' name the present," the very effort to say what postmodernism was indicated one did not understand it. Perhaps it was best understood as a phase of intellectual history. "The success story of the word postmodernism demands to be written, no doubt in best-seller format; such lexical neoevents, in which the coinage of a neologism has all the reality impact of a corporate merger, are among the novelties of media society," Jameson reflected later. "Why we needed the word *postmodernism* so long without knowing it, why a truly motley crew of strange bedfellows ran to embrace it the moment it appeared, are mysteries that will remain unclarified until we have been able to grasp the philosophical and social function of the concept, something impossible, in its turn, until we are somehow able to grasp the deeper identity between the two." In the meantime, theories ranging from antifoundationalism to deconstruction would be subsumed, perhaps wrongly, under the rubric of postmodernism.[10]

Though no one could say what postmodernism *was,* it was clearly "about language." The "postmodern moment" involved "an awareness of being within, first, a language, and second, a particular historical, social, cultural framework." Though no one could "prove" how the framework functioned, it carried endless possibilities for play. One need not subscribe to Lyotard's claim that postmodernism involved "incredulity towards metanarratives" of "legitimation" (and not everyone did), to agree with him that "the methodological approach" behind the postmodern perspective was one Wittgenstein developed, that of "language games." Drawing on the work of the later Wittgenstein and J. L. Austin, Richard Rorty had already popularized the phrase "linguistic turn" as shorthand for the theory that language created or produced meaning, consciousness, and thought, rather than reflecting or expressing them. "It is not as though we have meanings or experiences, which we then proceed to cloak with words; we can only have the meanings and experiences in the first place because we have a language to have them in."[11]

There was no unanimity about methodology. The "soft" linguistic turn characteristic of Cambridge historians, such as J. G. A. Pocock and Quentin Skinner, required a realization of the problematic relationship between language and the world. The "hard" linguistic turn taken by poststructuralists on the Continent threatened to dissolve that relationship altogether. Still other theorists subsumed the linguistic turn within an "interpretive turn," which concentrated on the roles of interpreter and culture in generating meaning.

The fascination with theory, culture, and language that led so many different individuals and movements to postmodernism in the 1970s and early 1980s blurred disciplinary boundaries in the very fields from which law professors sought guidance. Clifford Geertz remarked in 1980 that "the present jumbling of varieties of discourse has grown to the point where it is becoming difficult either to label authors (What *is* Foucault—historian, philosopher, political theorist? What Thomas Kuhn—historian, philosopher, sociologist of knowledge?) or to classify works." Boundaries between fields changed periodically, but something more momentous was transpiring. "It is a phenomenon general enough and distinctive enough to suggest that what we are seeing is not just another redrawing of the cultural map—the moving of a few disputed borders, the marking of some picturesque mountain lakes—but an alteration of the principles of mapping. Something is happening to the way we think about the way we think."[12]

Perhaps it was in other disciplines, but not in law. So far, law professors had simply flirted with interdisciplinary work. To be sure, Kuhn's *Structure of Scientific Revolutions* was one of their favorite books. All told, they have cited it in 521 law review pieces, and it has found its way into five federal cases. It was hip for law professors in the 1970s to extrapolate from Kuhn's argument that scientists abandoned old paradigms even when the evidence did not falsify them. It was chic to chatter of "paradigm shifts" in law.[13]

Law professors had simply seized on the least original aspect of Kuhn's thesis. Kuhn had pointed the way to history by demonstrating that "the proponents of competing paradigms practice their trades in different worlds." Instead of searching for "the permanent contributions of an older science" to knowledge, historians of science should contextualize them, focusing on "the historical integrity of that science in its own time." With their interest in change over time, historians, however, had long known about contingency and historicism. Kuhn later declared himself "puzzled" by those who liked his book "less because it illuminates science than because they read its main theses as applicable to many other fields as well. . . . To the extent that the book portrays scientific development as a succession of tradition-bound periods punctuated by non-cumulative breaks, its theses are undoubtedly of wide applicability. But they should be, for they are borrowed from other fields." Historians had traditionally used "[p]eriodization in terms of revolutionary breaks in style, taste, and institutional structure" as "standard tools."[14]

Kuhn's book proved noteworthy because he had shown "science" was "nonscientific." He had done so by applying historians' tools to science, not by inventing them. Consequently, as Mark Tushnet said in 1979, for law professors, Kuhn symbolized only "an ignorantly fashionable citation." They had not yet changed the way they thought about the way they thought.[15]

CHAPTER 4

CRISIS

In the 1980s, law professors were forced to confront different disciplines. They continued trying to coopt them. But they did change the way they thought about the way they thought. Combined with their divergent politics, the ensuing crisis polarized the legal academy.

FROM EPISTEMOLOGY TO HERMENEUTICS

Though law professors might have learned more from Kuhn, he and the historians seemed old-hat to some. Kuhn had praised historians for trying to recreate the past as it would have seemed to those who lived through it. "Consciously or not, they are all practitioners of the hermeneutic method," he declared. Theirs, however, was a nineteenth-century romantic hermeneutics designed to recover authorial intention. "It required that historians approach the text with minds as open and free from prejudice as possible and try to understand the text on its terms rather than in the terms peculiar to their own situations."[1]

The "new hermenutics" of Hans-Georg Gadamer, which underlay the growing interest in interpretation during the 1970s, underscored the difficulty of that task and any historical reconstruction. It emphasized that historians "are embedded in their own historical traditions ('History does not belong to us; we belong to it') and further that the texts they read are themselves a part of an interpretive tradition." Scholars who assumed a "gap between hermeneutics of the human sciences and legal hermeneutics" were mistaken; legal hermeneutics exemplified the "hermeneutical problem." The "hermeneutic circle" meant that Alexander Bickel could no more hope to reproduce the thought of James Madison than John Hart Ely could confront the counter-majoritarian difficulty without considering the glosses given it by constitutional scholars since Bickel.[2]

In short, law professors had to come to grips with their own involvement in interpretive activity. For them, Clifford Geertz and Richard Rorty proved most important in publicizing terms such as *hermenutics* and *interpretive turn*. One legal scholar thought that the work of Geertz and Rorty struck "many today with the force of revelation."[3]

Just as the legal realists had questioned whether their emperors, the judges, had clothes, so the posthumous publication in the 1960s of Malinowski's *A Diary in the Strict Sense of the Term* led Geertz to wonder whether his emperors, the ethnographers, did. The diary "rendered established accounts of how anthropologists work fairly well implausible," Geertz said in the early 1970s. "The myth of the chameleon fieldworker, perfectly self-tuned to his exotic surroundings, a walking miracle of empathy, tact, patience, and cosmopolitanism, was demolished by the man who had perhaps done most to create it." According to Geertz, however, the discovery that Malinowski had "rude things to say about the natives he was living with" had eclipsed the larger question his diary raised about the authority and objectivity of all ethnographic accounts. "[I]f it is not, as we had been taught to believe through some sort of extraordinary sensibility, an almost preternatural capacity to think, feel, and perceive like a native (a word, I should hurry to say, I use here 'in the strict sense of the term'), how is anthropological knowledge of the way natives think, feel, and perceive possible?" How could anthropologists stay loyal to Malinowski's "injunction to see things from the native's point of view . . . when we can no longer claim some unique form of psychological closeness, a sort of transcultural identification, with our subjects?"[4]

Defining his enterprise as one of "cultural hermeneutics," Geertz answered by advising anthropologists that "culture is not a power, something to which social events, behaviors, institutions, or processes can be causally attributed; it is a context, something within which they can be intelligibly—that is thickly—described." He urged his colleagues to commit themselves "to a semiotic concept of culture and an interpretive approach to the study of it." His student Sherry Ortner recalled: "Geertz's most radical theoretical move was to argue that culture is not something locked inside people's heads, but rather is embodied in public symbols, symbols through which the members of a society communicate their worldview, value-orientations, ethos, and all the rest to one another, to future generations—and to anthropologists." Geertz also rescued ideology. In his hands, it no longer constituted an insult reserved for dogmatists who disagreed with one's views. Instead Geertz neutralized it, making ideology just another necessary symbol system of modern society, and an especially valuable category of analysis now that it had lost its Marxist overtones. "Culture patterns—religious, philosophical, aesthetic, scientific, ideological—are 'programs,'" Geertz announced, furnishing "a template or blueprint for the organization of social and psychological processes, much as genetic systems provide such a template for the organization of organic processes."[5]

By studying the various symbol systems that constructed reality, anthropologists could see culture as a text and read it from the vantage point of the natives who made it. Anthropologists must place "the systematic study of meaning, the vehicles of meaning, and the understanding of meaning at the very center of research and cultural analysis," Geertz stressed. They should depict a culture in terms of constructions they imagined its inhabitants "place upon what they live through, the formulae they use to define what happens to them." Such accounts were not "part of the reality they are ostensibly describing; they are anthropological—that is, part of a developing system of scientific analysis. . . . In short, anthropological writings are themselves interpretations." Therefore, they were "fictions; fictions, in the sense that they are 'something made,' 'something fashioned'—the original meaning of *fictio*—not that they are false, unfactual, or merely 'as if' thought experiments."[6]

Geertz insisted that his program resisted subjectivism and relativism. According to him, this approach left anthropology a science. To view the anthropologist as interpreter "is to realize that the line between mode of representation and substantive content is as undrawable in cultural analysis as it is in painting; and that fact in turn seems to threaten the objective status of anthropological knowledge by suggesting that its source is not social reality but scholarly artifice." In a singularly opaque sentence, Geertz continued: "It does threaten it, but the threat is hollow."[7]

The interpretive approach did raise "some serious problems of verification," he acknowledged, "of how you can tell a better account from a worse one." That was its virtue. The anthropologist's audience cared more about the interpretation of facts, the "power of the scientific imagination to bring us into touch with the lives of strangers" than the uninterpreted raw data. "Anthropology, or at least interpretive anthropology, is a science whose progress is marked less by a perfection of consensus than by a refinement of debate."[8]

Richard Rorty was trying to move philosophy in an equally conversational direction. When Rorty edited *The Linguistic Turn* in the 1960s, he had announced that "philosophical problems are problems which may be solved (or dissolved) either by reforming language, or by understanding more about the language we presently use. This view is considered by many of its proponents to be the most important philosophical discovery of our time, and, indeed, of the ages." While he did not abandon his concern with language, Rorty later winced at the portentousness with which he had proclaimed the linguistic turn. "If there was ever any truth in the slogan 'the problems of philosophy are problems of language,' " he now said, "it was that the particular problems *about representation* which philosophers have discussed were pseudo-problems, created by a bad description of human knowledge, one that turned out to be optional and replaceable."[9]

Rorty's 1979 instant classic, *Philosophy and the Mirror of Nature,* reflected the change in his thinking. There, Rorty argued that the "notion of representation" should be set aside altogether in favor of "an anti-representationalist account . . . which does not view knowledge as a matter of getting reality right, but rather as a matter of acquiring habits of action for coping with reality." For, according to Rorty, neither the mind nor language could ever mirror reality. "The aim of the book is to undermine the reader's confidence in 'the mind' as something about which one should have a 'philosophical' view, in 'knowledge' as something about which there ought to be a 'theory' and which has 'foundations,' and in 'philosophy' as it has been conceived since Kant," he said. He condemned analytic philosophy "as an attempt to escape from history—an attempt to find nonhistorical conditions of any possible historical development."[10]

Kuhn was Rorty's hero, historicism Rorty's "moral." Nevertheless, Rorty criticized Kuhn for holding out hope for "a viable alternate to the traditional epistemological paradigm." Rorty believed that Kuhn should "have discarded the epistemological project altogether."[11]

Rorty pleaded with his colleagues to "drop the notion of the philosopher as knowing something about knowing which nobody else knows so well." According to him, "the desire for a theory of knowledge is a desire for constraint—a desire to find 'foundations' to which one might cling, frameworks beyond which one must not stray, objects which impose themselves, representations which cannot be gainsaid." Instead of seeking certainty, philosophers should seek wisdom. As Rorty put it, when there is no preinterpretive meaning, "Truth cannot be out there—cannot exist independently of the human mind—because sentences cannot so exist, or be out there. The world is out there, but descriptions of the world are not."[12]

Since "without absolutes, we cannot achieve 'a view from nowhere,' " Rorty called for philosophy to embrace "the hermeneutic insight that all perception is perspectival." His model was not the "cultural overseer who knows everyone's common ground—the Platonic philosopher-king who knows what everybody else is really doing whether *they* know it or not, because he knows about the ultimate context (the Forms, the Mind, Language) within which they are doing it."[13] Rather, his ideal philosopher was the "informed dilettante," who "comprised or transcended . . . [d]isagreements between disciplines and discourses . . . in the course of the conversation."

Rorty's exemplar, the "anti-foundationalist," moved "from epistemology to hermeneutics." The antifoundationalist denied "that there are foundations to serve as common ground for adjudicating knowledge-claims" and adopted a different role. "Hermeneutics sees the relations between various discourses as those of strands in a possible conversation, a conversation which presupposes no disciplinary matrix which unites the speakers, but where the hope of agreement is never lost so long as the conversation lasts," Rorty explained. "This hope is not a hope for the discovery of antecedently existing common ground, but simply hope for agreement, or, at least, exciting and fruitful disagreement." The purpose of philosophy should be "to keep the conversation going," rather than to locate "objective truth."[14]

Rorty maintained that his program did not spell the end of philosophy. All philosophers need do was continue the conversation, instead of insisting "upon a place for the traditional problems of modern philosophy within that conversation." Nor, he added, would the shift in emphasis mean the end of philosophers. "Professions can survive the paradigms which gave them birth."[15]

Proponents of the interpretive, or hermeneutical, approach rejected the existence of objective foundations while offering something to put in their place. They claimed that their approach "denies and overcomes the almost de rigueur opposition of subjectivity and objectivity." One insisted: "If we accept the notion that human activity can be understood only in the terms of the contexts that inform and limit the human agent's understandings of the social world in which she lives and her own activities in that world, we must also accept the premise that we can only understand these understandings in terms of the contexts which inform and limit our own practices of interpretation." Historical and cultural contexts situated the observer and observed. The meanings both attached to socially constructed practices were not just in their minds, but should be seen as "modes of social relations," a philosopher said. Other theorists agreed that "[t]hese meanings are intersubjective; they are not reducible to individual subjective psychological states, beliefs, or propositions. They are neither subjective nor objective but what lies behind both." And "intersubjectivity" was "not just a fancy term for mutual. It is meant to convey both the individual nature of experience and the collective nature of social systems that, in their turn, become individual experience."[16]

Hermeneutics provided hope. It proved there was no "absolutist foundation for truth, meaning and reason," while pointing to "the shared ground that prevents thinking from collapsing into subjectivism, relativism, or other sundry 'isms,' " one academic lawyer said. Thus Rorty and other hermeneuticists joined Geertz in scoffing at the suggestion they advocated either unwarranted skepticism or corrosive relativism. " 'Relativism' " is the view that every belief on a certain topic, or perhaps about *any* topic, is as good as every other," and save "for the occasional cooperative freshman," no one believed that, Rorty said. By abandoning the old obsessions with objectivity and scientific method, "we shall be able to see the social sciences as continuous with literature—as interpreting other people to us, and thus enlarging and deepening our sense of community."[17]

Having adopted this "new pragmatism," the individual could follow John Dewey in emphasizing the potential of knowledge for human improvement or Foucault in studying knowledge as an instrument of power. The two men differed "over what we may hope," Rorty wrote, but they "agree, right down the line, about the need to abandon traditional notions of rationality, objectivity, method, and truth." They stood united "in the attempt to free mankind from Nietzsche's 'longest lie,' the notion that outside the haphazard and perilous experiments we perform there lies something (God, Science, Knowledge, Rationality, or Truth) which will, if only we perform the correct rituals, step in to save us."[18]

Add Justice to the list of false messiahs, and Rorty's words resonated for law professors. After all, they were children of the legal realists, who had aligned themselves with Dewey, though they might not have anticipated Foucault. Joan Williams, who referred to Rorty's hermeneutics as "the new epistemology," for example, explained that "traditional epistemology, with its belief in the existence of transcendent, objective truth, has been replaced . . . by a 'new epistemology,' which rejects a belief in objective truth and the claims of certainty that traditionally follow." It followed that one of the "hard lessons of the new epistemology [was] that, in the absence of absolutes, sometimes we will not be able to persuade our opponents even of those convictions we hold so profoundly that we *know* they are right with every fiber of our being." Applied to the abortion debate, for example, that meant individuals had to disagree without being able to prove each other wrong. "Once I offer reasons, and my reasons fail to persuade, I must acknowledge that consensus on this issue is not in the cards."[19]

To another law professor, "the central point" to be gained from reading Rorty's antifoundationalist critique of epistemology and Kuhn's work on the historicity of scientific paradigms was "that all knowledge is humanly constructed and, therefore, contingent and provisional":

> Our beliefs about the phenomena we perceive depend on assumptions and categories that are the historically conditioned problems of human intellect rather than purely passive responses to physical data. What we take to be objective statements about the world around us derive their validity from criteria specified by belief systems that have been different in the past and can change in the future. Applied to the law, awareness of the contingency of our belief systems suggests a pervasive indeterminacy: if even scientific knowledge cannot be firmly grounded in objective reality, surely the pursuit of objective truth in legal reasoning is ephemeral. Understanding the law's meaning depends on intervening subjective judgment and emerges only through interpretive activity.[20]

But could legal scholars survive the end of the paradigm that had animated them for so long, the counter-majoritarian difficulty, if they moved from epistemology to hermeneutics? Preoccupied with the opportunities for subjectivity and relativism that judicial manipulation of law's more ambiguous phrases presented, law professors had long acted as if "meanings reside 'in' language." They assumed the text was "there," waiting to be acted on by the reader—who depending on his or her theory of decision making, might be a process theorist or interpretivist. They had ignored the possibility that "not even the simplest text is immune to interpretive controversy. The constitutional requirement that the president be at least thirty-five, for example, is 'clear' only so long as one assumes a consensus . . . about which calendar to use." The individual who was thirty-five according to the Gregorian solar calendar might be a different age under the Jewish, Muslim, or Chinese lunar calendars. What was necessary, some scholars were beginning to think, was greater attention to the act of interpretation.[21]

At the time of the 1981 Yale conference on legal scholarship, the only law professor to have taken the "interpretive turn" was critical legal scholar Paul Brest, and it had taken him in a direction many academic lawyers would have found frightening. As Brest examined the debate Raoul Berger had sparked, he saw that all of the proponents had espoused some sort of "originalism," a term Brest coined. While declaring he could tolerate "moderate originalism," Brest had used his 1980 article, "The Misconceived Quest for Original Understanding," to fight all originalism with hermeneutics. Depicting originalism as a "hermeneutical howler," Brest cited Gadamer in support of the proposition "that we can never understand the past in its own terms, free from our prejudices or preconceptions. We are hopelessly imprisoned in our own world-views; we can shed some preconceptions only to adopt others, with no reason to believe that they are the conceptions of the different society we are trying to understand." Instead of the Founders' original understanding as a touchstone for constitutional decision making, Brest proposed "a decidedly vague criterion: How well, compared to possible alternatives, does the practice contribute to the well-being of our society?"[22]

At the time, Brest stood "virtually alone . . . in attempting to provide a complete theory for disregarding original intent." Even professors who shared his politics acted as if insisting originalism was indeterminate meant naked normatives would be all that was left. " 'I like it' is not a very good statement, but 'the Constitution says so,' stated with appropriate emphasis and in a sincere tone can be persuasive," Mark Tushnet wryly acknowledged at the Yale conference. Brest, however, almost seemed content to say he liked it.[23]

Brest carried his argument further in New Haven, with a paper explicating the theories of substantive due process decisions, such as *Griswold* and *Roe*. "I shall argue that the controversy over the legitimacy of judicial review in a democratic polity—the historic obsession of normative constitutional law scholarship—is essentially incoherent and unresolvable," he announced. "No theory of constitutional adjudication can defend itself against self-scrutiny. . . . [A]ll are vulnerable to similar criticisms based on their indeterminacy, manipulability, and, ultimately, their reliance on judicial value choices that cannot be 'objectively' derived from text, history, consensus, natural rights, or any other source." How, then, should law professors spend their time? Brest spoke hopefully of working "toward a genuine reconstitution of society—perhaps one in which the concept of freedom includes citizen participation in the community's public discourse and responsibility to shape its values and structure." He noted, however, that the alternative requiring "the least dislocation is simply to acknowledge that most of our writings are not political theory but advocacy scholarship—amicus briefs ultimately designed to persuade the Court to adopt our notions of the public good."[24]

Surrender legal liberalism or admit law is simply preference: were those the choices? "If we can discover no ultimate normative premise, does it follow that there is no foundation for constitutional authority, and that we are therefore consigned to government by caprice?" asked the commentator on Brest's paper. Hermeneutics did enable one to answer that question in the negative. One could have said that the impossibility of foundational discourse made nonfoundational discourse impossible. One might also have urged law professors to recognize what W. V. O. Quine and Hilary Putnam (on whom Rorty "built") had already shown—that statements need be neither objectively true nor empirically verifiable to be rational. Law professors could make normative arguments without worrying about their truth, objectivity, or verifiability and without fretting that they were simply expressing subjective value preferences. Yet since in legal circles, philosophy, hermeneutics, and the interpretive turn would have all been associated with indeterminacy at first, the discussion about admitting them may only have heightened anxiety about normative judgments (as if increased anxiety were necessary).[25]

Further, the interpretive turn possessed the potential to carry individual disciplines in two different directions. Among insiders, it could lead to the "academic disorder" of "narcissism."[26] It encouraged scholarship about scholarship, or meta-scholarship. It also increased accessibility to outsiders by shifting the focus from the "substance" of a discipline to the act of interpreting it. The interpretive turn fostered real "interdisciplinarity."

The promise of "real" interdisciplinarity that made the interpretive turn so tantalizing to law professors, anthropologists, philosophers, and others also jeopardized their control over their own disciplines. As Roland Barthes said, "Interdisciplinarity consists in creating a new object that belongs to no one." It was "not about confronting already constituted disciplines (none of which, in fact, is willing to let itself go)." Thus

Rorty's colleagues feared how the uninitiated would react to his revolt against analytic philosophy. "They consider it iconoclastic and exciting, but few of them have had the time to feel the grip of what he [Rorty] rejects," one professor complained of students. More fundamentally, academics worried about the wisdom of toppling disciplinary boundaries. Though Alasdair MacIntyre celebrated the publication of *Philosophy and the Mirror of Nature* as "something of an event," he nevertheless fussed: "If I am doomed to spending the rest of my life talking with literary critics and sociologists and historians and physicists, I am going to listen to a great deal of philosophy, much of it inept." Martha Nussbaum also complained that "legal academics who pick up a bit of philosophy and do a thing or two in that field do it pretty badly." And what about time lags? In the 1980s, lawyers and historians made Geertz their "patron saint," just as he was challenged by younger anthropologists who found deconstruction after it had become "old hat" among English professors.[27]

Despite its dangers, the interpretive turn was still overdue in law. In the nineteenth century, Francis Lieber's *Legal and Political Hermeneutics* had Americanized hermeneutics. In the interim, however, legal scholars had let hermeneutics languish. Edward Corwin had not been certain how to spell the word when he appeared before the Senate Judiciary Committee to testify about Court Packing. One law professor griped at the beginning of the 1980s: "Not a single theorist has presented anything like a full-blown theory of what 'interpretation' really is." For all their talk about "what constitutional adjudicators ought to do," commentators had provided no accounts of what constitutional adjudicators "inevitably will do." Legal scholarship still lacked "even a rudimentary theory" of hermeneutics. There was also a flip explanation for the reason law should take the interpretive turn. Once "fancy European theorists started talking about 'texts,' 'interpretation,' and the like," who could expect American legal scholars to stay off the bandwagon? Yet though law professors were prone to jumping on and off intellectual bandwagons, in this instance they chose an appropriate one.[28]

In 1981, Yale Law School invited Geertz to give its annual Storrs Lectures, long an important part of intellectual life at the university. Grant Gilmore had delivered the most famous Storrs Lectures of the 1970s. Gilmore concluded:

Law reflects but in no sense determines the moral worth of a society. The values of a reasonably just society will reflect themselves in a reasonably just law. The better the society, the less law there will be. In Heaven, there will be no law, and the lion will lie down with the lamb. The values of an unjust society will reflect themselves in an unjust law. The worse the society, the more law there will be. In Hell, there will be nothing but law, and due process will be meticulously observed.[29]

Now, at his inaugural lecture, several months after the 1981 legal scholarship conference, Geertz espoused a very different conception of law. He pleaded with law professors to make

a shift away from functionalist thinking about law—as a clever device to keep people from tearing one another limb from limb, advance the interests of the dominant classes, defend the rights of the weak against the predations of the strong, or render social life a bit more predictable at its fuzzy edges (all of which it quite clearly is, to varying extents at different times in different places); and a shift toward hermeneutic thinking about it—as a mode of giving particular sense to particular things in particular places (things that happen, things that fail to, things that might), such that these noble, sinister, or merely expedient appliances take particular form and have particular impact. Meaning, in short, not machinery. . . . Although this "interpretive turn," as it has been called, the conceiving of human behavior and the products of human behavior as "saying something of something"—which something needs to be drawn out and explicated—has touched virtually every domain of cultural study, reaching even to such positivist strongholds as social psychology and the philosophy of science, it has not as yet had very much influence in legal studies.[30]

LAW TURNS INTERPRETIVE

The floodgates opened. Constitutional theorists now declared themselves engaged in interpreting the text and eager to explain the process by which they worked. Interpretation, rather than interpretivism, became the rage. That is, the focus shifted from interpretation of the

Constitution to the act and practice of reading and interpretation. Renouncing the interpretivist/noninterpretivist debate, Thomas Grèy said, "We are all interpretivists; the real arguments are not over whether judges should stick to interpreting, but over what they should interpret and what interpretive attitudes they should adopt." In a stunning 1982 book, providing an antifoundationalist answer to the question of what justified judicial review, Philip Bobbitt discarded "the notion that law takes place within a framework that is independent of the structure of legal argument" and announced "constitutional law needs no 'foundation.' " By locating "legitimation in a particular practice, rather than a prior, external rationale," he believed he had "solved" the counter-majoritarian difficulty.[31]

In the 1980s, constitutional scholars argued with philosophers, literary theorists and each other. They debated what Paul Brest called " 'the hermeneutic insight'—the view . . . 'that a sharp distinction cannot be drawn between understanding the text in its own terms and reading the interpreter's concerns into it.' " They differed over the value of hermeneutic method for interpretive strategies, the relevance of authorial intention to interpretation, the chance of interpretive objectivity. Was there a possibility "of an objective standard of criticism once it is conceded that there is no independent object by which to test interpretations"?[32]

The liveliest figure in the disputes, Stanley Fish, an English professor who would join the Duke law faculty in the mid-1980s, promised he could offer something just as appealing. Fish took issue with the idea of a stable text that became the subject of various interpretations. "I want to argue that there always is a text (just as there always is an ordinary world) but that what is in it can change, and therefore at no level is it independent of and prior to interpretation." Fish used the example of the sign on the door of the Johns Hopkins University Club: "PRIVATE MEMBERS ONLY." Students knew that "professors of English literature do not put things on boards unless they are to be examples of problematic or ironic or ambiguous language." So when Fish asked his literature students what the sign meant, the "most popular reading, perhaps because of its Disney-like anthropomorphism . . . [was:] 'Only genitalia may enter.' " As some "member" of the class always "rose" to say, however, Fish was just having fun. The sign obviously restricted entrance to those who belonged to the club. In fact, Fish maintained, there were only two things he did "not want to say about PRIVATE MEMBERS ONLY: that it has a literal meaning, and that it doesn't. It does not have a literal meaning in the sense of some irreducible content which survives the sea change of situations; but in each of those situations one meaning (even if it is plural) will seem so obvious that one cannot see how it could be otherwise, and that meaning will be literal."[33]

Fish confronted the implications of his argument. "The fear is of a world without principle, a world where might makes right, and personal preferences run roughshod over the rules and laws intended to constrain them," he acknowledged. "Does might make right?" The answer was yes, since if there was no perspective independent of interpretation, "some interpretive perspective will always rule by virtue of having won out over its competitors."[34]

But the outcome was not bleak, because the standards of judgment passing to some observers as "personal preferences," or force, and to others as "principles" proved "principled preferences," which arose by virtue of membership in "interpretive communities." In a series of essays, Fish repeatedly hammered home his point: "Since there are no independent grounds for interpretation [that do not derive from the act of interpretation itself], there is no escape from rhetoric, meaning the discourse of persuasion, the norms and constraints of which in every case are defined by one's membership in a given professional community of interpretation."[35]

While members of Fish's interpretive communities could produce rhetoric, they could not generate theory. Fish's definition of theory as "constraints that are more than the content of a practice from which they are indistinguishable" foreclosed theory's existence at the same time that the constraints themselves averted anarchy. "On the one hand, the condition of being without constraints is quite literally unimaginable and therefore need not be feared; but on the other, the constraints that are always in place are not fixed but interpretive—forever being altered by the actions they make possible—and there is no danger that they will forever hold us in the same position." In Fish's world, judges "are not using any epistemology (or theory) at all. They are merely registering what they see and proceeding in ways that seem to them to be obligatory and routine." There was nothing else for them to do. So much for the desire to solve the counter-majoritarian difficulty, which simply represented the vain hope to find a disinterested justification of the system in which legal actors were embedded, outside that system.[36]

If theory could not exist, it could not have consequences. Fish condemned what he called " 'anti-foundationalist theory hope,' the belief that because we now know that our foundations are interpretive rather than natural (given by God or nature) we will regard them with suspicion and shake ourselves loose from their influence." That implied the existence of a noninterpretive vantage point from which to survey interpretive foundations, which antifoundationalism itself made impossible.[37]

Within the legal community, as Fish recognized, he won few adherents. Because of his restrictive definition and "privileging of the interpretive community," as well as what was perceived to be his "paean to the status quo of judicial practice," his antifoundationalism held little appeal for critical legal scholars. Meanwhile a leading natural law theorist condemned Fish's "antimetaphysicial fetish," claiming that the interpretive turn was "a turn for the worse." Richard Posner maintained that Fish's most useful insights derived from Wittgenstein, and that literary theory itself could not illuminate law. And whatever their politics, the law professors who had so recently discovered theory, who were promoting it as a way of "transforming reality," and who believed the interpretive turn encouraged theory found Fish's contention theory lacked normative value or consequences "Fishy."[38]

The turn to interpretation, however, did attract liberal law professors. They apparently took the interpretive turn for several reasons: because they realized that developments in the social sciences and humanities about the understanding of language had ramifications for legal scholarship, because they could not abide the efforts of law and economics proponents to make interdisciplinary work "the property of the right," and because they saw the potential the interpretive turn possessed to fight claims of legal indeterminacy by critical legal scholars. To liberal academic lawyers, the interpretive turn proved a godsend, which allowed them to question the existence of objective foundations of justice without throwing up their hands. They could now argue that "objectivity does not depend upon determinacy." They need not travel through the tunnel of determinacy to reach the promised land of objectivity.[39]

Shifting his attention from Rawls to interpretation, Ronald Dworkin characterized legal interpretation as a "chain enterprise," in which the function of his mythical judge, still called Hercules, now resembled that of the "chain novel's" successive authors. As Hercules compared the new case before him to similar cases decided in the past, he "must regard himself . . . as a partner in a complex chain enterprise of which these innumerable decisions, structures, conventions and practices are the history; it is his job to continue that history into the future through what he does on the day. He *must* interpret what has gone before because he has a responsibility to advance the enterprise in hand rather than strike out in some new direction of his own." Only thus could Hercules pursue his goal and the goal of a "community of principle"—"law as integrity."[40]

Owen Fiss likewise now described judging as "interpretation," which he characterized as "neither a wholly discretionary nor a wholly mechanical activity." Membership in the interpretive community, "which recognizes and adheres to the disciplining rules used by the interpreter and that is defined by its recognition of those rules," checked and made possible interpretation, Fiss insisted. The "objective quality of interpretation is bounded, limited, or relative." To Fiss, the concept of "adjudication as objective interpretation" constituted powerful ammunition against critical legal studies. He wrote in 1982:

> A recognition of the interpretive dimensions of adjudication and the dynamic character of all interpretive activity and its capacity to relate constructively the subjective and objective . . . might enable us to come to terms with a new nihilism, one that doubts the legitimacy of adjudication—a nihilism that appears to me to be unwarranted and unsound, but that is gaining respectability and claiming an increasing number of important and respected legal scholars, particularly in constitutional law. They have turned their backs on adjudication and have begun a romance with politics. . . .
>
> Viewing adjudication as interpretation helps to stop the slide towards nihilism. *It makes law possible.* We can find in this conceptualization a recognition of both the subjective and the objective—the important personal role played by the interpreter in the

meaning-giving process, and yet the possibility of an inter-subjective meaning rooted in the idea of disciplining rules and of an interpretive community that both legitimates those rules and is defined by them.[41]

But Fiss's and Dworkin's were just two ways of reading Fish. Sanford Levinson drew on Fish's work to impugn Fiss and Dworkin. According to Levinson's reading of Fish, "meaning is created rather than discovered" in the process of interpretation. "Building on the views of Fish and Rorty," Levinson used his article "Law as Literature" (in the 1982 *Texas Law Review* symposium on interpretation) to insist on a convergence of the scholarship about interpretation produced by the new law and literature movement with cls work on indeterminacy. Anticipating judicial review in 1787, James Iredell had linked it to popular sovereignty, separation of powers, and simple necessity. Judges who struck down legislative acts were not exercising "usurped or a discretionary power, but one inevitably resulting from the constitution of their office, they being judges *for the benefit of the whole people,* not *mere servants of the Assembly,*" he said. "It really appears to me, the exercise of the power is unavoidable, the Constitution not being a mere imaginary thing, about which ten thousand different opinions may be formed, but a written document to which all may have recourse, and to which therefore, the judges cannot willfully blind themselves." Nearly two hundred years later, in what he later described as "for better or worse, the most quoted single sentence I have ever written," Levinson declared that "[t]here are as many plausible readings of the United States Constitution as there are versions of *Hamlet.*"[42]

Predictably, no one found anyone else's understanding of Fish, or interpretation of interpretive activity, plausible. Fish claimed that neither Dworkin nor Fiss understood the nature of interpretation, and that "Levinson actually makes the same mistake committed by those whom he is attacking." Fiss treated Levinson as a nihilist and claimed that "Stanley Fish and I actually stand united in defense of the middle ground."[43]

The editors of the *Texas Law Review* therefore opened their "pioneering . . . special issue on interpretation" with an apology. "Readers who plow through the offerings in this Symposium may be left feeling battered by the cacophony of it all," they warned in the introduction. "Not only do the authors disagree on substantive positions, they are unable to arrive at similar characterizations of each other's work. Although this abstract debate can appear quite distant from the day-to-day concerns of the practitioner, the questions discussed in this issue, will, for better or for worse, continue to haunt the legal profession in the coming years." Clearly in the editors' eyes, it was no step forward to claim that meanings of texts were "in part our own creations." Other legal scholars shared their view. Though law and literature had existed since James Boyd White published *The Legal Imagination* in 1973, its movement from text into theory with respect to constitutional interpretation made it seem dangerous now, even to some legal scholars schooled in literary theory.[44]

After all the law review symposia on interpretation, Paul Brest seemed sorry he had ever mentioned the word *hermeneutics*. The hermeneutic insight, he pointed out, had long pervaded constitutional interpretation and the moral reasoning that underlay it. So what if there was no "real" preinterpretive meaning out there waiting to be discovered? Brest now dismissed the hermeneutic insight as a "fancy" way of packaging the counter-majoritarian difficulty. "Although hermeneutics and moral philosophy aspire to right answers, their answers are not as 'objective' as many scholars, politicians, and citizens would like. The problem seems especially acute when federal judges, appointed with lifetime tenure, overturn the decisions of legislative majorities." What else was new? "The concern with objectivity in judicial interpretation, of course, antedates considerably contemporary legal academia's fascination with interpretation."[45]

Further, as Robert Cover eloquently emphasized in the mid-1980s, legal interpretation differed from literary interpretation in an important respect: "death and pain are at the center of legal interpretation." Harry Wellington criticized law professors' "wonderfully interesting articles written on such things as comparative normative hermeneutics" for their noncontextualism. They did not "come to grips with the stuff of adjudication; that is jurisdiction (or procedure in the large sense), power," or "with the fact that lawyers argue cases to win, not to establish true principles of interpretation, and that majority opinions are desperately negotiated documents and not the carefully crafted work of a philosopher." Martha Minow generously conceded that the controversy over interpretation sparked by law and literature had helped "to clarify what kinds of meaning or truth legal scholars fear law has lost." She also said, "for someone like me, who is drawn to the interpretive turn," Cover's "devastating and haunting insight" forced reexamination. "Legal scholars may have turned to the interpretive frame, which holds up a vision of communal efforts to create meaning, in an effort to demystify law and to rid it of its aura of objectivity. The interpretive frame, however, poses the danger of a new mystification, one that casts an aura of cozy conversation over official acts of domination and control."[46]

In the case of Minow, some of her fellow feminists, and others, antifoundationalism led to neopragmatism rather than to law and literature. Rorty's work created a resurgence of interest in pragmatism in the legal academy of the 1980s. Defining legal pragmatism as "a nonfoundational approach to law," involving the solution of legal problems through the use of "every tool that comes to hand, including precedent, tradition, legal text and social policy," scholars such as Daniel Farber argued that constitutional theorists should eschew "grand theory" for pragmatism. Farber pointed out that no grand theory had appeared to make judicial decision making principled or judicial review democratic. Pragmatists, he said, would stop worrying about whether judicial review could be reconciled with democracy, recognize that "judicial review *is* a part of a social system," and work to make it promote "a flourishing democratic society." To Thomas Grey, pragmatism offered "freedom from theory-guilt," while also stressing "the local and situated character of all theorizing." Quoting the lawyer and poet Wallace Stevens, Grey promised: "A pragmatic sense for context reminds us that jurisprudence is *not* poetics; law and poetry are 'beyond resemblance,' though between them remains 'this and that intended to be recognized.' " Acknowledging that thought was embedded in context and social practice would not lead to moral relativism, Minow pledged. Pragmatism offered "a refined sense of what factors should count in judgment, not an abandonment of the possibility of judgment." Nor would pragmatism prevent politics. "Instead, we can examine the expression of larger patterns of power, domination and exclusion in the particular details of each context." A "critical" as opposed to "complacent" neopragmatism could further social change. Posner, who recommended cautiousness toward wealth maximization and espoused "reasonableness" as the "judicial lodestar" after he was tapped for the Seventh Circuit Court of Appeals in 1981, rightly remarked on the "ideological diversity" of pragmatists. Yet the existence of pragmatism in law simply increased the cacophony as some law and literature adherents such as Dworkin claimed pragmatism lacked integrity, while others such as Fish asked why pragmatism would remove the bedrock so it could become a foundation. And while Minow thought some academics saw the interpretive turn of law and literature as a "frivolous . . . detour away from legal problems," other scholars dismissed pragmatism as a platitude. Rorty himself later characterized pragmatism as "banal in its application to law."[47]

Arguably, the "detour" represented by law and literature initially proved more significant than pragmatism. The interpretive turn threw open legal scholarship to outsiders, who frightened law professors and deepened their despair over justifying their practices. It pointed legal scholars toward a metatheory treating the Constitution "as an immense system of ventriloquism, in which each voice represents and usurps the next," which stopped trying to clothe the emperor and made his naked body "one more construction to be deconstructed," and which assumed a postmodern and ironic tone about law. To Jack Balkin, postmodern constitutionalism was "the rout of progressive forces, the increasing insularity, self-absorption, and fragmentation of progressive academic writing, and the increasing irrelevance of that writing to the positive law of the U.S. Constitution." Robert Lipkin sounded positively cheerful in comparison, when he announced that postmodern constitutionalism "encourages the very sort of 'discord' or 'tower of Babel' that some commentators decry."[48]

In this highly theoretical atmosphere, it was easy for Fish to use the pages of the *Yale Law Journal* to mock Posner's claim that literary theory had little to offer law. "His admonition—don't look for very much help from literary studies—comes too late; for as he surely knows, recent years have seen an unprecedented traffic between law and literary studies, with the former borrowing and appropriating far more than the latter and to considerable effect," Fish contended in the 1980s. "Not only is it now difficult to tell some numbers of the *Stanford Law Review* or *The Yale Law Journal* from *Diacritics* and *Critical Inquiry*, but the issues debated in their pages have . . . produced a general sense in the legal profession of a new crisis in which its authority—internal and external—is being put into question as never before." That was precisely what worried many law professors.[49]

Among the most concerned was Paul Carrington, Duke Law School's dean. In the 1970s, he had defended law schools against the "instantaneous practicality" implicit in proposals to emphasize skills training in legal education. He had also queried law and economics. In the 1980s, he came to agree with Fiss that some critical legal scholars subscribed to nihilism. In a widely publicized 1983 speech, Carrington suggested that such individuals had "an ethical duty to depart the law school, perhaps to seek a place elsewhere in the academy." As Carrington admitted, his were tough words "within a university, whose traditions favor the inclusion in house of all honestly held ideas, beliefs and values. When, however, the university accepted responsibility for training professionals, it also accepted a duty to constrain teaching that knowingly dispirits students or disables them from doing the work for which they are trained."[50]

Carrington spoke at a time when the culture wars had begun raging inside the university's walls. "A New Brand of Literary Criticism Has Scholars Everywhere Up in Arms," *Washington Post* headlines blared in 1983. "Alien spacecraft (rumored to bear the Air France emblem) have been sighted over college campuses from Yale to northern Alabama. Meanwhile, red-blooded young American scholars have begun speaking a strange language, thick with words like 'semiotics,' 'prosopoeia,' 'apotropaic,' and 'diacritical.' " An accompanying cartoon called up images of invasions from outer space and horror films: "Flanked by sinister spaceships in the shape of graduation caps, the monstrous figure of a tweed-clad 'alien being' wreaks deconstruction in a campus-turned terrordome, zapping hapless students with an unforgiving X-ray vision, all under the lurid banner 'Humanities vs. the Deconstructionist.' " Harvard's Walter Jackson Bate complained that a "nihilistic view of literature, of human communication and of life itself" frightened at least a quarter of the nation's English professors. In explaining why deconstruction proved so much more popular in the United States than in Britain,

Christopher Norris pointed to its obvious relevance to law: "The possession of a *written* Constitution whose principles are yet open to all manner of far-reaching judicial review . . . gives a political edge to questions of textual and interpretive theory that they do not have in the British cultural context." Defenders of the faith tried to mute the impact of deconstruction by making it an "ism," but they worried about winning. More generally, in literary studies, theory proved a sure route to tenure and to institutional success.[51]

Perhaps because law was a profession, and because critical legal studies threatened to gain a stronger toehold at the nation's most prestigious law school than deconstruction did in Bate's English department, traditional law professors had advantages denied their counterparts in other disciplines. Certainly the culture wars had politicized law schools most. "American legal thought has always been political, but legal academia today may be more openly politicized and more polarized than ever before," one critical legal scholar said in 1985. He continued: "Although the ideological divisions are clearly reflected in scholarship, the political conflict in the nation's law schools does not consist of mere skirmishing over intellectual orientations or interests. Rather, it amounts to a struggle for (and against) power on many fronts—in faculty meetings as well as at law reviews, over admissions and appointment decisions as well as over interpretations of legal doctrine and over the description and practice of the whole range of social relations." Intellectually and sociologically—in scholarship and on faculties—the veneer separating law from politics had been stripped away. In this atmosphere, tenure for a critical legal scholar was not the same foregone conclusion as promotion for the literary theorist. "Despite the relatively low tenure standards of American law schools, an alarming number of impressive critical legal scholars are being fired from law teaching positions," one sympathizer maintained. For its part, the right condemned critical legal scholars' style as one of "guerilla warfare." And at a time when some critical legal scholars liked to épater the meritocratic (and bourgeois) by, for example, proposing to transform Harvard Law School into a "counterhegemonic enclave" in which students were admitted by lottery and professors and janitors rotated through each other's jobs, the characterization stuck, even though some joked that "oppressed campesinos" had nothing more in common with the "spoiled yuppies" in cls than "a taste for goat cheese."[52]

Nowhere was the tension greater than at the peak of the hierarchy. Morton Horwitz thought there was "a crisis of legitimacy" at Harvard Law School; to Ralph Nader, the school was experiencing "a crisis of confidence on a directionless highway." The "Rome" of critical legal studies, Harvard had become "the Beirut of legal education." "Throughout its history, the HLS faculty has probably never been as divided as it is today," one observer said. At the time Carrington's speech was being reprinted, Calvin Trillin was reporting in *The New Yorker* that arguments over the hiring and promotion of critical legal scholars had turned Harvard into "the most unhappy place." Trillin explained that it "is about the only prominent law school where people involved in Critical Legal Studies have acquired a large enough base to be effective in faculty politics." His article spurred the Harvard Law School faculty to hold a discussion on critical legal studies for alumni at New York's Harvard Club. There, professors Robert Clark and Paul Bator vociferously attacked critical legal studies, while Duncan Kennedy, their colleague, vigorously defended it. Meanwhile, in an article entitled "War between Professors Pervades Harvard Law," the *Washington Post* was about to publicize Dean James Vorenberg's open letter to the alumni, which responded to "widespread concern that a 'war-like atmosphere threatens intellectual standards at the nation's most influential law school.' " Vorenberg's successor, Robert Clark, was complaining that "the attitude of the school that's emerging, at least as it presents its face to the outside world, such as to the alumni, is, 'Let a thousand flowers bloom, so long as they're all leaning sharply to the left.' " The *New York Times* was about to trumpet, "The Split at Harvard Law Goes Down to Its Foundations":

> Long the goal of law professors everywhere, the school has not been able to hire anyone laterally since 1981. Usually, that is because the Harvard faculty cannot agree on a candidate. In the rare instances when it has agreed, usually under a kind of "Missouri compromise" between the left and right, the candidate has declined. . . . Tenure decisions have proven equally divisive. Last year six committee members split three ways over one candidate.[53]

In this context, some condemned Carrington for red-baiting. "There is a deep fear (and I think Carrington and the critics of Critical Legal Studies are gripped by this fear) that the center (i.e., liberalism) will not hold," one of Carrington's critics wrote. In fact, the response to Carrington's attack might have been interpreted to demonstrate the enduring strength of legal liberalism. Critical legal scholars rushed to claim he had violated their rights in language that would have made Rawls proud.[54]

While most academics thought Carrington had impugned critical legal scholars' politics, Sanford Levinson claimed the dean was speaking about something different—"faith and belief. . . . The point is, that for Dean Carrington, law schools function as the divinity schools of our secular religion." As Levinson said, however, some of Carrington's detractors believed that "[l]aw schools should become ever more like departments of religion." Thus Owen Fiss claimed that "[l]aw professors are not paid to train lawyers, but to study the law and to teach their students what they happen to discover." After all, law schools had sought respectability within the university for a long time. "I am astounded by the distinction you make between the law school and the university of which it is part," Paul Brest chided Carrington. "One of the signal achievements of legal education in the past century has been to earn law schools a full and equal place in the university community." Carrington's view of legal education "would relegate law schools to the status of vocational training schools."[55]

The sense of upheaval in the law schools, which Carrington's cri de coeur accentuated, was the price of new political perspectives within the academy, but it was also the toll of interdisciplinary scholarship. "Today, you look back to C. P. Snow's complaint about the gulf between the 'two cultures,' and you think, *two?* Keep counting, C. P.," wrote Henry Louis Gates. "The familiar buzz words here are 'the fragmentation of humanistic knowledge.' " Though one might argue that the social sciences had diluted the new legal scholarship of the 1930s, "theory" did not tame the new legal scholarship of the 1980s.[56]

Theory also threatened traditional modes of scholarship that all law professors still employed. For example, lawyers thrived on footnotes, which they regarded as authoritative. Academic lawyers were using more of them in the 1980s. In the setting of the other disciplines to which they now referred, their footnoting practices seemed ridiculous. Law professors were "citing Rorty, Kuhn, and Wittgenstein as if they were citing a holding in an unanimous Supreme Court decision." The law professor who claimed it reasonable for a shipper to dump the cargo he carried overboard to save himself in a storm might cite Aristotle, but even if that reference settled the matter for other law professors, it would hardly do so for philosophers. Further, academic lawyers' footnoting customs seemed indefensible. Traditional legal scholarship was coming to seem tainted.[57]

From the standpoint of defenders of the faith, such as Carrington and Fiss, worse was coming. At least, the historian Joyce Appleby noted, "the idea of interpretive traditions undercuts the claim that words are uncontrollable. Repetition and communication form the essence of a tradition, and neither are assimilable to the notion of protean words dancing away with meaning before the author's ink can dry on the page." Now, the interpretive tradition that hermeneutics presupposed disappeared in poststructuralism. In the course of a long, published 1984 dialogue with another critical legal scholar that often sounded "like a pair of old acid heads chewing over a passage in Sartre," Duncan Kennedy renounced "the fundamental contradiction." Critical legal studies moved toward postmodernism, and some critical legal scholars traveled beyond structuralism to poststructuralism and deconstruction.[58]

More focused on "the text and its reading rather than the reader," deconstruction brought new challenges. Intertextuality reared its head; law professors now faced that endless play of signifiers leading from one text to another. As Fiss mistakenly interpreted it, deconstruction "expands the idea of text to embrace all the world and at the same time proclaims the freedom of the interpreter." Carrington was even less charitable. "There are those who do say that literary texts are what the reader chooses to make of them, and indeed that the creative process occurs in the minds of readers, not writers," he said. "I hope that it is not merely a revelation of a political bias when I confess sympathy for the view expressed that this is the sort of philosophy that has given bullshit a bad name."[59]

Anthropology professors were experiencing growing pains similar to those suffered by legal scholars. During the 1980s, literary theory supplanted anthropology, as it also replaced philosophy, in providing "a transfer point among the humanities." A new generation of anthropologists used the insights of deconstruction to attack Geertz's work. In the Geertzean text, "culture comprised a subtle code that only the canny anthropologist could decipher," an anthropologist complained. Whereas Geertz worried that Malinowski's text transformed the others ethnographers studied into the Other, "always capitalized, always singular," the Geertzean text bestowed "an equal apotheosis on the ethnographer, who could speak, *oracularly,* of worlds otherwise unknown." Spotlighting the politics of the ethnographer's text, a new generation emphasized the anthropologist's role in *constructing* "ethnographic truths," which James Clifford characterized as "inherently *partial*—committed and incomplete." Their postmodern ethnography foregrounded "dialogue as opposed to monologue," stressed "the cooperative and collaborative nature of the ethnographic situation in contrast to the ideology of the transcendental observer," and spurned "the ideology of 'observer-observed,' there being nothing observed and no one who is observer."[60]

Like Fiss and Carrington, and though it was he who had opened Pandora's box, Geertz was not amused. "The 'diary disease' is now endemic," he grumbled. "But what is to me anyway, finally most interesting about all . . . of these attempts . . . to produce highly 'author-saturated,' supersaturated even, anthropological texts in which the self the text creates and the self that creates the text are represented as being very near to identical, is the strong note of disquiet that suffuses them. There is very little confidence here and a fair amount of outright malaise." One of Geertz's younger colleagues admitted that "few anthropologists nowadays can ignore ethnography's loss of authority after the acts of authorship by which it has been constructed have been so astutely demystified."[61]

As some of the younger anthropologists realized, other disciplines were leading law professors to their own "ethnographic approach." Legal scholars' writing was changing. Though lawyers had always been "knee-deep in stories," once their style had been stiff. They relaxed only when they composed book reviews or incomplete, but nevertheless intriguing, tributes to dead friends. In the mid-1980s, however, law professors began to write about a subject they had always enjoyed discussing—themselves. In 1986, Patricia Williams published her reflections on "Spaceship Me." Susan Estrich's article "Rape," published that same year, began, "Eleven years ago, a man held an ice pick to my throat and said: 'Push over, shut up, or I'll kill you.' " David Kennedy's "Spring Break" attacked "the culture of law reviews" by "violating as many stylistic conventions as possible . . . [w]riting in the first person, avoiding footnotes, describing experiences, and discussing sexuality." Now law professors were ironic, sometimes even frivolous.[62]

The new trend encountered resistance at first. When Julius Getman acclaimed it and lamented the absence of the "human voice" in legal discourse, sturdy souls leapt forward in defense of ponderousness. They were outnumbered.[63]

Suddenly, law professors discovered the implications of "my most precious property, 'I' " for their scholarship. The vertical pronoun and "moi criticism" appeared everywhere. Legal scholars delighted in revealing their own multiple personalities. The reader learned, for example, whose child liked what television shows and whose hung an "S.S.D.D." (Same Shit, Different Day) sign in her room. On the one hand, such changes made the younger generation of academic lawyers seem almost folksy. On the other, they served to emphasize how much the professors differed from their predecessors.[64]

NO COVER

Surveying the field for his Stevens Lecture at Cornell in 1986, Owen Fiss proved despondent. As his colleague Bruce Ackerman had done in his own 1984 jeremiad, *Reconstructing American Law,* Fiss condemned both law and economics and critical legal studies. In "The Death of the Law?" Fiss declared the two trends more similar than different and warned that if either prevailed, "This will mean the death of the law, as we have known it throughout history, and as we have come to admire it." The movements rejected what Fiss had continued to defend, the view of law as embodiment of "public morality" or "public values." Fiss scored them for refusing "to take law on its own terms and to accept adjudication as an institutional arrangement in which public officials seek to elaborate and protect the values that we hold in common." He understood them "as a reaction to a jurisprudence, confidently embraced by the bar in the sixties, that sees adjudication as the process for interpreting and nurturing a public morality. Both law and economics and critical legal studies are united in their rejection of law as a public ideal." According to Fiss, one group "proclaims 'law is efficient,' the other that 'law is politics.' "[65]

Fiss proved especially hostile toward critical legal studies. Its advocates "revel in . . . (to use their favorite term) 'indeterminacy,' " he protested. Critical legal scholars, he said, were the ultimate nihilists. "The aim of their critique is critique," a program Fiss pronounced "politically unappealing and politically irresponsible." Critical legal scholarship created an illusion of judicial freedom. "What is required is that judges be constrained in their judgment, and they certainly are." According to Fiss, his beloved Warren Court justices were so restricted. "When I read a case like *Brown* v. *Board of Education,* for example, what I see is not the unconstrained power of the judges to give vent to their desires and interests, but rather public officials situated within a profession, bounded at every turn by the norms and conventions that define and constitute that profession." Sadly, while in the 1960s, "we undertook the Second Reconstruction and tried to build the Great Society, and we were drawn to law as public ideal, in the next decade we took refuge in the politics of selfishness: All normative matters became subjective." A "common morality" seemed unattainable.

> Locating these two jurisprudential movements within a specific historical context may also help us understand what must be done. Law has been threatened by the disintegration of public values in the larger society, and its future can only be assured by the reversal of those social processes. In order to save the law, we must look beyond the law. We will never be able to respond fully to the negativism of critical legal studies or the crude instrumentalism of law and economics until a regenerative process takes hold, until the broad social processes that fed and nourished those movements are reversed. The analytic arguments internal to law can take us only so far. There must be something more—a belief in public values and the willingness to act on them.

Whence would come those "public values and the willingness to act on them?" Fiss confided that the "historical vision" of the 1960s and his memory of "the role that the law played in the struggle for racial equality" sustained him as he spoke "of a public morality and the judiciary's responsibility for giving meaning and expression to those values." He conceded, however, that "for a generation born after *Brown,* after Ole Miss, after Birmingham, after Freedom Summer, and maybe even after Selma, this vision does not work." It stood "as a quaint and even touching remembrance of time past." He did see "a new cause taking hold," feminism, which might regenerate belief in public values.[66]

Unfortunately for Fiss, many of those academics in whom he staked his hopes had been born after *Brown* too. His vision did nothing for postmodernism's children. Though Fiss thought he had nodded to their sensibilities younger legal scholars mocked his use of the constitutive "we" and scorned him for ignoring the extent to which the individual, law, and truth were socially and culturally constructed. Focusing on the "time and place" from which Fiss talked, one postmodernist complained that Fiss's "authoritarian strategy . . . is attempting to force us to relive *the past . . .* and not just the past, but *his* past . . . and not just his past, but his past as *The Law.*" Nor did Fiss's vision inspire feminists: Clare Dalton skewered his legal liberalism, pointing out that it read "from start to finish as an appeal to faith—religious faith." On behalf of legal feminists, she shunned his invitation "to join his community of faith, and . . . to lead the congregation in prayer, as long as they will use his prayer book."[67]

Most sadly, for Fiss, surely, his vision did not even inspire his beloved colleague Robert Cover, who died the same year Fiss gave the Stevens Lecture. Fiss and Cover had recently appeared with Fish at an Association of American Law Schools "Law and Humanities" panel on constitutional interpretation. After long disquisitions about interpretive communities and disciplining rules by Fish, and by Fiss, who had thrown himself into the debate over interpretation, it was Cover's turn. "I can't imagine spending five minutes of my life reading the interpretations offered by Warren Burger of the Constitution of the United States were I interested only in the so-called 'meaning,' the interpretation which he has to offer," Cover began. "I, like most of you, go through this exercise for one reason only: Warren Burger is a violent man . . . and when he sits in a five or more person majority he has that violence to wield." That was what constitutional interpretation was about, "the mouthings of judges whose prose would otherwise be unworthy." Fiss, Cover charged, was living in the world of the Warren Court, circa 1967. Like Fiss, Cover had regarded *Brown* as paradigmatic case, but now it was time to move on. "I am not looking for disciplining rules," Cover said, because "the disciplining rules are part of the conditions that the violent community is asserting to control others." Describing himself as a legal realist, Cover characterized law as politics. The justices' political commitments in *Brown* were admirable, but an opinion that simply said, "let's end apartheid in America" would have been just as good, if not better than the one the Court produced. "I can't remember six words in a row of *Brown*," Cover said. ("I can," Fiss muttered, to laughter.) Like everyone else, judges responded out of commitments, Cover emphasized, not law. Craft skills determined style; politics shaped decisions. He would play Fiss's game of taking judicial mouthings seriously if it would do any good politically, Cover continued passionately, but no Warren Court would reappear in his lifetime, and "I don't see why we should legitimate the Court which is going to do what I hate, and which I'm committed against by trying to establish that what they are doing is part of [a] sacred process and putting them back in the position of priests." It was time to stop treating judges as prophets.[68]

It was a poignant exchange between two friends, perhaps even a moment of mutual betrayal. Anyone listening to the session could not miss the emotion in Fiss's voice as he accused Cover of trivializing two decades of judicial activism. In a note found after Cover's death and reprinted in the *Procedure* casebook that he, Fiss, and Judith Resnik coauthored, Cover stood firm:

> I am insistent that the apparent capacity of the courts to fashion a life of shared meaning is always seriously compromised and often destroyed by the violence which is the implicit or explicit threat against those who do not share the judge's understanding. I, like Owen, celebrate the achievements of federal courts in destroying apartheid in America. Like Owen, I favor federal courts taking a lead in reforming institutions when the other officials fail. But it is Fiss not Cover who is the romantic here. It is Fiss who supposes that these achievements emerge out of a shared community of interpretation that is national in character. I support those efforts because I believe them right and justified, because I

am sufficiently committed to them to join with others in imposing our will on those who disagree. At times the federal courts have been our allies in those commitments. There is every reason to believe that such a convergence of interests was temporary and accidental; that it is already changing and will soon be a romantic memory of the sublime sixties.[69]

Perhaps Fiss was constructing an enemy without in his Stevens Lecture to hide from the disintegration within. Whereas legal liberalism seemed fragile in 1980, by the middle of the decade it appeared dead, a historical relic. Almost precisely at this point, history came to the rescue.

CHAPTER 5

THE TURN TO HISTORY

"Wouldn't it be foolish for lawyers to ignore the 'republican revival' amongst American historians?" Bruce Ackerman asked recently. Lawyers did not. And it may be foolish for them to hope republicanism will help them find the answers they seek.[1]

THUNDER ON THE RIGHT

While law professors bickered, the Reagan administration was transforming the judiciary through the appointment of conservative judges and yoking its own activism to a "jurisprudence of original intention." According to originalist jurisprudence, Attorney General Edwin Meese said, "Where the language of the Constitution is specific, it must be obeyed. Where there is a demonstrable consensus among the Framers and ratifiers as to a principle stated or implied by the Constitution, it should be followed. Where there is ambiguity as to the precise meaning or reach of a constitutional provision, it should be interpreted and applied in a manner so as to at least not contradict the text of the Constitution itself." Concentrating on Founders' intent in the courts seemed good strategy—especially after the Republicans lost control of the Senate in 1986. The administration's crusade for originalism reflected an attempt to roll back *Roe* and the Warren Court's expansive reading of the Fourteenth Amendment. Again, the right joined the left in attacking the liberal vision of law. Conservatives offered more than the left; Meese pledged that originalism would "avoid . . . the charge of incoherence."[2]

Conservative academic lawyers blamed liberal judicial activism on the law schools. As one law professor said, most legal scholars "so distrust their fellow Americans, that they are willing to trust even Harry Blackmun more." The Supreme Court, he conceded, might not be academics' "ideal revolutionary institution, but it is the best that is currently available. Their policy preferences—that is, the policy preferences of the ACLU—regarding, say, abortion, busing, pornography, capital punishment, criminal procedure, school prayer, state aid to religious schools, flag desecration, and street demonstrations, are not nearly so likely to be enacted in this country any other way."[3]

The Reagan administration followed suit. In a 1984 address to the Federalist Society, Assistant Attorney General William Bradford Reynolds confided that "[t]hose of us in Washington sometimes feel like pioneers in the attempt to return the nation to its constitutional moorings." The past three years had "fully confirmed my worst suspicions that much of the anti-democratic, result-oriented jurisprudence of our time can be traced directly to our system of legal education." Law schools had failed "to inculcate in their students an appreciation of the role of the judiciary as the Framers of our Constitution saw it." Instead they trained students to "believe that it is judicial decision-making, and thus the courts, that should direct public policy." Reynolds contended there were few law professors to disabuse students of that idea. "Theirs is the political liberalism of the upper middle class, of the university and professional school educated. Theirs is the liberalism of a verbal elite. . . . out of touch with the mass of Americans." But Reynolds saw salvation ahead. He pointed out that the Federalist Society had not even existed a decade ago. "Its recent creation and the growth of its chapters at law schools around the country, in educational atmospheres that I know are not the most congenial, provide reason for hope." Reynolds was certain that its members appreciated "our history" and dared "to stand for principle." In 1976, Justice Rehnquist had espoused judicial deference to popularly elected branches of government (a deference his liberal critic, Owen Fiss, alleged Rehnquist rarely practiced), because it was "almost impossible, after reading the record of the Founding Fathers' debates in Philadelphia, to conclude that they intended the Constitution itself to suggest answers to the manifold problems they knew would confront succeeding generations." Now, members of the Reagan administration were explicitly enlisting the Founding Fathers and the Constitution on their side.[4]

The administration's originalist offensive seemed ridiculous to historians inside and outside the law schools, who could easily show that originalism was probably not the original understanding, and that, in any event, the surviving record was too fragmentary to permit definitive conclusions about the Founders' intent. "With its pressing need to find determinate meanings at a fixed historical moment, the strict theory of originalism cannot capture everything that was dynamic and creative—and thus uncertain and problematic—in Revolutionary constitutionalism; nor can it easily accommodate the diversity of views that, after all, best explains why the debates of this era were so lively," Jack Rakove said. Leonard Levy sounded like a critical legal scholar when he maintained that orginalism was indeterminate: "How the Supreme Court uses history, origins, and evolution, as well as original intent depends on those who serve on the Court. . . . That, not the original intent of the Framers, is our reality." Historians protested "that the cottage industry of original intent scholarship and analysis" diverted scholars' attention "from exploring the history of the Founding Period on its own terms." The best bibliographic essay on the literature of the bicentennial confirmed "the widening gap between historians' constitutional history and lawyers' constitutional history."[5]

Nothing more clearly suggested the threat lawyers' constitutional history posed to legal liberalism than the 1985 publication of Richard Epstein's *Takings: Private Property and the Power of Eminent Domain.* Wresting liberalism away from political liberals, Epstein reclaimed it for property rights. Though he never mentioned Hartz, Epstein, a law professor at Chicago, followed Hartz in arguing that the Founders were liberal, acquisitive Lockeans. According to Epstein, they had therefore envisioned a broad rather than narrow interpretation of the Fifth Amendment's eminent domain clause, which prohibited government from taking "private property for public use, without just compensation." Following their lead, Epstein took what he described as an "implacable stand against most zoning, rent control, collective bargaining, progressive taxation, and the like. . . . *All* regulations, *all* taxes, and *all* modifications of liability rules are takings of private property prima facie compensable by the state." He labeled most of the New Deal unconstitutional. "It will be said that my position invalidates much of the twentieth-century legislation, and so it does," he announced.[6]

Appalled legal liberals charged that Epstein was pimping for the Reagan administration and was abusing history to legitimate a "Malthusian Constitution." "What has your left wing critics so perturbed," one of Epstein's more sympathetic readers informed him, "is your desire to repeal the welfare state by using history." Bruce Ackerman thundered that Epstein had made "no effort to wrestle with anti-Hartz historiography, and consequently, no legitimate scholarly appeal to history." Though Epstein denied he used history, the appearance of and reaction to his book underscored the power of history as a weapon.[7]

Though historians dismissed originalism, law professors who had brushed aside Berger could not. The Reagan administration and Epstein campaigns caught them off guard. Perhaps legal scholars thought that in the process of dissolving the interpretivism/noninterpretivism debate, they had disposed of strict originalism, but they had not. To be sure, the strict originalism Meese advocated was a form of interpretivism, and some academics equated interpretivism with strict originalism. Yet whereas interpretivism concentrated on the Constitution as a document and inferences which could be drawn from it, originalism also focused attention on the intent of the Constitution's Framers and ratifiers, reducing the judge to a vessel in the process. "What am I?" Judge Richard Posner asked rhetorically—"A potted plant?" Sarcasm proved a poor weapon against originalism.[8]

While legal scholars floundered, Supreme Court justices who could once count on law professors to pick up the cudgels on their behalf had to fight their own battles. Justice Brennan took to the hustings to insist that "the genius of the Constitution rests not in any static meaning it might have had in a world that is dead and gone, but in the adaptability of its great principles to cope with current problems and current needs." Decrying its "political underpinnings," he derided originalism "as little more than arrogance cloaked as humility. It is arrogant to pretend that from our vantage we can gauge accurately the intent of the Framers on application of principle to specific, contemporary questions." Brennan complained "that the chorus of lamentations calling for interpretations faithful to 'original intention' . . . must inevitably come from persons who have no familiarity with the historical record." It was left for Justice Stevens to suggest that the Reagan administration was contending that the Fourteenth Amendment did not incorporate the First Amendment.[9]

Such responses proved a poor match for the calls for originalism from Reagan's justice department and conservative scholars. As Mark Tushnet admitted, "Meese's speeches strike a chord in our understanding of the Constitution, because they direct attention to our fear that judges, like other government officials, can do us serious harm. The dilemma is that Justice Brennan's confident liberalism, though it recognizes that governments and judges can do good, fails to express our concern that they do evil as well." Once the originalists had shanghaied the Founders and *The Federalist* for their public relations campaign equating democracy with majoritarianism, the majoritarian underpinnings that political conservatives gave originalism seemed to possess the potential to solve the counter-majoritarian difficulty and place judicial review in the service of democracy. "Reduced to its essence, the argument is this: If judges get their authority from the Constitution, and the Constitution gets its authority from the majority of the ratifiers, then the role of the judge is to carry out the will of the ratifiers." Conservatives such as Robert Bork and Bernard Siegan celebrated original intent, interpreting the Constitution as guarantor of laissez-faire and the Founders "as forerunners of Chicago-school economists." In the words of one colleague, Siegan used his "skills as a legal historian in establishing the historical pedigree for constitutionalizing economic liberties."[10]

As a bizarre by-product of the Reagan administration's advocacy of original intent, hermeneutics moved to the forefront of legal scholarship. "The 'originalist' position achieved the rare distinction in a hermeneutic theory (at least, in a secular polity) of becoming official government policy in the Justice Department," Robert Gordon said. Academic lawyer Sanford Levinson and English professor Steven Mailloux began their hermeneutics reader with a discussion of the impact of the 1985 controversy over originalism: "The emergence in the past decade of a vigorous right-wing conservatism has served, among other things, to move what had appeared to be merely esoteric debates about constitutional interpretation from the pages of the law reviews to the headlines of the nation's newspapers and magazines."[11]

A few liberal and left law professors did use hermeneutics against originalism. Examining the hermeneutical devices available to the Constitution's Founders, Powell argued that by the early nineteenth century, "Marshall and Madison accepted the common law understanding that the intent of a document is, at least in part, the product of the interpretive process; both accepted the authority of practice and precedent; and neither regarded historical evidence of the framers' personal intentions as a definitive or even particularly valuable guide to constitutional construction." Brest and Tushnet continued to maintain that hermeneutics halted conclusive ascertainment of the Founders' intent. As he had done since the early 1980s, Ronald Dworkin also pointed out that originalism provided no way of identifying the level of specificity at which the Founders intended constitutional provisions to be applied to contemporary situations.[12]

Neither the law professors' rejoinders, nor those of historians, however, dispelled the allure of originalism. So what if the surviving record of the Founding was fragmentary? "If historians were reduced to studying impeccably documented events, they would have little to do with their time." So what if the Founders were not originalists and expected those who followed to determine the meaning of the Constitution? So what if the Founders believed natural law was an adequate basis for judicial decisions? So what if the will of ratifiers in the past overrode majority preference in the present? So what if, as Justice Brennan warned, originalism forestalled the existence of a "living" Constitution, adjustable to changing circumstances? So what if it was impossible to determine the level of generality at which the Founders had intended the many broad-ranging clauses they included in the Constitution and the Bill of Rights to be imposed on the modern world? None of these complaints extinguished the normative argument for originalism. Its advocates need simply throw down the gauntlet. Though he admitted interpretivism presented "many difficulties," Michael McConnell, one of the most persuasive conservative originalists, defied anyone "to articulate an alternative view by which we can be assured that the judges are doing something other than reading their own personal, economic, moral, [and] political predilections into the Constitution." The bottom line was that legal liberals had not produced a "principled alternative to originalism." At least Bork's vague rule for determining the proper level of generality seemed to place originalism in the service of principled decision making: a "judge should state the principle at the level of generality that the text and historical evidence warrant." Fortuitously, that rule allowed Bork, as it did Meese and Siegan and almost every other originalist, to bow to history *and* argue that the seminal decision of their generation, *Brown,* was "compelled by the original understanding of the fourteenth amendment's equal protection clause."[13]

Most law professors considered originalism too valuable to surrender it to Bork. Recognizing the value of preserving it as a form of constitutional adjudication, they wanted to hang onto moderate originalism. The "dominant tradition of constitutional discourse" had emphasized "static originalism," rather than a "historically changing constitution." Consequently, "the most vehement critics of the specific-intention approach still feel obliged to tether their arguments to some form of original intent," one academic lawyer observed. "It seems difficult, in American political-legal culture, to make a persuasive case for nonoriginalism," another admitted. "That difficulty helps to explain why it is so hard to locate a real, live nonoriginalist, whether judge or, even, academic theorist."[14]

Therefore though hermeneutics may have enhanced legal scholars' image as intellectuals, it provided them with little help outside the ivory tower. The hermeneutic debate lacked fire because law professors wanted to have it both ways: save for a few who believed it possible to recover eternal truths from the Founding, almost all of them wanted to declare it impossible to determine original intent *and* they wanted to preserve originalism. With one breath they queried how their contemporaries could intuit original intent, whose intent should control, whether collective intent could be identified, how specific it need be, what should be done when no evidence of original intent existed, and whether a jurisprudence of original intent meant abandoning every progressive insight since the Founding. With another, they spoke authoritatively of the importance of honoring the wishes of those who framed and ratified the Constitution.[15]

Meanwhile, originalism flourished. The 1987 defeat of Robert Bork as Supreme Court justice suggested the Ninth Amendment was more than the inkblot Bork compared it to and represented a victory for the Warren Court decisions he had won the nomination by attacking. It did not constitute a defeat for originalism. Of all law professors Lawrence Tribe hurt Bork most. His 1985 book *Constitutional Choices,* focusing on the inevitability of choice in constitutional law, which one commentator described as "almost the perfect white paper of constitutional liberals," showed Tribe had little patience for originalism.[16]

But Tribe did turn to history. In another 1985 book, *God Save This Honorable Court,* which he called "the untold story of how the selection of our Justices has helped chart the course of American history," Tribe argued that in view of the "greying of the Court" and the probability President Reagan would make many Supreme Court appointments, the Senate retained the responsibility to ensure "a healthy mix of competing views" on the Court and to examine "how confirmation of the individual Justice would affect the overall balance of the Court." Robert Cover, who had long been interested in legal history, also showed a growing interest in the implications of history and narrative for constitutional law. Meanwhile the continued strength of originalism led other liberal law professors to turn to history as well.[17]

THE TURN TO HISTORY

Some legal liberals determined to appropriate originalism for themselves. They would meet the proponents of original intent on the battleground of history. They would advance alternative interpretations of the Founding to justify legal liberalism.

They had other reasons to turn to history. In 1969, C. Vann Woodward had used his presidential address to the American Historical Association to warn that history's popularity was waning. During the 1970s, philosophy, anthropology, and literary theory had sometimes seemed proudly ahistorical. "We're not concerned with the historical question here," Dworkin had said of himself and Rawls. "We're not concerned about how principles are in fact chosen. We're concerned about which principles are just." Some literary theory also made history irrelevant. When Derrida said "il n'y a pas d'hors texte" in *Of Gram-*

matology, he denied the possibility of access to external historical reality. Derrida spurned the "vulgar and mundane concept of temporality" and predicted "the end of linear writing."[18]

In the 1980s, Americans nevertheless embarked on one of their periodic love affairs with the past. Even so, at the bicentennial, NEH director Lynne Cheney was cautioning that erosion of "historical consciousness" could destroy the nation. "Knowledge of the ideas that have molded us and the ideals that mattered to us functions as a kind of civic glue," she testified.[19]

Allan Bloom's *Closing of the American Mind* appeared in time for the Bork battle and provided fodder for academics feeling besieged by liberals and the left. According to one law professor, "Bloom's work enraptured the book-buying public not because it was convinced by his plea for a return to Platonic dialogue and absolute values, but because it is enthralled by his marvelous depiction of the left-wing cowardice that has caused American universities to discard the values and principles that made them great." The culture wars were about to mushroom beyond the academy into a new phase, a battle between the university and its attackers.[20]

Although the new "political correctness" phase remained for the moment a gleam in the right's eye, some disciplines displayed renewed interest in history. Given Gadamer's emphasis on the "the historicity of all understanding," the interpretive turn led naturally to a "historic turn." Anthropologists were about to promise that "rehistoricization" would allow their field to recapture some of the authority it had recently lost. Historical sociology was experiencing a "revival."[21]

Literary theorists were also touting the new historicism, "a reciprocal concern with the historicity of texts and the textuality of histories," as "a response to that acceleration in the forgetting of history which seems to characterize an increasingly technocratic and commodified American academy and society." To some scholars who had come of age during the 1960s and had survived the revelations about Paul de Man's wartime activities as a collaborator, the new historicism apparently seemed more compatible than deconstruction with radical political critique. Whatever the reason for its emergence, the new historicism challenged deconstruction's domination of literary theory. Gayatri Spivak even charged that the new historicism was "a sort of academic media hype mounted against deconstruction." In his 1986 presidential address to the Modern Language Association, J. Hillis Miller complained about the "the so-called new historicism." Bemoaning the "shift from language to history," he decried literature's "sudden, almost universal turn away from theory in the sense of an orientation toward language as such and . . . [its] corresponding turn toward history, culture, society, politics, institutions, class and gender conditions, the social context, the material base."[22]

That was unfair: the new historicists knew their Derrida, as well as their Foucault, Geertz, and Marx. Their work transformed their teaching. Wesleyan now required potential English majors to enroll in a year of coursework organized around "two platitudes":

[E]very student should know how to read a text with careful and subtle attention to its language, and every student should be able to read a text with some appreciation of its historicity.

From this plain credo we developed two semesters of study with a chasm between them. In English 201 the students read mainly lyric poems in the way that became traditional after World War II. One poem per fifty minutes; no intentional fallacy, no context, little intertextuality; key in on voice, register, metaphor, syntax, dramatic situation, prosody, and so on. In English 202, suddenly, the texts are fat novels surrounded by journals, memoirs, documents, historical arguments, criticism, and so on, all somehow to be grasped as participating in the historical process. It is as if the English Department were kidnapped and taken en masse to a reeducation camp over winter break.[23]

Most law professors had shied away from historicism, new or old. In fact, at the 1981 Yale conference on legal scholarship, critical legal scholar Robert Gordon argued that "historicism, the recognition of the historical and cultural contingency of law, is a perpetual threat to the aims of our legal scholarship as conventionally practiced; that to defend against the threat (or to protect themselves from becoming aware of it) legal scholars have regularly and recurrently resorted to certain strategies of response and evasion; and finally that these strategies have so influenced the practice of legal scholarship as severely to limit its intellectual options and imaginative range." Few law professors seemed eager to confront Gordon's challenge.[24]

Neither English professors nor historians would point legal scholars to historicism. Those law professors who turned to literary theory in the early 1980s seemed unaware of the new historicism. They bypassed it for either Fish's or Derrida's forms of poststructuralism. And though adherents might credit the new historicism with making both context and text matter, it was too theoretical and acontextual for historians.[25]

Ironically, the turn to history in the social sciences and humanities came when history itself was in poor shape. Though politics had not polarized them, historians were anxious about the future of their discipline. Bernard Bailyn's 1981 presidential address to the American Historical Association deplored "the absence of effective organizing principles" in contemporary historical work. "[L]arge areas of history, including some of the most intensively cultivated, have become shapeless, and scholarship is heavily concentrated on unconnected technical problems. Narratives that once gave meanings to the details have been undermined and discredited with the advance of technical scholarship, and no new narrative structures have been constructed to replace the old." Bailyn's plea "to bring order into large areas of history and thus to reintroduce history in a sophisticated form to a wider reading public, through synthetic works, narrative in structure, on major themes, works that explain some significant part of the story of how the present world came to be the way it is" inaugurated an argument about the fragmentation of history and the wisdom of reviving synthesis.[26]

In many ways, this debate was a stand-in for one about the value of the social history that had proliferated in the 1960s and 1970s. It left historians with little time for law professors. Thus for legal scholars, the impulse to study history with an eye to its relevance for the present, along with an acknowledgment of the historicity of history, came from someone other than historians.[27]

In addition to Gadamer, the impetus for the turn to history may have come from Geertz and Rorty. Because of his emphasis on historians' beloved context, Geertz was becoming the patron saint of cultural historians. Rorty's neopragmatism may have also led law professors to context. In the mid-1980s, Rorty promised the law professors Gordon had spooked the possibility of having it both ways. "There seems to be a dilemma: either we anachronistically impose enough of our problems and vocabulary on the dead to make them conversational partners, or we confine our interpretive activity to making their falsehoods look less silly by placing them in the context of the benighted times in which they were written," Rorty said. "These alternatives, however, do not constitute a dilemma. We should do both of these things." Rorty turned attention from the general human condition to the human condition in the twentieth century. Legal scholars could focus on history's message for twentieth-century law, a project that would have seemed especially appealing at a time when law apparently lacked a future as an autonomous discipline.[28]

That enterprise meant law professors could conduct colloquies with the Founders *and* say something authoritative about the past. For example, Gregory Alexander explicitly accepted Rorty's challenge to make the dead "conversational partners." Bruce Ackerman reminded readers that the task "is to locate ourselves in a conversation between generations." Ackerman held out the hope history could be studied two ways. "My first aim is to place . . . [the] Founding . . . in historical context," he informed his readers. "My second aim is different, though not (I hope) inconsistent. I propose to use the Founding as the beginning of a dialogue between past and present which will serve as our central technique for constitutional discovery."[29]

THE REPUBLICAN REVIVAL

More probably, law professors' interest in history came not from Gadamer, Geertz, and Rorty, but from political theory, which was itself undergoing a surge of interest in republicanism and virtue. Writing in the early 1980s, Michael Sandel applauded his Harvard colleague John Rawls for taking on the utilitarians. "But in philosophy as in life, the new faith becomes the old orthodoxy before long," Sandel added. "Even as it has come to prevail over its utilitarian rival, the rights-based ethic has recently faced a growing challenge from a different direction, from a view that gives fuller expression to the claims of citizenship and community than the liberal vision allows." Sandel opened his own important book, *Liberalism and the Limits of Justice,* with a summary of the "deontological" liberalism of Kant and Rawls, which claimed the priority of right over good. "Its core thesis can be stated as follows: Society being composed of a plurality of persons, each with his own aims, interests, and conception of the good, is best arranged when it is governed by principles that do not *themselves* presuppose any particular conception of the good; what justifies these regulative principles above all is not that they maximize the social welfare or otherwise promote the good, but rather they conform to the conception of *right,* a moral category given prior to the good and independent of it."[30]

Sandel critiqued the Rawlsian vision as "flawed, both within its own terms and more generally as an account of our moral experience." According to Sandel, Rawls's theory of justice, with its difference principle exalting aid to the disadvantaged in the name of fairness, process, and neutrality, did not permit the right to trump the good. It was not neutral among competing principles of justice. Instead, and ironically, it accepted an "essentially utilitarian account of the good, however its theory of right may differ. . . . We cannot be persons for whom justice is primary and also be persons for whom the difference principle is a principle of justice." Sandel maintained that the difference principle Rawls made famous really adopted a "vision of the good life . . . endorsing some ends over others."[31]

More important, for Sandel, was that the difference principle rested on an antiquated concept of self. The self was not unencumbered, as Sandel said Rawls would have it, but situated. In the words of Alasdair MacIntyre, "the story of my life is always embedded in the story of those communities from which I derive my identity." Sandel considered the unencumbered self "a person wholly without character, without moral depth." In reality, character "draws me closer to some and more distant from others; it makes some aims more appropriate than others." The notion of the unencumbered self denied the possibility that a friend might understand one better than one knew oneself. "[T]o see ourselves as deontology would see us is to deprive us of those qualities of character, reflectiveness, and friendship that depend on the possibility of constitutive projects and attachments."[32]

At stake in "the debate between unencumbered selves and situated ones," Sandel claimed, lay "practical differences between a politics of rights and a politics of the common good" retrospectively. Sometimes the two types of politics would reach the same results by different means. For example, liberals could justify the civil rights movement of the 1960s in the name of increasing human dignity, while communitarians might explain it as action on behalf of fellow citizens wrongly excluded from national life. At other times,

> the two ethics might lead to different policies. Communitarians would be more likely than liberals to allow a town to ban pornographic bookstores, on the grounds that pornography offends its way of life and the values that sustain it. But a politics of civic virtue does not always part company with liberalism in favour of conservative politics. For example, communitarians would be more willing than some rights-oriented liberals to see states enact laws regulating plant closings to protect their communities from the disruptive effects of capital mobility and their sudden industrial change. More generally, where the liberal regards the expansion of individual rights and entitlements as unqualified moral and political progress, the communitarian is troubled by the tendency of liberal programmes to displace politics from smaller forms of association to more comprehensive ones. Where libertarian liberals defend the private economy and egalitarian liberals defend the welfare state, communitarians worry about the concentration of power in both the corporate economy and the bureaucratic state, and the erosion of those intermediate forms of community that have at times sustained a more vital public life.[33]

Sandel thereby reaffirmed the principles of justice derived from Rawls's "original position," while adding a communitarian dimension to them. "From the New Deal to the Great Society, the individualistic ethic of rights and entitlements offered an energizing, progressive force," he acknowledged. By the 1970s, however, that program no longer inspired Americans. "Lacking a communal sensibility liberals missed the mood of discontent. They did not understand how people could be more entitled but less empowered at the same time." Sandel had little positive to say for law or courts. He criticized "the advent in the United States of what might be called the 'procedural republic,' a public life animated by the rights-based liberal ethic. In the modern American welfare state, it seems, the liberal dimensions of our tradition have crowded out the republican dimensions, with adverse consequences for the democratic prospect and the legitimacy of the regime." Liberals could not prevail against cultural conservatives unless liberalism began defending "a vision of the common good," learning "the language of self-government and community," and cultivating "the kind of civic engagement that can flow from local attachments and communal ties."[34]

Without a doubt, the changing currents of philosophy and political theory in the 1980s enriched legal scholars' vision and critique of liberalism. Thomas Grey had claimed that Rawls's original position was nonneutral as early as 1973, and critical legal scholars had delighted in attacking liberalism. Nevertheless, as far as their fellow law professors were concerned, the 1970s had belonged to Rawls. By the early 1980s, however, academic lawyers were beginning to worry that talk about rights obscured talk of responsibilities. In this setting, the work of Sandel and other communitarians resonated for legal theorists and scholars in other fields.[35]

During a period "that invited cynicism, resignation and despair," the situated self made sense. It seemed disingenuous to deny the prejudices of which one was conscious. When I began this book by saying that I identify with historians more than lawyers and that I consider myself a legal liberal, for example, I rebelled against both the unencumbered self and foundationalism. I challenged the possibility of universalist scholarship, a casualty among historians by the 1960s and a relic by the 1980s. At the same time, I implied I possessed sufficient expertise and objectivity to make my discussion of legal liberalism valuable to someone besides me. I began from my position inside the world and tried (fruitlessly) to transcend it. Many other authors felt it imperative to locate themselves for their readers, and in the 1980s, many placed themselves in the communitarian camp.[36]

The emphasis on community appeared in sociology as well as political theory. Detecting "a profound ambivalence about individualism in America among its most articulate defenders," the five scholars who published *Habits of the Heart* in 1985 announced their hope of reversing "the slide toward the abyss." America's failure was one of "integration; we have failed to remember 'our community as members of the same body,' as John Winthrop put it. We have committed what to the republican founders of our nation was the cardinal sin; we have put our own good, as individuals, as groups, as a nation, ahead of the common good."[37]

But how exactly did that republicanism relate to liberalism? Was law professor Jordan Steiker correct in suggesting that republicanism offered the chance to create "a true community of liberals, a possibility seemingly foreclosed by liberal theory's emphasis on individual, rather than communal, self-definition" and that the "central attraction of civic republicanism may be its ability to promote the substantive commitments of liberalism that traditional legal doctrines, with their focus on neutrality or tolerance, are themselves unable to secure"? Didn't *some* liberals worry about the concentration of power in the corporate economy and the bureaucratic state too? What exactly did words such as *community* and *communitarian* mean, and how did they relate to republicanism? The difficulty of defining the categories employed in the liberalism/republicanism debate had a tendency to make all views fungible. For the time being, few scholars seemed to care.[38]

The Reagan administration's originalism made another problem more pressing: rooting the communitarian vision in history by proving America's Founders revered republicanism. Hartz's liberalism triumphant had long remained a liberalism unchallenged. Though historians may not have led law professors to history or historicism, once they discovered history, some academic lawyers expropriated historians' discovery of republicanism. Academics outside the law schools, such as Sandel, did too, of course. "Scholars became obsessed with virtue in the eighties because there was so little of it," Joan Williams said later. William Galston put it more circumspectly, simply observing that a "multidisciplinary revival of scholarly interest in the virtues" was in progress. Yet as Gordon Wood said, it was "legal thinkers like Cass Sunstein . . . who seemed most taken with the practical implications of the republican revival."[39]

With the publication of Bailyn's *Ideological Origins of the American Revolution* in 1967, Wood's *Creation of the American Republic* in 1969, and Pocock's *The Machiavellian Moment* in 1975, historians became fixated on toppling the consensus school and "forever ridding the college curriculum of the baleful influence of Louis Hartz." Under the influence of Bailyn, Wood, and Pocock, and in what may have been "the most stunning reversal in the history of political thought," "Locke et praetera nihil" became "omnia praeter Lockem."[40]

Influenced by Geertz's retrieval of ideology, Bailyn developed an "anthropological" approach to the American Revolution. In studying the pamphlets of the Revolution, "I began to see a new meaning in phrases that I, like most historians, had readily dismissed as mere rhetoric and propaganda: 'slavery,' 'corruption,' 'conspiracy,' " he reported in *The Ideological Origins of the American Revolution*. Bailyn came to believe that such words "meant something very real to both the writers and their readers: that there were real fears, real anxieties, a sense of real danger behind these phrases, and not merely the desire to influence by rhetoric and propaganda the inert minds of an otherwise passive populace." The Revolution showed that "ideas and words counted." Those that mattered were not those of Aristotle, Cicero, and other ancients: "The classics of the ancient world are everywhere in the literature of the Revolution, but they are everywhere illustrative, not determinative of thought." Nor were they simply the words of Locke, who was "cited often with precision on points of political theory, but at other times . . . referred to in the most offhand way, as if he could be relied on to support anything the writers happened to be arguing." The words were, above all, those of the old English Whig Opposition, which dated back to such seventeenth-century figures as James Harrington and Algernon Sidney and had been popularized by two "Cassandras," John Trenchard and Thomas Gordon. Using "Cato" as their pen name, Trenchard and Gordon "modified and enlarged this earlier body of ideas" and applied it to eighteenth-century English politics, attacking the " 'loss of pristine virtue.' " "[U]nited in criticism of 'court' and ministerial power," Trenchard and Gordon became "draftsmen of a 'country' vision of English politics." Americans loved it: "Opposition thought, in the form it acquired at the turn of the seventeenth century and in the early eighteenth century, was devoured by the colonists." The Revolution represented "an explosive amalgam of politics and ideology."[41]

Wood, a student of Bailyn, linked the Opposition vocabulary Bailyn had placed at the core of the Revolution to a one-word bundle, "republicanism"—conjuring up a tradition he traced back to the English Whigs, the Renaissance, and "classical antiquity, where the greatest republics in history had flourished," and making "republicanism" the dynamite that had precipitated the explosion. Wood demonstrated that republicanism's oft-stated goal of realizing the "public good" transformed Americans' "ideology"—a word that could be used once Bailyn and Geertz had reinterpreted ideology to focus on meaning—into something "truly revolutionary." Unlike Hartz, Wood found that "the sacrifice of individual interests to the greater good of the whole formed the essence of republicanism and comprehended for Americans the idealistic goal of their Revolution." Republicanism, "a more relaxed, secularized version of Puritanism," was "essentially anti-capitalistic." Like Hartz, however, Wood emphasized the triumph of liberalism and interest-group pluralism in 1787. "The Constitution represented both the climax and the finale of the American Enlightenment, both the fulfillment and the end of the belief that the endless variety and perplexity of society could be reduced to a simple and harmonious system."[42]

Wood almost suggested a way out of the counter-majoritarian difficulty. Recall that Bickel had said the Founders had blurred the counter-majoritarian difficulty by presenting the judiciary as agent of the people, labeling the word " 'people' so used" as an "abstraction" designed to obscure the antidemocratic nature of judicial review. Wood proposed that in the period after 1776, Americans "gave coherence and reality, even a legal reality, to the hackneyed phrase, the sovereignty of the people." They transferred sovereignty from the legislative bodies "to the people-at-large outside of all governmental institutions," he emphasized. In doing so, they fundamentally unsettled old notions about popular participation in republican governments: "The people no longer actually shared in a part of the government (as, for example, the people of England participated in their government through the House of Commons), but they remained outside the entire government, watching, controlling, pulling the strings for all their agents in every branch or part of the government." This explanation might have bridged the gulf between Wood's generation and that of the Founders by making the Constitution and judicial review agents of the people, and Wood did point to Hamilton's declaration in *Federalist 78* that judicial review would not "by any means suppose a superiority of the judicial to the legislative power. It only supposes that the power of the people is superior to both, and that where the will of the legislature, declared in its statutes, stands in opposition to that of the people, declared in the Constitution, the judges ought to be governed by the latter rather than the former." Recall too, however, that Wood thought everything had changed by the time the Convention ended in 1787 and Hamilton defended judicial review with those words in *Federalist 78*. As John Murrin said, "Wood made

Charles Beard credible." Wood was a neo-Hartzian *and* a neo-Beardian. In 1969, he seemed nearly as skeptical of the Founding Fathers as Beard, charging that to realize their hopes "for a high-toned government filled with better sorts of people," the Federalists had seized on "the most popular and democratic rhetoric available to explain and justify their aristocratic system," using words "that more rightfully belonged to their opponents."[43]

Consider the Bill of Rights. Writing some twenty years after Wood, another Bailyn student emphasized that Madison was the "key actor" in the adoption of the Bill of Rights. "Contrary to the usual story, the concessions that Federalist leaders offered to secure ratification in such closely divided states as Massachusetts, Virginia, and New York did not establish a binding contract to provide a bill of rights," Jack Rakove said. It was unclear a Bill of Rights must be enacted when the first Congress met in 1789. "Most Federalists had grown indifferent to the question, nor were former Anti-Federalists now sitting in Congress any more insistent, largely because they knew that the substantive changes they desired in the Constitution lay beyond their reach." Most of Madison's congressional colleagues wanted to table the topic. According to Rakove, however, as Madison came to see the educative value of bills of rights, he had begun to believe a Bill of Rights would promote governmental stability: "the principles encoded in rights . . . [would] restrain political behavior [of the majority], tempering improper popular desires *before* they took the form of unjust legislation." Rakove hypothesized that this reasoning may have lain behind Madison's claim that the First Congress must immediately consider adopting a Bill of Rights. "The logic of this demand was consistent with the concern with public opinion that drove his constitutional thinking. By closely linking the adoption of amendments with the ratification of the Constitution, and by treating both as extraordinary acts of reflection and choice, Madison hoped to attach to this conception of rights 'that veneration which time bestows on every thing, and without which perhaps the wisest and freest governments would not possess the requisite stability.' "[44]

Wood, however, had stuck largely to the traditional story. By his account, the Federalists' acquiescence in the Antifederalist demand for a Bill of Rights had been grudging; Madison had "surrendered to the pressure," then used the Bill of Rights for his own purposes. Where the

Antifederalists had intended the Bill of Rights to weaken "the power of the federal government in relation to the states in matters such as taxation," Madison focused on the potential of judicial enforcement of the Bill of Rights to protect personal liberties and to shield individuals and unpopular minorities from the tyranny of the majority. The Antifederalists thus found even their demand for a Bill of Rights, "the strongest of their objections to the Constitution, eventually turned against them." The net result of such Federalist machinations "was the beginning of a hiatus in American politics between ideology and motives that was never again closed," Wood maintained. The Federalists had "hastened the destruction of whatever chance there was in America for the growth of an avowedly aristocratic conception of politics and thereby contributed to the creation of that encompassing liberal tradition which has mitigated and often obscured the real social antagonisms of American politics. . . . They thus brought the ideology of the Revolution to consummation and created a distinctly American political theory but only at the cost of impoverishing later American political thought."[45]

Though it shared Wood's focus on republicanism, Pocock's *Machiavellian Moment* told a different story, one which stressed "Machiavelli at the expense of Locke." A "Machiavellian moment" was not just when Machiavellian thought or Florentine republicanism appeared. It was also Pocock's "name for the moment in conceptualized time in which the republic was seen as confronting its own temporal finitude, as attempting to remain morally and politically stable in a stream of irrational events conceived as essentially destructive of all systems of secular stability." According to Pocock, the "American founders occupied a 'Machiavellian moment'—a crisis in the relations between personality and society, virtue and corruption—but at the same time stood at a moment in history when that problem was being either left behind or admitted insoluble." Therefore the Revolution and Constitution did not represent an attempt to transform America into a liberal, capitalistic democracy. Rather they constituted "the last act of the civic Renaissance." "What we used to think of as the Age of Reason may just as well be called the Age of Virtue." The Founding Fathers became "the culminating generation of civic humanists and classical republicans." America had inherited from the Old World a "messianic and cyclical" approach to history and "the dread of modernity itself, of which the threat to virtue by corruption was the contemporary ideological expression."[46]

At the core of Pocock's thesis lay a "quarrel" between virtue and commerce, Country and Court. After following Bailyn by pointing to the development of "an ideology . . . variously known to historians as 'Old Whig,' 'Commonwealth,' or (the term to be used here) 'Country,' " in the reign of Charles II, Pocock rooted it in "a tradition of classical republicanism and civic humanism, anchored in the Florentine Renaissance, Anglicized by James Harrington, Algernon Sidney, and Henry St. John, Viscount Bolingbroke, but looking unmistakably back to antiquity and to Aristotle, Polybius, and Cicero . . . [in] interweaving . . . the themes of mixed government and personal independence." Court ideology belonged to the ruling Whigs and Robert Walpole.[47]

Both ideologies reflected the attempt to come to terms with the transition from agrarianism to modernity. On the one hand, "[c]ommerce," the Court's slogan, "denoted a world in which 'virtue had become historically obsolete,' since the growth of wealth had bred professional armies, the structures that maintained them, and the necessity of a politics that managed men no longer rendered independent by the private possession of arms." On the other hand, "virtue," the Country's rallying cry, "required an individual so independent of other men and their social structures that his dedication to the *res publica* could be wholly autonomous. It must be autonomous if he were not to be another man's creature, and so a source of illegitimate private, instead of public, power; therefore he must be master of his own family, property, and arms." Only that person could restore "an older, purer time of society as founded on principles from which any departure must be decay," or corruption. Country ideology "staked everything on a positive and civic concept of the individual's virtue."[48]

According to Pocock, Country ideology "ran riot in America." Most revolutionaries spoke a language "of virtue, corruption and reform, which is Machiavellian, classical, and Aristotelian, in which Locke did not figure." Country ideology did not cause the American Revolution, but characterized it. Yet Pocock, who had taken the linguistic turn, emphasized: "Men cannot do what they have no means of saying they have done; and what they do must in part be what they can and say and conceive that it is."[49]

Just as the language of Country ideology was distinct from that of Court ideology, so was the language of Country ideology distinct from that of liberalism. The vocabulary of liberalism was one of law, legalism, and individual rights. The "classical history of what we have come to term liberalism" was "the story of how rights became the precondition, the occasion and the effective cause of sovereignty, so that sovereignty appeared to be the creature of the rights it existed to protect." Pocock admitted "the law-centered paradigm" of liberalism remained an important tradition in political thought. "But it has long been the principal criticism of the liberal synthesis that because it defined the individual as rights-bearer and proprietor, it did not define him as possessing a personality adequate to participation in self-rule, with the result that the attempt to ground sovereignty in personality was not thoroughly carried out." Another tradition also remained crucial: "alongside the history of liberalism, which is a matter of law and right, there existed throughout the early modern period a history of republican humanism in which personality was considered in terms of virtue." Further, at least before eighteenth-century Scottish jurisprudence, "the two modes remained incommensurate." Pocock believed "[v]irtue was not reducible to right," and virtue could not be "assimilated to the vocabulary of jurisprudence."[50]

The implications of Pocock's displacement of Locke and his elevation of Machiavelli were significant. At a time when liberalism seemed "expendable," Pocock was saying America possessed a home-grown and nonsocialistic alternative to the liberal tradition. "[I]f Pocock is right, then maybe we Americans are not as inevitably individualistic and capitalistic as Hartz and others thought." Such implications became even more important when Pocock maintained that republicanism might well have survived into the present. "[T]he vocabulary of virtue and corruption persisted in American thought, not merely as a survival slowly dying after its tap-root was cut, but with a reality and relevance to elements in American experience that kept it alive and in tension with the consequences that followed its partial abandonment in so crucial a field as constitutional theory and rhetoric."[51]

Indeed, Pocock maintained, the recent challenge to the " 'Lockean consensus' " in historical scholarship, which had given rise to the republican revival, itself reflected a "Machiavellian note." It was the "jeremiad note" of apostasy, which sounded whenever "the chosen people failed of their mission." Arriving in the United States from New Zealand in the 1960s, Pocock had been struck by the fact that

> the American psyche, if not the governing structure, suggested less a nation of pragmatic Lockeans than one of tormented saints. The clamor of jeremiads, sick jokes, and enquiries as to what became of the dream at times became deafening and obsessive. And it seemed evident that the eighteenth-century quarrel between virtue and commerce, citizen and government, republic and empire was still going on in the twentieth century, and that historiography and political philosophy were still much involved in it. For this reason, it may be important to get the historical record straight.[52]

Pocock, then, showed greater interest in the aspirations of republicanism than did Wood. Drawing on Kuhn's work, Pocock explored the normative vocabulary and vision behind the republican paradigm. " 'Virtue,' which Wood read as self-denial, Pocock read as public self-activity—in which 'personality,' undergirded by sufficient property to give it independence, threw itself (for its own 'perfection' and the survival of the republic) into citizenship, patriotism and civic life." Put another way, "Participation in shaping the public good, not subordination to it, became for Pocock the highest expression of one's humanity." Unlike liberalism, which centered around rights, self-interest, and constraints on government, Pocock's republicanism bespoke commitment to common interest, civic virtue, responsibility, community values, deliberative democracy, and self-determination.[53]

Many academic lawyers adored Pocock. He had suggested republicanism still lived, and as they went about disregarding part of his message by assimilating virtue to jurisprudence and transforming republicanism into a law-centered paradigm, they interpreted him to have imbued the republican synthesis with a "prescriptive authority." *The Machiavellian Moment* has been mentioned in 181 law review articles (though it has been cited in only one relatively obscure Missouri Supreme Court case, and a dissent at that. The dissenter is one of the few judges to enlist Rawlsian theory in the service of calculating tort recovery). "The day seems to be coming when no student of constitutional law will lack her well-thumbed copy of Pocock," one Harvard Law School professor said recently.[54]

Because they focused on republicanism's normative language and vision, some law professors were as taken with the republican synthesis as they were with Pocock. Of course republicanism was not a vision that need be anchored in history and the republican synthesis. For example, in the 1980s, Michael Perry advocated realizing republican goals through neo-Aristotelianism. Challenging Rawls and Ackerman, he argued that judges could promote dialogue through nonoriginalist constitutional adjudication aimed at "a deliberative, transformative politics." Nevertheless, other legal scholars made history and the republican synthesis an important theme of constitutional law articles and casebooks. That enabled law professors to argue that "the constitution provides the framework for an organic community composed of socially constructed individuals, who join together in government to identify and pursue civic virtue." Who but "the most self-interested misanthrope" and most ardent antifoundationalist could oppose that, particularly when Epstein was reclaiming liberalism?[55]

Perhaps in part because not all law professors had enlisted in the republican revival, those who did possessed a missionary spirit. Robert Gordon urged revitalizing "the republican notion of the politically engaged lawyer with an identity autonomous from his client" in his 1985 Holmes Lectures at Harvard. The republican revival led others to write jeremiads of their own. Likening civic virtue to "[r]esponsibility, independence and community," one bewailed that everyone in contemporary society claimed rights, but no one accepted responsibility. "We have, indubitably, lost our virtue." Rights had overwhelmed it. Americans needed to "reinvigorate virtue."[56]

Sunstein inaugurated the rush to republicanism in 1985, the same year the Reagan administration began discussing originalism. It may be that Sunstein's important article, "Interest Groups in American Law," was in press before the Reagan administration began to trumpet the importance of honoring original intent. It may also be that Sunstein, a University of Chicago Law School professor, was simply recoiling against one luncheon too many with Richard Posner, Richard Epstein, and other disciples of law and economics or public choice. Yet Sunstein's argument in "Interest Groups" resonated for the reform-minded academic lawyers everywhere who had kept their faith in the Warren Court. He offered a way of coopting originalism by likening it to republicanism. Academic lawyers who read him need no longer bash Berger or cede the historical battleground to the right; Sunstein held out the promise that they too could be historically correct. The republican revival among academic lawyers reflected both their communitarian longings and a strategic move to steal the thunder of conservative originalists.[57]

Claiming that "republican thought played a central role in the framing period," Sunstein painted a picture of Madison boiling up a republican stew, which included a pinch of pluralism. Like other lawyers he became enamored of *The Federalist,* treating it as more momentous and sincere a document than Madison and his coauthors may have intended (and certainly as far more momentous and sincere a document than most historians interpreted it). For example, to Sunstein, Madison's *Federalist 10,* long assumed by political scientists to advance a theory of faction in which a large republic would sustain interest-group pluralism, "emphasized the capacity of a large republic to obtain public-spirited representatives who would have the virtue associated with republican citizens." In Sunstein's model, a nonrepublican Supreme Court ensured that a republican legislature made government a force of public good.[58]

Ironically, though Frank Michelman proved sensitive to history where republicanism was concerned, his 1986 *Harvard Law Review* "Foreword," titled "Traces of Self-Government," became a flash point in sparking the republican revival. In addressing the "problematic relationship between the two American constitutionalist premises—the government of the people by the people and the government of the people by laws," Michelman had long relied on political theory. Now he raised the prospect of popular sovereignty and the possibility of viewing the judiciary as agent of the people. But Michelman drew back from treating judicial review as an instrument of popular sovereignty, declaring that in "the final analysis, the People vanish, abstracted into a story written by none of us." Instead he turned to Pocock, a political theorist as well as historian, for assistance with the question, "In what sense is the United States Constitution, as construed, a charter of self-government?"[59]

Surveying America's history through the Founding, Michelman portrayed republicanism as a "counter-ideology" to liberal pluralism. A partner in a dialectic, republicanism figured "less as canon than ethos, less as blueprint than as conceptual grid, less as settled institutional fact than as semantic field for normative debate and constructive imagination." Making Pocock's vision of republicanism the version the colonists had carried with them across the Atlantic, Michelman implied that Bailyn and Wood might be right in saying that liberalism had triumphed in 1787. But what did that matter? To Michelman, originalism was a form of "authoritarianism," a "looking backward jurisprudence," which regarded "adjudicative actions as legitimate only insofar as dictated by the prior normative utterance, express or implied, of extra-judicial authority." He believed ideas had to stand on their own bottoms, and he tweaked Sunstein and others for trying to anchor the Constitution in the republican tradition.[60]

Nevertheless, Michelman acknowledged, "the republican tradition of civic dialogue retains a strong, if somewhat disguised and twisted, hold on American constitutional thought." And, he strongly implied, as long as the alternative was liberal pluralism, that survival was serendipitous. Republicanism responded to "the demand, said to be sweeping across the various fields of thought for recovery of practical knowledge, situated judgment, dialogue, and civic friendship." By offering "historical validation for the ideal of self-government realized through politics, along with visionary resources for critical comprehension of the ideal," it could help transform the Constitution into a charter of self-government.[61]

"[W]here, if anywhere, can we find self government inside the Constitution?" Michelman then asked. Unlike Sunstein, who rooted republicanism in the legislature, Michelman featured a republican Supreme Court acting as a polis in which nine citizens without prepolitical ends deliberatively and dialogically considered the public good. Instead of displaying knee-jerk responsiveness to the desires of "the people" and their representatives, the justices engaged in the dialogue and deliberation Madison had envisioned. They guaranteed that the nonrepublican legislature pursued their vision of the public good. According to Michelman, "the courts, and especially the Supreme Court, seem to take on as one of their ascribed functions the modeling of active self-government that citizens find practically beyond reach. Unable as a nation to practice our own self-government (in the full positive sense), we . . . can at least identify with the judiciary's as we idealistically construct it." Judicial review provided "traces of self-government."[62]

Maybe the traces were not that large. Michelman was fearful of a "pathology of Court-fetishism." In fact, read one way, he seemed to say "yes, the Court does provide America's last trace of self-government, and isn't that sad?" Read another, however, he seemed to displace the counter-majoritarian difficulty, as he stressed "more optimistic possibilities in the idea of the Court as a bastion of (its own) self-government."[63]

Indeed both Michelman and Sunstein's species of republicanism sought to swing some of the spotlight away from theories of judicial review and "the countermajoritarian difficulty as the true focus of democratic concern." Erwin Chemerinsky attributed republicanism's glamor to the fact that it "avoids viewing American democracy as primarily based on majority rule and . . . justifies judicial value choices based on its concept of 'civic virtue.' "[64] According to Michelman,

> For a citizen of Geneva it was perhaps imaginable that positive freedom could be recognized for everyone through direct-democratic self-government, a sovereignless civic process of ruling and being ruled, with no place for legal authority beyond the process itself. But for citizens of the United States, national politics are not imaginably the arena of self-government in its positive, freedom-giving sense. As a constituted nation we are, it seems, necessarily committed to the sovereign separation of rulers from not ruled. We ought not to deny the separation; government-fetishism is no better than court-fetishism. Congress is not us. The President is not us. The Air Force is not us. "We" are not "in" those bodies. Their determinations are not our self-government. Judges overriding those determinations do not, therefore, necessarily subtract anything from our freedom, although the judges also, obviously, are not us. Their actions may augment our freedom. As usual, it all depends. One thing it depends on, I believe, is the commitment of judges to the process of their own self-government.[65]

The republican synthesis also deflected attention from the incoherence and indeterminacy associated with legal realism and critical legal studies. Michelman and Sunstein saw their own republicanism as an effort to steer between objectivism and irrationalism. Using Richard Bernstein's rhetoric, Michelman described the republican synthesis as "on one reading, an historical projection of contemporary rebellion against a modern ethical dilemma that has been called the Cartesian Anxiety," the sense of being caught between foundationalism and relativism. In his and Sunstein's minds, republicanism rejected Kantian premises that political deliberation produced one right answer. It also avoided pluralism's tendency to interpret political outcomes as inevitably and entirely subjective. If the new epistemology made truth unattainable, the republican synthesis might yet make consensus possible. Like the interpretive turn, republicanism also stressed themes of "community and dialogue," while promising to move beyond the counter-majoritarian difficulty.[66]

All the while, republicanism offered the hope of a public interest that law could serve. Even when Michelman conceded in his text that the opposition of republicanism and liberalism was "more facile than interesting," and backed away from contrasting them in his footnotes, he was still using the text to maintain that "republicanism affirms, while liberalism denies, the notion of a statewide, substantive common interest or good. Accordingly, the special mark of republican constitutional thought is affirmation of 'an autonomous public interest independent of the sum of individual interests,' a common interest existent and determinable not just within the confines of a particular social group . . . but at the encompassing level of the sovereign or law-making state."[67]

Further, republicanism enabled those academic lawyers "haunted by the ghost of Earl Warren" to go beyond his Court's liberalism. As a "communitarian virus" swept constitutional theory, Paul Kahn saw academic lawyers using republicanism to "overcome the divide between the one and the many, the individual and majority." Instead of thinking in terms of individual rights versus majority and government, as Warren Court liberals had done, republicanism enabled law professors to understand self-interest and government as interconnected. Only through participation in public life and the display of civic virtue could the individual citizen maximize self-interest. Instead of speaking the language of negative freedom, which emphasized autonomy from government, republicanism permitted legal scholars to offer a more positive vision in which self-government became the route to freedom. In the meantime, republicanism would do as much as liberalism to protect individual rights. Thus liberal law professors marketed republicanism as a theory that could solve the counter-majoritarian difficulty, revive Warren Court liberalism, provide progressives with even more than they had received from the Warren Court, and had the Founders' imprimatur.[68]

NEOREPUBLICANISM

Modern Madisons left of center were trying to create a kinder, gentler republicanism. For all the differences between the various concepts of republicanism, Sunstein said in 1988, "republican theories tend to be united by four central commitments, and in any event it is in these commitments that the contemporary appeal of republican thought can be located." He defined them as faith in "deliberation," "political equality," a "universalism" that posited "the existence of a common good, to be found at the conclusion of a well-functioning deliberative process," and "citizenship and participation." Sunstein now labeled his theory "liberal republicanism," so it could explicitly include some of liberalism's more attractive aspects, such as its concern with rights. In the 1990s, Sunstein would switch names once again, and "liberal republicanism" would often become "deliberative democracy." In 1988, however, he was still riding the "republicanism" bandwagon, and he spoke of "a republicanism of rights."[69]

In their marketing attempts in *Yale Law Journal*'s 1988 symposium on the republican revival, Sunstein and Michelman acknowledged they advocated neorepublicanism. Influenced by Rorty's neopragmatism and the needs of those who formed their desired constituency, perhaps, they had pared republicanism of some of the attributes that made it objectionable in the past, such as sexism, authoritarianism, racism, and militarism, and added a focus on "tolerance and deliberation." In Michelman's words, "If republican thought does . . . as I believe, contain visionary resources of use to modern liberal constitutionalism, we need not fear drawing upon those resources because of their sometimes historical connection with an obnoxiously solidaristic social doctrine." At a time when the Supreme Court was upholding a law passed by the Georgia legislature that criminalized sodomy in *Bowers* v. *Hardwick* Michelman and Sunstein asked how Americans could be both free *and* subject to law. They provided some interesting answers. In a tour de force comparable to Michelman's gloss on *National League of Cities,* Michelman and Sunstein made privacy democratic. They claimed to have produced "[a]ll the components of the republican constitutional argument for an opposite result in *Bowers v. Hardwick.*"[70]

Bowers was just one example of neorepublicanism's promise. As William Fisher said, the second half of the 1980s witnessed "a spate of articles . . . suggesting that one or another field of law should be modified or altogether reconstructed in light of the lessons of republicanism. Among the recommendations that emerged from these analyses were these: cities and other arenas for the exercise of citizenship should be accorded more autonomy and power; greater protection should be accorded a more expansively understood zone of religious practice; pornography and other forms of expression corrosive of civic virtue should be more closely regulated . . . businesses should be discouraged from moving their bases of operation, thereby disrupting local communities; and courts should be more skeptical of statutes that derive from logrolling or pluralistic bargaining than they are of statutes that issue from an empathetic process of rational deliberation in which all the participants seek to identify and advance the common good." Neorepublicanism could even justify the modern administrative state. Miraculously, it could provide grounds for banning racial slurs and for revitalizing First Amendment doctrine to promote "democratic deliberation."[71]

In a sense, the hierarchical nature of the legal academy made the republican revival inevitable. Michelman had a chair at Harvard, Sunstein was a rising star, and once the *Yale Law Journal* had given neorepublicanism the benediction of a symposium, the rest followed naturally. Yet neorepublicanism also responded to the needs of law professors petrified of polarization.[72]

Neorepublicanism not only fascinated legal liberals such as Michelman and Sunstein but also attracted those critical legal scholars who believed it would enable them to sidestep the claim that "[c]ritique is all there is." It permitted them to answer the Carringtons and Fisses, who mourned the death of law. Writing in the early 1980s, critical legal scholar Roberto Unger had condemned the law school curriculum for its "cynical negativity. It teaches that a mixture of low-level skills and high-grade sophistic techniques of argumentative manipulation is all there is—all there is and can be—to legal analysis and, by implication, to the many methods by which professional expertise influences the exercise of state power." Law schools distracted "people by enticing them into the absurd attempt to arrange themselves into a hierarchy of smart alecks," Unger contended. He urged critical legal scholars to begin their "transformative activity . . . [in] the law school world." They should teach "superliberalism," which "pushes the liberal premises about state and society, about freedom from dependence and governance of social relations by the will, to the point at which they merge into a larger ambition: the building of a social world less alien to a self that can always violate the generative rules of its own mental or social constructs and put other rules and other constructs in their place." For Unger, "a doctrine of community" would "describe the political equivalent of love."[73]

Further, neorepublicanism appealed to both critical legal scholars and liberals because it accommodated their different ideas about the nature of law. It allowed liberals such as Sunstein to base law on public values, while it permitted critical legal scholars to point to the inevitable politicization of law. "If the Liberal idea of law was that it was a necessary evil, the price that individuals needed to pay for a reasonable degree of security, the Republican vision of law was as normative and constitutive of culture, and as potentially positive and emancipatory," Morton Horwitz said. "Law could create structures that enabled individuals and communities to fulfill their deepest aspirations."[74]

For 1960s liberals such as Owen Fiss, a neorepublicanism that enticed critical legal scholars and legal liberals was good news. In 1989, Fiss gave a second Stevens Lecture announcing that the law had been "regained." He even conceded that his earlier demonization of critical legal studies might have been misguided:

> I assumed that in proclaiming that "law is politics" the proponents of critical legal studies had in mind a rather base sort of politics—politics as market behavior, as nothing more than expressions of interest and preferences. In fact, they or at least some critical legal studies scholars may have been willing to entertain the possibility of a more noble and idealistic politics, one that is more an expression of public values, or of principle, or of

rights, than of private preference. This conception of politics is associated with the classic civic republican tradition that is now being rediscovered and revived by a number of legal scholars. Frank Michelman stands at the forefront of this group of scholars, although he has set for himself the singular task of trying to fuse critical legal studies with civic republicanism.[75]

To other scholars, nothing in Michelman was new. Instead, and ironically, it was republicanism for Rawls. "In this process-enhancing role, the Court facilitates rather than displaces or represents popular participation," a critic concluded. "Unfortunately, this insight yields little in the way of prescription that Michelman had not already taught us long before his journey in Pocock . . . when he argued that the Constitution compels government to provide 'a social minimum' of resources to every person so that he or she can function as a full participant in the political life of the community." Still other detractors delighted in demonstrating that for all their postmodern posing and emphasis on dialogue, Michelman and Sunstein still searched for objective foundations of justice and common good.[76]

But such jaded reactions overlooked the changed style of the neorepublicans' argumentation. That new style had consequences of its own. Just as historians had always mistrusted political scientists' use of history, so they would dislike any history constructed to suit law professors' communitarian yearnings. Once law professors made the historic turn, historians entered the fray to police their territory.

PART II

LAWYERS AND HISTORIANS

CHAPTER 6

LAWYERS V. HISTORIANS

For many years, a gulf separated lawyers from historians. We historians (for as a historian, I now explicitly become one of the subjects of my story) assumed that we were the only ones with expertise on our turf. "Lawyers are arrogant," we sniffed, "and they think they can do anything—even write history." Their reaction to Pocock, we believed, showed their susceptibility to what Tushnet has called "the 'lawyer as astrophysicist' assumption: We are people who have a generalized intelligence and can absorb and utilize the products of any other discipline in which we happen to become interested." In practical terms, "any lawyer can read a physics book over the weekend and send a rocket to the moon on Monday." Law professors who enlisted in the republican revival read Pocock and became authorities on republicanism. They made Pocock the Rawls of the 1980s. The gap between lawyers and historians has narrowed, but historians' reactions to the republican revival indicate it still exists.[1]

I contributed to the tension between lawyers and historians at a conference in Germany comparing German and American constitutionalism. There I commented on a paper by Clyde Summers on the Supreme Court and industrial democracy. That distinguished law professor, whose work was "marked by a passion for justice and concern with the rights of rank-and-file union workers," contended it was "painfully obvious" that "the role of the Supreme Court in industrial democracy has been to forget one of the central purposes of the National Labor Relations Act, to reach results that do not merely fail to foster, but frustrate, curtail, and ultimately deny industrial democracy as a statutory purpose or social value."[2]

In response, I conceded that "if I were a labor lawyer representing a union in a case requiring interpretation of the National Labor Relations Act, I would follow Summers in attempting to make the most out of the language in the act loosely referring to industrial democracy. As an historian, however, I can make a different, and I think, more historical argument." I then suggested that in enacting the National Labor Relations Act, most of Congress had intended primarily to promote industrial peace, not industrial democracy. Nor, I said, had the Supreme Court always played the villain.[3]

Replying, Summers declared "it is perfectly clear that lawyers look to history to help demonstrate what they hope was true or wish to be true. And so they do selective readings." Acknowledging that "industrial democracy was only a subsidiary goal of the National Labor Relations Act," he concluded with "a personal observation. I have always considered the study of comparative labor law a most difficult, nearly impossible subject because one cannot study comparative labor law without studying the political and economic institutions, the unions, the social structure. Now, speaking as an American lawyer who came here and is essentially on foreign ground when dealing with historians, I feel much more comfortable with German labor lawyers than with American historians." That was a sad commentary on the state of affairs. In succumbing to the temptation to score easy points by dismissing law professors' work as ahistorical, I had made Summers unnecessarily pessimistic.[4]

William E. Nelson has wisely differentiated between " 'lawyers' legal history,' written to generate data and interpretations that are of use in resolving modern legal controversies," and " 'historians' legal history,' written to provide and support new and interesting interpretations and bodies of data to advance exploration of the past." The distinction is useful as long as we recognize that it does not consign historians to one group, lawyers to another. Many legal historians teaching in law schools today, such as Nelson himself, belong to both professions, sporting both Ph.D. and J.D. degrees. Further, lawyers are not the only ones who produce lawyers' legal history. One need not have a J.D. to worry about the implications of one's work for the present. Nor need one possess a Ph.D. to write historians' legal history. University of Wisconsin Law School's Willard Hurst, considered by many to have preceded Horwitz in creating the field of modern legal history, with its focus on the relationship between law and social and economic change, had only a law degree. Many other law professors without graduate degrees in history who have written historians' legal history more recently than Hurst come to mind. I am afraid that if I listed those individuals I would curse myself for the rest of my life because I had forgotten some (and those I had omitted would curse me).[5]

One example may suffice. In a 1983 article exploring the birth of the modern First Amendment tradition, David Rabban, a law professor at the University of Texas, focused on Zechariah Chafee's 1919 *Harvard Law Review* article, "Freedom of Speech in War Time." Building on the work of other scholars, Rabban showed that Chafee there provided a bizarre gloss on the words Justice Holmes had written in the 1919 decision of *Schenck* v. *United States*. Holmes had taken advantage of *Schenck* to wrap the old "bad tendency" test he had long endorsed— which denied the existence of a First Amendment right to publish words having a "bad tendency" on the public welfare—in a new package. When he upheld the constitutionality of the wartime Espionage Act in *Schenck,* Holmes announced that Congress could punish words "used in such circumstances and . . . of such a nature as to create a clear and present danger that they will bring about the substantive evils that Congress has a right to prevent." Holmes considered "clear and present danger" in *Schenck* yet another way of saying that the judiciary must defer to the will of the majority. Chafee, a civil libertarian, saw that the words "clear and present danger," drained of the meaning Holmes meant to give them in *Schenck*, possessed more potential to protect speech than the "bad tendency" test. Deliberately misinterpreting Holmes's *Schenck* decision, misreading legal history, and ignoring a substantial body of prewar litigation, Chafee used "Freedom of Speech in War Time" to derive "an unfounded libertarian meaning from the phrase 'clear and present danger,' " claiming that Holmes intended the "clear and present danger test" he mentioned in *Schenck* to end punishment of words for their "bad tendency."[6]

Falling under the influence of Chafee and other civil libertarians who lobbied him, Holmes himself subsequently decided to argue in his *Abrams* v. *United States* dissent that the Court must intervene to protect speech. As Rabban explained, Holmes now "faced a major problem. Shackled by the heavy weight of restrictive precedents, including his own opinions . . . Holmes had to find legal doctrines to support the values he expressed in *Abrams* for the first time." Holmes seized on Chafee's misinterpretation of *Schenck* in "Freedom of Speech in War Time" to resolve his dilemma. "The myth Chafee created about the original appearance of 'clear and present danger' in *Schenck* allowed Holmes in *Abrams* to reject the 'bad tendency' theory without repudiating his own prior decisions that had relied so heavily on it," Rabban said. Chafee's "mediation" transformed "clear and present danger" from the "theory of judicial deference to majority will" it had been in *Schenck* into "a libertarian standard of constitutional adjudication in *Abrams*." In a stunning piece of historians' legal history, Rabban revealed a seminal article, Chafee's "Freedom of Speech in War Time" as lawyers' legal history. Rabban made Chafee "the key figure in the heroic but often disingenuous effort . . . to create a libertarian tradition out of . . . [the] restrictive past." On learning how Chafee had (mis) used history to manipulate Holmes into a libertarian interpretation of the First Amendment, I felt grateful to both Rabban and Chafee. (That I consider Chafee's work an example of Plato's "noble lie" probably only indicates the depth of my attachment to rights-based liberalism.)[7]

Did Chafee's article meet the scholarly criteria of "good" lawyers' legal history? "In his discussion of the crucial bad tendency theory, Chafee allowed the passion of his personal commitment to a libertarian construction of the First Amendment to overwhelm disinterested scholarship," Rabban concluded. While I would dispute the implication that "good" scholarship must or can be "disinterested," I would agree that Chafee did not produce "good" lawyer's legal history. There is a difference between using the past for presentist reasons and dissimulating. For example, as I suggest in the next chapter, one need not distort the history of abortion to conclude that the Founders did not intend to outlaw it. I believe the person who uses the past to make a pro-choice argument for the present can write good lawyers' legal history.[8]

As Nelson notes, the scholarly forms of lawyers' legal history and historians' legal history "are quite different, but neither is intrinsically superior." Though historians may be the only ones whose primary interest is in historicizing the past, why should we criticize others for using it in different ways? Just as " 'you can't make sociological omelettes without breaking a few historical eggs,' " so legal omelettes demand a forgiving recipe. But the turn to history of the law professors who participated in the republican revival perplexed—and, at times, infuriated—historians.[9]

DIALOGUE OF THE DEAF

Republicanism did represent a promising paradigm shift for historians, but the reasons were different from those for law professors. During the interwar years, idealist historians such as Charles McIlwain had stressed the impact of formal enlightenment and natural rights discourse on the constitutional process. Yet Arthur Schlesinger, Sr., and other Beard students dismissed ideas as epiphenomenal. Presenting the Revolution as "the movement of class minorities bent on promoting particular social and economic interests," they charged the revolutionaries dished out "cooked up pieces of thought served by an aggressive and interested minority to a gullible and unsuspecting populace. The concept of propaganda permitted the Progressive historians to account for the presence of ideas but it prevented them from recognizing ideas as an important determinant of the Americans' behavior." Because they viewed revolutionary rhetoric as propaganda weapons and stressed the difference between formal discourse and motivation, the materialists wanted ideas to take a back seat to social and economic forces. Then during the cold war, Daniel Boorstin managed to display a doctrinaire contempt for ideology. In making his case for consensus, not conflict, between the classes around the liberal tradition on which pragmatism fed, even Hartz barely mentioned ideology, hazarding only a rhetorical question about whether "the whole complex of 'Americanism' " was "an ideological question." At the same time, Hartz robbed the Revolution of its radicalism and challenged Beard's concept of Constitution as counterrevolution. As Gordon Wood asked, if Hartz was correct in saying that "revolutionary Americans were in fact already free and equal and did not have to experience a democratic revolution," what was the significance of the early republic? Bailyn tried to restore the Revolution to significance, rescue a reconfigured ideology, and use it to bridge rhetoric and reality. "Both views are wrong," he said of the old tension between idealists and materialists. Quoting Geertz, Bailyn added, "But both are resolvable into the concept of 'ideology,' which draws formal discourse into those 'maps of problematic social reality,' those shifting patterns of values, attitudes, hopes, fears, and opinions through which people perceive the world and by which they are led to impose themselves upon it." First Bailyn, then Wood and Pocock, made talk about the effect of belief systems on behavior during the formative years of the early republic acceptable.[10]

Seeing the potential of ideology to revive a social history drained dry of politics at a time when historians worried about the survival and continuing significance of their discipline, some historians fell on ideology as a solution to their field's problems. The rediscovery and retrieval of "ideology" which accompanied and made possible the republican synthesis helped to explain historians' fascination with republicanism. "The need of the moment was for means of investing the ethereal stuff of mind with convincing social power," Daniel Rodgers explained. "As the most recent intellectual construct to arrive on the scene, republicanism was the first to be rebaptized as ideology; through its attachment to the Revolution, it became a particularly forceful example of what an ideology could do." In calling attention to the appearance of republicanism as an alternative to the liberal consensus and Beardian paradigms, many historians overlooked a parallel development in the scholarship of Pocock, Wood, and Bailyn, the emergence of what Forrest McDonald described as "a host of works in the ideological vein." By 1986, Appleby referred to Pocock, Bailyn, and Wood as "the new ideological historians." She explained: "Instead of studying individuals and the ideas they articulated, the new ideological historians highlighted the ways that societies construct 'reality' through shared discourses." Instead of assuming "human nature endowed men with an independent capacity to size up reality, ideology—a concept that refers to the structuring of thinking—encloses human consciousness within a social skein of organized reasoning."[11]

Historians may have been more influenced by Bailyn and Wood, however, than by Pocock. As humanists, they judged work by scholarly and literary standards. While academic lawyers, with their talent for decoding dense prose, venerated Pocock, historians treated him less respectfully. Rodgers thought that the difficulty of *The Machiavellian Moment* "was so notorious that few actually scaled it," and J. H. Hexter parodied Pocock's "112-word sentences." Although Pocock impressed historians, he may have affected law professors more. Certainly historians who followed Pocock paid less attention to the normative vision and vocabulary of republicanism than he had.[12]

To be sure, some historians, such as Lance Banning, applauded the communitarian impulse they saw at republicanism's core and the revolutionaries' legacy, "a lasting commitment to ideas that were not part of a liberal consensus." In fact, Straussians, such as Thomas Pangle, complained about "this contemporary infatuation with 'classical republicanism,'" claiming that historians "in our 'post-sixties' era have become captivated by a romantic longing to discover, somewhere in the past, the roots of a prebourgeois and non-Lockean American soul." Pangle grumbled: "Never has there been so much chatter about 'community,' 'bonding,' 'empathy,' 'nurture,' and 'gentleness,' and never has there been so icy and thorough a disconnectedness between women and men, generations, fellow citizens, workers and neighbors." Other scholars were anxious about the significance of the republican resurgence too. Observing that republicanism offered "late twentieth century men and women an attractive alternative to liberalism and socialism," Joyce Appleby likened the concept to a magnet, which "has drawn to it the filings of contemporary discontents with American politics and culture." In time, according to her, "Like so many earlier organizing themes in American historiography, the wildfire success of republicanism began to illuminate contemporary concerns of historians more than the past, demonstrating anew the special tensions present when writing the history of one's own country."[13]

For most historians at first, however, the resonance of republicanism was simply a fortuitous by-product of its discovery. Historians' texts originally focused on other matters. They analyzed the sources and evolution of republican ideology; they studied the relationship between republican ideology and behavior; they pointed to republicanism's fears about the fragility of civil society and the omnipresent threat of corruption. They described republicanism's authoritarianism, its militarism, its elitism, its emphasis on patriarchy, and, in some instances, its nostalgic concern with the past and "country," as opposed to economic development. They asked what role republicanism played in American society after the Founding. In the process, historians developed an appreciation for republicanism's complexity. They became fond of quoting John Adams's observation that there "is not a single more unintelligible word in the English language than republicanism."[14]

Some historians also questioned the relationship between liberalism and republicanism. Was it sound, as a matter of historical interpretation, to oppose them? "None of the historical participants, including the Founding Fathers, ever had any sense that he had to choose or was choosing between republicanism and liberalism, between Machiavelli and Locke," Wood now stressed. The Founders could select whatever they liked of each. Though they might have spoken of republicanism, none talked of liberalism. "We ought to remember that these boxlike traditions into which the historical participants must be fitted are essentially our inventions, and as such are distortions of past reality." Wood condemned protagonists in the debate over eighteenth-century American political thought, such as Pocock, for having "invented too many 'paradigms' and forced too much material into them." Even Pocock challenged the "binary reading of the debate, in which the republican thesis is distorted and rigidified so that it may be set in opposition to an equally rigidified liberalism." But since so many law professors believed liberalism—be it classical, political or legal—had outlived its usefulness, some continued to think in terms of the "binary reading" and to work at retrieving republicanism.[15]

As the bicentennial of the Constitution approached, Stanford Law School's Robert Gordon decided to ask a member of a history department what she thought of the "republican revival" among law professors. He chose Joyce Appleby of UCLA, a prominent critic of the republican synthesis in history. Until Appleby was asked to participate in the 1987 Association of American Law Schools (AALS) panel, she had no idea that the lawyers were reading Pocock and Wood. She was surprised to find them citing her work. At a packed AALS session designed to present the theories of Sunstein and Michelman, "the legal avant garde," Appleby commented on recent legal work on republicanism.[16]

Law professors still recalled the event years later. Reconstructing it for me, David Rabban remembered that Appleby said, "Fellas, if you find late-eighteenth-century republicanism a useful source, OK, but don't be so ahistorical as to identify the republicans' views with yours." I listened to a tape of the discussion and found that Appleby had been more tactful. Nevertheless, Rabban had gotten the message: in a nice way, Appleby told lawyers they were not behaving like historians.[17]

Though he himself condemned originalism and sought to think like a political theorist rather than a historian, Michelman took the offensive when he responded. "Without the past . . . who am I?" he asked Appleby. "Who are we? . . . Without a sense of our identity, how do we begin to make a case for anything? Without *mining* the past, where do we go for inspiration?" The key words here were "mining" and "make a case," for Michelman had put his finger on what many of the law professors who capitalized on historians' discovery of republicanism were doing. Like the Founders themselves, they "ransacked" the past to find arguments for whatever vision of the social order they wished to promote.[18]

By mooring their vision in the Founding, law professors believed they could make a more powerful case for it. They could claim kinship with the Founders. Sunstein forthrightly told Appleby what he repeated in the *Yale Law Journal*: "the presence of a historical pedigree [originating in the Founding era] . . . adds force to the case for a republican revival."[19]

There was no historical pedigree, however. During the late 1980s, legal historians in law schools united with intellectual and political historians to deny its existence. Like Appleby, Wood dismissed the search for a pedigree as "ahistorical," claiming it showed no sense of "the ir-retrievability and differentness of the eighteenth-century world." Fur-ther, the claim to a pedigree distorted the historical record. Mark Tushnet pointed out that the complex of ideas constituting eighteenth-century republicanism "unravels once we attempt to disentangle the cur-rently attractive strands from the currently unattractive ones." For example, it was impossible to understand eighteenth-century republican thought without acknowledging the centrality of patriarchy to it. And how could the disparate individuals defined as "citizens"—a category the neorepublicans had broadened to include women and individuals of color—agree on the common good? Linda Kerber mocked Michelman's effort to develop an "inclusory republicanism": "Michelman seeks to cleanse 'We the People' of the ironies of classical republicanism (not the least of which is the fact . . . that there is no reference to equality in either the Constitution *or* the Bill of Rights), defuse it of its antique association with arms and violence, and offer an American republican-ism constructed by the Many, not the few."[20]

What was the relationship of Sunstein's "liberal republicanism" to the republicanism of the eighteenth century? Sunstein's "concern to join and even equate the liberal and republican themes leaves his search for a historical connection in some confusion," H. Jefferson Powell empha-sized. "Professor Sunstein identifies only a quite attenuated relationship between his ideas and specific schools of thought in the founding era." Like Powell, Kerber also showed that some of "the distinctive charac-teristics of republicanism to which Sunstein urges us to turn," were pres-ent in eighteenth-century liberalism as well. "Where," she asked, "is the historical pedigree we are promised?"[21]

Critics were gentler about noting that republican revivalists seemed fixated on judges. They did not explicitly accuse the neorepublicans of making civic republicanism the foundation for government by judiciary in the mode of the Warren Court. They did note that, ironically, Michel-man and Sunstein had shifted the focus of republican thought away from the people and their representatives to the judges. Paul Brest devoted a footnote to the possibility "that the civic republican revival is just an-other waystation in liberal constitutional law scholars' perennial quest for a defensible role for the judiciary." Paul Kahn contended that the "rejection of the focus on the countermajoritarian difficulty" in the republican revival and the new focus on "community as discursively constituted" marked the end of "modern" constitutional theory and "the emergence of a contemporary constitutional theory." To some scholars, however, it seemed unclear the counter-majoritarian difficulty had been discarded.[22]

Detractors also observed that neorepublicanism caricatured liberalism, making liberalism synonymous with interest group pluralism. Historically, liberalism had offered far more. Hendrik Hartog reminded readers that liberalism possessed "a transformative vision. . . . In these cynical days, when we identify [liberal] contractualism with the Baby M. case, we need to remember the liberating potential once identified with this idea of [individualistic], contractual, self-seeking, self-creating behavior."[23]

In contrast, as Wood said, even in 1776 republicanism "possessed a decidedly reactionary tone." Like the "manly, and warlike virtues" that Samuel Adams's cousin John sometimes extolled in republican society, the "Christian Sparta" Samuel dreamed of excluded many. Given republicanism's "elitist and patriarchal assumptions," Gregory Alexander observed there was "no reason to regret the loss of the republican tradition." Kerber noted that "it was not the civic humanists to whom women, blacks, Jews, and the marginalized groups of modern times have been able to turn for solutions." Dismissed from the realm of politics, they had been expected to defer to the civic humanists. Feminist legal scholars agreed, dismissing the neorepublicans' claims as "valiant but unpersuasive." So too, law professors of color concluded that "[s]kepticism is the necessary response for people of color who grapple with Frank Michelman's and Cass Sunstein's new republican concepts." Dialogue about hunger and other systemic social problems, they objected, would not solve them. And could "the egalitarianism" of dialogue be reconciled with "the authoritativeness of law"? Could deliberation and dialogue really change individuals' deepest beliefs?[24]

Had they but realized it, the neorepublicans might have seen that other new theories offered a more historically sensitive way of recapturing legal liberalism. Acknowledging that "rights rhetoric turns to dust time and again," legal scholars of color influenced by critical legal studies insisted on the historical importance of rights for minorities and emphasized that over time, judges' assertion and expansion of rights had provided at least formal protections. Richard Delgado identified the following themes in the critical race theory developed by professors of color: "(1) an insistence on 'naming our own reality'; (2) the belief that knowledge and ideas are powerful; (3) a readiness to question basic premises of moderate/incremental civil rights law; (4) the borrowing of insights from social science on race and racism; (5) critical examination of the myths and stories powerful groups use to justify racial subordination; (6) a more contextualized treatment of doctrine; (7) criticism of liberal legalisms; and (8) an interest in structural determinism—the ways in which legal tools and thought-structures can impede law reform." Critical race theory proved far more sympathetic to legal liberalism than critical legal studies was. For critical race theorists recognized that "liberal reform both transforms and legitimates," Kimberle Crenshaw said. " 'Rights' feels so new in the mouths of most black people," Patricia Williams stressed. "It is still so deliciously empowering to say. It is a sign for and a gift of selfhood that is very hard to contemplate reconstructing (deconstruction is too awful to think about!) at this point in history." When the dust settled, critical race theory "had retrieved and reconstituted liberalism in the face of critical legal scholars' challenge," Henry Louis Gates observed. For good or ill, depending on one's point of view, critical race theorists had shifted attention away from the preoccupation with theory in critical legal studies—"the great power of that shared generative moment" that "taking on the entire structure of legal scholarship" represented—to different problems, such as academic politics. Critical race theorists believed they had introduced a "critical pluralism" that respected both "difference and dialogue." In the process, they had caused some critical legal scholars to tone down their hostility toward legal liberalism. And for the most part, critical race theorists deserved high marks for their use of history.[25]

Yet while some neorepublicans, such as Michelman, acknowledged that "[a]lmost anybody who thinks about or teaches civil rights law has to be significantly affected" by critical race theorists' "skeptical, more victim-oriented outsider approach," not everyone was. Perhaps because they hoped to marginalize critical race theory, or because they distrusted critical race theorists' first-person narratives and emphasis on the significance of race to scholarship, some neorepublicans gave critical race theory short shrift. Feminist legal theorists who mistrusted communitarianism were also reconstituting liberalism. Together, the legal scholarship of feminists and critical race theorists was eclipsing that of their progenitor, critical legal studies, in part because they seemed more constructive. The neorepublicans still pressed forward with their enterprise.[26]

The chorus denying the pedigree for neorepublicanism and questioning the neorepublican vision only swelled in the 1990s. Horwitz added his voice to it, warning "against the dangers of a certain kind of lawyer's history, which involves roaming through history looking for one's friends." Contending that "the republican revival has by and large been very productive," he nevertheless worried "that it will develop into an unreflective growth industry. There is a danger of a simple-minded search for historical precedent, which becomes increasingly present-minded about the issues of the past and thereby presents an unsubtle, uncomplex, and partial picture of the past that will no longer convince any serious student of the past that there was a 'there' there." Observing that "the liberal individualistic tradition produces the ideology for tolerating difference," Horwitz also stressed that the republican tradition contained a "very limited version of pluralism."[27]

At the same time, historians' interest in republicanism was dwindling. As early as 1985, Kerber had warned that the word *republicanism* was "in danger of coming to signify too much and therefore to mean too little," though she was not persuaded it had outlived its usefulness. Seven years later, Daniel Rodgers believed it had. "The concept of republicanism was one of the success stories of the 1980s," he said in an article he obviously hoped would bury the term. "By 1990, it was everywhere and organizing everything, though perceptibly thinning out, like a nova entering its red giant phase." Historians had placed too heavy a load on republicanism, and they could not understand why law professors wanted it to carry even more.[28]

The exchange between historians and neorepublicans, I submit, is one that those who create historians' legal history can easily win on the merits, regardless of whether they prefer liberalism to neorepublicanism. Since any attempt to give history "presentist" implications is by definition ahistorical, it is as easy to show that lawyers' legal history is ahistorical as it is to shoot fish in a barrel. As Mark Tushnet has said in another context, however, "it is not a lot of fun watching people shoot fish in barrels; indeed, one sometimes begins to develop sympathy both for the fish, who are doing the best they can in trying circumstances, and for their pursuers, who are doing the only thing they know how to do." Like efforts at communication between historians and sociologists, those between historians and neorepublicans have proven a "dialogue of the deaf."[29]

A MATTER OF METHOD

The neorepublican episode suggests the nature of the disagreements dividing those who write historians' legal history from those who produce lawyers' legal history. For all their excursions into other disciplines, historians still favor context, change, and explanation.[30] Despite their acquaintance with Bailyn, Wood, and others, authors of lawyers' legal history value text, continuity, and prescription. The debates between historians and neorepublicans involve differing attitudes toward the past, paradigms, and the scholar's role.

Yale Law School's Robert Cover, whose interest in history grew out of his concern with the present, not the past (as Cover himself always made clear), was once asked whether his hero, Louis Brandeis, possessed a romantic view of history and the intentions of the Founders. "Of course," Cover answered. "If your view of history isn't romantic, then there is no *reason* for history to have any instructive power whatsoever. . . . Why in the world would you then use history as authority?"[31]

I doubt any historian considers the past authoritative. At best, it may be edifying, but to the historian, there are no "lessons from the past." True, Santayana said that those who did not understand the past were condemned to repeat it. He might have told us that study of the impact of "the Munich syndrome" on policymakers between the end of World War II and the Gulf crisis might inform the way politicians view the Bosnian crisis, but surely he would have reminded us that it would not reveal the stance today's politicians should assume toward Bosnia. For the historian, the past is relevant to the present insofar as it shows how other people lived their lives. It does not explicitly tell historians or their contemporaries how to conduct their own.[32]

In the neorepublicanism controversy therefore, historians did not understand why republican revivalists sought a pedigree. "It is anachronistic and unnecessary to reach back over the last two hundred years to claim the republicanism of the early modern era," Kerber said. To her, the prior existence of republicanism did not make the case for the adoption of neorepublicanism more persuasive. More important, from her historian's perspective, the search for a pedigree encouraged mischaracterization of the past. It permitted the present to overwhelm the past.[33]

To a historian, the word *anachronistic* stings. "The fallacy of anachronism . . . generally consists in the description, analysis, or judgment of an event as if it occurred at some point in time other than when it actually happened," historian David Hackett Fischer has explained.

> Consider the case of the Cox Commission report, an attempt by a group composed mostly of lawyers to produce something like a history of the student rebellion at Columbia University in 1968. The authors were able and intelligent men, but their honest attempt to understand the thought patterns of another generation was marred by analytical anachronism. They sought to explain the discontent of student rebels by quoting a character in J. D. Salinger's *Franny and Zooey*! My students laughed uproariously at this gaffe. They suggested that the Commission might as well have studied the works of Scott Fitzgerald.[34]

Not all of the anachronisms in lawyers' legal history are so funny. Even if they are, there may be utility to some, particularly those that invoke the Founding. Though Fischer condemned all presentism as anachronistic, many historians are more ambivalent about presentism. Indeed, behind historians' hostility to anachronism lies their own uncertainty about presentism. Historians take it as a truism that each generation must write its own history. The past may be real, but interpretations of it change. As Gadamer said, "Real historical thinking must take account of its own historicity." Even Karl Popper recognized historical contingency.[35]

True, generations of American historians have worked, often unsuccessfully, at achieving objectivity, and some continued to act as if truth is " 'out there'; something found, rather than made; unitary, not perspectival." By the mid-1980s, however, Rorty's antifoundationalism had encouraged scholars to think they possessed perspectives on reality and truth, instead of that they perceived reality and truth. Poststructuralism had undermined the dichotomy between objectivity and relativism, fact and value. These currents had indirectly influenced historians. "Perhaps the most striking feature of the way in which historians signaled their abandonment of traditional objectivist axioms," according to Peter Novick, "was the casual, matter-of-fact fashion in which they did so; the somewhat condescending attitude they adopted toward those who clung to what they regarded as outworn shibboleths."[36]

No one showed how often American history was remade better than Frances FitzGerald, whose analysis of history textbooks, *America Revised,* appeared in 1979. "To read the texts published over the two hundred years of United States history is to see several complete revisions in the picture they present of the country and its place in the world," she reported. "These apparently solid, authoritative tomes are in fact the most nervous of objects, constantly changing in style as well as in political content." A text that advocated internationalism in the 1930s preached anticommunism by the 1950s. Interpretations in historical scholarship have changed as frequently as interpretations in historical texts. To cite but one example, one generation's conflict becomes another's consensus.[37]

With the objectivist creed in decline in recent years, what lodestar would guide historians? Some, such as Simon Schama, turned to blending history with fiction. "It was bound to happen," Gordon Wood said. "Sooner or later a distinguished historian had to cross over, had to mingle the writing of fiction with the writing of history. The circumstances were ripe, the pressures were enormous. Everyone else was doing it." Docudramas had become commonplace, historical novels remained the rage. "Asked whether Emma Goldman and Evelyn Nesbit actually met, as they did in *Ragtime,* E. L. Doctorow answered, 'They have now.' " While I suspect that many historians of the late twentieth century are frustrated novelists, I doubt most think they write well enough to mix history and fiction. They would balk at being judged by whether they meet the standards of good fiction. They want to continue thinking of themselves as historians, and their concept of what historians do has remained largely untouched. Scholars in other disciplines would consider historians' epistemological handwringing slight. The recent appearance of books such as *That Noble Dream* and *Telling the Truth about History* suggests that a sense of epistemological "crisis" in history has grown.

Still, it has not paralyzed historians and has lacked the intensity of its counterpart in legal scholarship. For example, while acknowledging postmodernism raises "arresting questions about truth, objectivity, and history that simply cannot be dismissed," the authors of *Telling the Truth about History* endorse a "modified, or practical, realism," which encourages scholars "to get out of bed in the morning and head for the archives." Very few intellectual and cultural historians have so much as even acknowledged poststructuralist doubts.[38]

Some of the more methodologically innovative historians have adopted what James Kloppenberg has characterized as pragmatic hermeneutics. Historicist in its recognition that historians must try to view the past through the eyes of those who lived through it, pragmatic hermeneutics acknowledges that historians never can. Antifoundationalist in acknowledging that no two people will write history the same way and that the historian's perspective on the same topic changes constantly and in accordance with context, pragmatic hermeneutics also discourages travel down that road toward a denial of the Holocaust.[39]

I endorse this pragmatic, antifoundationalist hermeneutics. As Kloppenberg has admitted, however, some scholars would find it " 'Dewey-eyed,' at least as problematical as the old scientific history or the newest radical historicism. They may be right." Still others might say pragmatic hermeneutics is old wine in new bottles. Even most of those historians who have learned to speak the language of "fancy" social scientists and humanists have retained their native tongue and what Bruce Ackerman has rightly described as their "no-nonsense, original-source style." Perhaps that is no cause for celebration: it may be historians justifiably fear marginalization if they too obviously use their new vocabulary. But many historians would say the new language is unnecessary; they do not need Rorty and Gadamer to tell them that though they will never attain objectivity, interpretive ability equal to their subjects', or an unchanging perspective on an event, they must do the best they can.[40]

If objectivity has receded as a problem for historians, presentism has not. Its specter haunts us as we steer between acontextual presentism and overly contextual antiquarianism. On the one hand, presentism lends power and passion to historians' work. It is a temptation to which many—be we radical, liberal, centrist, or on the right—have succumbed. On the other hand, presentism has always embarrassed historians. (Why else would I use the word *succumbed?*) The radical historians of the 1960s defended their presentism by saying that it "had all the virtues of its faults." They would agree with Joan Williams:

> Of course, one implication of modernism is that all histories are either presentist or boring. Given that every interpretation reflects a particular viewpoint, historical interpretations that resonate do so because they speak to current concerns. But there is good presentism and bad, or, to state the distinction more accurately, at some point, the discussion cares so much about the present that it ceases to concern itself with a conscientious respect for the pastness of the past. At the extreme end of this insensitivity to incommensurability is not nonsense, but neither is it history.[41]

Those who write lawyers' legal history do not share historians' ambivalence. For them, presentism may be a virtue. Unlike historians, the creators of lawyers' legal history are more interested in the past than in history. C. Vann Woodward has relied on the work of J. H. Plumb to distinguish between "the past" and "history." The past "is used to sanction or sanctify authority, to control or motivate societies or classes, to endow elites and actions with a sense of destiny and mission, and therefore to bemuse and coerce and exploit." History, however, is neither ideology nor the past. "It is an intellectual process . . . [whose] future and true function are 'to cleanse the story of mankind from the deceiving visions of a purposeful past.' " While history is just one way of exploring what has gone before, the past is useful insofar as it helps to explain the present.[42]

Historians were accustomed to the presentism of lawyers' legal history. What was new about the republicanism debate was that law professors who participated in it *seemed* to be taking historians' scholarship seriously. Where once they cited Bailyn and Wood's history textbook to make the "case that the Framers of the Constitution expected that all political action would reflect a concern for the common good," they were now turning to Bailyn and Wood's scholarship, which they appeared to be treating with almost as much reverence as eighteenth-century sources. They were citing Bailyn, Pocock, Wood, Appleby, and others, in addition to *The Federalist Papers*. Even more significantly, they were differentiating between historians, rather than utilizing them as the suppliers of factoids to be plugged into legal arguments. But they were turning the historians themselves into factoids, talking heads who supplied one-sentence propositions from the past. The law professors who embraced the republican revival were assuming the same attitude toward historians' work that a prior generation of academic lawyers would have taken toward both other disciplines and the past. They appropriated historians for advocacy purposes.[43]

Again, the historian would recoil. The very task of making a case would compromise the historian. Of course historians make judgments, but they treat them as secondary to their work, smuggling them into it, rather than proudly declaring them. "Historians are most apt to find disconcerting the claim that we must now take a position on republicanism—that in Sunstein's terms we must 'support' it," Kerber warned. "Historians are more comfortable thinking of themselves as engaged in the act of uncovering, of eliciting from the discourse of past societies elements of argumentation which will enable us to understand these societies in all their distance and strangeness."[44]

Indeed one of the highest accolades one can award a historian is to say his or her work is so balanced it can be used to justify the opposite point the historian hopes to make. To quote Joan Williams again: "The criticism 'it's more complicated than that' is almost invariably a safe one in historical circles, while overly aggressive bonding of materials into a seamless thematic whole can easily raise eyebrows." In his presidential address to the American Historical Association, William E. Leuchtenburg reminisced:

> In 1974, John Doar, chief counsel of the congressional inquiry into the impeachment of Richard Nixon, commissioned Vann Woodward to prepare a report on allegations of wrongdoing by American presidents throughout our history, and Woodward in turn called on me to supervise the twentieth-century section. We had only a few weeks to complete this large task, and I turned to four of my former graduate students who I knew could be counted upon to do work of high quality in a hurry. . . . So intent were we on seeing Nixon deposed that we sacrificed all our own projects to that end. Some have concluded that the final report was, in the words of one historian, "a major salvo in the assault on

Richard Milhous Nixon," for it suggested how much more monstrous were Nixon's deeds than those of his predecessors, as indeed they were. But I have always thought that, so thorough-going
and fair-minded were the historians in revealing the many instances of wrongdoing in the past, that, if Nixon had actually
stood trial, the document in its total effect, would better have
served him than the prosecution.[45]

Leuchtenburg's compliment is the lawyer's insult. It is lawyers' business to build paradigms. Too much orderliness, however, makes historians suspicious. Our task, as Edmund S. Morgan explained to Felix
Frankfurter, is to reject "the demand for symmetry," which would permit "us to present sharp contrasts: between Puritans and Anglicans, between John Winthrop and Roger Williams, between Whigs and Tories,
Federalists and Republicans, between the radical Declaration of Independence and the conservative Constitution," while realizing that we do
so "at the peril of losing the reader."[46]

Historians delight in recreating the past in all its strangeness. Many
of us live for the chance to do archival research, to experience the romance of the document. Winifred Rothenberg put it well when she wrote
of a "kind of truth" that "has to do with something elusive I will call
authenticity:"

By that I do not mean historical scholarship, but rather a non-
verbal communication—an infusion—that passes from my farmers to me, through the documents they have left me. When I have
been long away from those documents I discover that I cannot
write about them, even though I have a complete data set taken
from them; I have lost the felt texture, the authenticity, of those
lives, and the data lack verisimilitude. I need to *steep* myself in
those books again. When I do that, I who have never farmed
become a farmer, and an eighteenth-century farmer at that. My
work may be full of numbers, but I do not write *from* numbers.
I write from the smell of manure that is still captured in an account book boxed since 1834; I write from the tear drop (I swear
it!) next to a young girl's signature when she was forced to surrender the keepsake her dead young lover left her in a will his
parents contested; I write from the account book in which a son

charged his father's estate $0.50 for the time he spent sitting with his mother at the funeral.[47]

Where those who write lawyers' legal history see forests, the archives lead historians to trees. Admittedly, focusing on trees is problematic. For example, it becomes more difficult to produce wide-ranging syntheses. Carl Degler opened a critical evaluation of David Riesman's use of history in *The Lonely Crowd* three decades ago by observing, "It seems to be either the fate or the opportunity of historians to be checking on how others use history. For it is the non-historians who write the broad interpretations of the American past." Though Degler himself has produced broad interpretations of American history, he made a good point. While others compose metanarratives, we brag about manuscript collections we have consulted, particularly when they are in out-of-the-way places, lapsing into "historians' machismo."[48]

But people do not become historians only because they like reading others' mail. As Henry Hart recognized, "History is the answer to the appeal to history." Historians of this century have realized that history can be liberating. "The central value of historical understanding is that it transforms historical givens into historical contingencies," Herbert Gutman emphasized. The past is so different from the present, Rorty has observed, that the historian's task is to try "to get out from under inherited contingencies and make his own contingencies, get out from under an old final vocabulary and fashion one which will be all his own."[49]

Those who proudly compare historians' use of evidence to that of lawyers and judges therefore miss the point. Yes, the "objective historian's role is that of a neutral, or disinterested judge: it must never degenerate into that of an advocate." Yes, many historians have abandoned the search for absolute objectivity, preferring to concentrate on attaining what they see as the more realistic goals of "qualified objectivity" and "measured relativism." Just as attorneys need not pursue "truth" in their advocacy, so historians may wonder whether truth exists. Yes, "the process of historical research and judgment on disputed issues of history is—indeed, must be—essentially adversarial." And yes, issues of evidence and proof are crucial for judges, attorneys, and historians. Like judges, lawyers gather evidence to make prescriptions for

the present. Like attorneys and some historians, those who write lawyers' legal history may straddle scholarship and politics. Still, significant
differences exist between lawyers' legal history and historians' legal history. Historians study change over time, "historical processes rather than
nonhistorical states—things that happen rather than things that are."[50]

Thus historians such as Jack Rakove emphasize that "the single most
important reservation or objection a historian can raise against the originalist belief is that it is false to the experience of the founding period
itself." Asking why, "in a society not otherwise known to defer to past
wisdom, do appeals to the original meaning of the Constitution and the
original intentions of its framers still play a conspicuous role in our legal
and political discourse," Rakove answers that the revolutionary era and
Constitution provide "Americans with the one set of consensus political
symbols that come closest to universal acceptance."[51] But Rakove and
other historians also like to quote Thomas Jefferson, as Joyce Appleby
did when she confronted the law professors:

> Some men look at constitutions with sanctimonious reverence,
> and deem them like the ark of the covenant, too sacred to be
> touched. They ascribe to the men of the preceding age a wisdom
> more than human, and suppose what they did, to be beyond
> amendment. I knew that age well; I belonged to it, and labored
> with it. It deserved well of its country. . . . Laws and institutions
> must go hand in hand with the progress of the human mind. As
> that becomes more developed, more enlightened, as new discov-
> eries are made, new truths disclosed, and manners and opinions
> change with the change of circumstances, institutions must ad-
> vance also, and keep pace with the times.[52]

Speaking for law professors, Robert Burt has answered Appleby and
Jefferson:

> Professional historians are often bemused by constitutional law-
> yers' obsession with the founding moment, pointing to the many
> vast differences in outlook between the founding generation and
> ours that limit any sensible capacity to transport lessons from one
> era to the next. But constitutional lawyers have grasped one con-
> tinuing, unsettling parallel between us and the founders, a parallel

that illuminates a persistent feature of our social life: the founders stared fixedly into the face of social anarchy because they were required to build their scheme of social organization from ground zero. This prospect of anarchy remains today always just barely visible in the premise of popular sovereignty, equality, and self-determination on which the founders' structure rests. We lawyers, in our professional concerns with practical questions of social action, can thus find lessons in the founding moment that historians, approaching these events with different purposes, would not find.[53]

This means that paradoxically, the past is more important and relevant to those who write lawyers' legal history. For one example, Ahkil Amar explained that the "neo-Federalist" label he assumed for himself "flags the fact that I am reading Federalist writings at a distance of two centuries and through a lens colored by intervening historical events (such as the Civil War, Reconstruction, and the civil rights movement) and current schools of legal thought (such as legal process and law and economics). Neo-Federalism attempts to offer a *usable* past—a set of Federalist doctrines in harmony with post-Federalist developments and the realities of twentieth-century life and law." The attempt to explore the past on its own terms makes little sense to those who write lawyers' legal history. They ask "why someone, such as a historian, would want to try to increase understanding if not to influence someone's behavior." They believe they can only achieve such influence by using the past. Though it is rarely dispositive, precedent confers legal authority. The authors of lawyers' legal history, who confuse history with precedent, have considered a pedigree for neorepublicanism vital to their case.[54]

Where it involves the Founders, the past is particularly important to lawyers. "In a sense, historians' recent rediscovery of republicanism has been appropriated by constitutional lawyers in the same way we always appropriate historical work, by converting it into a yearning for the restoration of what we have lost," Tushnet has said. "Concerned that we will be unable to develop cogent defenses for what we find attractive in republican thought, we re-present this thought to ourselves as valuable *because* 'the framers' thought it valuable."[55]

Despite lawyers' turn to history, they had hardly become historians. They were still mining the past and turning to historical figures as a pretext for talking about themselves. The more lawyers' legal history has changed, the more it has stayed the same. As I propose in the next chapter, perhaps that is appropriate.

CHAPTER 7

TRADING PLACES

Many of the criticisms that historians make of lawyers' history are indeed irrelevant to the lawyer's task. At least the immediate interest of historians is always in "historicizing" the past as much as possible, tamping it down firmly into departed times and places. For lawyers, this method is useful only half the time, when they want to get rid of some practice justified by tradition. At other times they want not to deaden the past but to make new, mythic, traditions out of it to use in current argument. It is pointless to say that such myths are "inaccurate" from the standpoint of conventional historiography, for they are so by definition. But that does not mean that all historicist criticism of legal rhetorics is irrelevant, because the critic could take the rhetorics on their own terms, instead of the conventional historian's terms and say, "This is bad mythmaking."[1]

Next to the word *context, historicism* sometimes seems to be historians' favorite term. Even historians, however, are beginning to recognize that originalism will continue to dog contemporary constitutional discourse. Other scholars realize this as well. "Dead or alive in academe, New Right constitutional theory is strong enough in other circles to constitute a continuing threat both to judicial power and constitutional theory," one political scientist observed recently. That New Right theory inclines "toward the study and writing of history" and to packaging its message "as the lesson of the nature's tradition."[2]

Clearly there are hazards to combining distinct perspectives. Methodological differences make law and history peculiar bedfellows. Yet assuming that legal liberalism survives, and that the "love affair" between law professors and Clio remains an important aspect of it (as, for example, when legal liberalism masquerades as the republican revival), can the relationship between historians and lawyers become more satisfactory? In this chapter, I suggest that historians may be trying to move beyond the academy toward an originalism they find tolerable, just as some liberal law professors reject that originalism as ahistorical.[3]

Though it is traditional for Supreme Court justices to rely on tradition, today some scholars and judges seem to pay more lip service to history and tradition than ever. Morton Horwitz has labeled the joint opinion of justices O'Connor, Souter, and Kennedy in *Planned Parenthood* v. *Casey* "perhaps unique in American constitutional history for its highly self-conscious discussion of the question of constitutional legitimacy." There the trio turned to constitutional history "to provide a standard for determining when overruling precedent is appropriate," and to rationalize the Court's strained attempt to avoid overturning *Roe* v. *Wade.* To Horwitz, that move reflected a "revival of interest in American constitutional history" in the legal community and academy, which itself revealed the depth of the crisis in contemporary constitutional theory. "[H]istory usually becomes the arbiter of constitutional theory only as a last resort in moments of intellectual crisis." And why not? "It seems so comfortingly legitimate to argue that because the government has done something since the beginning of the Republic, it must be constitutional."[4]

In *Michael H. v. Gerald D.*, for another example, Justice Scalia's plurality opinion for the Court maintained that a liberty interest would be deemed "fundamental" and protected by the due process clause only if it were "rooted in history and tradition," emphasizing that "[w]e refer to the *most specific level* at which a relevant tradition protecting, or denying protection to, the asserted right can be identified." Rebecca Brown has reported that "Justice Scalia has personally authored at least fifty-three opinions that relied expressly on tradition to resolve constitutional issues." Liberals content themselves with pointing to the difference between history and tradition and with pointing out that Justice Scalia's "use of tradition is but a thinly veiled effort to cut off all possibility of progressive interpretation of the past" and "to keep change at bay" at their peril. A recent law review article claims that "liberals must now learn to win the game by playing according to conservative rules, because that is the rulebook that will remain in use for potentially the next thirty years." "History and tradition" may be one of the few useful ploys legal liberalism has left.[5]

In his remarkable 1981 article on historicism, from which I have drawn the opening quotation of this chapter, Robert Gordon proposed one way of bridging the gap between historians' and lawyers' history. Yet, as he admitted, "the dialogue hypothesized has yet to take place." Fifteen years later, it still has not occurred. Perhaps Gordon never intended for it to do so. He may have had his tongue in cheek when he made that suggestion. Suppose, however, he was simply saying that historical arguments might vary according to context and purpose, something akin to what Karl Llewellyn called for as "situation sense." How dangerous is the proposal that historians evaluate lawyers on the basis of the quality and propriety of accounts of the past that lawyers create? "We have to learn to harass historical jurisprudence, not reject it," one legal historian has argued. "Historical adjudication is too convenient to be banished from decision writing. We should acknowledge that lawyers and judges can use history in a variety of ways and that not every exercise of historical jurisprudence deserves to be dismissed as law office history." Lawyers' job is to advocate. Perhaps historians should be satisfied if they can help lawyers to produce the most accurate and credible narratives the legal setting permits.[6]

Historians who shudder at the notion of appraising law professors' work according to the forum for which it is prepared, or according to whether it is good or bad "mythmaking," would do well to remember Bernard De Voto's statement that "American history began in myth and has developed through three centuries of fairy stories." Historians have perpetuated those myths in the name of national interest ever since Parson Weems informed readers that George Washington could not tell a lie. At the height of the cold war, the president of the American Historical Association reminded his colleagues that "not everything which takes place in the laboratory is appropriate for broadcasting at street corners. . . . Total war, whether it be hot or cold, enlists everyone and calls upon everyone to assume his part." In fact, historians probably have influenced society most when they were least objective.[7]

In his 1985 presidential address to the American Historical Association, William McNeill went so far as to advocate "mythistory." He said, "Myth and history are close kin insomuch as both explain how things got to be the way they are by telling some sort of story. But our common parlance reckons myth to be false while history is, or aspires to be true." Yet who still believed it possible to find truth? O'Neill asked. "[W]hat seems true to one historian will seem false to another, so one historian's truth becomes another's myth, even at the moment of utterance." Nevertheless, historians "undermined inherited myths that attempted to make the past useful by describing large-scale patterns, without feeling any responsibility for replacing old myths with modified and corrected general statements that might prove a better basis for public action."[8]

O'Neill called for the "care and repair of public myth." If historians persisted in "myth breaking" without "myth making," he warned, "others are sure to step into the breach." Michael Kammen agreed: "Any assertion that myths rob us of our real history might be countered with the declamation that myths give meaning to a culture and express its values." After all, as Macaulay said, a "history in which every particular incident may be true may on the whole be false."[9]

Both history and mythistory are too important to be left solely to nonhistorians. "Above all, history can give a sense of national identity," Arthur Schlesinger has written. Perhaps it is America's history, rather than its Constitution, as law professors maintain, which is its civil religion. That would explain why the battles over American history have become as fierce as battles over the meaning of the Constitution.[10]

What, then, is a "good myth," or good mythistory? Kammen emphasized that the most powerful myths have been based in history. "From the turn of the century until the coming of World War II . . . many Americans who seemed to be quite comfortable with what they knew to be patriotic national myths and patriotic symbols, nevertheless insisted upon their desire for historical accuracy, realism and authenticity in museums, restoration projects, pageants, and related phenomena." That reflected a desire for "collective memories to be at the same time sanguine and supportive but somehow unwarped and true." Even so, *myth* is a loaded word. Kammen conceded that many of his fellow historians were horrified by the call for "mythistory" at a time when the media was creating "a new mythology in which the U.S. government disappeared as a devastating force, the Vietnamese people ceased to be victims, and the principal focus of concern became psychic stress for those veterans who survived 'Nam and needed to reconstruct their lives." Historians who wrote mythistory would win little professional praise. Assuming they feel they have civic duties, how can historians fulfill them?[11]

SCHOLARS AS ACTIVISTS

Academics need not enlist their scholarship in support of their beliefs. Richard Hofstadter contended, for example, that "a historian can be a social activist without integrating his personal and professional lives." Yet I suspect many historians who are the least bit influenced by contemporary intellectual currents join me in considering themselves members of overlapping communities, including those of scholars and citizens. If "truth" is impossible, may we consider its consequences?[12]

In 1992, we watched the Bush administration turn away the Haitians who had fled to America. During one news broadcast, I recall that my husband turned to me and said, with evident frustration, "What happened to 'Give me your tired, your poor, your huddled masses yearning to be free?' " I responded with a lecture. He was conflating the Statue of Liberty, I said, with Emma Lazarus's words, inscribed on the statue's base by chance in 1903. I told him that the Statue of Liberty was never meant to represent the promise of asylum. Rather, in giving the statue to the United States, France had intended it to stand as a gesture to celebrate America's experiment with republicanism. It was the immigrants who arrived after the erection of the statue who changed its meaning. Then, as I remember, I paused and said, "I wonder if I would have told you the same thing if you were George Bush." I concluded I would not have done so; had I the opportunity, I would have quoted the words on the base of the Statue of Liberty to President Bush.[13]

In recent years, some historians who have observed that policymakers are influenced by perceived "lessons from the past" have moved beyond the academy. Establishing the field of "public history," which focuses on the use of history and historical method outside the university, a small but influential group has argued, beginning in the late 1970s, that historians must participate in the decisional process to prevent policymakers from "using" history irresponsibly. Just as law professors want to become players in the university, the public historians hope to become players in the policy arena. Since many who do not consider themselves public historians would concede that their personal perspectives inevitably affect their scholarship, some historians today may want to harmonize scholarship with activism through occasional forays into the realm of public history.[14]

For one example, historians have become increasingly common sights as expert witnesses in the courtrooms. Some have maintained that expert witnesses are hired guns, "paid liars," even "whores," who make the strongest possible argument for their side while ignoring countervailing evidence. The indictment is unfair. Politics has always affected historians' scholarship. Arguments may sound stronger in the courtroom than they do in the classroom: lawyers may favor sweeping interpretations more than nitpicking historians. That does not mean countervailing evidence can be slighted. As two law professors trained in both history and litigation have argued, "Lawyers with experience in appellate advocacy know that advocates ignore credible arguments or relevant facts only at their peril. The lawyer who fails to anticipate—and in defense, to re-interpret—arguments that the other side may put to good use generally comes out looking foolish, or worse."[15]

For this very reason, money may be the only gratification historians who serve as expert witnesses receive. In the celebrated employment discrimination case of *Equal Employment Opportunity Commission* v. *Sears, Roebuck & Company,* revolving around whether Sears had unfairly discriminated against women in awarding higher-paying commission sales jobs, two women's historians, Rosalind Rosenberg and Alice Kessler-Harris, squared off. Testifying on behalf of Sears, Rosenberg said that historically women had preferred noncommission sales jobs. Rosenberg was pilloried for undercutting the cause of women. Kessler-Harris endured professional humiliation: she undercut herself. Rosenberg and lawyers for Sears used the written scholarship of Kessler-Harris to rebut her testimony on behalf of the EEOC, and Kessler-Harris's own work was cited to justify the claim by Sears that women had not wanted commission sales jobs. The "withering cross-examination" of Kessler-Harris, Sanford Levinson and Thomas Haskell have said, "is probably the most poignant scene in the entire drama—at least from the perspective of working academics—for it shows a conscientious historian who had set out only to do her part for the EEOC being tripped up by her own research." When Levinson "presented the Kessler-Harris cross-examination to a diverse group of scholars interested in the topic of interpretation," his audience wondered "why anyone would want to be an expert witness. Among other things, this suggests that professional academics rarely face the intense scrutiny of their ideas that comes with full-scale cross-examination by a well-prepared lawyer."[16]

For historians, this scrutiny can prove painful, because whereas they are interested in explaining the past, lawyers will want to use those explanations to rationalize conditions in the present. Just because "many women's historians concentrated on documenting how domesticity cramped women's lives" that did not mean they believed women's lives should be cramped. Most women's historians consider themselves feminists. As Kessler-Harris dug herself in deeper and deeper, she found herself longing to say "that history was about change; that to drag the American revolution into today's labor market practices had no meaning at all."[17]

True, but sometimes life was better in the past for the groups with whom one sympathizes than one fears it may become. Although Horwitz is surely right in stressing the danger of "roaming through history looking for one's friends," history may at least indicate that one is not alone. In such instances, placing one's historical training at the service of lawyers may allow the historian opportunities to be objective and to do good, as he or she sees it.[18]

Even so, the expert witness route is a dangerous one. The historian who becomes an expert witness cannot control the use of his or her testimony. "To an individual accustomed to being a czar in the classroom, this subsidiary role in the courtroom may be hard to bear." The experience may bruise not only the historian's ego, but also the position he or she hopes to promote. Historians value a written culture, lawyers an oral one. Historians may be tripped up in exchanges with lawyers who think more quickly on their feet.[19]

Historians may increase their control and credibility, if not their savings, when they unite behind an amicus curiae brief that attorneys submit on their behalf. That is what historians inside and outside the law schools have done in recent cases involving abortion and civil rights discrimination. Such intervention makes sense in instances in which well-done history will support the political results historians wish to reach. Throughout its recent history, for example, the Supreme Court has repeatedly recognized that the Fourteenth Amendment must be interpreted in view of our "history and traditions." Historian James Mohr has observed that the doctrine of history and traditions, which "may be thought of as one of the most important bridges upon which lawyers and historians meet, deserves a great deal more extensive discussion and intensive analysis than it has heretofore received among historians." Who is better equipped to advise courts on the nation's history and traditions than its historians?[20]

Yet Mohr himself might never have become involved in litigation had attorneys not misread his work. It is difficult to close his book *Abortion in America* without concluding that eighteenth- and nineteenth-century Americans tolerated abortion. In *Webster* v. *Reproductive Health Services,* however, the solicitor general relied exclusively on Mohr's scholarship to support the proposition that "the right to abortion cannot be described as one that is 'deeply rooted in this Nation's history and tradition.' " Faced with a "situation in which, on the one hand the Supreme Court was threatening actually to reverse its policy, in clear disregard of what I considered to be the history of the republic, while on the other, people . . . believed that the Court might take seriously the so-called 'history and traditions' doctrine; that is, rights and privileges may be presumed to exist, and hence less easily erased, if they can be demonstrated to have been part of the 'history and traditions of the people,' " Mohr entered the realm of public history.[21]

With more than four hundred other historians, including both Kessler-Harris and Rosenberg, Mohr signed an amicus brief rebutting the solicitor general's historical argument and contending that a right to abortion was consistent with American history and traditions. The historians met with their attorneys—Professor Sylvia Law and two practitioners with historical training, Clyde Spillenger and Jane Larson—to lay out an outline of the brief and critique the drafts the attorneys prepared. They prevented their lawyers from making some arguments as specious as the solicitor general's. Law, for example, had insisted in her first draft of the brief for the historians "that the founding fathers probably all knew women who had abortions and would not have considered it [abortion] unusual." Historians deemed her claim indefensible. "As their lawyer, I listened and recognized that, as much as I loved the assertion, it could not be made," Law recalled. The final draft of the brief said, accurately: "At the time the federal constitution was adopted, abortion was known and not illegal."[22]

The historians' brief in *Webster* repaid the effort spent on its preparation. It received a great deal of attention. It proclaimed: "Never before have so many professional historians sought to address this Honorable Court in this way." The brief became a useful weapon in abortion advocates' war for public opinion: several newspapers reprinted an edited version of it, and many news stories stressed its key points. The *Webster* brief may also have healed some of the battle scars historians had acquired in *Sears,* and it signaled the existence of a coalition between women's historians and makers of social policy.[23]

As in the case of traditional legal scholarship, it is unclear whether amicus briefs actually influence the Court and how much. In this instance, at least, the lawyer for the Missouri abortion clinics actually relied on the historians' brief to contradict the solicitor general's claims in oral argument. Sylvia Law maintained that although the "*Webster* decisions say nothing about history . . . historians should take pride in having precluded the Court from using history in a shallow and deterministic way."[24]

The victory, however, was short-lived. Notably, though abortion rights advocates drastically reduced the number of briefs they submitted in *Planned Parenthood* v. *Casey,* among the few they filed was a brief prepared by Law, Spillenger, and Larson on behalf of 250 American historians. The brief recapitulated the historians' argument in *Webster.* Notably, too, Mohr refused to sign the historians' brief in *Casey.* This time the Rehnquist, White, Scalia, and Thomas portion of the opinion in *Casey* arguing that *Roe* v. *Wade* should be overruled cited Mohr's work in support of the claim: "Nor do the historical traditions of the American people support the view that the right to terminate one's pregnancy is 'fundamental.' " Even so, *Casey* was a victory of sorts for feminists: the Court there reaffirmed the right to abortion announced in *Roe,* while permitting the states further to restrict it.[25]

Mohr probably refused to add his name to the list of signatories in *Casey* because he had been dissatisfied with the final version of the *Webster* brief. Eventually he did sign the brief in *Webster,* emphasizing that it came closer to his own understanding of the past than the government's brief had done. But he charged that the historians' brief in *Webster* represented "advocacy" rather than "scholarship." The historians' brief was not "history, as I understand the craft," he said. "It was instead legal argument based on historical evidence. Ultimately, it was a political document. Those of us who signed it, signed as citizens, in my opinion, as well as historians." Mohr was particularly upset that the brief had made no mention of nineteenth-century feminists' opposition to abortion.[26]

Mohr's opposition of scholarship and advocacy, citizen and historian, could easily be deconstructed. Further, he himself admitted that the hostility of nineteenth-century feminists to abortion did not undercut the argument advanced by the drafters of the historians' brief in *Webster.* As Mohr said, they had "decided as lawyers that the complex attitudes of nineteenth-century feminists would not be worth explaining (or explaining away), even though they realized that historians certainly can and persuasively have analyzed what was going on." The Supreme Court restricted the length of amicus briefs, and the attorneys were low on space.[27]

For Estelle Freedman, the concentration on white, middle-class women and the silence about the experience of the poor and women of color in the *Webster* brief raised more fundamental problems. Her own historical scholarship showed that members of the latter two groups had frequently possessed powerful economic and religious reasons for reproducing. She agreed that abortion had been legal at common law. Yet "although the Constitution said nothing about abortion, and thus this right would, under the Ninth Amendment, be retained, I feel that the silence of the law cannot necessarily be read as acceptance, or even awareness, of social practice." She thought it dangerous to imply the Founders originally intended to accept abortion because historical evidence uncovered later might not bear out that claim. "Rather, I think the important fact is that at the time of framing of the Constitution, abortion was not a pressing issue because economic and social conditions discouraged its use. However, these conditions later changed to make abortion controversial and to necessitate the establishment of a right to abortion." Freedman had nevertheless signed the brief, and she recognized that "future research may well prove me wrong about the extent of abortion in the eighteenth century."[28]

Like the dichotomy between advocacy and scholarship, the dichotomy between change and continuity is false. Still, and regardless of what future scholarship shows, Freedman had raised the larger—and perennial—issue that lawyers and historians perceive divides them: where historians see change, lawyers search for continuity. Freedman would have preferred to argue that "the history of abortion practice in America is characterized more by change than by continuity, even though it is true that there have always been women who have attempted to abort." She questioned "the strategy of refuting one static historical argument with another." She probably spoke for many historians when she argued that their studies "should illuminate the ways the law needs to change in response to history, rather than the ways history supports a particular legal interpretation." She said: "I wish that lawyers could have found a legal basis to argue that women need reproductive choice today precisely because our lives *differ* from those of our foremothers even more than our lives resemble those of women in the past, despite our shared reproductive vulnerability."[29]

But the lawyers could not. For historians, the most satisfying constitutional theory might represent a combination of noninterpretivism with changed circumstances. Yet even a constitutional theorist as sensitive to history as Ahkil Amar dismisses such a theory. To paraphrase him, to convert actors in our legal culture, one must speak their language. As Freedman acknowledged, the "constraints of the legal theory within which we operate" made it essential for the historians' brief to rebut the solicitor general's "original intent" argument with another originalist version. If historians are to express their activist instincts by working with lawyers, they must play by lawyers' rules.[30]

Does that mean throwing scholarly integrity to the winds? I would argue it does not. We can be responsive to the spirit behind the calls of McNeill, Gordon, and Llewellyn if we acknowledge that there is a distinction between scholarly history and "public history" for nonacademic audiences.

"Good" public history uses history "responsibly." One scholar of constitutional law and history, H. Jefferson Powell, observed in the bicentennial year that in the case of originalism, although this task was difficult, it was not impossible. Emphasizing that "the turn to history does not obviate the personal responsibility of the originalist interpreter for the positions he takes, because historical research itself, when undertaken responsibly, requires of the interpreter the constant exercise of judgement," Powell proposed fourteen rules for originalists on historical method and conclusions, which I would say all those who use history for originalist purposes should follow.[31]

The first two rules point to "the difference between history and constitutional discourse." First, "[h]istory itself will not prove anything nonhistorical"—it cannot say whether Americans should honor Founders' intent. Second, the "pursuit of historical knowledge must not become an end in itself rather than a means." For the interpreter, as opposed to the constitutional historian, the "turn to history is legitimate only so long as it subserves the interpretation of, and fidelity to, the Constitution." It may be "that the clause's wording, its place . . . in the text as a whole, and its role in the broader 'Constitution,' invite or require a different conclusion from that based on history."[32]

The next five rules stress the difference between past and present and the need to avoid anachronism. Third: "History answers—and declines to answer—its own issues, rather than the concerns of the interpreter." It may not address the contemporary problems that moved the interpreter to look to history. Fourth: "Arguments from silence are unreliable and often completely ahistorical." Just because the Founders did not include a subject does not mean they intended to exclude it. Conversely, when they excluded something they did not necessarily mean to include it. For example, traditional interpretations of the Bill of Rights accent its counter-majoritarian nature, stressing the Founders' intention to protect individual rights against majorities. Ahkil Amar has developed an intriguing reinterpretation of the first ten amendments, which emphasizes instead the Founders' desire to structure the Constitution to spur majority rights, federalism, populism, and popular sovereignty with "phrases conjuring up civic republicanism, collective political action, public rights, and positive liberty." He only weakens his case, however, when he bases his argument in part on amendments the Founders considered but did not adopt. The fifth rule is: "To converse with the founders, you need a translator." Today's constitutional theorists should not treat Madison as a contemporary. It follows, sixth, that the "founders' comments on constitutional issues always are parts of a larger and intellectual whole." Nor, seventh, can the "original understanding of constitutional provisions . . . be neatly separated from their later use." For example, in some instances, the Founders intended for later generations to "fill in the meaning of the Constitution." Eighth: "If your history uniformly confirms your predictions, it is probably bad history."[33]

Rules nine through thirteen stress the "tentative and interpretative character of history." Ninth: "At best, history yields probabilities, not certainties." History proves nothing, not even "historical statements in the sense of demonstrating their truth with a degree of certainty that renders intelligent disagreement impossible." Similarly, rule ten notes: "History yields interpretations, not uninterpreted facts." The historian cannot provide "bare" facts, stripped of their preinterpretive meaning. Eleventh: "Consensus or even broad agreement among the founders is a historical assertion to be justified, not assumed"—it must be demonstrated. Twelfth: "History sometimes justifies plausible but opposing interpretations." Further, thirteenth, sometimes history "reveals a range of 'original understandings.' "[34]

The final and fourteenth rule sums up all of Powell's prior precepts. "History never obviates the necessity of choice." Treating the Founders' opinions as authoritative will never "preclude judges, and ourselves, from importing into constitutional interpretation our own values, preferences, individual viewpoints, and subjective and societal blindness and prejudice."[35]

I would say that, besides meeting the criteria set out in Powell's rules, "good" public history also shows "situation sense" by fortifying the argument in its particular context. Further, I would add one final criterion to avoid making "public history" the analogue of the "elaborate, systematized, jargon-filled, serious sounding deceptions" that scientists sometimes offer as expert testimony. Although the Supreme Court recently allowed "junk science" into the courtroom, public history risks losing its credibility if it becomes the equivalent. One opponent of junk science claims that the "ultimate test" of "scientific integrity" is the "readiness to publish and be damned." I suggest that any scholar, whether law professor or historian, who submits a brief or testimony on behalf of a client or cause should be willing to publish the conclusions in a scholarly journal or book under his or her own name. If a historian such as Freedman does not agree with a basic historical argument in a brief, she should not sign it (though Freedman did again add her name to the list of signatories in *Casey*). If her scholarship supports that argument, she should feel free to do so.[36]

The scholar's tone, however, need not match the public historian's. A thirty-page brief does not equal the space of any book or many articles, and arguments for the courtroom may prove both bolder and less nuanced than those for academic consumption. In this age of antifoundationalism, we should anticipate that scholars will assume one voice for an academic audience and another in the public realm. If a historian is unhappy with a brief, as James Mohr evidently was when he reviewed his experience in *Webster,* obviously he should not sign it. Yet the fact that a brief does not make an author's point in the same complex way he would make it in a book should not in itself prevent him from signing it. Likewise, his position as a federal court judge should not foreclose Richard Posner, a libertarian, from using his books and articles to maintain that the Court should overrule *Bowers* v. *Hardwick.*[37]

Yet some expect a constant voice. Ruth Colker spoke approvingly of Martha Minow's scholarly emphasis on dialogue. "Her academic tone is cautious, apparently reflecting her belief that there is no objective truth and that we must maintain openness in articulating our viewpoint." In her amicus brief in *Webster*, on the other hand, Minow flatly claimed that the Missouri abortion statute unconstitutionally violated the establishment clause of the First Amendment. "This criticism was not cautious; it was forceful and apparently confident of its accuracy," Colker complained. "Her legal argument about abortion does not appear consistent with her academic perspective about how to represent a point of view." Of course, Colker conceded, some lawyers and legal scholars would maintain "that an open voice is inappropriate for the courtroom—that there is no harm in speaking firmly in the courtroom and openly in an academic context. However, I reject that dichotomy."[38]

Why? As long as Minow is willing to say in an article or book that an antiabortion statute might violate the establishment clause, among other constitutional prohibitions, we should be satisfied. "Feminist litigation is not, and cannot be, as Professor Colker would have it, a dialogue." Other litigation cannot be, either. Traditional doctrinal work became stale in part because law professors produced scholarship that resembled briefs. While I do not deny that much advocacy is still "masquerading as scholarship," should we expect briefs to become scholarship?[39]

Nonetheless, the public historian's conclusion should not diverge from the scholar's. Harvard Law School's Randall Kennedy has compared the interpretation of the Civil Rights Act of 1866 in Eric Foner's book on Reconstruction to the historians' brief Foner signed in the recent Supreme Court case of *Patterson* v. *McLean Credit Union*. There, the Rehnquist Court upheld a 1976 decision of the Burger Court, which built on a Warren Court precedent, to say the Civil Rights Act of 1866 barred racial discrimination by private persons, as well as government, in the making and enforcement of contracts (though the Court in *Patterson* refused to extend the act to penalize racial harassment on the job). In his book Foner wrote that the drafter of the Civil Rights Act of 1866, Sen. Lyman Trumbull, knew what he wanted from the bill: "No state law or custom could deprive any citizen of what Trumbull called these 'fundamental rights belonging to every man as a free man.' " Nevertheless, Foner regretfully concluded, the bill "placed an unprecedented—and unrealistic—burden of enforcement on the federal courts. Once states enacted color-blind laws, these courts, despite their expanded jurisdiction, would probably find it difficult to prove discrimination by local officials. And despite its intriguing reference to 'customs' that deprived blacks of legal equality, the Civil Rights Bill was primarily directed against public not private, acts of injustice." The legislative history, Foner said, provided no definite answer regarding the legislative intent. The brief Foner signed in *Patterson,* however, promised "conclusively [to] demonstrate that the Act was intended by its framers . . . to protect the civil rights acts of both blacks and whites, notwithstanding [the identity of the violators]." Its argument contradicted Foner's own findings.[40]

Foner might have said instead in the brief that the ambiguity of the historical evidence emancipated the Court from the search for legislative intent. Of course this argument would have proved more overtly political than the one he made. As Foner said elsewhere in his book, "Whether the courts *should* be bound by the 'original intent' of a constitutional amendment is a political, not historical question." But it would have been a political argument that rested on Foner's evaluation that the historical data proved inconclusive and freed him to make a policy argument.[41]

Another historian who read that same data differently, however, might properly sign the historians' brief. Robert Kaczorowski, a law professor and historian, used the pages of the *Yale Law Journal* to contend "that interpretations of the Civil Rights Act of 1866 as limited to state action are anachronistic and historically incorrect because the framers did not intend, and probably could not have intended, to legislate within a concept of state action." Kaczorowski appropriately acted as counsel to the historians in *Patterson* v. *McLean.*[42]

Academic lawyers should stop viewing historians as repositories of useful facts and become more sensitive to the varieties of historical interpretation. Historian John Hope Franklin has said: "In virtually every area where evidence from the past is needed to support the validity of a given proposition, an historian can be found who will provide the evidence that is needed." That does not mean any history or historian is as good as any other. Like scholars, courts are free to reject history they deem inaccurate or incredible. Just as liberal law professors have made the counter-majoritarian difficulty their own bogeyman, so they have helped to plague historians with "the objectivity question" by treating them as walking encyclopedias, who speak "truth." The issue is counterfactual: historians might reply that objective history is impossible and pragmatic hermeneutics enables us to discard the ideal without cost.[43]

That does not make history irrelevant or efforts to be fair unnecessary. Suppose one sides with Mary Ann Glendon and Robert Nagel about the significance of the O'Connor-Kennedy-Souter plurality opinion in *Casey*, which refused to eliminate the right to abortion. To overturn *Roe* while that opinion was "under fire," the trio said, would jeopardize "the character of a Nation of people who aspire to live according to the rule of law." The plurality maintained that Americans' "belief in themselves as such a people is not readily separable from their understanding of the Court invested with the authority to decide their constitutional cases and speak before all others for their constitutional ideals." That conclusion invited Glendon's and Nagel's contempt. "Here, as in a late-night fit of drunken sentimentality, is revealed an important and disturbing truth about the self-image of some members of our high Court," Nagel said. "They believe that judicial sovereignty over constitutional issues is essential, not just to the Court's power or to the practical workings of government, but to our sense of ourselves as a people." Glennon decried "the plurality's grandiose pretensions of judicial authority." Alternatively, suppose that one agrees with Morton Horwitz, as I do, that the Court's decision in *Casey* "was as much about the legitimacy of constitutional change as it was about the right to abortion created by *Roe*," and that the plurality's theory of constitutional change in *Casey* "too narrowly defines when it is legitimate for changed factual circumstances to alter the application of fundamental law." In both instances, it follows that a historians' brief in the future might be devoted to a study of the historical role of the Supreme Court in American society, to an examination of when in its history the Court has found constitutional change appropriate, and to an evaluation of the O'Connor-Kennedy-Souter understanding of the Court's reaction to *Plessy* v. *Ferguson* and to *Lochner* v. *New York*.[44]

Though judges and other scholars may conclude a historical interpretation fails to meet the burden of proof, there is no immutable standard against which to evaluate the imperfect attempts of historians to achieve "accuracy." Historians must be judged against themselves. They may change their minds, but at all times, the conclusions they arrive at

as activists should substantively echo those they reach contemporane-
ously as scholars. We should recognize, however, that different forums
demand different voices.[45]

Does law professors' effort to give neorepublicanism a "historical
pedigree" in the eighteenth century represent good "situation sense" and
good public history? In the same article in which he invited historians
to differentiate between "good myths" and "bad myths" created by lawyers, Gordon addressed the implications of historians' discovery of republicanism for the legal community's understanding of the Founding.
He warned that the "lawyer who turns to the best available perspectives
on the thinking behind the American Constitution may find herself in
the position of the French humanist lawyers who hoped to uncover the
universal basis for their own jurisprudence by freeing the Roman Corpus
Juris from medieval corruptions, and then did such thorough scholarly
work as to persuade many of them of Rome's irrelevance."[46]

Gordon may have been right. G. Edward White's masterful history
of the early Supreme Court pointed to the impact of republicanism on
the Marshall Court. As White emphasized, however, members of the
Court during that era "not only worked in an environment that only
tangentially resembles that of current Justices, they also engaged in procedures clearly unacceptable by current ethical standards and in internal
practices notable for their informality and lack of accountability." In
addition, Marshall Court justices possessed a different theory of cultural
change and different attitudes toward class, toward the past and history,
and toward law. "It may be easier to fathom judges riding in stage-
coaches, or communicating to each other in handwritten letters with
eighteenth-century calligraphy, or wearing knee breeches beneath their
robes, or holding conferences in a boarding-house, than to imagine their
seeing their declarations of legal rules and principles as anything other
than creative law-making."[47]

What stood out was "the uniqueness and time-boundedness" of the
Marshall Court. "The years of the Marshall Court may have been the
first time in the history of American culture in which the possibility that
the future might never replicate the past was truly grasped." If Ameri-

cans understood that insight, they did not appreciate it. "History was still to an important extent perceived as an affirmation of first principles." Thus the Marshall Court was, "in the deepest sense a Court of its time." Similarly, H. Jefferson Powell has said that for Sunstein, at least, "the historical meaning of republicanism . . . does not matter in any crucial way." Like Powell's conclusion, White's work suggests that more generally, historical republicanism has little relationship to neorepublicanism. The search for the antecedents of neorepublicanism in eighteenth-century thought therefore seems foolish.[48]

Many critics have also declared the neorepublican vision futile or worse. It may be that the "present depiction of loggers as 'tree killers' and 'owl killers,' and the loggers' equally vehement dislike of environmentalists and the Forest Service has created an artificial gulf" between loggers and environmentalists, but can this gulf really be "overcome by dialogue"? Further, attractive as neorepublicanism is when one can imagine that Michelman and Sunstein, chaired professors at elite law schools, are participating in the policy discussions, they might not prevail. And, at least historically, rights may have given losers more protection than community has. Benjamin Barber may be correct in saying that the "Bill of Rights may do less to constrain a mob than would an appeal to the citizenship of its members, reminding them that they are embarked on a public course of action that cannot meet the objections of reasonable public discourse," but who can be sure? Rights may prove good fallbacks. Even Michelman once admitted "many readers" might think he was engaged in "a lunatic undertaking." Madison did caution us to beware of what will happen when "common passion unites a majority." The historian Robert Wiebe usefully reminds us that despite Madison's warning, "collective and individual democracy did interconnect" for a time in the nineteenth century, and "that nothing inherent to democracy sets majority rule and individual rights at odds." Yet in our society, I suspect *Bowers* v. *Hardwick* is all too consistent with majority rule and is just the sort of case we should fear under a republican revival. By this analysis, the republican revival has been useful insofar as it has swung attention away from procedural justice, neutrality, and rights. Yet it may fit Leo Strauss's conservative vision of America more than it does that of political liberals.[49]

It may be, too, that in making "community, democracy, equality, virtue" its "mantra," "contemporary antiliberalism" has done liberalism a disservice. As William Galston said recently, "For two generations, scholarly inquiry has been dominated by the belief that the liberal polity does not require individual virtue." He contended that what "is distinctive about liberalism is not the absence of a substantive conception of the good, but rather a reluctance to move from this conception to full-blown public coercion of individuals." I find Galston's liberalism more appealing than neorepublicanism. Had Franklin Roosevelt, Lyndon Johnson, and Earl Warren lived long enough to see Galston's work, and had they sat still long enough to read it, I imagine they would have too. Galston's "substantive liberalism" may not require as politically engaged a citizenry as civic republicanism, but it tolerates an individualistic and diverse populace, and his liberal virtues "circumscribe and check, without wholly nullifying, the promptings of self-aggrandizement." Stephen Holmes has forcefully reminded us that liberalism is not inevitably hostile to "communal values" or a "genuine shared common good." Nor do liberal rights preclude duties. Rather, Joseph Raz has claimed "rights are the grounds of duties."[50]

Perhaps the fragmentation of legal scholarship, which has damaged the sense of community among law professors, has caused the neorepublicans to romanticize the ideal of community. Dissenters who point to the community's potential for authoritarianism prefer liberalism. They note that liberalism enables us to recognize that we are a nation built "around diversity." Perhaps "liberal republicanism" would do so as well, but it might prove "oxymoronic." Such arguments suggest that neorepublicanism is "bad" mythmaking—for policy reasons. Add them to neorepublicanism's lack of pedigree, and there is a case against neorepublicanism.[51]

Yet like me, the historians who inveigh against the republican revival are generally more sympathetic to Michelman and the neorepublicans than they are toward conservative originalists. Therein lies a problem for many historians. Cass Sunstein has rightly pointed out that though "there is a freestanding, nonhistorical argument for deliberative democracy as a central political ideal," constitutional lawyers' argument in favor of it "draws substantial support from historical understandings." Gordon Wood acknowledged that "the stakes in these historical arguments about the eighteenth-century are very high—they are nothing less than the kind of society that we have been, or ought to become." As scholars, historians can show that the debate over original intent is stupid, fruitless, and anachronistic, just as they can demonstrate that the scavenging of the legal community in the eighteenth century for a republicanism that will prove "useful" today is ahistorical. To quote Wood: "It may be a necessary fiction for lawyers and jurists to believe in a 'correct' or 'true' interpretation of the Constitution in order to carry on their business, but we historians have different obligations and ends."[52]

Wood's words remind us that lawyers and judges do consider original intent a "necessary fiction." Conservatives certainly do: to them, as Frank Easterbrook has said, the "Constitution can mean one thing in a classroom and another in a Courtroom." Perhaps most Americans also value originalism. Wood has pointed to the many citizens who used the bicentennial to ask what Washington, Jefferson, and Adams would have thought about twentieth-century life. Those are not queries historians can shirk, Wood emphasized in one forum for historians, because in addition to understanding the past on its own terms, we are obliged "to connect the past with what came after . . . to describe the ways in which the future was created by the ideas and actions of the past." Although such questions may aggravate historians, "they are obviously meaningful to ordinary people. To that extent at least the classical standards that were alive in eighteenth-century America still have some relevance for us today." Wood's sensitivity to audience is laudatory. My impression is that when he is addressing historians he often accuses them of being insufficiently present-minded, but when he is speaking to lawyers or the general public, he warns against the dangers of presentism.[53]

Perhaps that dualism is the best answer. However problematic historians may find originalism, they recognize that if law professors advance a pedigree for neorepublicanism, they fight fire with fire. Like other scholars, Sunstein, Michelman, and others make their arguments for the present more powerful by allying themselves with the winners at the Constitutional Convention. They can maintain that it is they, the "modern republicans," who carry out the Founders' intent. Even Linda Kerber has admitted, "It may be useful to have these claims [for a contemporary neorepublican social order] made in the rhetoric of the Founders because, in practice, theirs are the voices to which we have been trained to listen." As she asks, what is preferable? "To ally oneself with Marxian dissent is to foreclose a hearing by centrist opinion in America; to ally oneself with the Antifederalists is to be caught on the losing side."[54]

Reduced to its essence, Kerber's position is that it is both imperative and impossible to justify neorepublicanism: it is imperative for us as citizens, impossible for us as historians. Do we opt to police our turf against the law professors, as Kerber did in the *Yale Law Journal*? Or do we opt to join law professors with whom we sympathize, as Kerber implied she would do in the *Yale Law Journal* and as she did in *Webster* and *Casey*? Perhaps the appropriate answer is hers: both.

NEOFEDERALISM

There may be more satisfying methods of fulfilling those dual obligations than through neorepublicanism. Consider the "neo-Federalist" theory of dualist democracy Bruce Ackerman advanced in his book *We the People*. Stressing his "opposition to the gross maldistribution of wealth that prevails in today's America" and commitment to "engaged national politics and activist government," Ackerman, who defined himself as a "liberal Democrat" and a "liberal republican—a republican in Pocock's sense, not Reagan's," took the theory of popular sovereignty advanced in *The Federalist* seriously. For all its "neo-Federalism," or neoliberalism, *We the People* also subscribes to some basic premises of the republican revival by intimating that at certain times—though perhaps not as frequently as other republican revivalists indicate—a deliberative citizenry can recast the Constitution outside the cumbersome procedure for constitutional amendment spelled out in Article V.[55]

Arguing that the Constitutional Convention represented a dodge around the state governments, Ackerman pointed to Madison's confession of the convention's illegality in a few of the papers in *The Federalist*. By Ackerman's account, Madison justified the illegality by explaining that at the convention, the Founders spoke in the name of what Madison called *"the people themselves,"* and what Ackerman described as "a People which normally does not exist—a People both mobilized and capable of sober deliberation." For Ackerman, Madison's move meant that when the Founders shifted sovereignty from government to the people, they were engaged in something more than "a legalistic shell game"; that they foresaw the People might act again; and that Gordon Wood was wrong to insist that at the Constitutional Convention in Philadelphia, the Founders appropriated and exploited their opponents' language. Instead, according to Ackerman, the Founders had "creatively elaborated a revolutionary language and practice in ways that allowed future Americans to take to the higher lawmaking track to challenge many of the verities held by the Founders themselves—while at the same time authorizing government to undertake the normal tasks of daily life. Not bad for a single generation." They had developed a "dualist Constitution" envisioning a "dualist democracy," which distinguished "between two different decisions that may be made in a democracy. The first is a decision by the American people; the second, by their government." During times of "normal politics," the latter occurs, as representatives stand in for the people and work "to deliver the goods for their constituents." At "constitutional moments," "*private* citizens become private *citizens*," and "mobilized deliberation" takes place: "Apathy will give way to concern, ignorance to information, selfishness to serious reflection on the country's future." "Higher lawmaking" in the name of "we the people," outside the ratification procedure involving congressional majorities and state approval for constitutional amendments spelled out in Article V of the Constitution, followed. The task, as Ackerman saw it, was to affirm what Wood had denied—"that the spirit of 1787 is not dead, that neo-Federalism is very much a live option for our own time," and that future generations had the ability to create "constitutional moments" of their own.[56]

Ackerman scorned the "Bicentennial myth" of American history as one republic, which stressed "the deep continuity of two centuries of constitutional practice" and suggested "the Founding Federalists had foreseen the works of Franklin D. Roosevelt" and the "judicial rediscovery of ancient truths" after 1937. Rather, he maintained that "we the people" displayed "liberal republicanism" by participating in higher lawmaking during the three foundings, republics, or constitutional moments, in American history. The first occurred when the Founders convened their illegal Constitutional Convention in 1787; second, during Reconstruction another legally problematic episode, "not only did the Republicans introduce new substantive principles into our higher law but they reworked the very process of higher lawmaking itself"; and third, the New Deal represented a "self-conscious" process of constitution making. "If the American people were ever endorsing a break with their constitutional past, they were doing so in the 1930s," Ackerman insisted of the New Deal. In his story, the 1930s contrasted sharply with the 1987 rejection of the Bork nomination, which Ackerman classified as "a failed constitutional moment." According to Ackerman, "the reformers returned to Washington with a clear victory at the polls" in 1936; they proclaimed that "the election results gave them a 'mandate from the people' and that it was time for the conservative Supreme Court to end its resistance"; and FDR threatened to pack the Court. The question for the Court was, "Should the conservatives . . . finally recognize that the *People had spoken?*" Ackerman claimed that the conservatives answered affirmatively. "Rather than escalating the constitutional crisis further, they decided, with evident reluctance, that further resistance would endanger too many of the very values they held fundamental. They made the 'switch in time' . . . the Supreme Court repudiated its doctrinal defense of laissez-faire capitalism and began to build new constitutional foundations for activist national government." The "switch in time" became a constitutional moment.[57]

Ackerman also emphasized "how much we may learn from the past once we orient constitutional theory away from the 'countermajoritarian' difficulty toward *the possibility of interpretation.*" He rejected both the "monistic democracy" of Ely and Bickel, in which democracy required "the grant of plenary lawmaking authority to the winners of the last general election" and treated "every act of judicial review as presumptively undemocratic," and he spurned the rights foundationalism of Dworkin, in which the Constitution was the source of fundamental rights and "[r]ights trump democracy—provided of course that they're the Right rights." Instead of the foundationalist's Constitution which was rights-protecting first and democratic second, "the dualist's Constitution is democratic first, rights-protecting second"; Ackerman's insistence on popular sovereignty made the people the source of rights and government. The down side of a dualist democracy in which the judiciary served as yet another voice of the people was that judges possessed no "general authority to protect the fundamental principles of dualist democracy against repudiation by the People." More positively, the job of judges, especially Supreme Court justices, in a dualist democracy was to preserve "the integrity of higher law making" by engaging in "an ongoing judicial effort to look backward and interpret the meaning" of constitutional moments which had gone before. Whereas traditionally commentators had strained "to save the Supreme Court from the 'countermajoritarian difficulty' by one or another ingenious argument," Ackerman's dualists saw judicial review itself as democratic, when preservationist, and "the discharge of the preservationist function by the courts as an essential part of a well-ordered regime. Rather than threatening democracy by frustrating the statutory demands of the political elite in Washington, the courts serve democracy by protecting the hard-won principles of a mobilized citizenry against erosion by political elites who have failed to gain broad and deep support for their innovations." Fearful that "American government is losing its historical roots in the practice of popular sovereignty," Ackerman thought the Court could "bring the power of historical memory into play," providing a reminder that higher lawmaking had taken place in the past. If citizens did not like the way the Court organized the "conversation between the present and the past about the future," they could mobilize again for higher lawmaking.[58]

By this account, *Brown* was not the "inspired act of political prophecy" legal scholars from Bickel onward had described. Rather, the case simply represented the Court's attempt to reconcile two constitutional moments, Reconstruction and the New Deal, by applying the affirmation of equality that marked Reconstruction to "the public school—an institution that had become emblematic of the New Deal's activist use of state power for the general welfare." Nor was *Griswold,* and by extension *Roe,* a milestone. Rather, *Griswold* simply read "the Bill of Rights to preserve the Founding concern with personal liberty in a way that endures in a post–New Deal world of economic and social regulation."[59]

Like Bickel, Ackerman believed that with *Brown* the Court had helped spark the civil rights movement. "Nonetheless," Ackerman warned, "on those happy occasions when a Court manages to provide constitutional symbols that new movements find inspiring, it would be a tragic irony if this success should allow lawyers to forget a crucial dualist truth." Though judges were uniquely situated "to preserve the past constitutional achievements of the American people, many other citizens are in better positions to lead the People onward to a better constitutional future." Ackerman accordingly produced a constitutional theory, which tried to justify *Brown* and *Roe, and* said judges were no substitute for higher lawmaking by "we the people."[60]

In a recent issue of the *Harvard Law Review,* law professor Suzanna Sherry critiqued *We the People.* At about the same time, historian Edmund S. Morgan evaluated Ackerman's book for the *New York Review of Books.* Compare their conclusions:

MORGAN

What Ackerman really wants is an exercise of judgment, a recognition of the rightful superiority of those higher laws that have a more plausible claim than others to be acts of the people themselves, even though the claim can be no more than plausible. He has exercised his own judgment in discerning the occasions when we should suspend our disbelief, give our faith, and say that the people have acted, when it is useful and indeed necessary to suppose that they have acted. In doing so, he has given us a fresh and convincing view not only of our constitutional history but of our will to believe.

The people do exist in our willingness to believe in them and to give force to the acts we attribute to them. Ackerman has provided us with a guide to the attributions. We may disagree with the particulars of his argument, but his distinction between normal and constitutional politics fits the way American government has operated over two cen-

SHERRY

At bottom, then, Ackerman's theory is merely originalism flying under liberal colors. . . . In this respect, Ackerman's whole book is designed to forestall, or at least condemn in advance, what Ackerman sees as an illegitimate counterrevolution by the Rehnquist Court.

Exposing that underlying motivation for Ackerman's project does more than undermine its legitimacy. Ultimately, Ackerman's originalism reveals the sad state of American liberalism. Unable to persuade the American people, or even the Supreme Court, of the substantive validity of liberal ideals, one of modern liberalism's most forceful spokesmen

turies. It cuts through the futile and absurd search for the "original intent of
the founders" as the way to discover the
will of the people. It recognizes that the
great and extraordinary occasions required for action by the people have not
been confined to a single instance in the
eighteenth century. It deflates the pretensions of politicians in normal politics
but magnifies the importance of constitutional politics when constitutional
politics is needed. It gives pragmatic
meaning to government, of, by, and for
the elusive, invisible, inaudible, but sovereign people.

is reduced to this last resort of conservatives. We
must retain the legacy of
the New Deal—as inter-
preted by modern liber-
als—not because it is
right, but because its founders told us to. There is
genuine pathos in seeing
what was once the most
optimistic and forward-
looking of the American
philosophies reduced to
this appeal to the authority of the past.[61]

Here are two stimulating reviews, which reached divergent conclusions.
How are we to explain the difference? Raoul Berger once hypothesized
that "[p]erhaps lawyers are more thick-skinned than historians." Maybe
historians are more likely than law professors to opt for politeness in
print. A friend, who is a law professor theorized that Morgan "copped
out."[62]

Morgan's generation of historians did value civility more than mine
do. The first time I understood the difference between historians and
lawyers with respect to civility was during my first year of graduate
school. I had just read John Morton Blum's *The Republican Roosevelt*
alongside Arthur Link's *Woodrow Wilson and the Progressive Era.* I
charged into Blum's office waving Link's book, which said that Wilson
had been the first president to strengthen his office and enjoy substantive
legislative achievements, and then accusingly pointed to *The Republican
Roosevelt,* which gave Theodore Roosevelt credit for those very accomplishments. Having come from the legal world, I expected Blum to attack
Link—to heap on his Princeton counterpart the abuse that, say, Mark
Tushnet had heaped on Lawrence Tribe or that Matthew Finkin was to
pile on Karl Klare and Katherine Stone. Blum smiled (rather serenely, as
I recall) and said: "Arthur and I disagree on that point." It is difficult

to imagine many historians of either generation writing the kind of mean-spirited polemics law professors periodically produce.[63]

Perhaps the difference in tone between historians and law professors relates to the standards by which they evaluate work. "While traditional history has had its share of controversies, controversy is not normally the mark of a successful study," Robert Fogel has stressed. "Success normally turns on how widely and how well a work is received. Although there are notable exceptions, strong attacks, especially if they come from distinguished colleagues, tend to undermine the credibility of a work even if the attack is empirically unwarranted."[64]

Yet strong attacks do not necessarily undermine the credibility of law professors' work, whether it be lawyers' legal history, historians' legal history, or any other kind of scholarship. Rather, such attacks suggest the work is "provocative" and, therefore, "important." For example, while historians acclaimed Horwitz's *Transformation of American Law,* it caused an uproar in the legal community. The book still remains a seminal text of American legal history and of legal scholarship. Law professors apparently expect their work to be challenged, just as they anticipate questioning the work of others. Perhaps that is one reason book reviews in law reviews are so much longer than they are in historical journals. I would guess that historians are still more likely than law professors to consider venomous published evaluations bad form.[65]

Not all historians of Blum's or my generation have eschewed acrimony for civility, but vituperative reviews do remain the exception rather than the rule. Morgan has, however, written some of them.[66]

Another historian friend who studied with Morgan advanced a more plausible explanation for the positive tone of his review of *We the People.* Ackerman's view of the Founding, at least insofar as Morgan interpreted it, she said, resembled the one Morgan articulated in *Inventing the People.* There Morgan emphasized the impact of "necessary . . . fictions," such as popular sovereignty, on political behavior. As the constitutional convention drew to a close, Morgan admitted, Madison did become nervous about the possibility of ever mobilizing the people effectively. Viewing the Founders more benignly than did the young Gordon Wood, however, Morgan insisted that Madison was not "trying to put one over on the public. He was a champion of popular rights and of republican, representative government." Toward that end, just as the

House of Commons "invented a sovereign people to overcome a sovereign king" in England in the 1640s, so Madison invented "a sovereign American people to overcome the sovereign states." In fact, Morgan's strongest criticism of *We the People*'s thesis was that "Ackerman, I think, accepts a little too readily Madison's contention [in *The Federalist*] that the people themselves acted in creating the Constitution." This admonition paled next to Sherry's withering assessment.[67]

Perhaps Morgan was simply reading Ackerman's work to support his own. Yet if Morgan and Ackerman do agree on some points, think of the grist Morgan could have given Ackerman for his mill. Since Ackerman has described himself as an "interdisciplinary scavenger," one might have expected him to ask Morgan for help. After all, for part of the decade during which he wrote *We the People,* the office of Yale's Sterling Professor of Law and Political Science Bruce Ackerman lay only half a block away from that of Sterling Professor of History Emeritus Edmund S. Morgan. Further, Ackerman himself has observed that "law professors trade on a university name, built up by historians, classicists, and theoretical physicists. We put ourselves forward as professors of law at *Yale* University (to pick a name at random). Yet even knowledgeable outsiders do not always recognize that lawyers become professors on the basis of a publication standard that embarrasses their colleagues in the rest of the university."[68]

Still, it is unclear Ackerman is interested in aid historians could provide. In *We the People,* he harangued historians for wasting their time on "a dismal kind of dating game—in which the debate concerns the precise moment that the (Neo-) Classical Republican Ideal was conquered by the increasingly aggressive forces of Liberalism." And the only member of a history department Ackerman singled out in the long list of those to whom he expressed gratitude was Eric Foner![69]

Ironically, Ackerman's history apparently has impressed Morgan and other historians more than it did the law professors who branded it ahistorical. Though Stanford historian Jack Rakove agreed with Sherry that Ackerman advanced liberal originalism, his assessment in the *Journal of American History* of the history in Ackerman's account was more positive than the critiques written in law reviews by academic lawyers, such as Sherry, William Fisher, Michael Klarman, David Dow, Frederick Schauer, and even Eben Moglen. "I believe his appeal to history is normatively sound, in the sense that later generations should prefer the example of the Founders over their gloomier doubts about our likely fallibility," Rakove emphasized. The Founders' skepticism should not bind those who followed. Rakove's sympathies obviously lay more with Ackerman "the legal reconstructionist" rather than Ackerman the historian, but he recognized that the two Ackermans were interdependent. He provided documentation from the Founding Ackerman had missed which would have "fortified his case" that the Founders envisioned a dualist democracy, just as I would have provided documentation strengthening Ackerman's argument that the New Deal represented a constitutional moment. Similarly, Richard Bernstein singled out Ackerman's work as evidence that "it is possible for legal and constitutional theorists to draw on both the newest research in original sources and the newest interpretative products of historians' constitutional history to advance the inquiries and research agenda of constitutional law."[70]

Perhaps Ackerman is onto something. Perhaps Article V is nonexclusive, and constitutional amendment can occur outside its straitjacket. Law professors might still ask, with Thomas Landry, why Ackerman has apparently concluded we have reached "a point in American history at which the States are obsolete entities for purposes of establishing or amending the national Constitution." They might agree with H. Jefferson Powell that "Ackerman's constitutionalism rests, in the end, on a simple ontological mistake: he posits the existence of a 'People' that acts in identifiable ways and speaks in comprehensible tones." They might argue, with Terrance Sandalow, that "in Ackerman's 'dualist democracy' it is the Justices, not the People, who make the crucial constitutional decision," and that Ackerman is engaged in yet another attempt to rationalize and revive the Warren Court. They might join Avi Soifer in pointing out that a theory such as Ackerman's did not explain "why the KKK, the Red Scare, McCarthyism, Reaganism, etc. are not also [constitutional moments]." They might concur with Robert Lipkin that "[n]othing in Ackerman's theory provides future justices with a reliable guide for knowing when higher lawmaking occurs," and that "Ackerman's basic problem is his desire to combine originalism and majoritarianism, on the one hand, with progressive change, on the other." They might side with Lawrence Lessig in saying that we need no constitutional amendment to constitutionalize the New Deal. They might mourn, with

Frank Michelman, that Ackerman's theory prevents the Court from exercising its "prophetic" role. They might conclude that, like neorepublicanism, the dualist democracy of neofederalism risks majority tyranny. Yet they might also decide it is more historically plausible than neorepublicanism and that it possesses the potential to move constitutional theory beyond the counter-majoritarian difficulty.[71]

TRADING PLACES

Just as historians seem ready to accept the necessity of liberal originalism, Ackerman may be about to desert it for their side. Consider the current debate about the legality of the Constitution, which engages Ackerman and his Yale colleague Ahkil Amar and enrages Lawrence Tribe. In his 1984 Storrs Lectures and *We the People,* Ackerman claimed "that the Constitutional Convention was acting illegally in proposing its new document in the name of We The People," and defined a convention as "an assembly whose legal right to make constitutional proposals is open to good-faith legal doubt; but which, nevertheless, proposes to ratify these proposals by a procedure that *plainly departs* from pre-existing constitutional understandings." By Ackerman's theory, such conventions are substitutes for the people themselves, and they will only occur on the rare occasions the American people channel "mass energy into a deliberative politics that is *more* rational and public-spirited than the norm."[72]

This may represent good strategy. Morgan's and Wood's work supports the conclusion constitutional moments will be infrequent. "As these historians have pointed out, early American constitutionalists eventually hit on the idea that procedurally irregular—even extralegal—conventions paradoxically conferred more legitimacy on constitutions than legislatures could in part because their very irregularity suggested greater civic fervor and representativeness," one legal historian has observed. "This insight helps Ackerman first because irregularity in the abstract suggests infrequency, and second because conventions in this sense occurred only during times of crisis in fact, or at least as far as Anglo-American history to 1787 is concerned."[73]

Such historians might also contend, however, that Ackerman's preoccupation with legality leads him toward a dead end. There were justifiable challenges to the legality of both convention and Constitution, and Antifederalists made them, but the need to develop a national government and the idea of popular sovereignty—a concept that admittedly did not unfold either "deliberately or evenly"—rendered them inconsequential. Without *legitimacy,* and regardless of legality, the Constitution would become an anachronism. The problem for the Founders, then, was not so much legality, or even "acceptance" of the Constitution, Stanley Elkins and Eric McKitrick say in their massive history of the early republic, "but the more fundamental problem of legitimacy," which was conferred by the sending of Federalist majorities to the new Congress after ratification of the Constitution by specially elected conventions, by the unanimous election of Washington as president, and by the spectacularly rapid transformation of Constitution into cultural totem.[74]

Ackerman now seems to recognize this. In a 1995 article, "Our Unconventional Founding," he persuasively establishes the illegality of the Founding while subordinating legality to legitimacy. But the historian reading the exchanges between law professors over legality versus illegality may feel that the whole debate might have been avoided. The question of the Constitution's legality distracts attention from the more crucial one of legitimacy.[75]

Some legal scholars, however, continue to make legality and legitimacy synonymous. To his fellow publicist for popular sovereignty Ahkil Amar, Ackerman's charge of illegality "betrays the founding generation's extraordinary accomplishment of fully legalizing revolution by channeling it through precise legal procedures." Concluding that Ackerman "has tinkered with his criteria in a result-oriented fashion to constitutionalize the 'New Deal,' " Amar portrays Ackerman as mad political scientist. "If James Madison's and James Wilson's Constitution violated preexisting legal rules, how was it any different from Jefferson Davis's Confederate Constitution, except that Madison and Wilson succeeded, ex post, and Davis did not?" he asks. "Ackerman's 'laws of amendment,' seem more laws of political science—empirical regularities, like the 'laws' of supply and demand—than formal, legal, procedural laws that specify an ex ante rule of recognition."[76]

Amar claims to have produced a "less nebulous and government driven—more formalistic and plebiscitary" version of Ackerman's neofederalism, or dualist democracy. He disparages Ely's dismissal of the theory of popular sovereignty advanced in *The Federalist* as "largely a fake" and urges "sophisticated theorists" to stop smirking at the phrase "We the People." Even more emphatically than Ackerman, Amar treats the judiciary as property of the people. "All three branches of government derive, with various degrees of directness; all three are agencies of the People," Amar insists. "Each represents the People in a different and ultimately problematic way. . . . The ultimate power to reassess those costs, and redefine the terms of agency, if deemed appropriate, must always rest with We the People Ourselves—you, me, and our fellow citizens, here and now." Amar dissolves the counter-majoritarian difficulty by following Morgan in treating popular sovereignty as something more than a sham and in contending that the Founders intended the judiciary to function as yet another voice of the people. Further, Amar gives the people the option of following the Founders' example. When a majority of the electorate petitions Congress to call a convention to propose constitutional amendments, Congress must do so, and any resultant amendment can be ratified by a simple majority of American voters. To Amar, the legality of the convention and Constitution, for which he makes an ingenious, technical argument, is crucial: if the Constitution was the product of a legal process it tells us something "about the People's *legal* right to alter or abolish." Article V notwithstanding, " '[t]he People retain the legal right to change the Constitution by legal mechanisms akin to the legal mechanisms by which they ordained and established it.' My claim is that the Constitution is best read as saying exactly this, only in different words . . . and in the act of legal ordainment and establishment itself." In fact, "the popular sovereignty amendment path is legally *higher* than Article V," which "only supplements, but can never supplant, majority rule popular sovereignty."[77]

As Amar admits, this is "strong stuff. My argument here about the right of a current majority to amend our Constitution may scare you. To be honest, it scares me a little too." Amar concluded, however, that if exercised, popular sovereignty would not promote majority tyranny or instability, and would force us "to educate ourselves, and each other."[78]

Both Ackerman and Amar democratize judicial review and argue constitutional amendment can occur outside Article V—Ackerman because the Constitution was illegally adopted, Amar because it was legally adopted. According to Lawrence Tribe, the " 'all-roads-lead-to-Rome' character of this debate suggests that both Professor Ackerman and Professor Amar seek to draw vastly more from the explosive historical event of the Constitution's adoption than that event will yield for purposes of deciding whether the Constitution may be amended outside Article V's procedures." To Tribe, Ackerman's and Amar's work signals "the emergence of a distinctive new 'Yale school' of constitutional interpretation," characterized by "a willingness to treat even the architecture-defining, power-conferring provisions of the Constitution as merely suggestive." Anything goes.[79]

This, Tribe intimates sadly, is where interdisciplinary research has brought law professors. That Ackerman and Amar are shifting their focus from constitutional interpretation "to the meaning of the American Revolution, of the Civil War experience, of the New Deal," he alleges, is not "just another interesting conversational gambit. Rather, that change in subject—whatever its other values—should be seen for what it is: a complete departure from the enterprise of interpreting the Constitution of the United States." Tribe maintains that "it is wrong to assume that theories that account for our nation's most extreme moments can generate principles capable of accounting, either normatively or descriptively, for more ordinary constitutional episodes." Whatever the value of Ackerman's theory as history, "it has no role to play in resolving any question of constitutional interpretation." Tribe maintains "that there are legal truths out there, or at least legal falsehoods, that simply cannot be wished away, and that legal discourse itself imposes serious constraints, enforced by the interpretive community that engages in that discourse." He condemns scholars such as Ackerman and Amar who cease making constitutional interpretation "truly a *legal* enterprise, genuinely disciplined."[80]

In contrast, I would argue that the new "Yale school" Tribe decries is marked not so much by "free-form" constitutional interpretation as by greater sensitivity to history and a more *disciplined* approach to interdisciplinary work. That is, their scholarship does more than show off their forays outside the law school. It has the potential to move constitutional theory beyond a powerful myth—the conviction the anti-democratic nature of judicial review is rooted in history—and, by explaining how constitutional change has occurred, to illuminate how it may take place.

Imagine the appeal of neofederalism to one who trusts, as I do, that the Founders viewed the people and popular sovereignty with hope as well as horror. Rakove has shown that they believed in popular sovereignty and feared it, much as critical legal scholars thought relations with other people were necessary to and incompatible with the individual's freedom. I think the Founders had some shy hope for popular sovereignty; that they perceived popular sovereignty could legitimate judicial review; that they believed the judiciary would help establish a workable federalism; and that they hoped that in addition to preventing the governed from government, the judiciary would operate to protect individual and minority rights from the majority acting through government (while anticipating judges might not fulfill this mission). These beliefs will not be sufficiently definite for lawyers, but lawyers must realize historians will never be able to provide them with definite answers. As Rakove has said, historians "revel in . . . the ambiguities of the evidentiary record" and seek to explain how and "why 'contrasting meanings' were attached to the Constitution from its inception."[81]

In this instance, ambiguity holds potential. To anyone who shares these views about the Founders, history can be liberating because it suggests that as a way of understanding how they operated, the counter-majoritarian difficulty may be counterfactual; they did not necessarily view judicial review as antidemocratic. Ackerman's and Amar's work becomes crucial because its rescue of popular sovereignty points toward an interpretation of the past that an obsession with the counter-majoritarian difficulty has precluded law professors from acknowledging. Because law professors attribute so much significance to the Founding, and because Bickel grounded the counter-majoritarian difficulty in it, the counter-majoritarian difficulty has held them in its thrall and distracted them from more constructive modes of inquiry. Once they recognize that the problem Bickel identified is not necessarily anchored in the birth of the nation, or is rooted only shakily there, perhaps the hold of the majoritarian paradigm over law professors will lessen. It may survive, though public choice theory and recent elections make me nearly as nervous about Congress as I am about the Rehnquist Court. But constitutional theorists might be more likely to worry about the tension between constitutionalism and democracy in the present, as I think they should, rather than taking the counter-majoritarian difficulty as a troublesome historical given.

I do not advocate neofederalism. Tribe is correct: history and constitutional theory are not one and the same. I despise the argument that because events have followed a certain pattern in the past, they must do so in the future. Yet history does confer legitimacy on constitutional theory, and in the two hundred–odd years since the Founding, the meaning of the Constitution has changed more than its twenty-six amendments suggest. The idea of amendment outside Article V, as adumbrated by Ackerman and Amar, sets us to thinking about when and why. Granted, I suspect the Founders took a less certain and rosy view of the people and popular sovereignty than Ackerman and Amar contend. As Rakove has pointed out, Ackerman glossed over those *Federalist* papers in which Madison "expressed deep pessimism about the consequences of mobilizing public opinion on constitutional issues—and which therefore weigh most heavily against the larger argument of his work." In his book on original meanings Rakove observes:

> Whereas other Federalists and even Anti-Federalists argued that a clear and lucid Constitution would enable the people to police the boundaries of power, Madison literally went out of his way in *Federalist* 49 and 50 to explain why the people should never act as arbiters of constitutional disputes through . . . "occasional" or "periodical appeals" to their authority. . . . Their judgment "could never be expected to turn on the true merits of the question itself." It would inevitably be connected with the spirit of preexisting parties, or of parties springing out of the question itself. Such appeals, if repeated, sap the very legitimacy of the Constitution. Equally important, the logic of Madison's entire theory of faction led to the conclusion that the most likely source of constitutional encroachment was the House of Representatives, where the people's impulses would be felt most quickly and powerfully.[82]

There are other problems with neofederalism. I am as nervous about popular sovereignty as I am about neorepublicanism. "If ever there were a fit candidate" for eligibility as one of Ackerman's constitutional amendments outside Article V, as Elizabeth Mensch and Alan Freeman said in 1989, it might be "the Nixon/Reagan redirection of the federal courts (from bottom to top)." As a legal liberal, I also like to believe the Founders hoped the Court would assume a "prophetic" role, in addition to a "preservationist" one. Yet neofederalism rattles the historical foundation on which Bickel rested the counter-majoritarian difficulty and his majoritarian paradigm. In this respect, Ackerman's and Amar's work represents an imaginative use of another discipline to shed new light on their own.[83]

But where will history lead members of the "Yale school"? It may simply take them toward a more professionalized and academic history. While Ackerman applauds the emphasis on popular sovereignty in Amar's work and commends his colleague for persuasively arguing "that the American Founders should not be read as insisting upon a monopoly for their rules of revision," he faults Amar for treating the debate over the legality of the Constitution "as if he were arguing before a hypothetical Supreme Court; he provides a document that resembles a legal brief seeking to assure the nonexistent justices that the Federalist end run was perfectly legal." To Ackerman, Amar's whole discussion of amending the Constitution outside Article V shows Amar has "his eyes firmly focused upon the eighteenth century and seeks to establish that the Founding generation had a clean and crisp answer." Ackerman writes:

> I deny that the *lawyerly* search for appropriate supplements to Article V should focus exclusively on the eighteenth century. It is more important to consider the ways that Americans moved beyond Article V to revise the Constitution during Reconstruction and the New Deal. These great historical precedents must be analyzed thoroughly by any serious legal effort to elaborate the modern American law of lawmaking. Thus far at least, Amar has not attempted such an analysis, but he seems to suppose that he may adopt eighteenth-century precedents to the twenty-first century without fundamental efforts by the American People to exercise their popular sovereignty. To this extent, Amar is far more *originalist than historicist* in his constitutional sensibility.[84]

What are we to make of this criticism? In one sense it is unfair. Ackerman may now celebrate the difference between legality and legitimacy, but it is he who, beginning with his 1984 Storrs Lectures, focused debate among law professors on the illegality of the Constitution.[85]

Further, it may be Ackerman who is more preoccupied with the lawyer's past, precedent, than Amar. Recognizing one legal constitutional convention to date, Amar leaves open the possibility of others in the future. Ackerman, however, sees one constitutional moment, whose illegality and legitimacy justified the two constitutional moments that followed and any more that may yet come. One possible explanation for the difference between the two scholars is that Ackerman's explanation may enable him to justify more precedents, insofar as the term relates to cases, and more constitutional moments. Ackerman, who dedicated one of his first books to "Alex Bickel, who taught me to disagree," may remain enough of a prudentialist to venerate precedent more than Amar, whose hero is Charles Black. Amar may care more about seeing that the people follow rules in exercising popular sovereignty than about whether the Court follows precedent. He may have no problem with retrospectively declaring cases wrong at the time they were decided. The desire to be able to say cases such as *Lochner* and perhaps *Plessy* were both soundly decided and soundly overruled may lead Ackerman, however, to say his three constitutional moments invalidated results reasonably reached. For example, Ackerman seeks to rehabilitate the judges of the period between Reconstruction and 1937, long portrayed as "blunderers or worse," by arguing that "the Constitution they were interpreting was importantly different from the transformed Constitution left to us by the New Deal."[86]

That would make Ackerman's approach historicist, though historicist for originalism's sake. Perhaps Ackerman is building historicism into originalism (which might bring us back to a noninterpretivism based on changed circumstances). Ackerman exhorts us to "try to see how it might have seemed *sensible* to judges in different eras to view the principles of constitutional liberty expressed at the Foundation and Reconstruction quite differently from the way we do today," while keeping an eye to continuity. "Though the languages of constitutional liberty have shifted over time from property and contract to privacy and equal opportunity, we should be trying to glimpse the deeper continuities."[87]

For my purposes, however, the language Ackerman uses to condemn Amar's inquiry into legality is most significant. Amar, he complains, is "lawyerly" and "originalist," not "historicist." Consider the irony: some historians who have long complained of lawyers' originalist approach to the past now do seem to recognize the inevitability of originalism and to be willing to help lawyers develop it for their tool-box. With their help, Ackerman and Amar could be on the verge of arriving at a theory of originalism historians might find credible as both scholars and activists. Yet precisely at this point law professors take to hurling the word *originalist* at each other as an insult. Sherry dismisses Ackerman as an originalist, Ackerman disparages Amar as an orginalist. Meanwhile Ackerman and Amar imply each other speaks for the field historians love to hate (along with sociology), political science. Once again, historians and law professors are talking past each other in their dialogue of the deaf. This time it is the historians who are trying to be pragmatic, the law professors who want to be academic. Given the intellectual history of both disciplines during the past generation, this scenario is hardly surprising. The price may be high.

LIBERALISM, HISTORY, AND LAW PROFESSORS

Our distance from the founders makes translation necessary;
what we have in common with them makes translation
worthwhile.
H. Jefferson Powell, "Rules for Originalists" (1987)

As a high school senior in 1970–71, I read Tom Wolfe's *Radical Chic.*
I recall laughing aloud at the description of wealthy, white New Yorkers
affirming the Black Panthers' struggle with shouts of "Right on!" I
owned a tie-dyed cashmere turtleneck, and I had a classmate and friend
who faithfully drove her Mercedes to SDS meetings. But rich people's
radicalism seemed ridiculous to me. "Limousine liberalism," however, a
recently coined and equally sarcastic reference to upper-class and upper-
middle-class liberals, made more sense. I came to maturity too late to
understand why liberals would have linked reform at home to globalism
abroad, and their commitment to the war in Vietnam antagonized me,
as it did so many of my generation. (I had supported Eugene McCarthy
in 1968, but was wearing a "little people for Humphrey" button by

November.) Further, it seemed obvious that liberalism was inherently conservative insofar as it made preserving capitalism its goal. Yet capitalism had been good to my family; as a Jew, I was brought up to give something back; liberalism was humorous about its own limitations; liberalism was on the defensive (as it has been ever since), and I liked underdogs. I decided that for me, domestic liberalism contained the right amounts of self-interest and self-sacrifice, idealism and realism, and I retain my faith in it still.[1]

To such a person, the Court was wonderful because of its embrace of equality and ousiders. When I attended law school in the mid-1970s, I thought it represented liberalism at its loftiest, a belief I continued to hold as a graduate student interested in reform movements. Certainly, the Warren Court's agenda had limits, but so did liberalism. All the hackneyed words used to describe the Constitution—*beacon, lighthouse, symbol*—reflected the role I thought the Court played in changing the meaning of the Constitution to spark social reform. Its success seemed less significant than the intensity of its effort.

For law professors with my politics, the Warren Court proved still more important. As Malcolm Feeley has said, the idea of a liberal and powerful Supreme Court "is functional for the legal profession, particularly the elite of the profession," including professors at leading law schools and federal judges. By promoting the idea "of extraordinarily powerful judges," who make law "a powerful agent of the good," they foster faith in "extraordinarily powerful lawyers, law professors, and law students" who fight injustice.[2]

If the Warren Court was more important for law professors than it was for me as a historian of liberalism, it was also more troublesome. In the years since 1954, both legal liberalism and the counter-majoritarian difficulty so worrisome to process theorists proved the starting points of constitutional theory. Whether or not one agreed with their premises, one had to take them into account. Robert Nagel has noticed that though no one can produce a satisfactory theory to justify contemporary judicial review, everyone loves judicial power. Even Robert Bork sought it so he could undo what he disliked about American society. Kenneth Karst's recent book *Law's Promise, Law's Expression: Visions of Power in the Politics of Race, Gender, and Religion* is a moving expression of a liberal law professor's continuing confidence in the Court's ability to bring about social change.[3]

There are also signs that the preoccupation with the Siamese twins of judicial power and counter-majoritarianism may be waning. While murmuring that the counter-majoritarian difficulty represents the wrong nerve center has suffused constitutional theory for the last four decades, some constitutional scholars have joined republican revivalists and neo-federalists in more aggressively exposing the problems with Bickel's majoritarian paradigm. For example, just as there may be reason to doubt legislatures are bastions of majoritarianism, so may there be reason to believe the Supreme Court has practiced majoritarianism.[4]

Yet the eclipse of the obsession with judicial power and counter-majoritarianism would not necessarily bode well for constitutional theory, which H. Jefferson Powell believes "has worked itself into a conceptual and moral quagmire from which it does not appear to have the resources to escape." In four decades, at least forty bright constitutional theorists have produced variations on two significant themes—process theory and interpretivism. Neither can promise to make judicial decision-making principled or reconcilable with contemporary democracy.[5]

Nor would it necessarily follow that faith in *Brown* and a vision of the Supreme Court as the great engine of social reform so integral to legal liberalism are still justified. Like the critical legal scholars of the 1970s, critical race theorist Giradeau Spann declared in 1993 that the "veiled majoritarianism" of the Supreme Court has precluded it from protecting the interests of minorities and has "perpetuate[d] the subordination of racial minorities for majority gain." At the same time, Elizabeth Mensch and Alan Freeman condemned *Roe* as "legally problematic at best, sociologically inaccurate, and politically disastrous." Arguing that the legalization of abortion "was happening anyway (albeit more gradually)," they scored "*Roe*'s private 'rights' formulation of the issue" for abruptly "rendering moral/religious debate irrelevant for purposes of public policy." The following year, Robin West damned "our habitual reliance on courts" and maintained that "progressive understandings of the Fourteenth Amendment do not lend themselves to judicial enforcement." Insisting that "[w]e have, in effect, alienated the responsibility for public morality to the courts," she urged the invigoration of "nonconstitutional moral public discourse. . . . The key, of course, is to create a progressive Congress, and behind it a progressive citizenry." That may be practical. In a July 1995 *New York Times* article entitled "Farewell to the Old Order in the Court: The Right Goes Activist and the Center Is a Void," Linda Greenhouse observed that the current Court includes "no liberal in the mold of Justices Thurgood Marshall and William Brennan, Jr. who both retired in the early 1990's and who sought to use the Court as an engine of social change." Ronald Collins and David Skover made a compelling argument that, given the current Supreme Court, liberal legal scholars should spend less time dreaming about the Warren years and trying to justify federal judicial review, and more time thinking about national and state reform legislation, state constitutional law and common law, and liberating liberal theory from its fixation on individual rights consciousness.[6]

The obsession with *Brown* may be equally misplaced. Though historians have long emphasized that the civil rights movement started before *Brown* and that *Brown* represented the first time in the Court's history that it had asserted a constitutional right, while delaying its exercise, law professors have treated the case as the spark that kindled the civil rights movement as well as constitutional theory. Even process theorists venerated *Brown*. Now a new anthology on critical race theory opens with one of its most eloquent advocates announcing that Alexander Bickel's 1969 prediction of *Brown*'s irrelevance has come true.[7]

Certainly, as the *New York Times* notices, *Brown* is no longer "sacred." If Justice Thomas has his way, we may be headed back toward separate but equal. As long as there are no discriminatory inequalities in allocation of resources, *de facto* school segregation "does not constitute a continuing harm after the end of *de jure* segregation," he said in his concurrence in *Missouri* v. *Jenkins*. " 'Racial isolation' itself is not a harm; only state-enforced segregation is. After all, if separation itself is a harm, and if integration is the only way that blacks can achieve a proper education then there must be something inferior about blacks. Under this theory, segregation injures blacks because blacks, when left on their own, cannot achieve." To Thomas, "that conclusion is the result of a jurisprudence based upon a theory of black inferiority."[8]

While Earl Warren spins in his grave at the low esteem in which some of his successors may hold his Court's precious property, *Brown*'s stock may also be sinking in the law school world. "[I]ntegrationism has failed to help African-Americans to achieve progress in this society," critical race theorist Alex Johnson declared in 1993. The "decision in *Brown* v. *Board of Education* was a mistake." Young constitutional law professors raised in the shadow of a conservative Court, trained in other disciplines, and unencumbered by cls baggage have also called *Brown* into question, saying the imperatives of the postwar American political economy and the cold war made *Brown* an easy case for the Court. Michael Klarman's celebrated 1994 "backlash" thesis, which gains support from a new biography of George Wallace, suggests that "*Brown* was indirectly responsible for the landmark civil rights legislation of the mid-1960s by catalyzing southern resistance to racial change." Propelling "southern politics far to the right" and causing race to be "exalted over all other issues," *Brown* created a political environment in which elected officials used any means to resist racial change. "The predictable consequence was a series of violent confrontations between white supremacist law enforcement officials and generally nonviolent demonstrators, which provoked an outcry from national television audiences, leading Congress and the President to intervene with landmark civil rights legislation."[9]

In some ways, the current generation may threaten legal liberalism and *Brown* more than other legal scholars ever did. Like legal liberals, for example, critical legal scholars argued from theory. Gerald Rosenberg, who has a law degree yet identifies with political scientists, uses empirical evidence to argue that Supreme Court decisions such as *Brown* generally played no significant role in producing major social change. Acknowledging that "Supreme Court decisions sometimes have symbolic importance," Klarman, who possesses a doctorate in history but identifies with process theorists of the Constitution, uses history to go even further, when he contends that "transformative racial change was bound to come to the United States regardless of *Brown*." In the short run, and perversely, according to Klarman, "*Brown* probably did accelerate that change" by creating hostility in the South to civil rights.[10]

Certainly the road from treating *Brown* as "paradigmatic event" to presenting it as the jurisprudential analogue of the Tet Offensive is long. Born in 1959, just five years after Sunstein, Klarman may be the precursor to a new generation of constitutional law professors. If 1937,

1954, and 1973 were the pivotal moments for the last three generations of constitutional law professors—the Wechslers, the Covers and Michelmans, the Sunsteins—what will be the decisive moment for members of this new generation?[11]

Will they lose the faith in judicial power as an effective force of social change, a belief that allowed their intellectual fathers and grandfathers to unite behind *Brown?* Will they give up, as Rosenberg has exhorted them to do, "the endless attempt to canonize a case"? Will they conclude the Court is largely irrelevant to reform? William Eskridge and Philip Frickey began their *Harvard Law Review* "Foreword," "Law as Equilibrium," by observing that with "the confirmation of Justice Stephen Breyer to the United States Supreme Court, the legal process school has quietly attained what every Supreme Court litigator seeks: a majority on the Court" and by maintaining that "legal process theorizing about public law has enjoyed a renaissance." Though Eskridge and Frickey justified *Brown* by suggesting that the Court was simply fulfilling its role of preserving law's equilibrium by enforcing "national norms against recalcitrant or slow-moving states," other process theorists may prove indifferent to the case. For example, if Klarman has his way, we have a process theory drained of legal liberalism that makes little effort to defend *Brown.* That is a pity: Even if *Brown* was easy and did spur a "backlash" against civil rights, it is important as a symbol of commitment to equality and outsiders. The prospect of Klarman's *Brown* frightens me, as it must legal liberals at law schools who see *Brown* as foundational and derive a sense of purpose from it.[12]

That fear, I have suggested, animates the republican revival in constitutional theory. I have argued that the republican revival represents an effort to enlist history and the Founders in the service of legitimating judicial review by a liberal judiciary. I have also maintained that the neofederalism of Bruce Ackerman and Ahkil Amar may offer a better way of responding to scholars such as Bickel who mocked Madison's majoritarianism. But though history can suggest that the countermajoritarian dilemma may not be rooted in the Constitution because the Founders may have hoped judicial review would serve as yet another instrument of popular sovereignty, history can never do as much as law professors want. Constitutional historian Leonard Levy has made an intriguing proposal: "If history is so crucial to constitutional interpretation, at least with respect to questions that have a historical dimension, Congress should create the Office of Historian to the Supreme Court. The official historian and his staff would tell the Court not how to decide cases but how to answer questions of history asked by the Justices." Given the nuanced, tentative, and subjunctive shape of historians' explanations, how often would the official historian be able to give an answer that did not start with "maybe"?[13]

Still, there are times when history does help. For example, if it can assist in diminishing the counter-majoritarian difficulty, I believe it makes sense for constitutional theorists to pursue historical inquiry. Further, there is no sign originalism is abating. In fact, a renewed offensive may have begun. For years, originalism has foundered *because* it could not offer a persuasive explanation for the seminal case of modern constitutional law, *Brown*. In the May 1995 issue of the *Virginia Law Review*, Michael McConnell, a respected conservative who has produced important originalist studies, has written the most interesting originalist defense of *Brown* advanced yet—one cited by Justice Thomas in his *Missouri* v. *Jenkins* concurrence. If McConnell's account of *Brown* is judged successful, originalism may be revitalized. Meanwhile the May 1995 *Columbia Law Review* features William Treanor explaining how the Founders understood the takings clause, and the *New York Times* shows Chief Justice Rehnquist and Justices Scalia, O'Connor, and Thomas costumed in clothes the Founders might have worn.[14]

In this setting, I have come to appreciate the value of pragmatism in constitutional theory. To be sure, its "counsel to 'be contextual' merely urges us to do what we cannot help doing anyway." Still, it is good for lawyers, who are notoriously acontextual, to be reminded that they are inevitably contextual. Besides exploring the prospect of realizing liberalism through legislatures, state constitutional law, and common law, and revitalizing it by taming its obsession with rights consciousness, I believe pragmatism must continue to find a place for grand constitutional theory. Granted, solving the counter-majoritarian dilemma, traditionally the focus of such constitutional theory, now might only serve to justify activism by a conservative court. The pragmatist would recognize, however, that the counter-majoritarian dilemma has been an important intellectual problem for law professors and that simply telling them to drop it will not ensure that they do so. Further, if the wheel turns and an activist liberal Court committed to making law a tool of social reform emerges, it would probably be able to work more effectively if it is not dogged by the counter-majoritarian bogeyman.[15]

Pragmatists might also observe that law professors often turn to history when historical political theory would serve them better. As I have shown, the communitarian genie came out of the bottle in a variety of disciplines ranging from sociology to history in the 1980s. Historical political theory might imply that communitarianism and neorepublicanism are grounded in a misunderstanding of liberalism and republicanism. For example, in large part because historians have repeatedly pointed to the militarism, sexism and patriarchy at the heart of classical republicanism, republican revivalists in law have largely stopped describing themselves as republican. They now prefer to speak of their "liberal republicanism" or their "republicanism of rights." Historical political theory can give them liberal republicanism or republican liberalism—or anything else. Instead of ceding classical liberalism to libertarians, why not adopt Stephen Holmes's reading of classical liberal texts, which stresses "the compatability between classical liberalism and modern welfare politics"? Instead of assuming that "liberal" means "bourgeois," why not rely on Steven Dvoretz's case for "the theistic Locke," who believed in "private, individualistic thought as a requisite for salvation," as against the "bourgeois Locke"? Dvoretz contends that, like political theorists ranging from Leo Strauss on the right to C. B. Macpherson on the left, Pocock took "Locke at his *worst*: the possessive individualist, the apologist for bourgeois excess, the corrupt prophet of the 'spirit of capitalism.' Lockean liberalism thus seemed to be the ideological source of a serious modern problem: the egoistic commercialization of American life." Instead of treating liberalism as antithetical to virtue, why not rely on Richard Sinopoli's demonstration that the "particular liberal statesmen who wrote *The Federalist* were clearly concerned with civic virtue and offered a compelling conception of it"? Alternatively, instead of assuming republicanism was antithetical to rights, why not follow Michael Zuckert in reading those two "sponsors" of classical republicanism, Trenchard and Gordon, as having fused Locke with republicanism to promote a "natural rights republicanism"? Where historians pick apart paradigms, historical political theorists build and remodel them. Political theory may have more potential to do what law professors want, and I suspect that like Michelman, many backed into history via political theory anyway. If political theorists can make Isaiah Berlin into someone who undercuts the Enlightenment project, just imagine what they can do with Madison![16]

Perhaps, however, legal scholars turned to history because political theory seemed as malleable as constitutional law. If political theorists could come up with so many plausible readings, how much authority could political theory have? And who serves better as talking head—Stephen Holmes or James Madison? In constitutional interpretation, Madison trumps everyone—which is why the pragmatist sometimes gives in to the temptation to dress him as the prototype of John Dewey. Therefore many law professors have surrendered to the allure of anchoring theory in history and especially the Founding—both of which they have sometimes assumed were unmediated by historians. The pragmatist might decide that though historical political theory appears more compatible with constitutional theory than does constitutional history, law professors will sometimes dress up political theory as history or turn to history for purely rhetorical reasons. On other occasions, the motivation may be less cynical; H. Jefferson Powell has eloquently observed, "[o]ur distance from the founders makes translation necessary; what we have in common with them makes translation worthwhile."[17]

Pragmatism would therefore recognize history and originalism as sometime building blocks. To quote one pragmatist; "Although originalism is unsatisfying, its rivals have also been subject to withering criticism." Because we are stuck with originalism, the pragmatist would accept it on occasion. Pragmatism would emphasize, however, that history is only one potential tool among many.[18]

If originalism is a valuable form of constitutional interpretation, if history does confer authority on constitutional interpretation, it matters what historians think about the Founding, and law professors should pay more heed to historians. Neither history nor political theory can ever make Madison the talking head. Like pragmatic hermeneutics, pragmatic originalism must recognize that historians do interpret and that their interpretations, like those of political theorists, are subject to change. As Katharine Bartlett puts it, "the past, like the present, is always in flux and part of the process of negotiation about who we are, what matters, and what constitutes improvement. It is always 'before us,' not behind us, and is something 'one can never predict." Whether the just compensation clause of the Fifth Amendment was drafted by believers in the "bourgeois Locke" has obvious implications for an originalist's "take" on takings jurisprudence. Allowing for time lags between disciplines, the legal scholar in the early 1980s might well assume Madison did personify Lockean liberalism, as William Treanor did. He or she might well conclude, on the basis of historical scholarship during the next decade, that liberalism and republicanism coexisted at the Founding, as Treanor did also. That approach does not negate the originalist enterprise. It is sophisticated originalism.[19]

It is also good interdisciplinary scholarship. Such work neither treats other disciplines as window dressing nor is absorbed by them. Surely the possibility of developing a more constructive relationship between law professors and scholars in other fields deserves further exploration. If a little interdisciplinary scholarship is dangerous, though, too much is, as well. I believe law professors should pursue and be wary of interdisciplinarity. Those who turn to other disciplines should remember why they did so. Law professors are not paid twice as much as historians to dismiss the work of other academic lawyers as insufficiently originalist and overly historicist. The task is to inquire how work in other disciplines can improve legal discourse. For example, historians' participation in the abortion cases suggests that it is possible for law professors to "use" other disciplines more sensitively than they have in the past *and* to enlist history in support of law—if they want to do so.

But do they want to? It is not clear that lawyers want to make better use of other disciplines. This book has explored the breakdown of agreement about the function, purpose, and appropriate audience of legal scholarship, a collapse of consensus about the community to which law professors belong and for which they write. I have addressed this issue by focusing on the intellectual history of legal liberalism and recent constitutional theory. I have tried to explain how law professors came to consider integration with the university necessary and how membership in the various communities of the university fragmented the community of legal scholars.

Currently there is a backlash against interdisciplinarity. It is not just the word itself that is considered unfortunate. Too often, the tale of cross-fertilization between disciplines turns out to be "the story of the mutual enlightenment that never happened." Interdisciplinary borrowings rarely please the lenders. It is fashionable to derogate scholars who appropriate "useful" theories in other disciplines for paying no attention to the context in which those theories were advanced or to their current standing. In fact, some scholars have noted that theories become popular elsewhere just as they are about to be banished from their first homes. This book responds to the recent call for more histories of disciplines, focusing on disciplinary boundaries. In many fields, interdisciplinary work has both caused and reflected internal disorder. I maintain that in law, along with the breakdown of political consensus on law faculties, interdisciplinary scholarship has helped cause and reflect a crisis in legal liberalism.[20]

To lawyers, professors, and students in Britain, our law schools are enviable. Though American law professors have historically lacked the prestige or influence of their German counterparts, they have certainly led better lives than their English ones. In his 1994 manifesto *Blackstone's Tower: The English Law School,* William Twining acknowledges American law schools have their problems. He perceptively observes that in "all Western societies law schools are typically caught in a tug of war between three aspirations: to be accepted as full members of the community of higher learning; to be relatively detached, but nonetheless engaged, critics and censors of law in society; and to be service-institutions for a profession which is itself caught between noble ideals, lucrative service of powerful interests and unromantic cleaning up of society's messes." Twining considers such tensions healthy, and he calls for modernizing British legal education by accelerating "assimilation of law schools into the academy," transforming law schools into "multipurpose centres of learning," and making the law school "the legal system's, as opposed to the legal profession's House of Intellect." For Twining, interdisciplinary work is a boon: "neither legal education nor legal scholarship can afford to be self-contained."[21]

At home, the expansion of legal scholarship into other disciplines looks less inviting. For legal liberals are not the only ones who fret. The turn to history by legal liberals in order to justify activism by a liberal Court is a subset of a larger crisis involving the nature of legal scholarship.

"If judges make law, so do commentators," Edward Corwin said in 1920. Thirty years ago, most law professors were doctrinal scholars who made law. By picking apart the decisions of the Supreme Court and lower courts, before which they might also argue cases for a legal community broadly conceived to include judges, practitioners, and colleagues, law professors had the opportunity most academics lacked to affect society. They were public intellectuals with practical expertise. As recently as 1975, Robert Gordon said that "law teachers think of themselves as lawyers as much as professors, and usually more so." Their scholarship remained largely doctrinal, and it may have influenced the Court.[22]

Today everything seems different. Doubtless, many law professors continue to till the fields of doctrine, to argue cases, and to consider it their mission to train the young to practice law. Yet the law reviews suggest a possibility that the vicissitudes of legal liberalism may themselves be part of a larger crisis of the law school. At the 1993 annual Association of American Law Schools meeting, participants spoke of living in a "tension-filled moment" of the intellectual history of the legal academy.[23]

Whatever their politics, many law professors do appear troubled. Larry Alexander talks of the "identity crisis" facing the "typical lawyer-teacher," while Steven Winter announces that the entire "legal academy is experiencing a state of epistemological crisis." Mary Ann Glendon blames the defeat of Lani Guinier's nomination as assistant attorney general on "a legal academic establishment" that shows "growing disdain for the practical aspects of law [and] a zany passion for novelty." Julius Getman grouses that whereas once young law professors at elite schools responded to pressure "by developing writing blocks, currently they are more likely to write pretentious and meaningless articles." Civility, never at a premium among law professors, has declined. Richard Posner gives counsel, which may not be tongue-in-cheek, to those submitting articles to law reviews: "Write in a superior, arrogant, dismissive, sarcastic manner [and] insinuate that only a fool, or a person untutored in the mysteries of the law would disagree with you." Traditional and nontraditional academic lawyers attack each other's work. Pierre Schlag sums up the atmosphere: "the mainstream scholars rage," and the "fancy scholars" are "livid." According to Robert Post, "Traditional legal scholarship is being challenged on the one side by the emergence of a new form of external scholarship, and it is being undermined on the other by the collapse of any internal consensus as to the purposes and function of law."[24]

Ironically, law professors today are publishing more at a time when they seem to think their work matters less. Some assail all legal scholarship, whatever its form, for its prescriptiveness, or "irreducible normativity." "How does a text that is in fact nothing more than a rather mediocre amicus brief come to be held up as a paradigm of legal scholarship?" they ask. They propose that "all those *normativos* . . . hold a garage sale" for their "normative manuscripts about love, compassion, equity, fairness, and so on, nearly ready to be mailed out, with the usual, predictable normative letter explaining why, dear editor, this article is the most normative of all and worthy of your esteemed pages." Others inveigh against student-edited law reviews, blaming the editors for the "sorry state" of legal scholarship. They claim "general agreement" that "[p]ublished articles lack originality, are boring, too long, too numerous, and have too many footnotes, which also are boring and too long." They are filled with "lawreviewese." A notable understatement of the president of the *Harvard Law Review* remains appropos: "The *Review* has yet to field a team of Hemingways."[25]

Though many legal scholars apparently assume their work goes unnoticed, this assessment may be unduly grim. Even Pierre Schlag has said that law professors' normative work may still affect law practice. A survey published in the 1992 *Stanford Law Review* concluded: "[A]pproximately 54% of professors [in the sample] said that they had consulted law reviews more than 25 times in the last six months, compared to less than 3% of attorneys and 6.4% of the judges." But only 18.3 percent of judges and 33.6 percent of attorneys reported that they had not consulted law reviews at all in the past six months. "In sum, professors read law reviews frequently and use them primarily for academic purposes, while attorneys and judges read law reviews less frequently and use them primarily for more practical purposes." It is possible that the survey's designers were overly optimistic. I recently showed my father the phrase *shanda fur de Goyim* in the text of one of Mark Tushnet's essays. In a footnote, Tushnet explained: "The phrase describes a scandalous situation within the Jewish community about which it would be a shame for the non-Jewish community to learn. Roughly, although it loses something in this version, it means 'Don't wash dirty linen in public.' " Remembering his own brushes with the profession's anti-Semitism, my father smiled at seeing Yiddish in a law review. Then he told me that "lawyers don't read law reviews anymore." The implication was clear: law reviews have become so useless to practitioners that professors can use their articles to give Yiddish lessons instead of to elaborate doctrine.[26]

Perhaps only loyal friends and contemptuous colleagues do read legal scholars' articles. Long before his death in 1994, even Erwin Griswold, once Harvard Law School's most devoted dean, a man who personally met ninety-five presidents of the *Harvard Law Review* and wrote "pithy comments to the president upon receipt of each issue," may have stopped "drumming his fingers on his desk waiting for a copy of the latest edition [of the *Harvard Law Review*] to be delivered." Attorneys may still glance at the reviews, but they do not like what they see. Professor Kenneth Lasson's biting attack on the pretentiousness of legal scholarship in the *Harvard Law Review*, "Scholarship Amok: Excesses in the Pursuit of Truth and Tenure," elicited rare raves from practitioners. Consider the extraordinary response to Judge Harry Edwards's 1992 article, "The Growing Disjunction between Legal Education and the Legal Profession," with its thesis that "law schools and law firms are moving in opposite directions" and that the legal academy is filled with " 'law professors' hired from graduate schools, wholly lacking in legal experience or training, who use the law school as a bully pulpit from which to pour scorn upon the legal profession." It inspired a symposium on whether contemporary legal education has in fact changed and whether change is desirable.[27]

Few law professors would mind abandonment by "brain dead" practitioners. They do clearly fear they no longer influence the judges. Probably most judges do not consult law reviews now, but how does one know? Does one follow Richard Posner in measuring reputation by citation? Even if judges do read law reviews, can they follow the "esoteric and interdisciplinary character of much recent constitutional theory"? Even if judges do understand it, is that cause for celebration? Challenging the view that law professors no longer impress judges, William Fisher has argued that legal scholars have influenced the Supreme Court's interpretation of the Bill of Rights. According to Fisher, "the combination of the diversity of the professors' proposals and the Court's tendency to pick up bits and pieces from each has contributed to the jumbled, intellectually unsatisfying character of current doctrine." Fisher concludes that we should be "dismayed to find in Supreme Court opinions shards of the various seemingly incommensurable normative theories developed by law professors."[28]

Legal scholars have long worried about who reads what they write, but today they have an especially severe case of "legalarboraphobia (fear of . . . a law review article falling in an empty forest)." Outsiders are sent mixed signals. On the one hand, they are informed that the Constitution is America's civil religion. On the other, they see the professors who make such declarations frantically reaching out to other disciplines. Charles Collier observes that "wholly gratuitous discussions of Nietzsche, Saussure, Derrida, and Foucault are now de rigueur in law review articles about section 1983, contract doctrine, poverty law, and even Uruguayan prisons."[29]

At a time when both the Prince of Wales and Pope John Paul II have discovered postmodern rhetoric, we might expect law professors to embrace disciplines which do so too. There is something deeper to academic lawyers' frenzied interdisciplinary work, however, than their desire for trendiness. As one of them says, "legal scholars are desperately groping for an external, non-legal source of legitimacy or authority."[30]

Some law professors would say they are not finding it and that law remains an autonomous discipline. They would apply my observation about most lawyers' legal history to legal scholarship and education as a whole: the more it changes, the more it stays the same. The "law student who fell asleep in 1963 and awoke in 1993 would not be astonished by his new surrounds," Stanford Law School Dean Paul Brest maintains. "If he had fallen asleep holding a law review—the soporific power was no weaker in those days—the nature and language of some of the articles would bewilder him, but he would find much that was familiar." John Schlegel grieves: "Until one takes the 'and' out of 'law and . . . ' there is no point in talking." Pierre Schlag grumbles that "when traditional legal thought goes traveling (in the footnotes) through the university, it never seems to encounter much of anything except itself. The interdisciplinary travels of traditional legal thought are like a bad

European vacation: the substance is Europe, but the form is Mc-
Donald's, Holiday Inns, American Express." Perhaps that is universal.
"Despite the recent millenarian calls to interdisciplinarity, disciplines will
prove remarkably resilient and difficult to kill," Stanley Fish predicts.[31]

Nevertheless, the interdisciplinary gropings of law professors worry
some of the humanists that the legal scholars most admire. To put it
colloquially, the humanists have responded: "Don't fool around with
the rule of law and justice." Richard Rorty cautioned one adoring law
professor: "I must confess that I tremble at the thought of Barthian
readings in law schools. I suspect that civilization reposes on a lot of
people who take the normal practices of the discipline with full 'realistic'
seriousness." We also encounter postmodernism's prophet Jean-François
Lyotard "arguing that 'consensus has become an outmoded and suspect
value' but then adding, rather surprisingly, that since 'justice as a value
is neither outmoded nor suspect' (how it could remain such a universal,
untouched by the diversity of language games, he does not tell us), we
'must arrive at an idea and practice of justice that is not linked to that
of consensus.' "[32]

And we find English professor Jennifer Wicke, the keynote speaker
at a conference on postmodernism and the law, cautioning that "these
bedfellows could make strange politics." The "more than thirty-one fla-
vors of postmodernism," she warns, all promise indigestion for law. According to Wicke, in postmodernism "the legal text ceases to emanate
from an origin, point of timeless authority or as a singular transmis-
sion." Postmodernism insists that "[l]anguage games are all that are
left," and it highlights the schizophrenic existence of the individual who
lives in multiple worlds. Those characteristics endanger law's integrity
and potential for social change. Postmodern analysis may clash "with
the need to deploy a language of the legal subject, in other words, a
language of rights and a language of cultural identity, in securing cultural justice."[33]

Wicke's warning may only increase the appeal of postmodernism for
many law professors. What is law if not "Word-Magic"? Who is the
law professor if not a schizophrenic, even pathologically so? As the gap
between the law school and the university narrows, that between the
law school and the profession may widen. Yet for all the disjunction
between the legal academy and the profession, that between law profes-

sor and student is greater. University legal education has never prepared students for law practice. Even nearly thirty years ago, as Thomas Bergin saw, the law teacher was "a man divided against himself," a victim of the belief "that he can be, at one and the same time, an authentic academic and a trainer of Hessians" who practice law.[34]

Today that schizophrenia is still more intense. Bergin spoke at a time when most law professors agreed that an "authentic academic" did doctrinal analysis. Now, however, as doctrinalists battle with those who would make the law school "a colonial outpost of the graduate school," doctrinal work may be dismissed as unprestigious and anti-intellectual. Law professors contest the very definition of authenticity. Further, though its connection with the Supreme Court has always made the work of academic lawyers more overtly political than that of scholars in other disciplines, the legal academy became polarized in the 1980s. Nor is today's law professor "divided against himself"—more likely, he or she feels fragmented.[35]

Most law professors have learned postmodernism from other disciplines and have been speaking it for a long time. In fact, one scholar who surveyed postmodernism's influence concluded: "Legal theory is an arena where post-modern views of epistemology and method have created one of the most severe crises." Law professors have been speaking other languages as well. Some believe "there is much to be gained by introducing Barthian readings into the law schools." Perhaps we cannot expect academic lawyers to remain at the barricades valiantly holding culture together, while those outside the law schools pick it apart. But it would be unfortunate if law professors desert the barricades just as academics in other fields, such as historians, begin to show signs of appreciating what legal scholars are doing, and wanting to help.[36]

NOTES

1. I emphasize that I mean "political liberalism" not in the sense that John Rawls used the phrase in his book *Political Liberalism* (1993), but in the admittedly amorphous sense it has been used by politicians and political historians in recent American political discourse. My principal purpose is not to examine whether political liberalism possesses what Ronald Dworkin would characterize as a "constitutive morality." Dworkin, *A Matter of Principle* 184 (1985). Insofar as political liberalism has a "constitutive morality," this characteristic seems to me to be best articulated by William Galston, *Liberal Purposes: Goods, Virtues, and Diversity in the Liberal State* (1991); but I am a political historian, not a political theorist.

   When I speak of classical liberalism, I refer to Enlightenment liberalism. Here I draw my definition from Rogers Smith, who emphasizes: "Liberalism's most distinctive feature is . . . its insistence that government should be limited so as to free individuals to undertake private as well as public pursuits of happiness, even if this option erodes public spiritedness in practice. While this characteristic is often traced to an inherent methodological, psychological, or philosophical individualism in liberalism, for the early liberals it was at bottom a normative political commitment, an espousal of a society that would promote some public and personal goods and not others. As a political ideology at least, . . . liberalism rested not so much on the vulnerable philosophic premises that liberals reshuffled freely in different contexts as on the basic ends that they shared, despite their important differences over relative priorities, immediate means and ultimate justifications. . . . To a surprising degree early liberals conceived of popular governance, religious tolerance, the rule of law, and other forms of liberty only as means to their basic goals. They also did not equate liberalism with fair legal and constitutional procedures, or with the pursuit of the maximum freedom imaginable, as many liberals do. Instead, liberals originally held that only a specific and limited conception of liberty deserved to be an end in itself. And they were attached to other specific ends, for which liberty was a means—essentially peace, prosperity through economic growth, and intellectual progress." Smith, *Liberalism and American Constitutional Law* 14–15 (1985).

2. "Those specific social reforms" is from Gerald Rosenberg, *The Hollow Hope: Can Courts Bring about Social Change?* 4 (1991) (emphasis in the original). See also *Brown* v. *Board of Education,* 347 U.S. 483 (1954) (*Brown I*) and *Brown* v. *Board of Education,* 349 U.S. 294 (1955) (*Brown II*). Unless otherwise indicated, all references to *"Brown"* are to *Brown I.* I discuss some different, contemporary interpretations of *Brown* in the epilogue. Jackson is quoted in Rosenberg, *Hollow Hope,* at 1. The judge was Stephen Reinhardt in, "Guess Who's Not Coming to Dinner!!" 91 *Michigan Law Review* 1175, 1181 (1993). The law school dean was Gene Nichol of the University of Colorado in "Constitutional Judgment," 91 *Michigan Law Review* 1107, 1117 (1993). "[T]he quest for racial justice" is from Ira Lupu, "Intergenerationalism and Constitutional Law," 85 *Michigan Law Review* 1390, 1396 (1987).

3. Robert Cover, "The Origins of Judicial Activism in the Protection of Minorities," 91 *Yale Law Journal* 1287, 1316 (1982) ("paradigmatic event"); Steven Keeva, "Demanding More Justice," 80 *American Bar Association Journal* 46, 48 (August 1994) (quoting Howard; emphasis in the original); Mary Ann Glendon, *A Nation of Lawyers: How the Crisis in the Legal Profession Is Transforming American Society* 155 (1994) ("a sign"); C. Vann Woodward, *Thinking Back: The Perils of Writing History* 84 (1986); Woodward, *The Strange Career of Jim Crow* 149 (1957 ed.).

4. Owen Fiss, "A Life Lived Twice," 100 *Yale Law Journal* 1117, 1118 (1991) (emphasis added).

5. Rosenberg, *Hollow Hope,* at xi, 338; Lillian De Vier, "Judicial Restraint: An Argument for Institutional Design," 17 *Harvard Journal of Law and Public Policy* 7, 8 (1994); Gerald Rosenberg, "Hollow Hopes and Other Aspirations: A Reply to Feeley and McCann," 17 *Law and Social Inquiry* 761, 776 (1992). For a canvassing of the literature on the relationship between law and social change as of the 1980s, see Carl Auerbach, "The Relation of Legal Systems to Social Change," 1980 *Wisconsin Law Review* 1227; Steve Bachmann, "Lawyers, Law, and Social Change," 13 *New York University Review of Law and Social Change* 1 (1984–85).

6. Ronald Brownstein, "4 Decades Later, Legacy of Brown vs. Topeka Is Cloudy," *Los Angeles Times,* May 15, 1994, A1, A15; Cass Sunstein, 1994 Tanner Lectures on Human Values (a portion of Sunstein's first lecture has been published under the title "Incompletely Theorized Agreements," 108 *Harvard Law Review* 1733 [1995]); Richard Posner, "Legal Scholarship Today," 45 *Stanford Law Review* 1647, 1652 (1993).

7. See John Brigham, *The Cult of the Court* (1987). For an excellent introduction to the literature that question has spawned, see, in addition to Rosenberg's *Hollow*

Hope, the bibliographic sources cited in Malcolm Feeley's review of *Hollow Hope,* "Hollow Hopes, Flypapers, and Metaphors," 17 *Law and Social Inquiry* 745 (1992); Michael McCann, "Reform Litigation on Trial," id. at 715.

8. *Lochner v. New York,* 198 U.S. 45 (1905). Quotations are from Herbert Packer, Book Review, *New York Times,* March 1, 1970, 3, 3; William La Piana, "Thoughts and Lives," 39 *New York Law School Review* 607, 634 (1995); George Braden, "The Search for Objectivity in Constitutional Law," 57 *Yale Law Journal* 571, 572 n.5 (1948). Historians have challenged law professors' tendency to understand *Lochner* as a prototype of the kind of decisions the Court handed down at the turn of the century. See, e.g., Michael Les Benedict, "Laissez-Faire and Liberty: A Re-Evaluation of the Meaning and Origins of Laissez-Faire Constitutionalism," 3 *Law and History Review* 293 (1985).

9. Alexander Bickel, *The Least Dangerous Branch: The Supreme Court at the Bar of Politics* 16 (1962).

10. David Garrow, *Liberty and Sexuality: The Right to Privacy and the Making of Roe v. Wade* 342, 379, 386, 591 (1994); *Roe v. Wade,* 410 U.S. 113 (1973).

11. Pamela Karlan, "Harry A. Blackmun," 108 *Harvard Law Review* 13, 14 (1994).

12. John Hart Ely, "The Wages of Crying Wolf: A Comment on *Roe v. Wade,*" 92 *Yale Law Journal* 920, 947, 935–37 (1973). Emphasis in the original.

13. Id. at 926; Stephen Presser, *Recapturing the Constitution: Race, Religion, and Abortion Reconsidered* 5, 288 (1994); Guido Calabresi, "What Clarence Thomas Knows," *New York Times,* July 28, 1991, section 4, at 15, quoted in Owen Fiss, "Thurgood Marshall," 105 *Harvard Law Review* 49, 51 (1991).

14. Ronald Collins and David Skover, "The Future of Liberal Legal Scholarship," 87 *Michigan Law Review* 189, 189 (1988).

15. Suzanna Sherry, "Responsible Republicanism: Educating for Citizenship," 62 *University of Chicago Law Review* 131, 133 (1995). For a summary of the diverging views about the constituency of republican revivalists, see Miriam Galston, "Taking Aristotle Seriously: Republican-Oriented Legal Theory and the Moral Foundation of Deliberative Democracy," 82 *California Law Review* 331, 333–35, 340–41 (1994). The group of individuals I identify as republican revivalists may seem small, but it is almost the size of the number of individuals Ackerman pointed to in the first attempt at identifying a "Legal Process" school. Ackerman included twelve individuals in the Legal Process School: Alexander Bickel, Ronald Dworkin, Paul Freund, Lon Fuller, Henry Hart, Louis Jaffe, Edward H. Levi, Karl Llewellyn, Herbert Packer, Albert Sacks, Harry Wellington, and Herbert Wechsler. Bruce Ackerman, "Law and the Modern Mind," 103 *Daedalus* 123, 128 n.26 (winter 1974).

16. Linda Greenhouse, "Blowing the Dust off the Constitution That Was," *New York Times,* May 28, 1995, section 4, at 1 (discussing *United States v. Lopez,* 115 S.Ct. 1624 [1995]).

17. See Alexander Macmillan, *Hymns of the Church: A Companion to the Hymnary of the United Church of Canada* 196–97 (1945). I am grateful to Allen Guelzo for this citation.

18. Carol Rose, "The Ancient Constitution vs. The Federalist Empire: Anti-Federalism from the Attack on 'Monarchism' to Modern Localism," 84 *Northwestern University Law Review* 74, 83 n.38 (1989).

1. William Fisher, Morton Horwitz, and Thomas Reed, *American Legal Realism* xiii–xv, 3–4, 9, 26 (1993); Oliver Wendell Holmes, Book Review, 14 *American Law Review* 234 (1880) (Langdell as "theologian"). See also Joseph Singer, "Legal Realism Now," 76 *California Law Review* 465 (1988); Morton Horwitz, Book Review, 75 *Journal of American History* 299 (1988). Both are reviews of my book, *Legal Realism at Yale, 1927–1960* (1986), in which I downplayed the originality of realism. As critical legal scholars, Singer and Horwitz have a stake in defining realism broadly. My own concern with presenting legal realism as a jurisprudence and as a past phase in intellectual history, and with laying out its genealogy, led me to a different and narrower conception of realism in *Legal Realism at Yale* from that held by most law professors on the left or the right. It seems to me that if we are to have a broad definition of realism, process theory must be included within its parameters. Therefore I differ from Horwitz and others insofar as I stress the continuity between legal realism and process theory. Compare, e.g., Morton Horwitz, *The Transformation of American Law, 1870–1960: The Crisis of Legal Orthodoxy* 253 (1992).

2. John Schlegel, "A Tasty Tidbit," 41 *Buffalo Law Review* 1045, 1064, 1067–69 (1993); Schlegel, *American Legal Realism and Empirical Social Science* 7, 20–21 (1995). For example, Llewellyn, who is always labeled a realist, is generally said to have written only one essay on constitutional law, "The Constitution as an Institution," 34 *Columbia Law Review* 1 (1934) (but see Note, "Legal Realism and the Race Question: Some Realism about Realism on Race Relations," 108 *Harvard Law Review* 1607 [1995] [discussing Llewellyn's scholarship on race relations, at id. 1611–15]). The big-tent definition of realism allows us to add to the realists Walton Hamilton, Thomas Reed Powell, Frankfurter, and Robert Hale, all of whom did write about public law.

3. Ronald Rotunda, *The Politics of Language: Liberalism as Word and Symbol* 14 (1986) (see also pp. 32–80). The discussion of rights is taken from Robert Wiebe, *Self-Rule: A Cultural History of American Democracy* 225–26 (1995).

4. Alan Brinkley, *The End of Reform: New Deal Liberalism in Recession and War* 6, 170, 166, 106, 10, 226, 268–71 (1995). See also John Morton Blum, *V Was for Victory: Politics and American Culture during World War II* (1976). For the argument that Roosevelt freed the presidency from party politics by replacing "constitutional government with an administrative state" and that he established an "administrative constitution, in which government programs were viewed as tantamount to rights and thus worthy of protection from the vagaries of party politics and elections," see Sidney Milkis, *The President and the Parties: The Transformation of the American Party System since the New Deal* 145, 11 (1993). For the classic indictment of the reform liberalism of the 1930s, see Barton Bernstein, "The Conservative Achievements of Liberal Reform," in *The New Deal,* ed. Otis Graham, 147, 149 (1971): "[T]his is not to deny the changes wrought by the New Deal—the extension of welfare programs, the growth of federal power, the strengthening of the executive, even the narrowing of property rights. But it is to assert that the elements of continuity are stronger, that the magnitude of change has been exaggerated. The New Deal failed to solve the problem of depression,

failed to raise the impoverished, it failed to redistribute income, it failed to extend equality and generally countenanced racial discrimination and segregation. It failed generally to make business more responsible to the social welfare or to threaten business's pre-eminent political power. In this sense, the New Deal, despite the shifts in tone and spirit from the earlier decade, was profoundly conservative and continuous with the 1920s."

5. For the study results, see Wesley Sturges and Samuel Clark, "Legal Theory and Real Property Mortgages," 37 *Yale Law Journal* 691 (1928). The quotation is from Grant Gilmore, *The Ages of American Law* 81 (1977). Sturges's colleague, Thurman Arnold, for example, likened the traditional formation of legal concepts to classification according to the possession of a "trunk": "Originally the word 'trunk' was applied to trees. Suppose later a writer on the science of things in general classifies 'elephants,' 'trees' and 'tourists' under the same heading. The reason for such a classification is that all three possess trunks. The answer to the objection that the trunks are of different kinds can easily be met by saying that to a nicely based analytical mind, they all have one inherent similarity, i.e., they are all used to carry things. The elephant's trunk carries hay to the elephant's mouth, the tree trunk carries sap to the leaves and the tourist trunk carries clothing. The soundness of the new abstraction cannot perhaps be disputed but nevertheless the classification would create at least verbal confusion and the necessity for a great many fine distinctions." Thurman Arnold, "Criminal Attempts—The Rise and Fall of an Abstraction," 40 *Yale Law Journal* 53, 57–58 (1931).

6. Definition of doctrinal scholarship is from Larry Alexander, "What We Do, and Why We Do It," 45 *Stanford Law Review* 1885, 1886 (1993); "in the habit" and "in the past" are from Walter Wheeler Cook, Book Review, 38 *Yale Law Journal* 405, 406 (1929).

7. Veblen is quoted in John Schlegel, "Langdell's Legacy or, the Case of the Empty Envelope," 36 *Stanford Law Review* 1517, 1517 (1984). Hutchins is quoted in Schlegel, "American Legal Realism and Empirical Social Science: From the Yale Experience," 28 *Buffalo Law Review* 459, 489 (1979). For the discussion in this section see also Kalman, *Legal Realism,* chap. 1.

8. Horwitz, *Transformation,* at 209–10. On the other hand, perhaps the second step did not suppress the radicalism of the first. See Schlegel, "A Tasty Tidbit," at 1069–70; and Schlegel, *American Legal Realism.*

9. See Jerome Frank, "Realism in Jurisprudence," 7 *American Law School Review* 1063 (1934), reprinted sub. nom "Experimental Jurisprudence and the New Deal," 73 *Congressional Record* 12412–14 (1934). For realists in the New Deal, see Peter Irons, *The New Deal Lawyers* 6–9 (1982); Laura Kalman, *Abe Fortas: A Biography* 29 (1990); Mark Barenberg, "The Political Economy of the Wagner Act: Power, Symbol, and Workplace Cooperation," 106 *Harvard Law Review* 1381, 1409 (1993); and G. Edward White, "From Sociological Jurisprudence to Realism: Jurisprudence and Social Change in Early Twentieth Century America," 58 *Virginia Law Review* 999 (1972). But see Neil Duxbury, *Patterns in American Jurisprudence* 155–158 (1995) (challenging the notion of legal realism as jurisprudential analogue of the New Deal). On the realists, New Dealers, and the public/private distinction see, e.g., Singer, "Legal Realism," at 477–95; Morton Horwitz, "The History of the Public/Private Distinction," 130 *University of Pennsylvania*

Law Review 1423, 1426–27 (1982). Though I stress the contribution of New Dealers in this paragraph, Morton Horwitz has made a compelling argument that progressives such as Pound, Wilson, Brandeis, and Cardozo were the real midwives of the contemporary constitutional order because they created "the intellectual framework for the progressive view" in which constitutional meaning changed along with circumstances. Indeed, Horwitz argued that "this progressive elaboration of a theory of a changing constitution in reaction to the *Lochner* Court's static view of constitutional meaning ground to a halt after 1937," which is when realists began to be appointed to the Court. Horwitz, "The Supreme Count, 1992 Term—Foreword: The Constitution of Change: Legal Fundamentality without Fundamentalism," 107 *Harvard Law Review* 30, 54, 56 (1993).

10. "[V]ehicle" is from Milkis, *The President,* at 51 (see generally id. at viii–ix, 4–5, 51–146). Harrington is quoted in *The Commonwealth of Oceana,* reprinted in *The Political Work of James Harrington,* ed. J. G. A. Pocock, 171 (1977). Landis is quoted in Donald Ritchie, *James M. Landis* 177 (1980). Natalie Hull has shown that realists Karl Llewellyn and Jerome Frank originally labeled Landis as one of the "realists-in-part-of their work" and then dropped him from their list of realists. Hull, "Some Realism about the Llewellyn-Pound Exchange over Realism: The Newly Uncovered Private Correspondence, 1927–1931," 1987 *Wisconsin Law Review* 921, 968. Jerome Frank echoed Landis's sentiments about the regulatory state in his book dedicated to William O. Douglas, *If Men Were Angels: Some Aspects of Government in a Democracy* (1942). See also Alan Brinkley, "The New Deal and the Idea of the State," in *The Rise and Fall of the New Deal Order, 1930–1980,* ed. Steve Fraser and Gary Gerstle, 85, 87–94 (1989). According to Brinkley, "There was an unrecognized irony in this enthusiasm for an expanded regulatory state. On the one hand, the 'New Dealers' [of the late 1930s] had a view of what government could hope to achieve that was in many ways more modest than those of some earlier reformers. . . . The state could not, liberals had come to believe, in any fundamental way 'solve' the problems of the economy. But the very limits of their ultimate ambitions made their vision of government more aggressive and assertive than that of many of their progressive predecessors. The inevitability of constant conflict and instability in a modern capitalist economy was all the more reason for government to become an active regulatory force." Brinkley, *End of Reform,* at 63. The capture of regulatory agencies by corporate interests during World War II caused some New Dealers to lose their enthusiasm for the regulatory state. Blum, *V Was for Victory,* at 117–46. On the New Dealers' passion for meritocracy see G. Edward White, "Felix Frankfurter, the Old Boy Network and the New Deal: The Placement of Elite Lawyers in Public Service in the 1930s," 39 *Arkansas Law Review* 631 (1986); and G. Edward White, "Recapturing the New Deal Lawyers," 102 *Harvard Law Review* 489, 513 (1988).

11. "Indeed" is from Cass Sunstein, "What Judge Bork Should Have Said," 23 *Connecticut Law Review* 205, 236 (1991); see also Sunstein, "Constitutionalism after the New Deal," 101 *Harvard Law Review* 421 (1987). "[S]eemed to be a road block" is from Norman Silber and Geoffrey Miller, "Toward 'Neutral Principles' in the Law: Selections from the Oral History of Herbert Wechsler," 93 *Columbia Law Review* 854, 924 (1993). For discussion of the populists' and progressives' hostility toward the Court see William Ross, *A Muted Fury: Populists, Progressives and Labor Unions*

Confront the Court, 1890–1937 197–98, 309–10 (1994). Roberts and Stone are quoted in *United States* v. *Butler,* 297 U.S. 1, 62, 87 (1936) (for a recent sympathetic discussion of Roberts's textualism in *Butler* see William Van Alstyne, "Interpreting *This* Constitution: The Unhelpful Contribution of Special Theories of Judicial Review," 35 *University of Florida Law Review* 209, 225–29 [1983]). "[S]uper-legislature" is from *Burns Baking Co.* v. *Bryan,* 264 U.S. 504, 534 (1924), quoted in Robert Harrison, "The Breakup of the Roosevelt Court: The Contribution of History and Biography," 3 (1987)(unpublished Ph.D. dissertation, Columbia University).

12. See, e.g., Drew Pearson and Robert Allen, *The Nine Old Men* (1936); Henry Hart, "The Gold Clause in United States Bonds," 48 *Harvard Law Review* 1057 (1935); Henry Hart, "Processing Taxes and Protective Tariffs," 49 *Harvard Law Review* 610 (1936); Felix Frankfurter and Henry Hart, "The Business of the Supreme Court at October Term, 1934," id. at 68 (1935). On Hart and the *New Republic* see Henry Hart to Bruce Bliven, May 26, 1933, Box 29, Folder 1, Henry M. Hart Papers, Harvard Law School (hereafter cited as Hart Papers) (indicating that he is offering an essay at Frankfurter's suggestion); Bliven to Hart, March 29, 1933, id. ("I hope you will query me freely on subjects regarding which you would like to write for The New Republic"); Hart's unsigned editorials are collected in id., Folders 1–3. "[S]traitjacket for the status quo" is from Hart, "Unshackling the Tax Power," *New Republic,* January 30, 1935, id., Folder 3. The remaining quotations are from Hart, "The United States Supreme Court: An Argument on the President's Side," *Harvard Alumni Bulletin,* Box 30, Folder 8, Hart Papers.

13. Corwin is quoted in William Leuchtenburg, *The Supreme Court Reborn: The Constitutional Revolution in the Age of Roosevelt* 162 (1995); Robert McCloskey, *The American Constitution* (2d ed., revised by Sanford Levinson) 207 (1994).

14. Recently, some republican revivalists among the realists' descendants argued that the traditional interpretations of the Court's switch in 1937, which focus on its "endorsement of 'judicial restraint,'" miss the point. For example, Cass Sunstein has argued that the significance of "the revolution of 1937" lay in the fact that the Court denaturalized the common law, recognizing that "ownership rights, and everything that accompanied them had been created by the legal system." More specifically, it scrapped "a particular conception of neutrality, one based on existing distributions of wealth and entitlements." The Court recognized that "ownership rights and the status quo were products of government," that the principles of the common law "amounted to a controversial regulatory system that created and did not simply reflect the social order," and that the "status quo had been a legal creation." Thus it abandoned the use of the common law and "of the status quo as the baseline from which to distinguish partisanship and neutrality, or government action and inaction. Rejecting that view, the New Deal period deepened the original constitutional commitment to deliberative democracy, seeing the status quo, like everything else, as subject both to deliberation and to democracy." Sunstein, *The Partial Constitution* 41–42, 50–57, 66–67 (1993). Sunstein here incorporated critical legal scholars' claims that the realists had destroyed the public/private distinction in constitutional theory. While Ackerman's recent work suggests he would surely agree with this point, he goes further. In chapter 7 I discuss his view of 1937 to suggest that Article V of the Constitution is nonexclusive.

15. On Brandeis, see his partial concurrence in *Ashwander* v. *Tennesee Valley Authority,* 297 U.S. 288, 341, 346–48 (1936). "[I]mposing its own view" is from Hart, "United States Supreme Court." Frankfurter is quoted in Harrison, "Breakup," at 333. The description of process theory is from Gary Minda, *Postmodern Legal Movements: Law and Jurisprudence at Century's End* 34 (1995). Here, however, I follow Neil Duxbury in treating process theory not solely as the postwar response to legal realism, which it has been traditionally perceived to be by Minda and others, but as a response to the crisis caused by the Court's arrogation of power in the early and middle 1930s. Duxbury, *Patterns,* at 5, 208, 232–34. See also Eugene Rostow, "The Democratic Character of Judicial Review," 66 *Harvard Law Review* 193 (1952); *United States* v. *Carolene Products Co.,* 304 U.S. 144, 152–53 n.4 (1938); Cover, "Origins of Judicial Activism," at 91; Alpheus Mason, "Judicial Activism: Old and New," 55 *Virginia Law Review* 385, 405–6 (1969). "[H]igh ground" is from Bruce Ackerman, "Beyond *Carolene Products,*" 98 *Harvard Law Review* 713, 715 (1985). "One important side-effect [of Stone's footnote 4] probably was an elevation in the stature of law schools as the institutional loci of constitutional theory understood as means of insuring judicial fidelity to democracy." H. Jefferson Powell, *The Moral Tradition of American Constitutionalism* 151 n.331 (1993). Fittingly, Stone, the author of footnote 4 in *Carolene Products,* had once been dean of Columbia Law School.

16. Braden, "Search for Objectivity," at 571–72, 580–82.

17. "[I]nternal goods" is from Powell, *Moral Tradition,* at 117; "gave even" from Edward Purcell, *The Crisis of Democratic Theory: Scientific Naturalism and the Problem of Value* 172 (1973); Holmes, Hobbes, Hitler from Francis Lucey, "Natural Law and American Legal Realism; Their Respective Contributions to a Theory of Law in a Democratic Society," 30 *Georgetown Law Journal* 493, 531 (1942). On the realists' ethical pluralism, see William Fisher, "The Development of Modern American Legal Theory and the Judicial Interpretation of the Bill of Rights," in *A Culture of Rights: The Bill of Rights in Philosophy, Politics, and Law—1791 and 1991,* ed. Michael Lacey and Knud Haakonssen, 266, 279–83 (1991).

18. The discussion of anthropology is from Elvin Hatch, *Culture and Morality: The Relativity of Values in Anthropology* 35, 108 (1983); that of abstract expressionism from David Harvey, *The Condition of Postmodernity: An Enguiry into the Origins of Cultural Change* 37 (1990).

19. Cleanth Brooks is quoted in Gerald Graff, *Professing Literature: An Institutional History* 188, 171–79 (1987). See also Terry Eagleton, *Literary Theory: An Introduction* 50 (1983).

20. Stephen Feldman, "Republican Revival/Interpretive Turn," 1992 *Wisconsin Law Review* 679, 685 (1992).

21. Charles Beard, *An Economic Interpretation of the Constitution of the United States* 73, 164, 161 (1913, 1986 ed.). For a discussion of the history of Beard's reputation see, e.g., Forrest McDonald, "A New Introduction," id. at vii. Beard's celebration by his contemporaries for destroying "patriotic banalities" is discussed by John Diggins, "Power and Authority in American History: The Case of Charles Beard and His Critics," 86 *American Historical Review* 701, 702 (1981).

    As Gordon Wood explained, historians before Beard had placed a "constant and at times extravagant emphasis on the idealism of the Revolution." Wood, "Rhetoric and Reality in the American Revolution," 23 *William and Mary Ouarterly* 3d ser.,

3, 7 (1966). See also Lester Cohen, "Creating a Usable Future: The Revolutionary Historians and the National Past," in *The American Revolution: Its Character and Limits,* ed. Jack Greene, 309 (1987). Though Beard shifted the focus to class conflict in his scholarship, interestingly, Charles and Mary Beard emphasized consensus among Americans in their American history textbook. In some respects, this is unremarkable. According to Frances FitzGerald, "many of the texts omit or contradict the very interpretations of history which their supposed authors made famous: Charles and Mary Beard's school history scants economics as a factor in the making of the Constitution; the nineteen-thirties textbook that bears Commager's name contains no intellectual history at all." Frances FitzGerald, *America Revised: History Schoolbooks in the Twentieth Century* 20–21, 155 (1979). Though FitzGerald implied many historians did not actually write their textbooks, the Beards did write theirs, McDonald, "A New Introduction," at xxii. Notwithstanding the intellectual reasons Beard gave for not mentioning economic factors in the textbook, Beardianism may have been downplayed because it would not sell. Id. "[E]ver since the thirties the texts have been written without conflicts." Class confict has always been inadmissible to them—it is un-American." Thus consensus became a cult long before consensus historians were deemed a school.

22. Louis Hartz, *The Liberal Tradition in America: An Interpretation of American Political Thought since the Revolution* 9–11 (1955). As Peter Novick noted, *The Liberal Tradition* had "an ambiguously . . . Marxist cast." Novick emphasized that consensus history was not "intrinsically or necessarily conservative." Novick, *That Noble Dream: The "Objectivity Question" and the American Historical Profession* 333–34 (1990). Historians have debated the reasons for the popularity of consensus history. According to Novick, it represented in part "a natural swing of the scholarly pendulum. The Progressive Historians had, as Hofstadter said, 'pushed polarized conflict as a principle of historical interpretation so far that one could go no further in that direction without risking self-caricature.' " Id. Cf. the discussion of consensus history in "American History," in *History: The Development of Historical Studies in the United States,* ed. John Higham with Leonard Krieger and Felix Gilbert, 147, 221 (1965); "Historians in an age of unceasing international peril, when national security and the capacity for survival are fundamental concerns, can hardly avoid a somewhat conservative view of their country's history. They can hardly avoid an appreciation of its more cohesive and deeply rooted qualities."

23. Daniel Boorstin, *The Genius of American Politics* 94–95, 132, 179 (1953) (emphasis in the original); Daniel Bell, *The End of Ideology: On the Exhaustion of Political Ideas in the Fifties* 350, 400–402, 14–17 (1988 ed.). (Bell has denied critics' accusations that his book defended "the status quo," "sought to substitute technocratic guidance by experts for political debate in the society," and "sought to substitute consensus for moral discourse." He has also rejected the suggestions that the book "was an instrument of the Cold War" and that it was "disproved by the events of the sixties and seventies, which saw a new upsurge of radicalism and ideology in Western Societies as well as in the Third World." Bell, "Afterword, 1988: The End of Ideology Revisited," id. at 409, 420–21. The afterword presents an excellent evaluation of the intellectual and political context in which the "end of ideology" theme emerged.) The other quotations are from Wiebe, *Self-Rule,* at 218–19; W. H. Morris-Jones, "In Defence of Apathy," 2 *Political Studies* 25 (1954); David Truman, *The*

Governmental Process: Political Interests and Public Opinion 514, 483, 498 (1951); Seymour Lipset, *The First New Nation: The United States in Historical and Comparative Perspective* 11, 93, 313–17 (1963); Reinhold Niebuhr and Paul Sigmund, *The Democratic Experience: Past and Prospects* 179 (1969). Wiebe's *Self-Rule* provides a fascinating history of the concept of American democracy.

24. Robert Dahl, *A Preface to Democratic Theory* 32, 142–43, 3, 50, 68, 132–33, 82–84, 132–33, 58–59, 111, 137, 146, 150–51 (1956). See also Dahl, "Decision-Making in a Democracy: The Supreme Court as a National Policy-Maker," 6 *Journal of Public Law* 279 (1957).

25. Quoted in Bell, "Afterword," at 419. The speech was drafted in part by Arthur Schlesinger, Jr., who had attended the famous "end of ideology" conference in Milan in 1955, which also attracted Bell, Lipset, Raymond Aron, Michael Polanyi, Edward Shils, and C. A. R. Crosland. Id. at 412, 419.

26. Mark DeWolfe Howe, "The Supreme Court, 1952 Term—Foreword: Political Theory and the Nature of Liberty," 67 *Harvard Law Review* 91 (1953). "[M]aximizing total satisfaction," is from Hart and Sacks, *The Legal Process,* as quoted in Duxbury, *Patterns,* at 254. See id. at 236 for the notion of jurisprudence "as quality control." Duxbury maintains that "this was something different from legal realism." Id. and see id. at 212.

27. *Brown I,* at 492–95, and *Brown II,* at 301. At the time *Brown* was handed down, most scholars outside the South apparently assumed it overruled *Plessy.* Cf. Michael Klarman, "An Interpretive History of Equal Protection," 90 *Michigan Law Review* 213, 248 (1991): "[A]n honest reading of *Brown,* given its emphasis on the importance of education, did not support invalidation of segregated recreational facilities." For the argument that as in *Brown,* the majority in *Plessy* v. *Ferguson,* 163 U.S. 537, 551 (1896), relied on prevailing social science data in saying segregation did not stamp African Americans with a "badge of inferiority," see Herbert Hovenkamp, "Social Science and Segregation before *Brown,*" 1985 *Duke Law Journal* 624 (1985). Nor, Charles Lofgren has suggested, was the majority's history in *Plessy* "jarringly inaccurate." Lofgren, *The Plessy Case: A Legal-Historical Interpretation* 198 (1987).

28. The standard history of *Brown* is Richard Kluger, *Simple Justice: The History of Brown v. Board of Education and Black America's Struggle for Equality* (1975). See also Morton Horwitz, "The Jurisprudence of *Brown* and the Dilemmas of Liberalism," 14 *Harvard Civil Rights–Civil Liberties Law Review* 599, 602 (1979).

29. For Tushnet's discussion of Frankfurter and *Brown* see Mark Tushnet, "Public Law Litigation and the Ambiguities of *Brown,*" 61 *Fordham Law Review* 23, 26–28 (1992); and Tushnet, with Katya Lezin, "What Really Happened in *Brown* v. *Board of Education,*" 91 *Columbia Law Review* 1867, 1883–84, 1893–96, 1909–20, 1925–30 (1991). *Brown's* impact on the South is explored in Del Dickson, "State Court Defiance and the Limits of Supreme Court Authority: *Williams* v. *Georgia* Revisited," 103 *Yale Law Journal* 1423, 1478–81 (1994).

30. "Frankfurter, despite" is from Gerald Gunther, *Learned Hand: The Man and the Judge* 668–69 (1994); "No good society" and "would it" from Bickel, *Least Dangerous Branch,* at 64, 174, 71, 236; "100%" from Gerald Gunther, "The Subtle Vices of the 'Passive Virtues'—A Comment on Principle and Expediency in Judicial Review," 64 *Columbia Law Review* 1, 3 (1964); "the whole thing" from Alexander

Bickel to Robert Bork, October 9, 1968, Box 10, Folder 193, Alexander Mordecai Bickel Papers, Yale University Library (hereafter Bickel Papers); "a little priestly" from Bickel to Felix Frankfurter, April 24, 1964, Part III, Reel 14, Felix Frankfurter Papers, Harvard Law School Library (hereafter Frankfurter Papers). Bickel's first book, *The Unpublished Opinions of Mr. Justice Brandeis* (1957), had celebrated the prudentialism of Brandeis. For a discussion of how the theme of prudentialism unified Bickel's political philosophy and career, see Anthony Kronman, "Alexander Bickel's Philosophy of Prudence," 94 *Yale Law Journal* 1567 (1985). See also Lawrence Wiseman, "Alexander Bickel and the Idea of Prudence: Value Choices in Modern Constitutional Theory," 1987 (Ph. D. dissertation, University of California, Berkeley). Bickel's inconsistency (or prudentialism) was evident to others among his contemporaries besides Gunther. In his review of *The Least Dangerous Branch,* Mark DeWolfe Howe suggested "that there are serious difficulties in his [Bickel's] apparent effort to have the cake of activism and eat it too." Howe, Book Review, 77 *Harvard Law Review* 579, 581 (1963). To Samuel Krislov, Bickel's "ideal court" was rather like "the spinster saving herself for a destined husband, ignorant of the fact that she is training herself never to find him." Krislov, Book Review, 56 *Cornell Law Review* 1031, 1034 (1971). Wellington's prudentialism is reflected in his current advocacy of a "common law method of constitutional adjudication," which exercises "a function that differs from the legislative and executive functions." Harry Wellington, *Interpreting the Constitution: The Supreme Court and the Process of Adjudication* 127, 78 (1990). I believe Frankfurter preferred the prudentialists to the theologians. Irritated by Hart's insistence on the utility of diversity jurisdiction, for example, Frankfurter once complained to Hart about "your theoretical and, I believe largely unreal arguments—unreal in the actualities of life," and he told Paul Freund that Hart "seems to me to become more and more Thomistic or geometric in his thinking." Frankfurter to Hart, February 11, 1959, Part III, Reel 16, Frankfurter Papers; Frankfurter to Freund, Box 3, Folder 3, copy in Hart Papers.

31. "[P]roduced a sharply critical" is from Horwitz, *Transformation,* at 258 (a charge repeated by Minda, *Postmodern,* at 37–38, 47); Gary Peller, "Neutral Principles in the 1950's," 21 *Journal of Law Reform* 561, 568, 586 (1988). See generally Duxbury, *Patterns,* at 264–65.

32. "[T]he boundaries for" is from Peller, "Neutral Principles," at 602 (Peller pointed out that process theorists believed "common-law courts might consider both policy and principle," at 603); "morality of function" from Hart, "The Morality of Function," n.d., Box 23, Folder 3, Hart Papers; "probably the most important" from Ahkil Amar, "Law Story," 102 *Harvard Law Review* 688, 688 (1989). The legal process materials did not mention *Brown,* and Hart never revised his casebook on the federal courts. Id. at 703 n.71. The cartoon and note are in Frankfurter to Hart, n.d., Box 3, Folder 3, Hart Papers. Earl Warren described *Baker* v. *Carr,* 369 U.S. 186 (1962), as his most important case in *The Memoirs of Earl Warren* 306 (1977). Bernard Schwartz noted: "Whether there was a cause and effect relationship between his defeat in that case and the Justice's [Frankfurter's] physical collapse can, of course, never be known." Schwartz, *Super Chief: Earl Warren and His Supreme Court* 427 (1983). Hart's personal papers contain three letters from students suggesting that *Baker* v. *Carr* sent him over the edge. Richard Dyson to Hart, March 27, 1962, Box 2, Folder 12, Hart Papers; Richard Rubenstein to Hart, October 29, 1962, Box 6,

Folder 8, id.; Bernard Harvith to Hart, October 30, 1962, Box 3, Folder 27, id. According to Sacks, the "gentle" Hart would "grow so indignant over unprincipled or unreasoned decisions that he would hurl verbal thunderbolts akin to those of the biblical Jehovah." Albert Sacks, "Henry Hart," 82 *Harvard Law Review* 1593, 1594 (1969). In a letter to Hart, his colleague Thomas Reed Powell alluded to "the hell-bentness of your mood when you are in sociological heat with its tendency to find turpitude where there may have been just stupidity or neglect." Powell to Hart, October 18, 1937, Box 5, Folder 18, Hart Papers.

33. "[A]dmission ticket" is from Louis Seidman, *"Brown* and *Miranda,"* 80 *California Law Review* 673, 675 (1992). The student was Richard Dyson (in his March 27, 1962, letter), who continued: "I do not suggest that your distinctions are unsound from a technical standpoint. But the similarities should also be noted: there also the social need was great, the administrative difficulties were enormous, and the precedent was opposed. And there also the Supreme Court acted with courage in the conviction that the American people would arrive at a solution, however gradual and painful, which conformed with the ethical imperative contained in the decision. The problem of remedies will indeed be difficult; the battle has undoubtedly just begun. But just because the ultimate outcome is not clear does not mean that the fight is not worth it. And the venturing of the federal courts into uncharted territory does not signal their doom; they have been there before, and the country is better for it. With all respect, I am completely confident that *Baker* v. *Carr* is right—and that you are wrong." The scholar was Michael McConnell, "Originalism and the Desegregation Decisions," 81 *Virginia Law Review* 947, 1136 (1995). For Sacks on *Brown* see Albert Sacks, "The Supreme Court, 1953 Term—Foreword," 68 *Harvard Law Review* 96, 96–98 (1954). Even the bizarre 1958 resolution on federal-state relationships by state supreme court chief justices begging the Court to "exercise one of the greatest of all judicial powers—the power of judicial restraint" contained "not one iota of criticism" of *Brown.* Philip Kurland, "The Supreme Court and Its Judicial Critics," 6 *Utah Law Review* 457, 457 (1959).

34. Frankfurter to Sacks, November 29, 1954, Part III, Reel 18, Frankfurter Papers.

35. Sacks to Frankfurter, January 7, 1955; Frankfurter to Sacks, January 11, 1955, both in id. "Although his relations with his colleagues were not always smooth, Frankfurter was a superb mentor for his law clerks, many of whom became academics. His correspondence with former clerks is replete with evidence that he was warm and caring toward them and their families, and the clerks reciprocated by conveying to the legal academy the sense that Frankfurter was a wise and insightful person. A somewhat less attractive aspect of the correspondence is that it suggests that Frankfurter was able to develop these loyalties by offering his law clerks a sense that they were privileged insiders." Tushnet, "What Really Happened," at 1883; Isidore Silver, "The Warren Court Critics: Where Are They Now That We Need Them?" 3 *Hastings Constitutional Law Commentary* 373, 387 n.66 (1976). It was not unusual for Frankfurter to show his former clerks an internal Court memorandum prepared after they had left the Court. See, e.g., Bickel to Frankfurter, January 10, 1956, Part III, Reel 14, Frankfurter Papers (acknowledging receipt of Frankfurter's memorandum in *Naim* v. *Naim*). Though Bickel maintained that "the clerks, arriving every year, *are* a conduit from the law schools to the Court," Frankfurter used his clerks more

effectively than they used him. Alexander Bickel, *Politics and the Warren Court* 143 (1965) (emphasis in the original).

To some extent, the argument between Frankfurter and his followers, on the one hand, and more activist members of the Court, such as Douglas and Black and their followers, on the other, can be viewed as a Harvard-Yale debate. To outsiders, such as Fred Rodell of Yale and Justice William O. Douglas, a onetime Yale law professor, Frankfurter's clerks appeared to be his claque. To Bickel and others trained at Harvard, Rodell was part of a Douglas-Black claque. Douglas told the editor of the *New Republic* that Bickel was a "propagandist" (presumably for Frankfurter), and Bickel was once told that Douglas had said "he would never sign an opinion which cited any work of mine." Douglas to Gilbert Harrison, March 22, 1960, Box 2, Folder 45, Bickel Papers; Bickel, Memorandum for the File, November 2, 1968, Box 82, Folder 23, id. For their part, Harvard Law School faculty members rejected a recommendation by the Holmes Committee that Justice Black be asked to give the Holmes Lectures in 1957. See Henry Hart to Erwin Griswold, n.d., Box 3, Folder 13, Hart Papers, and Kalman, *Legal Realism,* at 201–7.

36. "[M]ake-weight excuse" is from Schwartz, *Super Chief,* at 161; Gunther, *Learned Hand,* at 670, 666 (see generally 652–72); "greatest crisis" and "efforts at dismantling" from Horwitz, *Transformation,* at 260. See *Naim* v. *Naim,* 350 U.S. 891 (1955); 350 U.S. 985 (1956); and Learned Hand, *The Bill of Rights* 6, 54–55, 69 (1958). Like his publication of the Roberts memorandum in 1955 indicating that Justice Roberts had not switched sides in 1937 as a result of political pressure, and like his memorial tributes to Justice Jackson, Frankfurter's enthusiasm for the Holmes Devise History of the Supreme Court in the 1950s can be seen as an attempt to increase support for the Court. See Felix Frankfurter, "Mr. Justice Roberts," 104 *University of Pennsylvania Law Review* 311 (1955); Frankfurter, "Foreword," 55 *Columbia Law Review* 436 (1955); Frankfurter, "Mr. Justice Jackson," 68 *Harvard Law Review* 937 (1955); Michael Ariens, "A Thrice-Told Tale, or Felix the Cat," 107 *Harvard Law Review* 620, 625, 652–75 (1994); Sanford Levinson, Book Review, 75 *Virginia Law Review* 1429, 1429–30 n.2 (1989). On attacks on the Court during the 1950s generally see Louis Pollak, "The Supreme Court under Fire," 6 *Journal of Public Law* 428 (1957); Paul Freund, "Storm over the Supreme Court," 21 *Modern Law Review* 28 (1958).

37. Duxbury, *Patterns,* at 273; Wechsler, "Toward Neutral Principles of Constitutional Law," 73 *Harvard Law Review* 1, 32, 34–35 (1959); Silber and Miller, "Neutral Principles," at 927. Other scholars have been far more critical of Wechsler than I am, alleging that his "proceduralist paradigm," like those of other process theorists in the 1950s, was "deeply conservative." See, e.g., Peller, "Neutral Principles," at 566.

38. Henry Hart, "The Supreme Court, 1958 Term—Foreword: The Time Chart of the Justices," 73 *Harvard Law Review* 84, 98–100, 125 (1959); Harry Wellington to Hart, November 20, 1959, Box 28, Folder 8, Hart Papers; Hart to Wellington, December 3, 1949, id.

39. Charles Black, "The Lawfulness of the Segregation Decisions," 69 *Yale Law Journal* 421, 425 (1960); Alexander Bickel, "The Original Understanding and the Segregation Decision," 69 *Harvard Law Review* 1, 65 (1955) (emphasis added); Charles Fairman, "The Supreme Court, 1955, Term—Foreword: The Attack on the Segregation

Cases," 70 *Harvard Law Review* 83, 94 (1956); Edmond Cahn, "Jurisprudence," 30 *New York University Law Review* 150, 167, 169 (1955); Hart, Memorandum for Ernest Brown, February 24, 1959, Box 35, Folder 10, Hart Papers; Hart, Notes, n.d. (c. April 1958), Box 5, Folder 13, Hart Papers (noting "burned up since Hand's lectures"); Wechsler, "Neutral Principles," at 31–32; Gunther, *Learned Hand,* at 660. Hart had special reason to be annoyed with Hand's lectures. Though Hand did not mention William Crosskey, his Holmes Lectures were haunted by Crosskey's *Politics and the Constitution in the History of the United States* (1953). There Crosskey announced that the Founding Fathers had intended the scope of judicial review to be quite limited. Though at first the reaction to *Politics and the Constitution* was favorable, the tide turned after Hart savaged it in his book review, 67 *Harvard Law Review* 1439, 1461 (1954). Philip Bobbitt examined the reaction to Crosskey's work in *Constitutional Fate: Theory of the Constitution* 15–21 (1982), as did Robert Power in "The Textualist," 84 *Northwestern University Law Review* 711, 713–16. Doubtless Frankfurter, who considered *Politics and the Constitution* "a fundamentally arrogant and foolish concoction," was responsible for at least some of the hostility to the book. Frankfurter to Arthur Sutherland, January 29, 1954, Part III, Reel 18, Frankfurter Papers.

40. As Anthony Lewis said, in the academic criticism of the Court during the 1950s, occasionally "[t]he strictures are so harsh, the language so sweeping as to give the impression that the craftsmanship of the Court is at an all-time low." Lewis, "The Supreme Court and Its Critics," 45 *Minnesota Law Review* 305, 324–35 (1961). "[T]amed realism" is from Peller, "Neutral Principles," at 589. The defenders are William Eskridge and Philip Frickey, "The Making of *The Legal Process*," 107 *Harvard Law Review* 2031, 2050 (1994). See Alexander Bickel and Harry Wellington, "Legislative Purpose and the Judicial Process: The Lincoln Mills Case," 71 *Harvard Law Review* 1, 2–3 (1957). Their article is described as the "classic" indictment in Silver, "Warren Court Critics," at 374. Hart quoted the Bickel and Wellington critique and commented on it in his *Harvard Law Review* "Foreword," "Time Chart," at 100–101. (Perhaps significantly, Hart's "Time Chart" was highly critical of the Court's habeas corpus decisions, a source of joy to political liberals.) Hart's statement, which Neil Duxbury has described as the most "strident" exposition of process theory up to that point, could be taken as a statement from Harvard. Duxbury, *Patterns,* at 240. As Frankfurter told Fairman, the annual forewords of the *Harvard Law Review* carried with them "certainly more than any other signed contributions, an implication of institutional expression." Frankfurter to Charles Fairman, August 23, 1956, Part III, Reel 15, Frankfurter Papers. See generally Mark Tushnet and Timothy Lynch, "The Project of the Harvard *Forewords:* A Social and Intellectual Inquiry," 11 *Constitutional Commentary* 463 [1994–95].) The Wechsler quotation is from his "Neutral Principles," at 15. See also Wechsler, "The Courts and the Constitution," 45 *Columbia Law Review* 1001, 1011–12 (1965).

41. Silber and Miller, "Neutral Principles," at 925, 926–29. See, e.g., Eugene Rostow, *The Sovereign Prerogative: The Supreme Court and the Quest for Law* 28 (1962): "To me, Professor Wechsler's lecture . . . represents a repudiation of all we have learned about law since Holmes published his *Common Law* in 1881."

42. "[T]he most influential scholar" is from Anthony Kronman, *The Lost Lawyer: Failing Ideals of the Legal Profession* 24 (1993); *"writtenness"* from Thomas Grey, "Do We

Have an Unwritten Constitution?" 27 *Stanford Law Review* 703, 707 (1975); the remaining quotations are from Bickel, *Least Dangerous Branch,* at 15–16, 104, 2–3, 128 (and see pp. 4–14, 73–75). See also *Marbury* v. *Madison,* 5 U.S. (1 Cranch) 137, 177 (1803). Martin Flaherty, who follows customary historical practice in referring to the "Founding" as "the efforts that culminated in the drafting and ratification of the Federal Constitution," has made a persuasive argument for departing from tradition by speaking of the Founders rather than the Framers: "Strictly speaking, 'Framers' applies only to the fifty-five men who participated in the Philadelphia Convention, which drafted the document. In historical terms, speaking of the 'Framers' leaves out numerous individuals—John Adams and Thomas Jefferson to name two—who were critical to early American constitutional thinking. According to most theoretical accounts, moreover, the views that merit greater weight are not those of the Framers, who merely proposed a plan of government, but those who ratified that plan in state conventions." Flaherty, "History 'Lite' in Modern American Constitutionalism," 95 *Columbia Law Review* 523, 527 n.17 (1995).

43. Bickel, *Least Dangerous Branch*, at 15–17. "[M]ajoritarian paradigm" is from Erwin Chemerinsky, "The Supreme Court 1988 Term—Foreword: The Vanishing Constitution," 103 *Harvard Law Review* 43, 70–71 (1989). Chemerinsky defines the majoritarian paradigm as "the philosophy . . . that American democracy means majority rule; that the legislatures and executives are majoritarian, but the Court is counter-majoritarian; and that as a result, the Court should invalidate government actions only when they violate clear constitutional principles that exist apart from the preferences of the Justices." Id. at 61 n.77.

44. Bickel, *Least Dangerous Branch*, at 17–19.

45. Bickel to Eugene Rostow, Box 9, Folder 166, Bickel Papers; Bickel, *Least Dangerous Branch*, at 36 (see also *McCulloch* v. *Maryland*, 17 U.S. [4 Wheat.] 316 [1819]; *Cohens* v. *Virginia* 19 V.S. [6 Wheat.] 264 [1821]); William Van Alstyne, "A Critical Guide to *Marbury* v. *Madison*," 1969 *Duke Law Journal* 1, 44 (1969) (quoting Holmes, and see id. at 37–38); Rakove, personal communication (see also Rakove, *Original Meanings: Politics and Ideas in the Making of the Constitution* 175–77 [1996]). Democracy as a "central legitimating concept" is from Horwitz, "Foreword: The Constitution of Change," at 57, 63. According to Horwitz, democracy "began to be considered a foundational concept around 1940." Id. at 61; Horwitz and Orlando da Campo, "When and How the Supreme Court Found Democracy—A Computer Study," 14 *Quinnipiac Law Review* 1, 17–18 (1994). On Bickel's lack of evidence see William Haltom and Mark Silverstein, "The Scholarly Tradition Revisited: Alexander Bickel, Herbert Wechsler, and the Legitimacy of Judicial Review," 4 *Constitutional Commentary* 25, 30–36 (1987): "There are grounds for suspecting that neutral principles have little or nothing to do with public reactions to the Court's decisions. For example, congressional attempts to punish the Court for unwelcome decisions are often unrelated to whether the decisions were principled and cogently justified in the opinions. Social scientists have demonstrated the obvious fact that most citizens lack the minimal prerequisites for thoughtful assessment of judicial opinions." In fact, Haltom and Silverstein suggest that "substantive agreement with the Court suffices to ensure popular approval of a decision." Id. at 30, 33.

With the development of the controversy over original intent in the last decade, the ever-simmering debate about the origins of judicial review has boiled over among political scientists. The position advanced in the text accompanying this note is at odds with some recent scholarly studies taking a very different position toward *Marbury* and early judicial review from what Bickel, and certainly I, would.

Attacking "the conversion of *Marbury v. Madison* into a mythical symbol of modern judicial review" by Bickel and others, for example, Robert Clinton insisted in 1989: "Nothing in the opinion contradicts the restrictive conception of judicial power which is embodied in the Constitution. Specifically, I contend that *Marbury* was not a political decision but was based on sound constitutional doctrine and existing legal precedent. In short, it was precisely the sort of case that the Founders considered appropriate for the exercise of judicial review. . . . A close reading of *Marbury* itself supports no more than . . . [the] narrow view . . . that federal courts are entitled to invalidate acts of Congress and the president with finality only when to let such acts stand would violate constitutional restrictions on judicial power." Clinton treated the suggestion that the Marshall Court intended to promote nationalism in cases such as *McCulloch* equally contemptuously. See, e.g., Robert Clinton, *Marbury v. Madison and Judicial Review* 139, 79, ix–x, 5, 192–97 (1989). According to him, the "mythical *Marbury* imparts a flavor of legitimacy to the modern, activist conception of judicial review," which just is not there. Id. at 138, 224, 230. Christopher Wolfe made an equally strong case that Marshall contemplated only "moderate judicial review," which "was different from 'judicial supremacy.' It acknowledged definite limits on itself in an effort to harmonize judicial power and independence with the legitimate autonomy of coordinate branches and the ultimate authority of the people." By this reading, Marshall in *Marbury* said only that "judges have a power to refuse to give effect to unconstitutional acts in cases that come before them." He did not say judges had the power "to choose from among reasonable competing interpretations of the Constitution and impose that one view on the legislature." Wolfe maintained that after the Civil War, the understanding of judicial review began to change, and by the time Earl Warren became chief justice, "the distinction between judicial review and judicial supremacy had become blurred." Wolfe, *The Rise of Modern Judicial Review* 101–16, 61, 77 (1986). J. M. Sosin contended that there was no Anglo-American foundation for judicial review before *Marbury*, in *The Aristocracy of the Long Robe: The Origins of Judicial Review in America* (1989).

While maintaining that Bickel and modern commentators misunderstood *Marbury*, Sylvia Snowiss made a more Bickelian argument for contemporary judicial review in *Judicial Review and the Origins of the Constitution* (1990). She insisted that at the time of *Federalist 78* judicial review "was limited to the concededly unconstitutional act." Marshall played a crucial role in transforming the scope of judicial review, and not in *Marbury*, "which was only a peculiarly reworded restatement of the ground already won." Rather, after *Marbury* and in the 1810s and 1820s, Marshall revised the justification for judicial review, broadened its scope, and ensured judicial supremacy by transforming the Constitution from "explicit fundamental law [unenforceable by courts except under extraordinary political circumstances], different in kind from ordinary law [enforceable by the courts], into supreme written law, different only in degree." Americans had accepted his treatment of the written Constitution as supreme ordinary law by the middle of the nineteenth century. "Marshall did not, as is widely assumed, simply reinforce or extend ideas partially or wholly accepted. Modern judicial review is Marshall's judicial review, as developed in the contract and supremacy clause cases, and not that of Iredell, Hamilton . . . or even *Marbury*. It developed slowly and did not reach its mature form until sometime after Marshall left the Court." Snowiss followed Bickel in concluding that contemporary constitutional law must involve "the defense of fundamental values broadly understood," while emphasizing that "[c]onstitutional law, as an ongoing enterprise committed to the defense of long-term principle, necessitates more ongoing judicial implementation of principle than Bickel contemplated or seemed ready to accept." But she emphasized that "the judicial defense of fundamental values needs to be coupled with some form of restraint." Snowiss, *Judicial Review,* at 3–6, viii, 195, 208–16.

46. See Bickel, *Least Dangerous Branch,* at 35; Bruce Ackerman, "Constitutional Politics/ Constitutional Law," 99 *Yale Law Journal* 453, 463 n.17 (1989); Michael Klarman, "The Puzzling Resistance to Political Process Theory," 77 *Virginia Law Review* 747, 768 n.102 (1991). On Bickel's predecessors, see, e.g., G. Edward White, *Justice Oliver Wendell Holmes: Law and the Inner Self* 487 (1993); James Thayer, "The Origin and Scope of the American Doctrine of Constitutional Law," 7 *Harvard Law Review* 129 (1893); and also Kurland, "Supreme Court," at 466: "Judicial *activism* is undemocratic" (emphasis added).

47. Bickel, *Least Dangerous Branch,* at 24–25, 244, 128, 251–54, 258. Later in the 1960s, as the Warren Court pursued majoritarianism in the reapportionment cases, Bickel became more pessimistic about majoritarianism and more optimistic about pluralism. See Bickel, *The Supreme Court and the Idea of Progress* 83–88, 116–17 (1970). Judge Skelly Wright thought that in that book, Bickel took a "rosy view of the pluralist political system" and noted that "[u]ntil a few years ago, Bickel's pluralist and wholly complacent view of the political system dominated academic political science." J. Skelly Wright, "Professor Bickel, the Scholarly Tradition, and the Supreme Court," 84 *Harvard Law Review* 769, 789 nn.67–68 (1971). Lawrence Wiseman discussed Bickel's attitude toward pluralism in *Alexander Bickel,* at 172–74, 265–79.

48. Bickel, *Least Dangerous Branch,* at 82, 84; Philip Kurland spoke of his own debt to the realist tradition in *Politics, the Constitution and the Warren Court* 18–19 (1970). The phrase "scholastic mandarins" was J. Skelly Wright's. Wright, "Professor Bickel," at 777. (In addition to Bickel, Wright included in this group Ernest Brown, Erwin Griswold, Louis Henkin, Henry Hart, and Philip Kurland. Id. at 770 n.6. Silver described Bickel, Kurland, Paul Freund, and Wechsler as "the most eminent and in many ways the most representative" of the Court's critics. Silver, "Warren Court Critics," at 374.) "[I]nstrumental effectiveness" is from Hans Linde, "Judges, Critics, and the Realist Tradition," 82 *Yale Law Journal* 227, 238 (1972) (Linde suggested that these criteria were not "adequate measure of the substance of constitutional decisions," at id.). The "image of a Supreme Court" is from Alan Barth, "Some Dissenting Opinions," *Washington Post Times-Herald Book Week,* December 19, 1965, Box 14, Folder 26, Bickel Papers. Barth applied that criticism to the early Bickel, and it might be applied to some of Bickel's followers as well. For example, in his 1992 book *The Constitution in Conflict,* Robert Burt theorized that it was the technique of announcing a right and deferring its exercise until other branches of government decided to enforce it in 1964 that made *Brown* a paradigmatic and

correct Warren Court decision. Burt, *Constitution in Conflict,* at 301–3, 311, 329–30. But see Burt, "Alex Bickel's Law School and Ours," 104 *Yale Law Journal* 1853, 1864–69 (1995) (stressing the difference between the views his generation and Bickel's took toward *Brown*).

Of all Warren Court critics, Bickel may have had the most interesting relationship to legal realism, in part because he taught at Yale, long regarded as the center of realism. Edward Purcell noted that by 1969, Bickel had abandoned "his earlier denigration of legal realism" and "now argued that a group of 'progressive realists,' which included originally both Brandeis and Frankfurter, had begun to dominate American jurisprudence during the early twentieth century." But, as Purcell said, one can also see Bickel's acknowledgment of his debt to the realist tradition in his earlier work, such as *The Least Dangerous Branch*. Edward Purcell, "Alexander Bickel and the Post-Realist Constitution," 11 *Harvard Civil Rights–Civil Liberties Law Review* 521, 542–43, 549 (1976). In his personal correspondence, Bickel classified himself as a realist but also resisted identification with any jurisprudential group. He once referred to "the unpardonable sin of constructing a camp and taking anyone into it." Bickel to Eugene Rostow, November 8, 1961, Box 9, Folder 166, Bickel Papers. Responding to Harvard Law School professor Louis Jaffe's criticism of one of Judge David Bazelon's activist decisions in the field of criminal justice, for example, Bickel wrote: "I don't agree that it makes no difference who is a realist. . . . You and I are I think realists (I am because you are and because your teachers were), and that is why we can have discourse. What I for my part deplore is the expression 'you people.' There is no such animal. At least I am no such animal. Some of my colleagues here address me as you people, meaning me and Herbert Wechsler and you and Henry Hart and god knows what other devils. And you address me as you people meaning at least a little bit me and [activist Judge David] Bazelon. . . . Well, I am none of them fellows, nor any of you fellows." Bickel to Louis Jaffe, September 30, 1965, Box 9, Folder 176, Bickel Papers. See also Bickel to Wallace Mendelson, November 26, 1962, Box 9, Folder 167, Bickel Papers (predicting trouble over *The Least Dangerous Branch* "at Harvard with what one might call the 'neutralists' "); Bickel to Yosal Rogat, May 20, 1965, id., Folder 174 (describing Thomas Reed Powell and Felix Frankfurter as realists); Bickel to Peter Strauss, March 9, 1966, id., Folder 180 (asking Strauss, a Brennan clerk: "Why is it you fellows don't recognize that I am on your side? Probably because you cannot rid yourselves of the presumption that I would be unlikely to be on your side").

49. Hart is quoted in "Time Chart," at 99. See also Hart and Albert Sacks, *The Legal Process* 177–78 (tentative ed. 1958). I have found the following discussions of process theory especially useful: Duxbury, *Patterns,* at 206–99; Peller, "Neutral Principles," at 567, 588–89, 620; G. Edward White, "From Realism to Critical Legal Studies: A Truncated Intellectual History," 40 *Southwestern Law Journal* 819, 825–30 (1986); G. Edward White, "The Evolution of Reasoned Elaboration: Jurisprudential Criticism and Social Change," 59 *Virginia Law Review* 279 (1973); William Eskridge and Philip Frickey, "Legislation Scholarship and Pedagogy in the Post–Legal Process Era," 48 *University of Pittsburgh Law Review* 691, 694–701 (1987); Eskridge and Frickey, "The Making of *The Legal Process*"; Tushnet and Lynch, "Harvard *Forewords*," at 474–80; Minda, *Postmodern,* at 33–47.

50. Though process theory was the most significant jurisprudence of the immediate post-

war years, policy science also sought to tame the realist insight and constrain judicial discretion by emphasizing the democratic values of shared power, knowledge, and respect. See Kalman, *Legal Realism,* at 176–87, and Duxbury, *Patterns,* at 162–203, 207.

51. "[A] takeoff" and "far too much" are from "With the Editors," 83 *Harvard Law Review* vii (no. 4, 1970) (see also Louis Henkin, "Infallibility under Law: Constitutional Balancing," 78 *Columbia Law Review* 1022 [1978]). The point that neutral principles did not guarantee neutral attitudes toward principles was made by Arthur Miller and Ronald Howell, "The Myth of Neutrality in Constitutional Adjudication," 27 *University of Chicago Law Review* 661, 664 (1960). Schwartz discussed the impact of Frankfurter's retirement on the Warren Court in *Super Chief,* at 446–49.

52. "[C]ultural phenomenon" and "independent political actor" are from Mark Tushnet, "The Warren Court as History: An Interpretation," in *The Warren Court in Historical and Political Perspective,* ed. Mark Tushnet, 3, 16 (1993). The remaining quotes are from David Trubek, "Back to the Future: The Short, Happy Life of the Law and Society Movement," 18 *Florida State University Law Review* 1, 8, 9, 23 (1990). See also David Trubek and Marc Galanter, "Scholars in Self-Estrangement: Some Reflections on the Crisis in Law and Development Studies in the United States," 1974 *Wisconsin Law Review* 1062, 1070–80 (1974). Like many critical legal scholars, Trubek, however, referred to legal liberalism as liberal legalism. As a political and legal liberal, I find the phrase "liberal legalism" unduly pejorative. Nor do I consider President Kennedy a liberal.

53. Tushnet, "Warren Court" at pp. 19–20; Owen Fiss, *History of the Supreme Court of the United States: Troubled Beginning of the Modern State, 1888–1910* 393 (1993); Anthony Lewis, "Earl Warren," in *The Warren Court: A Critical Analysis,* ed. Richard Sayler, Barry Boyer, Robert E. Gooding, Jr., 1, 1 (1969); Hannah Arendt, *The Origins of Totalitarianism* 296 (1973 ed.) (I am grateful to Stephen Whitfield for linking Arendt's emphasis on "the right to have rights" to the Warren Court). "[T]he importance of individual dignity" is from David Rudenstine, "Justice Brennan, the Constitution, and Modern American Liberalism," 10 *Cardozo Law Review* 163, 176 (1988). According to Bernard Schwartz, "it may be said that for the first time in our history [beginning in 1963], the first amendments to the Constitution were given effective practical meaning." Schwartz, "The Judicial Lives of Earl Warren," 15 *Suffolk University Law Review* 1, 20 (1981). On the Court and the Vietnam War see Rodric Schoen, "A Strange Silence: Vietnam and the Supreme Court," 33 *Washburn Law Review* 275 (1994). Perhaps the Court failed to find the war unconstitutional for prudential reasons, fearing a loss of its prestige if it could not enforce the decision. I think it is equally likely, however, that the justices acted as they did because they shared Lyndon Johnson's views about the war. Given globalism's importance to post–World War II American liberalism, the Warren Court's refusal to rule on the constitutionality of the Vietnam War was consistent with liberalism. See William O. Douglas, *The Court Years: 1939–1975* 151–52 (1980) (talking of his frustration at his colleagues' refusal to rule on constitutionality of the war in Vietnam). Douglas attacked the war itself in *Points of Rebellion* (1969), but he did not discuss the Warren Court's reaction to the war or its opinions involving dissent against the war at length there. For the argument that the Vietnam War really was constitutional, though the wars in Laos and Cambodia were not, see John Hart Ely,

War and Responsibility: Constitutional Lessons of Vietnam and Its Aftermath (1993). On the Warren Court and protest against the war see, e.g., *U.S. v. O'Brien,* 391 U.S. 367, 376 (1968). As Steven Shiffrin said, in invalidating draft-card burning, the Court there "put its head in the sand. . . . *O'Brien* is a first amendment horror story." Shiffrin, *The First Amendment, Democracy and Romance* 81 (1990). See generally Russell W. Galloway, Jr., "The Third Period of the Warren Court: Liberal Dominance (1962–1969)" 20 *Santa Clara Law Review* 773 (1980); Edward Heck, "Justice Brennan and the Heyday of Warren Court Liberalism," id. at 841. For a more extended exploration of the relationship between the Warren Court's liberalism and that of Lyndon Johnson's Great Society see John Morton Blum, *Years of Discord: American Politics and Society, 1961–1974* 187–217 (1991), and Kalman, *Abe Fortas,* at 277–92.

54. See, e.g., Kalman, *Abe Fortas,* at 250–55; Donald Horowitz, *The Courts and Social Policy* 171–219 (1977) (children); *Gray v. Sanders,* 372 U.S. 368 (1963) and *Reynolds v. Sims,* 377 U.S. 533 (1964) (in these voting cases, the rhetoric of "one man, one vote" covered over the fact that reapportionment benefited city dwellers); *Engel v. Vitale,* 370 U.S. 421 (1962) (declaring school prayer unconstitutional); A. Kenneth Pye, "The Warren Court and Criminal Procedure," 67 *Michigan Law Review* 249, 256 (1968); *Loving v. Virginia,* 338 U.S. 1 (1967) (striking down the state miscegenation laws Frankfurter had tried to evade in the 1950s); Gerald Gunther, "The Supreme Court, 1971 Term—Foreword: In Search of Evolving Doctrine on a Changing Court: A Model for a Newer Equal Protection Legacy," 86 *Harvard Law Review* 1, 8–10 (1972) (Warren Court's equal protection record); *Shapiro v. Thompson,* 394 U.S. 618, 630 (1969) (for later critiques of the Warren Court's failure to declare class a suspect classification, along with race, see, e.g., J. M. Balkin, "The Footnote," 83 *Northwestern University Law Review* 275, 308–9 [1989]; William Taylor, "*Brown,* Equal Protection, and the Isolation of the Poor," 94 *Yale Law Journal* 1700, 1726–29 [1986]). Ronald Kahn made the case "the level of innovation by the Warren Court in the fundamental rights and interests strand" was exaggerated, in Kahn, *The Supreme Court and Constitutional Theory, 1953–1993* 40 (1994). "[G]roup perspective on the victim" is from Owen Fiss, "The Supreme Court, 1978 Term—Foreword: The Forms of Justice," 93 *Harvard Law Review* 1, 19 (1979); "the first Court in American history" from Morton Horwitz, "The Warren Court and the Pursuit of Justice," 50 *Washington and Lee Law Review* 5, 10 (1993). For a penetrating discussion of the "impoverished" tendency of American constitutional law "to marginalize the role of groups," see Aviam Soifer, *Law and the Company We Keep* 101 (1995). On the Warren Court and state and federal courts see, e.g., *Fay v. Noia,* 372 U.S. 391 (1963); *Dombrowski v. Pfister,* 380 U.S. 479 (1965); Robert Glennon, "The Jurisdictional Legacy of the Civil Rights Movement," 61 *Tennessee Law Review* 869 (1994). "Barriers" is from Larry Yackle, *Reclaiming the Federal Courts* 31 (1994). Of all its decisions, according to Justice Brennan, the Warren Court opinions "binding the states to almost all of the restraints in the Bill of Rights" proved most significant for "the preservation and furtherance of the ideals we have fashioned for our society." William Brennan, "The Bill of Rights and the States: The Revival of State Constitutions as Guardians of Individual Rights," 61 *New York University Law Review* 535, 536, and see 540–45 (1986).

55. Kathleen Sullivan, "The NonSupreme Court," 91 *Michigan Law Review* 1121, 1121

(1993); William Brennan, "The Role of the Court—The Challenge of the Future," in *William J. Brennan, Jr.: An Affair with Freedom,* ed. Stephen Friedman, 315, 332 (1967); the critic was Richard Funston, in *Constitutional Counterrevolution? The Warren Court and the Burger Court: Judicial Policy Making in Modern America* 309 (1977); Anthony Lewis, "Earl Warren," in *Justices of the United States Supreme Court 1789–1969,* ed. Leon Friedman and Fred Israel, 4: 2721, 2726 (1980) (Warren as "the closest thing"); Lewis, "Earl Warren," in *The Warren Court,* at 30 ("present"); *Reynolds* v. *Sims,* at 620; Michael Boudin, Book Review, 67 *Virginia Law Review* 1251, 1255 (1981) ("a continuing constitutional convention"); Fred Graham, *The Self-Inflicted Wound* 321 (1970). Thus Judge Henry Friendly, for example, worried publicly that the Court did not recognize "there is danger in moving too far too fast." Friendly, "The Bill of Rights as a Code of Criminal Procedure," 53 *California Law Review* 929, 930 (1965).

56. *Griswold* v. *Connecticut,* 381 U.S. 479, 484–85 (1965); Garrow, *Liberty,* at 245–54.

57. Garrow, *Liberty,* at 237, 78, 251–55. The concurrence was that of Justice Byron White. Id.

58. Stephen Feldman discussed the atypical nature of *Griswold* in "From Modernism to Postmodernism in American Thought: The Significance of the Warren Court" (forthcoming). For the reference to "unprincipled penumbralist" and the argument that "penumbral reasoning is more common than is generally realized and is used regularly by judges generally regarded as conservative," see generally Glenn Reynolds, "Penumbral Reasoning on the Right," 140 *University of Pennsylvania Law Review* 1333, 1336–37 (1992). H. Jefferson Powell has made an interesting argument that the return to *Lochner* did not occur until Brennan reinterpreted the meaning of *Griswold* for the Burger Court in *Eisenstadt* v. *Baird,* 405 U.S. 438, 453 (1972). In Powell's narrative, *Roe* is important because it "unveiled the meaning of *Eisenstadt.*" See Powell, *Moral Tradition,* at 173–79.

59. Mark Tushnet, "Judges and Constitutional Theory: A View from History," 63 *University of Colorado Law Review* 425, 439, (1992) ("constitutional theory"); Tushnet, *Red, White, and Blue: A Critical Analysis of Constitutional Law* 133 (1988) ("Earl Warren"). "Yes, Counsel" is from Bobbitt, *Constitutional Fate,* at 135. As Bobbitt noted, "The famous question is widely quoted but less easily verified." Id. at 267 n.56. "With five votes" quoted in Fiss, "Objectivity and Interpretation," 34 *Stanford Law Review* 739, 758 (1982).

60. Kalman, *Abe Fortas,* at 272, 276.

61. Horwitz, "Warren Court," at 11. "Of course, 'real reasons' such as you speak of always operate. But it is our business to analyze their [the judges'] business as if those reasons did not operate, for it is our business to see that those reasons operate as little as possible, and the way to achieve that is to write as if they didn't. At least so I have been taught to believe, though the belief may very well be self-serving, since the academic branch of the legal profession would be out of business otherwise." Bickel to Frederick Wiener, December 13, 1961, Box 9, Folder 166, Bickel Papers.

62. Sanford Kadish, "A Note on Judicial Activism," 6 *Utah Law Review* 467, 467 (1958) ("a notable school"); Herbert Wechsler, Remarks, 74 F.R.D. 219, 294 (1976). For a critique of the assumption that the Warren Court hurt the institutional legitimacy of

the judiciary see, e.g., Erwin Chemerinsky, *Interpreting the Constitution,* 133–37, (1987).

63. Quotes from Martin Shapiro, "Fathers and Sons: The Court, the Commentators, and the Search for Values," in *The Burger Court: The Counter-Revolution That Wasn't,* ed. Vincent Blasi, 218, 219 (1984); Silber and Miller, "Neutral Principles" at 926. On Bickel's "can't help" see Silver, "Warren Court Critics," at 385–86; Bickel to Frankfurter, July 29, 1961, Part III, Reel 14, Frankfurter Papers (regarding *Mapp* v. *Ohio,* 367 U.S. 643 [1961]).

64. Charles E. Clark and David Trubek, "The Creative Role of the Judge: Restraint and Freedom in the Common Law Tradition," 71 *Yale Law Journal* 255, 267–68, 270 (1961); Clark, "The Limits of Judicial Objectivity," 12 *American University Law Review* 1 (1963); Thurman Arnold, "Professor Hart's Theology," 73 *Harvard Law Review* 1298, 1313 (1960); Rostow, "The Democratic Nature of Judicial Review," in *Sovereign Prerogative,* at 168; Charles Black, *The People and the Court* 52–53 (1960); Black, *Structure and Relationship in Constitutional Law* 7, 72, 95 (1969); Black, "On the Failure and Success of Courts," reprinted in Black, *The Humane Imagination* 140, 146 (1986). Another Warren Court apologist was Archibald Cox. See, e.g., Cox, *The Warren Court: Constitutional Decision as an Instrument of Reform* (1968). Martin Shapiro identified Vincent Blasi, Paul Brest, Jesse Choper, John Ely, Owen Fiss, Thomas Grey, Frank Michelman, Henry Monaghan, Lawrence Tribe, and William Van Alstyne as members of a new generation of Supreme Court scholars concerned with how the Court should act, whose "consciousness-shaping crisis was not 1937 but 1954." All were born in the 1930s or 1940s. "Ronald Dworkin (1931) and Kenneth Karst (1929) are the elder statesmen of the group." Shapiro, "Fathers and Sons," at 220, 309 n.5.

The generation shaped by 1937, whose members pleaded for better craftsmanship, is examined in Silver, "Warren Court Critics," at 375–421. Silver observed, however, that "there is strong evidence that, for some critics [in the 1937 generation, who urged better craftsmanship] the plea served to cloak disagreements with the substantive decisions of the Supreme Court." Id. at 378. Further, the Warren Court critics often expressed their disapproval in audacious fashion. Philip Kurland was especially snotty. Wright cited Kurland's 1963 *Harvard Law Review* foreword as "a prime example of the usual haughty derision merging into almost scurrilous disrespect." Wright, "Professor Bickel," at 778 n.33. He should have seen Kurland's private correspondence! Kurland wrote Bickel: "That Skelly Wrong should use your book as a focus for his Harvard Law Review article and ignore mine is ignominy indeed. I thought of writing the reply article for the Harvard Law Review to gain my own place in the sun. I even wrote the first sentence: 'For the simple-minded all things are simple.' And I was prepared to tell how each night as my girls go to bed, they say to me: 'Please Daddy, tell us again, the story of how Judge Wright desegregated the public schools in the District of Columbia.' " Kurland to Bickel, April 16, 1971, Box 4, Folder 87, Bickel Papers.

65. Alexander Bickel, "The Kennedy Cause," *New Republic,* July 20, 1968, 42; Bickel to Anthony Lewis, July 16, 1968; Bickel to William Hackett, June 18, 1968, Box 10, Folder 191, Bickel Papers; Bickel to Burke Markshall, June 6, 1968, id. At first, Bickel had little use for Kennedy. "Bobby makes me sick," he wrote Frankfurter in 1960. Bickel to Frankfurter, December 29, 1960, Frankfurter Papers. See Bickel, "Robert

F. Kennedy: The Case against Him for Attorney General," *New Republic,* January 9, 1961, 15. Bickel's "sense of the impropriety of the Kennedy candidacy" led him to support Kenneth Keating against Robert Kennedy in the 1964 Senate race. At the time, he classified Robert Kennedy as a carpetbagger who had little respect for due process and who was responsible for the Kennedy administration's appointment of segregationist judges in the South. Bickel, Draft Letter to Editor, *New York Times,* October 23, 1964, Box 9, Folder 173, Bickel Papers. As Bickel said, Kennedy, "the world and I all changed." Bickel to Anthony Lewis, July 16, 1968, Box 10, Folder 191, Bickel Papers. Kennedy's opposition to the war in Vietnam won over Bickel. He wrote Harold Leventhal in 1968: "I know that it is very risky to abandon an otherwise liberal, sitting democratic President, and I am proud to this day of never having been tempted to desert Truman in 1948, but I am sick at heart with the Vietnam war and with all it has done to the country, and that for me is almost the single issue." Bickel to Leventhal, January 10, 1968, Box 10, Folder 148, Bickel Papers. Bickel originally supported McCarthy in 1968. Statement, May 17, 1968, Box 35, Folder 4, id. In 1969, Bickel wrote Daniel Patrick Moynihan, a former Robert Kennedy campaigner who had gone to work for the Nixon White House, "I think now—and I really didn't think so then [spring 1968]—that our man would be President if he had been allowed to live." Bickel to Moynihan, October 20, 1969, Box 10, Folder 200, id.

Did Bickel change again and, if so, when? According to Maurice Holland, Bickel's "rank apostasy" to liberalism came when he delivered "The Supreme Court and the Idea of Progress" as the Holmes Lectures at Harvard in October 1969. Holland, "American Liberals," at 1026. "To the evident shock of his audience, he argued that on the two greatest issues which it [the Warren Court] dealt with—schools and voting—the Court misread the American future," Anthony Lewis reported in "The Heavenly City of Professor Bickel," *New York Times,* October 10, 1969, Box 14, Folder 34, Bickel Papers. In the published version, Bickel turned his back on the role for the Court he had set out in *The Least Dangerous Branch* with a message just as bleak: "I have come to doubt in many instances the Court's capacity to develop 'durable principles,' and to doubt, therefore, that judicial supremacy can work and is tolerable in broad areas of social policy." Bickel, *Supreme Court,* at 99. According to the dust jacket for *The Supreme Court,* Bickel condemned the Court for "irrationality, inconsistency, and at times, incoherence; of overconfidence in itself and in the rule of the majority; and of unwise decisions which lead to undue centralization of government"; in the text, he speculated *Brown* "may be headed for—dread word— irrelevance." Id. at 151. Rereading the book, however, I am struck by its unhysterical tone. The lectures that constituted its basis had apparently been written before intense campus unrest occurred in the Ivy League. Initially scheduled for April 1969, they were postponed because "Harvard blew up." Bickel to Robert Bork, April 28, 1969, Box 10, Folder 194, Bickel Papers.

I think Bickel's "rank apostasy" to liberalism did not occur until the campus disturbances in 1970, which culminated in the New Haven Panther trials in the spring. See Bickel, "The Tolerance of Violence on the Campus," *New Republic,* June 13, 1970, 15. Bickel's personal correspondence in 1970 indicated that he was becoming increasingly unhappy at Yale and was considering accepting one of several offers he had received elsewhere. See, e.g., Bickel to Ronald Dworkin, January 19, 1970,

Box 10, Folder 203, Bickel Papers. I see a real difference between Bickel's acknowledgment that if the Warren Court proved correct "it isn't going to matter that . . .
its reasoning is . . . faulty" in *The Supreme Court and the Idea of Progress* (at 99)
and his suggestion in *The Morality of Consent* (1975) that the Warren Court led
naturally to Watergate (at 120–22). Nevertheless, it seems clear that at the time, the
Holmes Lectures and *The Supreme Court and the Idea of Progress* were perceived
as Bickel's break with liberalism. Wright, "Professor Bickel," at 771–72; Leon Friedman, "Judicial Activism," *Commentary,* May 1970, 94; William Wiecek, Book Review, *Saturday Review,* April 4, 1970, 37; Joseph Alsop, "Warren Court Attacked
Again, This Time by the U.S. Left," *Washington Post,* December 3, 1969, Box 14,
Folder 40, Bickel Papers; Silver, "Warren Court Critics," at 418.

66. Silver, "Warren Court Critics," at 407. See also the concluding paragraph of Kurland,
Politics, at 206: "The Nixon Court has awesome tasks before it: To match the Warren Court attainments in the protection of individuals and minorities that today justifies the Court's existence; to restore the confidence of the American public in the
rule of law. One or the other is not enough." Of the two other Warren Court critics
Silver studied, Freund "seemed never to attack the Court," and by the late 1960s,
Wechsler had "almost vanished from the scene." Silver, "Warren Court Critics," at
419–20. Though Freund was apparently reluctant to publish criticism of the Court,
he criticized it to Frankfurter, in speeches, and to Harvard students. See, e.g., Freund
to Frankfurter, July 13, 1962, Part III, Reel 15, Frankfurter Papers ("In your absence
your Brethren seem to have gone off on a spree. It's as if they felt like the emancipated
Negro whom Zech Chafee liked to quote: 'There's a looseness 'bout this freedom
that I like.' Of course I have in mind the prayer case especially"); Richard Hannaway,
"Freund: *Engel* Basis 'Unfortunate,' " *Harvard Law Record,* November 29, 1962.

67. Jerry Berman and Edgar Cahn, "Bargaining for Justice: The Law Students' Challenge
to Law Firms," 5 *Harvard Civil Rights–Civil Liberties Law Review* 16 (1970) (challenge to corporate law firms); Richard Posner, *Overcoming Law* 82 (1995) ("moved
easily"); Alexander, "What We Do," at 1901 (law professors' belief they ran the real
world). Quotations about law and society are from Trubek, "Future," at 48, 39 ("a
union"; "liberal legal agenda"); Robert Kidder, "From the Editor," 22 *Law and
Society Review* 625, 625 (1988) ("defeated, diverted"). For an overview of the relationship between the law and society movement and liberalism in law, see Trubek's
essay "Future," and White, "Critical Legal Studies," at 830–36. Lawrence Friedman
provides an illuminating discussion of the marginalization of law and society inside
and outside the law schools in "The Law and Society Movement," 38 *Stanford Law
Review* 763, 773–79 (1986). "[G]rowing incidence" is from Arthur Miller, "On the
Need for 'Impact Analysis' of Supreme Court Decisions," reprinted in *The Impact of
Supreme Court Decisions: Empirical Studies,* ed. Theodore Becker, 7, 14 (1969). On
Tom Emerson see, e.g., Guido Calabresi, "Tom Emerson: The Scholar as Hero," 101
Yale Law Journal 315 (1991) and the other tributes in that volume. See also Stephen
Werber, "On Defining Academic Scholarship," 40 *Cleveland State Law Review* 209,
211 (1992) (repeating Kalven's observation about *New York Times* v. *Sullivan,* 376
U.S. 254 [1964]); Charles Reich, "The New Property," 73 *Yale Law Journal* 733
(1964); *Goldberg* v. *Kelly,* 397 U.S. 254 (1970); Charles Reich, "Commentary," 100
Yale Law Journal 1465 (1991); Fred Shapiro, "The Most-Cited Articles from the
Yale Law Journal," id. at 1449, 1462. See also Harry Wellington, "Challenges to

Legal Education: The 'Two Cultures' Phenomenon," 37 *Journal of Legal Education* 327, 328 (1987): "The legal scholarship of 25 or 30 years ago that could be used ideologically was used by those practitioners on the bench and at the bar who were liberals or who represented liberal causes." It did not always get them as far as they wanted to go. "[U]ltimately Charles Reich failed to convince the Court that entitlements of the welfare and regulatory state, because they serve the same function as traditional property, should be accorded similar constitutional treatment." Margaret Radin, *Reinterpreting Property* 238 n.59 (1993).

Later, people too young to have gone to law school in the 1960s described the law school world of that period more critically. See, e.g., Guyora Binder, "On Critical Legal Studies as Guerilla Warfare," 76 *Georgetown Law Journal* 1, 24 (1987): "The staid, professional education the law students were receiving was not only at odds with the party going on elsewhere on campus, but it prevented them from joining it. Going to law school in the late sixties was like having to go to summer school while your friends were out playing ball."

68. Tushnet suggested Warren Court decisions hurt the Great Society, in "Warren Court," at 20. Quotations are from Alexander Bickel to Gilbert Harrison, October 28, 1958, Box 18, Folder 4, Bickel Papers; Frederick Bernays Wiener to Bickel, August 6, 1970, Box 9, Folder 151, id. ("Nine Old Men"); Frankfurter to Bickel, March 18, 1963, Box 82, Folder 25, id.; Bickel to Kenneth Tollett, October 5, 1965, Box 9, Folder 177, id.; ("moratorium"); Philip Kurland, "The Supreme Court, 1963 Term—Foreword: 'Equal in Origin and Equal in Title to the Legislative and Executive Branches of the Government,' " 78 *Harvard Law Review* 143, 175–76 (1964). Bickel's insistence that he "generally functioned without regard to the question of aid and comfort" to Warren Court enemies is from Bickel to Anthony Lewis, June 6, 1974, Box 11, Folder 243, Bickel Papers. Bickel continued: "Now Tony, Tony, how often have I been told that to say this or that is to give comfort to one or another son-of-a-bitch. I was a very young man when Bill Coleman and others charged me—in friendship and good nature, to be sure—with giving comfort to Jimmy Byrnes, and suggested that I should not have published my article on *The Original Understanding of the Segregation Decision*." Id. Yet when Byrnes cited that article in support of the argument that the Court had misread the history of the Fourteenth Amendment, Bickel said publicly he had been misrepresented. James F. Byrnes, "The Supreme Court Must Be Curbed," *U.S. News and World Report,* May 18, 1956, 50; Bickel, "Frankfurter's Former Clerk Disputes Byrnes's Statement," id., June 15, 1958, 132. For other defenses of the Warren Court by Bickel to the public see, e.g., Bickel's critique of the Southern Manifesto, "Ninety-Six Congressmen versus the Nine Justices," *New Republic,* April 23, 1956, 11, 13; and "An Inexplicable Document," September 29, 1958, 9 (about state court chief justices' report criticizing the Court), "Court-Curbing Time," May 25, 1959, 10, "Barry [Goldwater] Fights the Court," October 10, 1964, 9, "Voting the Court Up or Down: Fortas, Johnson and the Senate," September 28, 1968, 21, all in the *New Republic* (of the last piece, an ambivalent endorsement of Johnson's nomination of Fortas as chief justice, Bickel wrote Anthony Lewis: "I turned chicken." Bickel to Lewis, October 22, 1968, Box 10, Folder 193, Bickel Papers).

69. "With the Editors," 83 *Harvard Law Review* vii–viii (no. 4, 1970). See also "With the Editors," 82 *Harvard Law Review* vii (no. 7, 1969): "[A]ttempts to come to

intellectual terms with issues central to the judicial process, however uncertain of success, will always represent a memorial to Professor Hart."

70. Richard Dyson to Hart, March 27, 1962, Dedication, 83 *Harvard Law Review* 1 (1969); Editorials, "Lawyers as 'Hired Guns,' " November 14, 1969, 8, "Ralph Nader . . . ," November 7, 1968, 8, "The Day After," March 5, 1970, 8, "The Nixon Court," March 4, 1971, 10, all in *Harvard Law Record;* Fiss, "Life Lived," at 1129. The same page on which *Harvard Law Review* editors dedicated the issue to Warren featured Archibald Cox's celebration of Warren. Cox, "Chief Justice Earl Warren," 83 *Harvard Law Review* 1 (1969). "[T]o my knowledge nothing of this anti-intellectual, indeed anti-mind sort has ever before appeared in the pages of the *Review,*" Bickel grumbled privately. Bickel to Frederick Wiener, December 15, 1969, Box 10, Folder 202, Bickel Papers. Richard Parker recalled asking Freund to write the article on Warren; Freund refused, telling Parker the editors should not even dedicate the issue to Warren. Conversation with Richard Parker, December 6, 1994.

71. President's Page, 22 *Stanford Law Review* (January 1970) ("[G]lossy admissions brochures," "law, long dominated," and "altruism"); Yackle, *Federal Courts,* at 213 ("Federal courts are special"); Glendon, *Nation,* at 89 ("law seemed like a romance," quoting from Thomas Geoghegan, "Warren Court Children"); Dedication, 84 *Yale Law Journal* 405 (1975); Bickel to David Reisman, February 25, 1974, Box 11, Folder 239, Bickel Papers ("vision"); Dedication, 84 *Yale Law Journal* (December 1974) ("little Earl Warrens" and "little Alexander Bickels"); Mark Tushnet, "Critical Legal Studies: A Political History," 100 *Yale Law Journal* 1515, 1535 (1991) (Tushnet suggested, however, that for "red diaper babies" Warren may not have played a pivotal role. "The formative legal experience for this group, I believe, was the law's half-hearted defense of civil liberties against McCarthyism, not the civil rights movement; the paradigmatic judge was Irving Kaufman, not Earl Warren." Id. at 1535); Alan Freeman, "Racism, Rights and the Quest for Equality of Opportunity: A Critical Legal Essay," 23 *Harvard Civil Rights–Civil Liberties Law Review* 295, 302 (1988) ("We did not notice"); Wright, "Professor Bickel," at 804. See also Cox, "Chief Justice Warren," at 4: "[T]he strongest support for the decisions of the Warren Court comes from the rising generation, as is partly evidenced by the Editors' decision to dedicate this issue of the *Harvard Law Review* to the retired Chief Justice"; Vincent Blasi, "A Requiem for the Warren Court," 48 *Texas Law Review* 608, 621–22 (1970): "[I]n the final analysis they [the young] may be what the Warren Court was all about. . . . With the promise of judicial activism, legal skills became important tools of social reform and idealists were increasingly attracted to the law."

72. Paul Savoy, "Towards a New Politics of Legal Education," 79 *Yale Law Journal* 444, 444 (1970) ("small but articulate"); John Griffiths, Book Review, 77 *Yale Law Journal* 827, 827 (1968) ("Our judges"). Savoy discussed the critique of the Warren Court's attitude toward dissent from the left in "New Politics," at 450: "The discontented students in our current law school classes are raising not only a direct challenge to the viability of our educational institutions, but a frontal assault upon certain venerable legal doctrines nourished by middle-class liberal values. For students who have experienced the Free Speech Movement at Berkeley, the march on the Pentagon, the Democratic National Convention in Chicago, the rebellion at Columbia and the confrontation over People's Park in Berkeley—to say nothing of the countless number of demonstrations, protests and draft resistance movements that have struck almost every

campus in the country—the refusal of the law to accord the same degree of constitutional protection to symbolic conduct that it has conferred upon conventional speech is an insistence that lawful speech be lifeless speech. Thus the recent decision of the Supreme Court in the draft card cases and its timid opinions in the flag-burning and black armbands cases are not merely 'unhappy' chapters in the chronicles of a liberal Court. They are powerful satires of the mystifying rhetoric of political repression." See also the complaints about the Warren Court's symbolic speech decisions voiced by book reviewers of Abe Fortas's pamphlet *Concerning Civil Dissent and Civil Disobedience* (1968), which defended those decisions. Terrance Sandalow, Book Review, 67 *Michigan Law Review* 599, 606–9, 611–12 (1968); Michael Tigar, Book Review, at 612. Bickel anticipated the critique that Warren Court decisions did not foster community and spoke of "a reaction to the steady unification and nationalization of recent years, a movement toward a decentralization and a diversity of which the as yet unacknowledged prophet—due, I should suppose, for a revival—is Brandeis," in *Supreme Court,* at 115–16. The Brandeis revival did not occur until the 1980s. See Helen Garfield, "Twentieth Century Jeffersonian: Brandeis, Freedom of Speech, and the Republican Revival," 69 *Oregon Law Review* 527 (1990).

73. Howard Zinn, *Disobedience and Democracy: Nine Fallacies on Law and Order* (1968); Stuart Scheingold, *The Politics of Rights: Lawyers, Public Policy, and Political Change* 5, 211 (1974); Joan Roelofs, "The Warren Court and Corporate Capitalism," 39 *Telos* 94, 94 (1979).

74. Anthony Chase, "A Note on the Aporias of Critical Constitutionalism," 36 *Buffalo Law Review* 403, 418–19 n.32 (1988) ("very few"); Savoy, "New Politics," at 444 ("student revolts"). Former Harvard Law School dean Erwin Griswold declared himself "happy to say that, on the whole, law schools have been less engulfed in the group neurosis than other parts of the universities." Griswold to Bickel, June 12, 1970, Box 3, Folder 65, Bickel Papers. As legal historian Jerold Auerbach put it, "the timbers of legal education" might have "rattled," but "the foundation held firm." Auerbach, "What Has the Teaching of Law to Do with Justice?" 53 *New York University Law Review* 457, 466 (1978). Perhaps the foundation held firm at other professional schools as well.

75. Tushnet, "Critical Legal Studies: Political History," at 1531 n.63 ("commune"); Louis Pollak, Memorandum to Alumni and Other Friends of the Law School, June 1, 1970, reprinted in 16 *Yale Law Report* 1, 2 (summer 1970) ("any attempt"); Bickel, "Tolerance of Violence," at 16; "With the Editors," 81 *Harvard Law Review* vii (1967–68); The Editors, "Symposium in Memory of Dr. Martin Luther King, Jr.," 68 *Columbia Law Review* (June 1968); Joel Seligman, *The High Citadel: The Influence of Harvard Law School* 6–7 (1978) (quoting Harvard Law School dean Derek Bok); Richard Hoffman, "Harvard Sit-In Stirs Students," *Harvard Law Record,* April 24, 1969, 1; Walter Metzger, "The Crisis of Academic Authority," 99 *Daedalus* 568, 571 (winter 1970). In 1968, a committee chaired by Ellen Peters held hearings on student dissatisfaction at Yale Law School. As at Harvard, the dissatisfaction apparently centered around grading, student participation in governance, and alienation. See J. G. Deutsch, Memorandum, March 12, 1968, Box 63, Folder 26, Bickel Papers; First Year Demand Committee, Memorandum to the Faculty and Students of the Yale Law School, April 30, 1968, id.: "If Yale has lost some of the magic of the thirties, perhaps we can help it to construct a greater relevance for the 60's and 70's."

It may well be that the atmosphere in the law schools during the late 1960s and early 1970s was more roiled than I suggest here. For another example, in 1969, the *Harvard Law Review* published a statement it said had been approved by two-thirds of its membership declaring the war in Vietnam "immoral" and calling for withdrawal of American troops. See "With the Editors," 82 *Harvard Law Review* vii (no. 3, 1969). Since only two of the fourteen members of the board of overseers of the *Harvard Law Review* believed it appropriate for the editors to state their political views in that fashion, the editors may have thought that in publishing the statement, they risked damaging their careers. J. William Doolittle to the president, *Harvard Law Review*, May 5, 1969, Box 3, Folder 48, Bickel Papers. But how risky could they have thought it was? The statement was unsigned, and Doolittle simply asked the president to place his letter "in the files of the Review for whatever value it may have for future Board of Editors." Id. Like their counterparts at Yale, "almost the entire [Harvard] Law School community" responded to Nixon's 1970 incursion in Cambodia "with active and personal political involvement. Often at real sacrifice, faculty and students both put aside immediate work and plans, undertook writing projects and mail campaigns, collected funds and signatures and joined primary campaigns and peace demonstrations." Editorial, "November Electioneering," *Harvard Law Record,* November 15, 1970, 10; Derek Bok, Harvard Law School Occasional Newsletter to Alumni, no. 2, May 14, 1970; Pollak, Memorandum to Alumni and Other Friends of the Law School. Again, in comparison to the activities of students elsewhere on campus, those of law students seemed tame.

The issue of how much the political unrest of the late 1960s and early 1970s affected legal education remains important because of the debate over whether the critical legal scholars of the 1970s and 1980s were "tenured radicals" who had attended law school in the 1960s and early 1970s. Compare Chase, "A Note," at 418–19 (suggesting that most prominent critical legal scholars were "too old or too young" to have been 1960s radicals and that the "frequent characterization of CLS professors as 1960s hippies or radicals who have gotten tenure in the law school could not be farther off the mark") with Maurice Holland, "A Hurried Perspective on the Critical Legal Studies Movement: The Marx Brothers Assault the Citadel," 8 *Harvard Journal of Law and Public Policy* 239, 243 (1985) (charging that the critical legal studies movement was composed mostly of "anti-war, student radicals who, fifteen years after their halcyon days are now accoutered with tenure and other perquisites of a system they affect to despise").

76. "Karl, Come Home" from Carol Brown, "The Early Years of the Sociology Liberation Movement," in *Radical Sociologists and the Movement: Experiences, Lessons, and Legacies,* ed. Martin Oppenheimer, Martin Murray, and Rhonda Levine, 43, 44 (1991); McCawley quoted in Randy Harris, *The Linguistics Wars* 206 (1993); "political complicity" from Graff, *Professing Literature,* at 240; "the 1968 charge" from Paul Lauter, *Canons and Contexts* 139 (1991).

77. Paul Buhle, "*Radical America* and Me," in *History and the New Left, Madison, Wisconsin, 1950–1970,* ed. Paul Buhle, 216, 226 (1990) ("If undergraduates" and "search for allies"); Buhle, "Madison: An Introduction," id. at 1, 29 ("struggles of the past"); David Hackett Fischer, *Historians' Fallacies: Toward a Logic of Historical Thought* 135 (1970). On the emergence of social history see John Higham, "Intro-

duction," in *New Directions in American Intellectual History,* ed. John Higham and Paul Conkin, xi, xiii (1979). "[W]hat happened in the 1960s was like the bursting of a dam. Social history had accumulated over the decades but it had been contained. It had never seemed powerful. Now an earthquake split the dam and released a flood of waters across the entire terrain of scholarship."

It must be emphasized that some social historians had nothing to do with the New Left. Though intellectuals associated with the New Left helped to originate and popularize the concept of corporate liberalism, social history preceded the New Left and might have been equally influential had there been no New Left. Nevertheless, some critics seem to suggest that social historians' connections with the political left taint the entire field of social history. See, e.g., Gertrude Himmelfarb, *The New History and the Old* (1987).

It is equally important to stress that not all radical historians espoused presentism. Those who did probably alienated other members of the profession because of their politics rather than their presentism. "The radical caucus's critique of the profession was expressed most fully in [Jesse] Lemisch's essay 'Present-Mindedness Revisited: Anti-Radicalism as a Goal of American Historical Writing since World War II,' presented at the 1969 AHA meeting," Jon Weiner said later. "The piece was a passionate response [to the argument of Eugene Genovese and others that historians should not condemn the Vietnam War or 'take an official stand' on any political issue], documented with 305 notes, to the argument that radical historians' political commitments undermined their work as scholars. Lemisch demolished the claim that the Left was injecting politics into a profession otherwise characterized by objectivity and political neutrality. Leading historians had often taken political positions in their work, Lemisch showed: they tended to be cold warriors who enlisted history in the fight against communism." Weiner, "Radical Historians and the Crisis in American History," 76 *Journal of American History* 399, 422–24 (1989).

Lemisch submitted his essay to the *American Historical Review.* In rejecting it, the editor wrote that Lemisch had " 'unjustly' convicted 'a good many of my close friends' of 'historical derelictions.' " Lemisch then submitted his piece to the *Journal of American History.* Its editor, Martin Ridge, told Lemisch that the "essay more than any I have read in several years has disturbed me." Ridge told Lemisch to read the story of Diego Rivera. A Communist, Rivera had included a portrait of Lenin in a 1933 mural he was commissioned to paint for Rockefeller Center. Rockefeller objected, and when Rivera refused to delete Lenin's face, Rockefeller had the mural destroyed. "The message intended for Lemisch was clear: the *Journal,* like the Rockefeller Center, was not a proper medium for expressing a certain point of view." One outside reader of Lemisch's piece wrote Ridge, "I don't know how you can tell him that he simply cannot do this, and that he certainly cannot do it in the pages of the *Journal.* He probably believes he can, which says something about how far he and his ilk are estranged from civilization." Lemisch's manuscript remained underground and "surfaced only through the efforts of a left publisher" in 1975. Thomas Schofield, "Introduction," in Jesse Lemisch, *On Active Service in War and Peace: Politics and Ideology in the American Historical Profession* 1, 3 (1975).

78. Buhle, "Madison," at 28–29, 3, 36 n.50. Bernstein's "Conservative Achievements of Liberal Reform" said as much about the 1960s as it did about the New Deal.

79. Theodore Lowi, *The End of Liberalism: The Second Republic of the United States* 51, 57, 233–36, 92–113 (1979 ed.). "It is liberalism because it is optimistic about government, expects to use government in a positive and expansive role, is motivated by the highest sentiments, and possesses a strong faith that what is good for government is good for the society. It is interest-group liberalism because it sees as both necessary and good a policy agenda that is accessible to all organized interests and makes no independent judgment of their claims. It is interest-group liberalism because it defines the public interest as a result of the amalgamation of various claims." Id at 51. Other political scientists also expressed dissatisfaction with liberalism. See Philip Green and Sanford Levinson, eds., *Power and Community: Dissenting Essays in Political Science* (1969); Kahn, *Supreme Court and American Constitutional Theory*, at 102, 251, 82–92. For earlier discussions of the conservatism of liberalism by historians see John Morton Blum, *The Republican Roosevelt* (1954), and Richard Hofstadter, *The Age of Reform* 252–53 (1955).

80. "[P]olitical authority," "the very basis," and Warren's remark are from "Rights and Responsibilities: The University's Dilemma," 99 *Daedalus* v, xi (winter 1970). Of the many paeans that appeared around the time of Warren's retirement, two of the most thoughtful are Blasi, "Requiem," and Charles Black, "The Unfinished Business of the Warren Court," 46 *Washington Law Review* 3 (1970). Philip Kurland's skeptical assessment in "Earl Warren, the 'Warren Court,' and the Warren Myths," 67 *Michigan Law Review* 353 (1968) spurred an impassioned response indicating that Warren was "a superb Justice." See Francis Beytagh, "On Earl Warren's Retirement: A Reply to Professor Kurland," 67 *Michigan Law Review* 1477, 1483 (1969). The new courses, of course, grew out of student demands in the late 1960s. Robert Bork joked that the Yale Law School catalogue should be rewritten to say: "Because of its colonial, capitalist, white racist inheritance, as laid bare in the preceding history of the school, most of the faculty and curriculum of the school are irrelevant to the central issues of our time. No more than 20% of the course and seminar offerings are even peripheral to the problems of the inner city. These insignificant offerings are overbalanced by traditional exercises in repression, not even concealed under such headings as Commercial Law, Criminal Law, and Debtors' Estates." Bork to Bickel, May 23, 1968, Box 10, Folder 193, Bickel Papers. For a more sober version of Bork's critique see Charles Black, "Some Notes on Law Schools in the Present Day," 79 *Yale Law Journal* 505, 510 (1970).

81. Michael Parrish, "Earl Warren and the American Judicial Tradition," 1982 *American Bar Foundation Journal* 1179, 1179 (1982).

82. "An Editorial Statement," 5 *Harvard Civil Rights–Civil Liberties Law Review* (1970); Michael Tigar, "The Supreme Court, 1969 Term—Foreword: Waiver of Constitutional Rights: Disquiet in the Citadel," 84 *Harvard Law Review* 1, 24, 27 (1970); Russell Caplan, "The Paradoxes of Judicial Review in a Constitutional Democracy," 30 *Buffalo Law Review* 451, 456 (1981) ("judicial Camelot").

83. The reference is to Justice Stewart's too frequently quoted comment on hard-core pornography in his concurrence in *Jacobellis* v. *Ohio*, 378 U.S. 184, 197 (1964), which I trot out again here: "I shall not today attempt further to define the kinds of material I understand to be embraced within that shorthand description; and perhaps I could never succeed in intelligibly doing so. But I know it when I see it."

84. Early on, Gerald Gunther saw a Burger Court "divided, uncertain and adrift." Gunther, "Foreword: In Search of Evolving Doctrine," at 1. L. A. Powe suggested the Warren era may have lasted through 1973, in "The Court between Hegemonies," 49 *Washington and Lee Law Review* 31, 35-36 (1992). Mark Tushnet mentioned renaming the Warren Court the Brennan Court in Tushnet, "Foreword," 77 *Virginia Law Review* 631, 634 (1991) (Tushnet might have added that the Brennan Court also decided that the death penalty, as it was then administered in the United States, was unconstitutional. *Furman* v. *Georgia*, 408 U.S. 238 [1972]). Cf. Tushnet, "Warren Court" at 33: "That, however, makes too much of Brennan's role within the Court. Labelling Courts is an exercise in cultural analysis, and the real question is what the public understands about the Supreme Court and its history. Brennan was primarily a tactician, devising ways to implement a vision clearly and properly associated with Warren. In that sense there was a Warren Court, and not a Brennan Court."

85. Blasi, "Rootless Activism of the Warren Court," in *The Burger Court*, at 198, 209–10; Ely, "Crying Wolf," at 944 ("Lochnering," and distinguishing methodology in *Roe* from that generally used by Warren Court, at 943); Gary Leedes, "The Supreme Court Mess," 57 *Texas Law Review* 1361, 1437 (1979) ("classic example"); Bobbitt, *Constitutional Fate*, at 157; Posner, *Overcoming Law*, at 180; Albert Alschuler, "Failed Pragmatism: Reflections on the Burger Court," 100 *Harvard Law Review* 1436, 1449 (1987) ("pragmatic issue"). On Tribe's changing rationales for *Roe*, compare, e.g., Lawrence Tribe, "The Supreme Court, 1972 Term—Foreword: Toward a Model of Roles in the Due Process of Life and Law," 76 *Harvard Law Review* 1, 10–11, 15 (1973), with Tribe, "Structural Due Process," 10 *Harvard Civil Rights–Civil Liberties Law Review* 269, 317–18 (1975); Tribe, *American Constitutional Law* 928–32 (1978). Garrow summarized the negative academic reaction to *Roe*, which he blamed in large part on Ely, in *Liberty*, at 609–16. The political scientist Ronald Kahn provided a revisionist account of the Burger Court, defending it against the claim that it simply refined "Warren Court doctrine in an activist but rootless manner," in *Supreme Court and Constitutional Theory*, at 137. According to Kahn, the "Burger Court had more complex views of polity malfunction and more innovative definitions of rights than the Warren Court." Id. at 181. I have not drawn heavily on his analysis because my task is to describe how law professors who would have characterized themselves as legal liberals perceived the Burger Court.

86. *Gedulig* v. *Aiello*, 417 U.S. 484, 496 (1974). For a list of examples of the Court's wavering see Alschuler, "Failed Pragmatism," at 1438–41.

87. Powell, *Moral Tradition*, at 179 ("epistemological crisis"); Nichol, "Constitutional Judgment," at 1108 ("significant constitutional actors" and "minor oracles"). Cf. id. (suggesting that academic lawyers perceived their mission as one of demonstrating that "*Brown* and *Roe* had been correctly decided, and that *Lochner* was not").

CHAPTER 2. "LAW AND"

1. Paul Samuelson, "The Convergence of the Law School and the University," 44 *American Scholar* 256, 258, 269 (1974); Novick, *That Noble Dream*, at 574. Admittedly, Samuelson, an economist who spent much of his professional career at a university without a law school, was no expert on the legal academy. But he was a good trend-

spotter. Martha Minow discussed the impact on law professors of the lack of jobs in the humanities and social sciences in "Law Turning Outward," 73 *Telos* 79, 91 (1987). See also Alvin Kernan, "Plausible and Helpful Things to Say about Literature at a Time when All Print Institutions Are Breaking Down," in *English Inside and Out: The Places of Literary Criticism,* ed. Susan Gubar and Jonathan Kramholtz, 9, 19 (1993): " 'Gypsy scholars' who are sometimes paid as little as $400 a course, the number of hours they can teach capped so that the university will not have to pay fringe benefits, are often forced to work at second and third jobs to earn enough to live. . . . But as the poor got poorer, professors taught less and less, and more of the teaching was done by the new academic proles." No one would dispute the emergence of gypsy scholars, but the notion that established academics in the humanities and social sciences were teaching less in the 1970s for more money is controversial. Compare Stanley Fish, "The Unbearable Ugliness of Volvos," in *There's No Such Thing as Free Speech . . . and It's a Good Thing Too* 273–74 (1994) (maintaining that in the mid-1970s "American academics stopped buying ugly Volkswagens and started buying ugly Volvos." In explaining that affluence, Fish pointed to the extra income from the lecture and conference circuit, "something that was not in place when I was a graduate student in the late fifties and early sixties"), with Frank Freidel, "American Historians: A Bicentennial Appraisal," 63 *Journal of American History* 5, 12 (1976) (observing that senior faculty members were beset by inflation in the 1970s. Freidel neglected to say that in many parts of the country, inflation and the real estate boom meant that the houses academics had bought earlier were worth a great deal more and that if they could find jobs in the 1970s, many young academics could not buy houses).

2. This information was taken from Law School Admission Services reports and Harry First, "Competition in the Legal Industry (I)," 53 *New York University Law Review* 311, 311 (1978).

3. Griswold quoted in Seligman, *High Citadel,* at 123 ("traditional" and "high grades"). Julius Getman compared mediocre grades in legal education to "original sin in Calvinist doctrine—something which could not be overcome by future good works." Getman, *In the Company of Scholars: The Struggle for the Soul of Higher Education* 254 (1992). See generally Richard Posner, "The Decline of Law as an Autonomous Discipline: 1962–1987," 100 *Harvard Law Review* 761, 766–77 (1987). Posner, however, dated the beginning of the decline to the 1960s.

4. Lawrence Tribe, *American Constitutional Law* iii–v, 1098, 9–13, 13, 414, 47 (1978); Thomas Cooley, *Treatise on the Constitutional Limitations Which Rest upon the Legislative Power of the States of the American Union* (1868). See Ethan Bronner, *Battle for Justice: How the Bork Nomination Shook America* 129–34 (1989), for a discussion of Tribe's activities outside the classroom.

5. Arthur Leff, "Law And," 87 *Yale Law Journal* 989 (1978); Richard Posner, Book Review, 37 *University of Chicago Law Review* 636, 636 (1970).

6. John Rawls, *A Theory of Justice* (1971). Cf. Robert Nozick, *Anarchy, State, and Utopia* (1974). Rawls now explicitly characterizes "justice as fairness" as a political, not moral, theory. See Rawls, *Political Liberalism,* at xvii, xxix. For further discussion of academic lawyers' discovery of philosophy see Lawrence Wiseman, "The New Supreme Court Commentators: The Principled, the Political, and the Philosophical," 10 *Hastings Constitutional Law Quarterly* 315 (1983); Richard Parker, "The Juris-

prudential Uses of John Rawls," in *Nomos XX: Constitutionalism*, ed. J. Roland Pennock and John Chapman, 269 (1979). Mark Tushnet discussed the link between Rawls's work and political liberalism in "Truth, Justice, and the American Way," 57 *Texas Law Review* 1307, 1316–17 (1979).

7. Rawls, *Theory of Justice*, at 31, 560, 136–37, 27, 14–15, 120, 251–57.

8. Id. at 14–15, 235 n.20, 204. The law professor was Richard Parker, in "Jurisprudential Uses of John Rawls," at 270–76.

9. Frank Michelman, "The Supreme Court, 1968 Term—Foreword: On Protecting the Poor through the Fourteenth Amendment," 83 *Harvard Law Review* 7, 9, 14–15 (1969); Michelman, "Property, Utility and Fairness: Comments on Ethical Foundations of 'Just Compensation' Law," 80 *Harvard Law Review* 1165, 1219–21 (1967); Michelman, "The Advent of a Right to Housing: A Current Appraisal," 5 *Harvard Civil Rights–Civil Liberties Law Review* 207, 209 (1970); Michelman, "Constitutional Welfare Rights and a Theory of Justice," in *Reading Rawls: Critical Studies on Rawls' A Theory of Justice*, ed. Norman Daniels, 319 (1989). "Michelman's 1969 Foreword, appropriating John Rawls's *Theory of Justice* as a theory of the equal protection clause, redefined the project" of the *Harvard Law Review* "Forewords." Though legal process theory and doctrinal analysis did not disappear, the new style was that of substantive critique, in which the author asked whether the Supreme Court "got it right" and generally offered "a theory or model external to constitutional doctrine. This model, like Michelman's, is often interdisciplinary, incorporating ideas from philosophy, political science, or economics. These substantive, nondoctrinal models provide the criteria by which the author evaluates the Supreme Court's opinions. The cases and doctrines discussed in these Forewords typically show no more than that the theory has some descriptive accuracy, if that. The substantive theories appear as ends in themselves." Tushnet and Lynch, "Harvard Forewords," at 484–87, 495.

10. See, e.g., *Williams* v. *Illinois*, 399 U.S. 235 (1970); *Tate* v. *Short*, 401 U.S. 395 (1971); *Bullock* v. *Carter*, 405 U.S. 134 (1972); Frank Michelman, "Welfare Rights in a Constitutional Democracy," 1979 *Washington University Law Quarterly* 659, 663. Gerald Gunther made the point that the Warren Court had only anticipated this move in dicta, in "Foreword: In Search," at 10. The 1973 case was *San Antonio Independent School District* v. *Rodriguez*, 411 U.S. 1; for *Washington* v. *Davis*, see 426 U.S. 229 (1976). For Fiss on *Washington* v. *Davis*, see Fiss, "Forms of Justice," at 23 n.49; Fiss, "Equality in Education," 74 F.R.D. 219, 276 (1976); and generally Fiss, *The Civil Rights Injunction* 36–37 (1978). See also David Strauss, "Discriminatory Intent and the Taming of *Brown*," 56 *University of Chicago Law Review* 935, 954 (1989): "*Washington v Davis* tamed *Brown*. The precedents—*Brown*, the cases decided in the two decades after *Brown* . . . —all left open the possibility that Brown would stand for a principle that mandated relatively far-reaching changes in society. In *Washington v Davis*, the Court closed off that possibility."

11. See Owen Fiss, "Thurgood Marshall," 125 *Harvard Law Review* 49, 51 (1991); Warren Burger, "The Special Skills of Advocacy: Are Specialized Training and Certification of Advocates Essential to Our System of Justice?" 42 *Fordham Law Review* 227 (1973). Burger's comment about young people is quoted in David Broder, *Changing of the Guard: Power and Leadership in America* 235 (1980). For Rehnquist's attack, see William Rehnquist, "Observation: The Notion of a Living Constitution,"

54 Texas Law Review 693, 706 (1976). "[I]nterlocking directorate" is from Paul Campos, "Advocacy and Scholarship," 81 *California Law Review* 817, 819 (1993). According to Richard Parker, law clerks' hostility to Burger led them to talk to Woodward and Armstrong, thereby making *The Brethren* possible. Conversation with Parker; Bob Woodward and Scott Armstrong, *The Brethren: Inside the Supreme Court* (1979).

12. Richard Posner, "Lawyers as Philosophers: Ackerman and Others," 1981 *American Bar Foundation Research Journal* 231, 233; Posner, *Overcoming Law*, at 101. Theodore Lowi made a similar point with respect to Ackerman's later shift to economics and "Constructivism" in *Reconstructing American Law* (1984). Lowi, "Deconstructing American Law," 63 *Texas Law Review* 1591, 1595 (1985).

13. Thus Robert Stevens argued that Ronald Dworkin's *Taking Rights Seriously* signaled the arrival of neoconceptualism, in *Law School: Legal Education in America from the 1850s to the 1980s* 274 (1983). For an extended discussion of the relationship between Dworkin and process theory, see Vincent Wellman, "Dworkin and the Legal Process Tradition: The Legacy of Hart and Sacks," 29 *Arizona Law Review* 413 (1987). See Allan Hutchinson, "Inessentially Speaking (Is there Politics after Postmodernism?)" 89 *Michigan Law Review* 1549, 1566 (1991) for the suggestion law professors "go no more a-courting" judges.

14. On the shift to lower federal courts and from federal courts to state courts see, e.g., Abram Chayes, "The Role of the Judge in Public Law Litigation," 89 *Harvard Law Review* 1281, 1284, 1298, 1313 (1976); William Brennan, "State Constitutions and the Protection of Individual Rights," 90 *Harvard Law Review* 489 (1977). See *National League of Cities* v. *Usery*, 426 U.S. 833 (1976); *overruled, Garcia* v. *San Antonio Metro Transit Authority*, 469 U.S. 532 (1985). "[A] step back" is from Bobbitt, *Constitutional Fate*, at 191; the students' comment from Dedication, 86 *Yale Law Journal* (no. 6, 1977). For the Michelman article, see Frank Michelman, "States' Rights and States' Roles: Permutations of 'Sovereignty' in *National League of Cities* v. *Usery*," 86 *Yale Law Journal* 1165, 1194, 1174 (1977); for other cues that Michelman was using *National League of Cities* as "a joker to play (or is it a joke?)," see id. at 1183, 1166, 1180, 1191. Michelman was not the only one to take this approach. See Lawrence Tribe, "Unravelling *National League of Cities*: The New Federalism and Affirmative Rights to Essential Government Services," 90 *Harvard Law Review* 1065 (1977). Michelman mentions his article's "kinship" to Tribe's in "States' Rights," at 1165.

15. Bruce Ackerman, "Regulating Slum Housing Markets on Behalf of the Poor: Of Housing Codes, Housing Subsidies and Income Redistribution Policy," 80 *Yale Law Journal* 1093 (1971). Wright cited Ackerman in *Robinson* v. *Diamond Housing Corporation*, 463 F. 2d 853, 860 (D.C. Cir. 1972).

16. Bruce Ackerman, *Social Justice in the Liberal State* 25, xi, 378, 368, 361–62 (1980); Ackerman, "Neutralities," in *Liberalism and the Good*, ed. R. Bruce Douglass, Gerald Mara, and Henry Richardson, 29, 38 (1990) ("popularize"). Michael Sandel juxtaposed the two quotations from Ackerman, "hard truth" and "Big Questions," in *Liberalism and the Limits of Justice* 176 n.2 (1982).

17. Ronald Dworkin, *Taking Rights Seriously* 132, 145–49, 105, 273, 87 (1977); Dworkin, *A Matter of Principle* 191, 359 (1985) (reiterating commitment to "equal concern and respect" and describing rights as "trumps"); Dworkin, *Rights*, at 149

("Constitutional law"). I do not intend to suggest that Dworkin followed Rawls on everything. See, e.g., Dworkin, "The Original Position," in Daniels, *Reading Rawls,* at 16, 17, 26.

18. Wellington is quoted in Paul Brest, "The Fundamental Rights Controversy: The Essential Contradictions of Normative Constitutional Scholarship," 90 *Yale Law Journal* 1063, 1069–70 (1981); Michelman quotations are in Frank Michelman, "In Pursuit of Constitutional Welfare Rights: One View of Rawls' Theory of Justice," 121 *University of Pennsylvania Law Review* 962, 1010, 1018 (1973). See also id. at 968. When law professors did find deconstruction, "the subjective/objective dichotomy" was one of the first targets. See Gerald Frug, "The Ideology of Bureaucracy in American Law," 97 *Harvard Law Review* 1276, 1287 (1984); James Boyle, "Is Subjectivity Possible? The Post-Modern Subject in Legal Theory," 62 *University of Colorado Law Review* 489 (1991).

19. Quotation is from Richard Saphire, "The Search for Legitimacy in Constitutional Theory: What Price Purity?" 43 *Ohio State Law Journal* 335, 378 n.191. Ackerman notes that philosophers found Rawls problematic, in *Social Justice and the Liberal State,* at 337. Ackerman's admission is in Ackerman, *We the People: Foundations* 11 (1991).

20. The characterization of legal history as a "Dark Continent" was Daniel Boorstin's and is quoted in Stephen Botein, "Professional History Reconsidered," 21 *American Journal of Legal History* 60, 60 (1977). On the professionalization of legal history in the 1970s see William E. Nelson, "1976," in *The Literature of American Legal History,* ed. William E. Nelson and John Reid, 201, 207–8 (1985). In speaking of "history for law professors," I mean only that the authors I disuss in this section, Horwitz and Berger, envisioned law professors as an important element of their audiences. Other historians, such as Pocock, Wood, and Bailyn, did not, and therefore it took some time for law professors to discover their work.

21. Horwitz, *Transformation,* at 253-54; Mark Tushnet, "Critical Legal Studies: An Introduction to Its Origin and Underpinnings," 36 *Journal of Legal Education* 505, 506 (1983). Robert Gordon maintained that Horwitz's "story lines" were "staple crops of mainstream Atlantic culture—so much so that I'm staggered by hearing their use in Horwitz' book so constantly called 'Marxist.' For God's sake, at any bar dinner you can listen to the most conservative lawyers talking about how the fellowship of the bar (community), sense of professionalism (craft ethic), and devotion to the public good (republicanism) have declined as the practice of law has become a business devoted to making money. Other legal historians had sounded these themes as well." Gordon, "Critical Legal Histories," 36 *Stanford Law Review* 57, 97 n.96 (1984). See Wythe Holt, "Morton Horwitz and the Transformation of American Legal History," 23 *William and Mary Law Review* 663 (1982), for a review of the critical reaction to Horwitz's work and an assessment of the book's importance; and see G. Edward White, "Transforming History in the Postmodern Era," 91 *Michigan Law Review* 1315, 1317, 1319–20 (1993).

22. Horwitz, *Transformation,* at xii; Stephen Presser, "Confessions of a Rogue Legal Historian: Killing the Fathers and Finding the Future of the Law's Past," 4 *Benchmark* 217, 219 (1990) ("excitement and drama"); Eben Moglen, "The Transformation of Morton Horwitz," 93 *Columbia Law Review* 1042, 1059 (1993) ("impieties" and

"dominated"). A Horwitz detractor might say that Horwitz did not give law professors reason to hold up their heads, but made historians look bad by showing how easily lawyers could mislead them.

23. Mark Tushnet, "Following the Rules Laid Down: A Critique of Interpretivism and
Neutral Principles," 96 *Harvard Law Review* 781, 787 (1983) ("better off"); Mark
Tushnet, "Constitutional Interpretation, Character, and Experience," 72 *Boston University Law Review* 747, 754-56 (1992) (quoting Frankfurter to Fairman and describing Frankfurter's view of history); Bickel to J. R. Pole, December 19, 1963, Box
9, Folder 170, Bickel Papers; Bickel to Robert Bork, October 9, 1968, Box 10, Folder
193, id.; Bickel, *Least Dangerous Branch,* at 103 ("No answer"); Aviam Soifer, "Reviewing Legal Fictions," 20 *Georgia Law Review* 871, 885 (1986) ("fabric of
fiction"); Arthur Miller, "The Elusive Search for Values in Constitutional Interpretation," 6 *Hastings Constitutional Law Quarterly* 487, 499 (1979) (quoting Warren); Alfred Kelly, "Clio and the Court: An Illicit Love Affair," 1965 *Supreme Court
Review* 119 (1965); Charles Miller, *The Supreme Court and the Uses of History*
(1969).

24. Miller, *Supreme Court and History,* at 6 ("inept and perverted," "trappings"); Kelly,
"Clio and the Court," at 122–23; William Wiecek, "Clio as Hostage: The United
States Supreme Court and the Uses of History," 25 *California Western Law Review*
227, 254 (1987) ("tended uniformly"). For a discussion of the outcry over Black's
dissent in *Adamson* v. *California,* 332 U.S. 92 (1947), see Kelly, "Clio and the
Court," at 120–21. "On those sporadic occasions" is from Klarman, "An Interpretive
History of Equal Protection," at 253. John Reid summarized the principal objections
to "law office history" in "Law and History," 27 *Loyola of Los Angeles Law Review*
193, 201–3 (1993): "Law office history is not history according to the canons of the
academic historical method"; "Law office history 'asks questions of the past that the
past cannot answer' . . . Too often law office history is a blatant use of the historical
method." For a fascinating discussion rooting the Court's need to use history in
cognitive dissonance theory see Theodore Blumoff, "The Third Best Choice: An Essay
on Law and History," 41 *Hastings Law Journal* 537 (1990).

25. Leonard Levy, *Constitutional Opinions* 193, 229 (1986); Vincent Blasi, "Creativity
and Legitimacy in Constitutional Law," 80 *Yale Law Journal* 176, 192 (1970) (noting
that Charles Black's structural theory of constitutional law might provide a liberal
version of original intent, a suggestion no one effectively followed up on until Ahkil
Amar); Miller, "Elusive Search," at 508.

26. Grey, "Unwritten Constitution," at 703, 706–8, 717, see also Grey, "Origins of the
Unwritten Constitution: Fundamental Law in American Revolutionary Thought," 30
Stanford Law Review 843 (1978); Grey, "The Constitution as Scripture," 37 *Stan-
ford Law Review* 1, 5, 19–23 (1984); Grey, "The Original Understanding and the
Unwritten Constitution," in *Toward a More Perfect Union: Six Essays on the Con-
stitution,* ed. Neil York, 145 (1988); Suzanna Sherry, "The Founders' Unwritten
Constitution," 54 *University of Chicago Law Review* 1127, 1170–72, 1175–76
(1987) (extending period of reliance on natural law up until Marshall's opinion in
Dartmouth College v. *Woodward,* 17 U.S. [4 Wheat.] 518 [1819]); Sherry, "Natural
Law in the States," 61 *University of Cincinnati Law Review* 171, 221 (1992) (state
court judges in Virginia, Massachusetts, New York, and South Carolina appealed to
natural law concepts "for a considerably longer period of time" than did federal

judges). But see, e.g., Wolfe, *Modern Judicial Review,* at 108–13 (contending reliance on natural law was "very rare" in early American history). Sherry's "Natural Law in the States" provides a good overview of the differing opinions about the reliance on natural law in the early republic. See generally William E. Nelson, "Emulating the Marshall Court: The Applicability of the Rule of Law to Contemporary Constitutional Adjudication," 131 *University of Pennsylvania Law Review* 489 (1982). For relatively early arguments that the interpretivist/noninterpretivist distinction begged the question and should be abandoned, see Paul Brest, "The Misconceived Quest for Original Understanding," 60 *Boston University Law Review* 204, 204 n. 1 (1980) ("Virtually all forms of constitutional decision making . . . require interpretation"). Ronald Dworkin, "The Forum of Principle," 56 *New York University Law Review* 468, 472 (1981): "Any recognizable theory of judicial review is interpretive in the sense that it aims to provide an interpretation of the Constitution as an original, foundational legal document, and also aims to integrate the Constitution into our constitutional and legal practice as a whole."

27. Martin Shapiro, "Morality and the Politics of Judging," 63 *Tulane Law Review* 1555, 1574 (1989); *McCulloch* v. *Maryland,* 17 U.S. (4 Wheat.) 316, 407 (1819); Grey, "Unwritten Constitution," at 703, 705–6.

28. Grey, "Unwritten Constitution," at 706, 717; Thomas Grey, "Property and Need: The Welfare State and Theories of Distributive Justice," 28 *Stanford Law Review* 877 (1976).

29. Leonard Boudin, *Government by Judiciary* 2: 545–56 (1932); Raoul Berger to James Thomson, September 11, 1982, Box 2, Folder 6, Raoul Berger Papers, Harvard Law School (hereafter cited as Berger Papers) ("Warren converted" and "academicians loved it"); Berger, *Government by Judiciary: The Transformation of the Fourteenth Amendment* 245, 408, 371 (1977) ("revised," "utterly unrealistic," "convert"); Berger to Alpheus T. Mason, March 14, 1976, Box 2, Folder 3, Berger Papers ("not insensible").

30. *Time,* November 14, 1977, 102; Louis Lusky, " 'Government by Judiciary': What Price Legitimacy?" 6 *Hastings Constitutional Law Quarterly* 403, 404 (1979) ("crystallized for millions"); Larry Alexander, "Modern Equal Protection Theories: A Metatheoretical Taxonomy and Critique," 42 *Ohio State Law Journal* 3, 4 (1981) ("all constitutional theorists"); Walter Murphy, "Constitutional Interpretation: The Art of the Historian, Magician, or Statesman?" 87 *Yale Law Journal* 1752, 1760–61 (1978) ("intelligent and patriotic"). The Hastings symposium "Government by Judiciary," in which Lusky's article was included, contained a representative sampling of criticism.

31. J. M. Balkin, "Constitutional Interpretation and the Problem of History," 63 *New York University Law Review* 911, 913 (1988) ("darling"); Charles Bosworth, "Professor Calls Court Rulings 'Lawless,' " May 3, 1981, *St. Louis Post Dispatch,* Berger Papers ("said to have helped"); and Berger to Willard Hurst, December 25, 1976, Box 1, Folder 19 ("torn"), Berger to Anthony Lewis, September 5, 1977, Box 2, Folder 2 ("recoil"), Berger to David Grais, September 24, 1977, Box 2, Folder 21 ("scant sympathy"), all in Berger Papers. For a sampling of Berger's earlier work, which had hurt Republicans, see Raoul Berger, *Impeachment: The Constitutional Problems* (1973), and his *Executive Privilege: A Constitutional Myth* (1974). Berger had also delivered the death blow to Crosskey's thesis about the illegitimacy of ju-

dicial review in a book (dedicated to the memory of Henry Hart) whose conclusions anticipated some of the findings he reached about the scope of judicial review in *Government by Judiciary*. See Berger, *Congress v. The Supreme Court* 340, 346 (1969).

Interestingly, Willard Hurst, whom I identify later here as the father of modern American legal history, had been the reader on Berger's "Government by Judiciary" manuscript for Harvard University Press. Though Hurst's reader's report "warned the press to expect some carnage" (Hurst to Berger, February 2, 1978, Box 1, Folder 19, Berger Papers), Hurst later expressed surprise "at the extent to which some critics have tried—vainly, I believe—to challenge you on your history. To my mind the only real course open to those who disagree with what the book lays out is frankly to state and argue for a flatly different set of values regarding the politically legitimate or socially useful role of the Court. Such a different valuation of the Court's role— one toward which I am very suspicious—can be stated intelligibly and argued rationally. But it has been disingenuous or naive of critics to attack your history because they want a different value premise for the Court's place in the system." Hurst to Berger June 9, 1981, id. "The acerbic and inflamed nature of most of the responses [to Berger] suggests that we are witnessing more than a 'mere' historical debate." Henry Monaghan, "Our Perfect Constitution," 56 *New York University Law Review* 353, 376 (1981). Monaghan warned that "Berger's uncomfortable and unfashionable analysis is an important one. It will not do, as some have already done, to brush it aside in a preremptory matter." Monaghan, "Commentary: The Constitution Goes to Harvard," 13 *Harvard Civil Rights–Civil Liberties Law Review* 117, 124 (1978). Berger's papers leave no doubt that he was, as he said, having "a corking good time" with the controversy. Berger to Alpheus T. Mason, June 21, 1981, Box 2, Folder 3, Berger Papers. He published a rebuttal to virtually every critique of his book and claimed that the scholars who praised the book possessed "higher stature" than those who criticized it. Berger, "Bruce Ackerman on Interpretation: A Critique," 1992 *Brigham Young University Law Review* 1035, 1050 (1992).

32. Balkin, "Constitutional Interpretation," at 914 ("increasing frustration"); Raoul Berger, "Constitutional Interpretation and Activist Fantasies," 82 *Kentucky Law Journal* 1, 15 (1993–94) (classifying himself as "a political 'liberal' "); Berger, "History, Judicial Revisionism and J. M. Balkin," 1989 *Brigham Young University Law Review* 759, 761 (1989) ("As long ago" and "credo"); Berger to James McClellan (*"labels"*), October 21, 1982, Box 2, Folder 4, Berger Papers (and continuing: "Nothing more shakes my confidence in my analysis than to learn that I am [Senator Jesse] Helms' darling. No scholar is responsible for the use others make of his learning"); James McClellan to Berger, October 8, 1982, id. ("not one darn constitutional scholar").

33. Brest, "Fundamental Rights," at 1087.

34. Regarding publishing practices, see, e.g., Berger to Arthur Rosenthal, May 26, 1973, Box 1, Folder 18, Berger Papers. Labeling legal history "the step-child of the law," Berger here generously suggested to Rosenthal, the director of Harvard University Press, that the proceeds of his prize money for his book on impeachment go toward the establishment of a prize "for the best legal-historical essay for each of five years" written by a Harvard law student. It is probable he intended legal history to include constitutional history. Since Harvard Law School dean Albert Sacks appointed Horwitz to select the recipient, however, and he and everyone else were writing about

private law at the time, the award probably had the effect of lowering the status of constitutional history still further. Albert Sacks to Arthur Rosenthal, July 3, 1973, Box 1, Folder 21, id. Both Rosenthal and Stanley Katz, the American Society for Legal History editor at the time, spoke appreciatively of the wide audience for Berger's work. See, e.g., Arthur Rosenthal to Berger, September 27, 1974, Box 1, Folder 18, id. ("Of course you made the year for everybody at the press"); Stanley Katz to Berger, August 30, 1973, Box 1, Folder 25, id.

    See Harry Scheiber, "American Constitutional History and the New Legal History: Complementary Themes in Two Modes," 68 *Journal of American History* 337, 338, 342 (1981); Paul Murphy, "Time to Reclaim: The Current Challenge of American Constitutional History," 69 *American Historical Review* 64 (1963) ("blocking"); William E. Nelson, "The Role of History in Interpreting the Fourteenth Amendment," 25 *Loyola of Los Angeles Law Review* 1177 (1992); Nelson, *The Fourteenth Amendment: From Political Principle to Judicial Doctrine* 8, 197–99 (1988); Nelson, *Americanization of the Common Law: The Impact of Legal Change on Massachusetts Society, 1760–1830* (1975); Nelson, *Dispute and Conflict Resolution in Plymouth County, Massachusetts, 1725–1825* (1981); Nelson, *The Roots of American Bureaucracy: 1830–1900* (1982); John Reid, *Constitutional History of the American Revolution: The Authority of Rights* (1986); Reid, *Constitutional History of the American Revolution: The Authority to Tax* (1987); Reid, *Constitutional History of the American Revolution: The Authority to Legislate* (1991); Reid, *Constitutional History of the American Revolution: The Authority of Law* (1993); Reid, *The Concept of Liberty in the Age of the American Revolution* (1988); Reid, *A Better Kind of Hatchet: Law, Trade, and Diplomacy in the Cherokee Nation during the Early Years of European Contact* (1976); Reid, "In an Inherited Way: English Constitutional Rights, the Stamp Act Debates and the Coming of the American Revolutions," 49 *Southern California Law Review* 1109 (1976); Reid, " 'In Our Contracted Sphere': The Constitutional Contract, the Stamp Act Crisis, and the Coming of the American Revolution," 76 *Columbia Law Review* 21 (1976); Reid, "In the First Line of Defense: The Colonial Charters, the Stamp Act Debate, and the Coming of the American Revolution," 51 *New York University Law Review* 177 (1976); Reid, *Law for the Elephant: Property and Social Behavior on the Overland Trail* (1980).

35. The law professor was Martin Flaherty in "History 'Lite,' " at 542. For a review of this work, which includes the law review articles Reid wrote in the 1970s, see id. at 542–46; Jack Greene, "From the Perspective of Law: Context and Legitimacy in the Origins of the American Revolution: A Review Essay," 85 *South Atlantic Quarterly* 56 (1986).

36. Dworkin, "Forum of Principle," at 476–99; "dogmas" is from Tushnet, "Following the Rules," at 784. Berger expressed his suspicion of process theory in a letter to Ward Eliot, April 24, 1976, Box 1, Folder 13, Berger Papers.

37. Michael Perry, *The Constitution, the Courts, and Human Rights: An Inquiry into the Legitimacy of Constitutional Policymaking by the Judiciary* 75, 101, 162 (1982) (see also Perry, Book Review, 78 *Columbia Law Review* 685 [1978]; Raoul Berger, "Michael Perry's Functional Justification for Judicial Activism," 8 *University of Dayton Law Review* 465, 466 [1983]; Berger to Perry, January 20, 1979, Box 2, Folder 8, Berger Papers). For the reaction to Perry's work see, e.g., symposium on *The Constitution, the Courts, and Human Rights*, "Judicial Review and the Constitu-

tion—The Text and Beyond," 8 *University of Dayton Law Review* 443 (1983). On constitutional law professors' indifference to history, see Monaghan, "Our Perfect Constitution," at 377–78:

"My impression is that few of the present generation of constitutional theorists are concerned with what the relevant history 'really' shows with respect to original intent, or with the difficulty of any undertaking along that line. They simply do not care. This is the direct result of the current dominance of law professors in constitutional law scholarship. Until the 1940s constitutional law was a subject of importance to both political scientists and historians, and they—Lowell, Beard, Corwin, Willoughby, McLaughlin—made substantial contributions to our understanding of this subject. Political scientists, have, however, become increasingly concerned with the study of political sociology, a shift which necessarily diminished their interest in the doctrinal work of the supreme court. Law professors now occupy this field virtually alone, and few if any of them have either an interest in or the background for meticulous historical scholarship. Moreover, law professors are problem solvers by training. Their eyes are on the present, not the past. By disposition, therefore, they are unsympathetic to being bound by the chains of the past." I would agree with the entire passage, except for the last sentence. I maintain that lawyers want to *appear* "bound by the chains of the past"; therefore, it is all the more important to them to manipulate it.

38. Miller, "Elusive Search," at 508. I do not mean to suggest that Bork altogether neglected originalism in the 1970s. See Bork, "Neutral Principles and Some First Amendment Problems," 47 *Indiana Law Journal* 1 (1971). But Bork's remarks there were avowedly "tentative and exploratory" (id. at 35), and, as Bruce Ackerman observed of Bork's espousal of original intent in *The Tempting of America: The Political Seduction of the Law* (1990), "Few reader's of Bork's major book, *The Antitrust Paradox,* would guess that its author would next try to make a name for himself by championing the use of historical methods against the seduction of abstract theory. Indeed, one question left unresolved in *Tempting* is the extent to which Bork himself is aware of the tension between the ostentatiously theoretical methods of *Paradox* and the putatively historical concerns of *Tempting.*" Ackerman, "Robert Bork's Grand Inquisition," 99 *Yale Law Journal* 1419, 1423–24 (1990). On Bork's (ab)use of history in the antitrust area, compare his *Antitrust Paradox: A Policy at War with Itself* 61–63 (1978) with the sources cited in Daniel Ernst, "The New Antitrust History," 35 *New York Law School Review* 879, 882 n. 23 (1990).

39. Bob Brown, "McGovern Sweeps Poll with 83%," *Harvard Law Record,* October 20, 1972, 1, 4 (in 1964, only two of sixty-one law professors polled had supported Goldwater against Lyndon Johnson. Robert Grayson, "Two Profs for Goldwater," id. at October 22, 1964, 1); Freeman, "Racism, Rights," at 300.

40. Richard Posner, *Economic Analysis of Law* (1972); Bork's *Antitrust Paradox* followed six years later. The quotes are from Richard Posner, Book Review, at 646; Posner, "Volume One of the Journal of Legal Studies—An Afterword," 1 *Journal of Legal Studies* 437, 437 (1972) ("to encourage"). Posner's language about making law a science bore a striking resemblance to that of Harvard Law School dean Christopher Columbus Langdell, the father of modern legal education. Langdell based his theory of legal education on two postulates he described in 1886: "first that law is a science; secondly, that all the available materials of that science are contained in

printed books." Like Langdell, Posner and many realists hoped to make law a science. They did not agree, however, that all materials of that science were contained in printed books and could be mastered through doctrinal analysis. For an extended examination of the roots of law and economics in legal realism see Edmund Kitch, ed., "The Fire of Truth: A Remembrance of Law and Economics at Chicago, 1932–1970," 9 *Journal of Law and Economics* 163, 164–76 (1983). (But see Duxbury, *Patterns,* at 309, contending that though law and economics bears "superficial affinities" to realist legal thought, it is "profoundly distinct" from realism. For Duxbury's excellent intellectual history of law and economics, see id. at 301–94.) Posner identified Becker, Calabresi, and Coase as founders of modern law and economics, in Posner, "Economic Approach to Law," 53 *Texas Law Review* 757, 759–61 (1975). See Gary Becker, *The Economics of Discrimination* (1957); Guido Calabresi, "Some Thoughts on Risk Distribution and the Law of Torts," 70 *Yale Law Journal* 499 (1961); and Ronald Coase's seminal article, "The Problem of Social Cost," 3 *Journal of Law and Economics* 1 (1960).

41. "[U]nstinting confidence" is from James Krier, Book Review, 122 *University of Pennsylvania Law Review* 1664, 1665 (1974); Posner quotations are from his "Economic Approach," at 761–65. Compare Ackerman, "Regulating Slum Markets," at 1099, with Neil Komesar, "Return to Slumville: A Critique of the Ackerman Analysis of Housing Code Enforcement and the Poor," 82 *Yale Law Journal* 1175, 1187 (1973). In my judgment, John Donohue rightly attributed "the most influential role in expanding the scope of law and economics throughout the legal academic community" to Posner and law and economics' rapid growth to "the clarity and accessibility of all of Posner's work." John Donohue III, "Law and Economics: The Road Not Taken," 22 *Law and Society Review* 903, 911–12 (1988). Doubtless what Ronald Coase described as the "triumphal advance" of economics into other social sciences in the 1970s helped to explain the popularity of law and economics as well. Coase, "Economics and Contiguous Disciplines," 7 *Journal of Legal Studies* 201, 209, 203 (1978). William Eskridge suggested that the oil shortages and inflation of the 1970s also helped to explain the popularity of law and economics: "The rediscovery of scarcity by our political and economic culture has coincided with an increased emphasis on scarcity in our legal culture. In academic law this has been most apparent in the law and economics movement, which starts with the fact of scarce resources and asks how we can structure rules and procedures to maximize the happiness we can achieve through enjoyment of those scarce resources." Eskridge, *Dynamic Statutory Interpretation* 301 (1994).

42. For Posner on normativity see his "The Uses and Abuses of Economics in Law," 46 *University of Chicago Law Review* 281, 285–87 (1979); "little operational content" and "risk aversion" are from Posner, *Economic Analysis,* at 218–20; "Rawlsism," "indefiniteness," and "empirical hunches" are from Posner, "Utilitarianism, Economics and Legal Theory," 8 *Journal of Legal Studies* 103, 118–19 (1979); the definition of efficiency is from *Economic Analysis,* at 4. Donohue quotation is from "Law and Economics," at 918; "strongly conservative," "legislation designed," and "capital punishment deters" from Posner, "Economic Approach," at 775. Arthur Leff parodied Posner's insistence he was nonjudgmental, in Leff, "Economic Analysis of Law: Some Realism about Nominalism," 60 *Virginia Law Review* 451, 460–61 (1974). For his part, Posner complained that his critics were playing foul. "The oddest thing

... is that economic research that provides support for liberal positions is rarely acknowledged, at least by liberals, as manifesting political bias.... In any event, the criticism is wide of the mark. The law and economics scholars have been scrupulous—more scrupulous I would argue than their critics—in respecting the line between positive and normative analysis." Posner, "Economic Approach," at 775–76. For a discussion of the "anti-antitrust" perspective of law and economics and its influence, see Duxbury, *Patterns,* at 348–63.

43. Leff, "Economic Analysis of Law," at 452, 459, 454. On Manne's summer institute see Marilyn Bender, "Lawyers and Economics," *New York Times,* July 11, 1971, section 3, at 1.

44. Leff, "Economic Analysis of Law," at 456, 481. Thomas Heller similarly claimed that "much of the current attraction of law to economics seems to lie in the hope of finding a technocratic, value free, nondiscretionary method to resolve social problems." Heller, "The Importance of Normative Decisionmaking: The Limitations of Legal Economics as a Basis for a Liberal Jurisprudence—As Illustrated by the Regulation of Vacation Home Development," 1976 *Wisconsin Law Review* 385, 388 (1976). Perhaps twenty years ago, Leff could be more confident his readers knew Latin than he would be today. In mourning the replacement of "the humanists" by "the mechanics" in the legal profession, Sol Linowitz grumbled: " 'Fiat justitia ruat coelum!' thundered Lord Mansfield; how many contemporary economists—or lawyers—would know what that means?" The translation is "Let justice be done though the Heavens may fall." Sol Linowitz with Martin Mayer, *The Betrayed Profession: Lawyering at the End of the Twentieth Century* 67, 136 (1994).

45. Posner, "Utilitarianism," at 105, 116–17 ("wealth maximization," "moral monstrousness," and "moral squeamishness"); remaining quotations are from Posner, *The Economics of Justice* 133, 124 (1981). See also Posner, "The Ethical and Political Basis of the Efficiency Norm in Common Law Adjudication," 8 *Hofstra Law Review* 509 (1980).

46. Posner, *Economics of Justice,* at 128, 133, 138–39. See also Elizabeth Landes and Richard Posner, "The Economics of the Baby Shortage," 7 *Journal of Legal Studies* 323 (1978).

47. Richard Schmallbeck, "The Justice of Economics: An Analysis of Wealth Maximization as a Normative Goal," 83 *Columbia Law Review* 488, 493, 500 (1983) ("King Midas" and "whether a policy will maximize"); Cass Sunstein, "Incommensurability and Valuation in Law," 92 *Michigan Law Review* 780, 852 (1994) ("too thin"). For a sampling of the controversy Posner provoked, see "Symposium on Efficiency as a Legal Concern," 8 *Hofstra Law Review* 485 (1980), and "A Response to the Efficiency Symposium," id. at 811.

48. "[W]illingness to write things" is from Schmallbeck, "Justice of Economics," at 489 n.9. Gary Minda provided a survey of the diverse second-generation law and economics movements, while acknowledging none possessed the significance of the first generation of law and economics scholars, which included Posner, in "The Jurisprudential Movements of the 1980s," 50 *Ohio State Law Journal* 604–14 (1989). One progressive second-generation scholar of law and economics bitterly acknowledged: "[T]he fact that it is Posner who has popularized and largely become synonymous with law and economics has one significant feature. In the minds of many, law and economics is an ideological crusade: if one does not embrace the Chicago school

vision of the world then there is little of value to be found in this area of scholarship. It is as though the first individuals to read Daniel Defoe's classic work denounced the novel as a literary form simply because they disliked the story of Robinson Crusoe." Donohue, "Law and Economics," at 912. The influence of law and economics may have peaked. Compare, for example, Robert Ellickson, "Bringing Culture and Human Frailty to Rational Actors: A Critique of Classical Economics," 65 *Chicago-Kent Law Review* 23, 27–31 (1989) (suggesting it has), with Yale Law School dean Anthony Kronman, *Lost Lawyer,* at 226 (describing law and economics as "the most powerful current in American law teaching today"). For a more tentative assessment than Kronman's but still optimistic see William Landes and Richard Posner, "The Influence of Economics on Law: A Quantitative Study," 36 *Journal of Law and Economics* 385, 424 (1993).

49. Preface, 1 *Harvard Journal of Law and Public Policy* (1978). Beginning in 1984, the journal made "an effort to provide an outlet for conservative law students at other campuses to assist the nation's only conservative student-run legal journal." Preface, 7 *Harvard Journal of Law and Public Policy* (1984).

50. Frank Michelman, "Political Markets and Community Self-Determination: Competing Judicial Models of Local Government Legitimacy," 53 *Indiana Law Journal* 145, 148, 186, 201–6 (1977–78). Bernard Grofman characterized public choice as a "kissing cousin" to law and economics. Grofman, "Public Choice, Civic Republicanism, and American Politics: Perspectives of a 'Reasonable Choice' Modeler," 71 *Texas Law Review,* 1541, 1543 (1993). I have benefited from the excellent study by the "Minnesota truth squad" (Jerry Mashaw, "The Economics of Politics and the Understanding of Public Law," 65 *Chicago-Kent Law Review* 123, 142 [1989]), Daniel Farber and Philip Frickey, *Law and Public Choice: A Critical Introduction* (1991). Bruce Ackerman and Neil Duxbury explored how public choice illuminated the assumptions of process theory in Ackerman, *Reconstructing American Law* 39–40 and Duxbury, *Patterns,* at 263.

51. Trubek is quoted in White, "Critical Legal Studies," at 834 ("Of all the issues that were to demarcate Critical Legal Studies from the Law and Society movement, the association of objective empiricism with positivism was the most explosive and the most clearly joined." Id. at 835; and see Trubek and Galanter, "Scholars in Self-Estrangement," at 1082; Trubek, "Where the Action Is: Critical Legal Studies and Empiricism," 36 *Stanford Law Review* 575, 615–22 (1984); Duxbury, *Patterns,* at 437–46). For Tushnet's characterization of cls as a "political location" see Tushnet, "Critical Legal Studies: Political History," at 1516, 1518. Nathan Glazer emphasized the strangeness of the "late radicalization . . . of the legal professorate," as compared to other disciplines, in "Marxism and the Law School: A Nonlegal Perspective," 8 *Harvard Journal of Law and Public Policy* 249, 249 (1985). Robert Gordon provided an intellectual biography of the typical critical legal scholar in "New Developments in Legal Theory," in *The Politics of Law: A Progressive Critique,* ed. David Kairys, 413 (1990), as did Binder, "Critical Legal Studies as Guerilla Warfare," at 13–33. John Schlegel discussed the Yale "purge" and "summer camp" in "Notes toward an Intimate, Opinionated, and Affectionate History of the Conference on Critical Legal Studies," 36 *Stanford Law Review* 391, 392 n.5, 401 (1984). Among those generally included in the group are Richard Abel, Lee Albert, John Griffiths, Robert Hudec, Larry Simon, and David Trubek. Id. It remains unclear whether all of them were

denied tenure because of their politics. John Griffiths left Yale long before he would have come up for tenure (though he may have left because he thought he would not get tenure). Hudec, who taught at Yale for six years, never believed that his politics, which he considered more moderate than those of most law professors at the time, affected consideration of his promotion. Personal communication. The first outreach letter to colleagues who might be interested in what would become the cls conference was signed by an organizing committee that included two members of the Yale group, among others: Richard Abel, Thomas Heller, Morton Horwitz, Duncan Kennedy, Stewart Macaulay, Rand Rosenblatt, David Trubek, Mark Tushnet, and Roberto Unger. Mark Kelman, *A Guide to Critical Legal Studies* 297 n.1 (1987).

52. The quotation is from Fisher, "Modern American Legal Theory," at 292. Critical legal scholar Gary Peller explicitly noted that the realists might not have recognized themselves from critical legal scholars' definition, when he distinguished between two strands of realism: "the deconstructive approach," which was available to "debunk the false sense of necessity inherent in the reification of representational terms," and a "constructive" strand, which was "incorporated into mainstream legal discourse." According to him, "this second strand of realism conceived that social meaning could be determined by looking at the consequences of legal decisions. . . . Law was 'political,' as the deconstructive arguments suggested, but 'politics' itself was re-translated from the notion of wide-open subjective ideology to closed, determinate issues of technique." Peller admitted, however, "there is nothing to suggest that the realists themselves conceived of their practice this way. . . . I have found no discussion in realist work of the divergent political implications that I have associated with the two strands. Instead, the separation of these aspects of realism is a construct of an interpretive interest in evoking what strike me as two different feelings one gets from the realist work—on the one hand a sense of engaged and passionate struggle, and on the other hand a sense of dry and lifeless engagement and observation." Peller, "The Metaphysics of American Law," 73 *California Law Review* 1151, 1222, 1225–26 (1985). David Kennedy provided the fullest description of critical legal scholars' idea of their lineage in "Critical Theory, Structuralism and Contemporary Legal Scholarship," 21 *New England Law Review* 209, 210 n.1 (1985–86): "The intellectual legacies of the school extend beyond Legal Realism and include inter alia: (1) Marxism; (2) New Left anarchism; (3) Sartrean existentialism; (4) Structuralism; (5) Neo-Progressive historiography; (6) liberal sociology; (7) radical social theory; and (8) empirical social science." According to Kennedy, "Methodologically, the major contribution of critical theory for legal scholarship seems to be its encouragement of a habit of radical distance from the materials of legal culture. Once attuned to the possibility of 'false' consciousness and the mechanisms of social 'legitimation,' it seems difficult to speak about the law in the normalizing rhetoric common to much legal scholarship." Id. at 245. "Thinking about law like a structuralist changes one's stance toward the materials one analyzes. The legal structuralist sets aside questions of law's origin, consequence and meaning. He focuses on the relationships within legal texts rather than between law and its content. . . . [S]tructuralism has by and large been imported into legal scholarship to assist in the hermeneutics of doctrinal interpretation." Id. at 267, 270.

53. "[L]aw varies" is from Joseph Singer, "The Player and the Cards: Nihilism and Legal Theory," 94 *Yale Law Journal* 1, 5 (1984). For an excellent critique of critical legal

scholars' generally structuralist approach toward history see Joan Williams, "Culture and Certainty: Legal History and the Reconstructive Process," 76 *Virginia Law Review* 713 (1990). "[M]anipulable" is from James Boyle, *Critical Legal Studies* xix (1992). As I indicate later, cls critiques of law and economics are legion. For an interesting example, see Duncan Kennedy, "Cost-Benefit Analysis of Entitlement Problems: A Critique," 33 *Stanford Law Review* 387 (1981) (discussing the relevance of the indeterminacy principle to the work of Calabresi and other liberals in law and economics). Kennedy's judges were likened to Houdini in Scott Altman, "Beyond Candor," 89 *Michigan Law Review* 296, 308–9 (1990). Tushnet quotation is from his "The Dilemmas of Liberal Constitutionalism," 42 *Ohio State Law Journal* 411, 424 (1981); "no torts" and "welfare queen" are from Barbara Woodhouse, "Mad Midwifery: Bringing Theory, Doctrine, and Practice to Life," 91 *Michigan Law Review* 1977, 1989 (1993). For cls explications of the indeterminacy thesis see, e.g., Charles Yablon, "The Indeterminacy of the Law: Critical Legal Studies and the Problem of Legal Explanation," 6 *Cardozo Law Review* 917 (1985); David Kennedy, "Spring Break," 63 *Texas Law Review* 1377, 1417–23 (1985). Kronman pointed to Kennedy's admiration of Skelly Wright in *Lost Lawyer,* at 244 (citing Duncan Kennedy, "Form and Substance in Private Law Adjudication," 89 *Harvard Law Review* 1685, 1777 [1976]; and see Duncan Kennedy, "The Effect of the Warranty of Habitability on Low Income Housing: 'Milking' and Class Violence," 15 *Florida State University Law Review* 485 [1987]; Joseph Singer, "Catcher in the Rye Jurisprudence," 35 *Rutgers Law Review* 275 [1983] [praising the liberal judicial activism of Justice Morris Pashman of the New Jersey state supreme court]). Kennedy described himself as a "doctrinal teacher" in his "Discussion on Critical Legal Studies at the Harvard Law School," presented by the Harvard Society for Law and Public Policy and the Federalist Society for Law and Public Policy Studies, Harvard Club, May 13, 1985, at 31.

54. "By its own criteria" is from Singer, "The Player and the Cards," at 6; "Take specific arguments" from Mark Kelman, "Trashing," 36 *Stanford Law Review* 292, 292 (1984) (emphasis in the original), in which he provides an answer to those who trashed trashing, at 297. For a gleeful discussion of trashing see Alan Freeman, "Truth and Mystification in Legal Scholarship," 90 *Yale Law Journal* 1229, 1230 (1981).

55. "[M]ost often-cited" is from Kelman, *Guide to Critical Legal Studies,* at 17; definition of "fundamental contradiction" is from Duncan Kennedy, "The Structure of Blackstone's Commentaries," 28 *Buffalo Law Review* 209, 211–13 (1979).

56. See William Bratton, "Manners, Metaprinciples, Metapolitics and Kennedy's *Form and Substance,*" 6 *Cardozo Law Review* 871, 890–91 (1985).

57. "[L]aw is politics" is from Tushnet, "Critical Legal Studies: Political History," at 1526. "[P]erson on the street" is from Carrie Menkel-Meadow, "Durkheimian Epiphanies: The Importance of Engaged Social Science in Legal Studies," 18 *Florida State University Law Review* 91, 102 n.43 (1990), law as "a mechanism" from Singer, "The Player and the Cards," at 5–6. Martin Shapiro pointed out that political scientists had yawned at critical legal scholars' message in "Morality and the Politics of Judging," at 1556. See also Gene Nichol, "The Left, the Right, and Certainty in Constitutional Law," 33 *William and Mary Law Review* 1181, 1182–83 (1992): "It takes no great legal mind, in fact it barely takes consciousness, to make out a claim

that constitutional law is indeterminate. A fancy theorist may be required to demonstrate that all legal reasoning is unstable—that good lawyers and good judges can make any case or virtually any case come out any way they wish. But every first year law student has an exceptionally strong sense that *constitutional* law is unstable. No candid theorist can actually work *Brown, Bakke, Bowers, Buckley, Bowsher, Baker, Bethel, Brandenburg, Broadrick, Branzburg,* and *Bivens* into a coherent whole and still say anything meaningful about the controversies presented. And that is limiting myself, obviously somewhat arbitrarily, to cases that start with a 'B.' " Emphasis in the original. In contrast, critical legal scholars' claims about the indeterminacy of private law probably would have startled persons on the street—provided they ever heard about the claims and did not consider them exaggerated—and first-year law students alike.

58. John Schlegel discussed Horwitz as an exception in "A Tasty Tidbit," at 1051–52. For an excellent example of critical labor law scholarship see Katherine Van Wezel Stone, "The Post-War Paradigm in American Labor Law," 90 *Yale Law Journal* 1509 (1981). For a discussion of relative autonomy see Gordon, "New Developments in Legal Theory," at 417.

59. "[S]ophistries" and "hocus-pocus" are from Roberto Unger, "The Critical Legal Studies Movement," 96 *Harvard Law Review* 561, 574–75 (1983), though Unger's hostility to liberalism came through most clearly in *Knowledge and Politics* (1975); "Future legal historians" is from Morton Horwitz, "Law and Economics: Science or Politics?" 8 *Hofstra Law Review* 905, 905 (1980); "Helms to Tsongas" is quoted in Lee Christie, "Prof. Frug Urges Critical Look at Law," *Harvard Law Record,* December 3, 1982, 9; "most powerful rhetorical means" is from Joan Williams, "Critical Legal Studies: The Death of Transcendence and the Rise of the New Langdells," 62 *New York University Law Review* 429, 487 (1987) (describing "cLS's term 'liberalism' " as "just the kind of huge, ultimately contentless word that confuses rather than promotes conversation." Id. at 488 n.418). For extended critiques of the cls reading of liberalism see Don Herzog, "As Many as Six Impossible Things before Breakfast," 75 *California Law Review* 609 (1987); Jeffrey Blum, "Critical Legal Studies and the Rule of Law," 38 *Buffalo Law Review* 59 (1990); Andrew Altman, *Critical Legal Studies: A Liberal Critique* (1990).

60. Karl Klare, "Law Making as Praxis," 40 *Telos* 123, 132 n.29 (1979).

61. "[I]solated rights bearers" is from Richard Delgado, "The Ethereal Scholar: Does Critical Legal Studies Have What Minorities Want?" 22 *Harvard Civil Rights–Civil Liberties Law Review* 301, 305–7 (1987); "internally inconsistent" from Duncan Kennedy, *Legal Education and the Reproduction of Hierarchy: A Polemic against the System* 23 (1983); "Rights are indeterminate" from Fisher, "Modern American Legal Theory," at 294. See also Peter Gabel, Book Review, 91 *Harvard Law Review* 302, 314 (1977): "If we were to take Dworkin with complete seriousness by applying his value-system to the facts of the hard cases discussed in [*Taking Rights Seriously*] . . . we would have to assume that the sort of goods and opportunities that people really want from their lives can be captured by such phrases as the right to collect damages for injuries, the right to go to law school, the right to get an abortion . . . the right not to be jailed for touching someone passionately, and so on. However important these limited powers may be to the litigants who assert a claim to them, they are largely irrelevant to the truly serious problem that these litigants share with

almost everyone, an everyday life of operating machines, disseminating clerical knowledge, and ingesting televised images. Yet from the legal-distributive point of view, they express the full meaning of 'human dignity' and 'equal concern and respect.' " Alan Freeman provided an important examination of rights from a critical perspective in Freeman, "Legitimizing Racial Discrimination through Antidiscrimination Law: A Critical Review of Supreme Court Doctrine," 62 *Minnesota Law Review* 1049 (1978); and see Symposium on Rights, 62 *Texas Law Review* 1363 (1984).

62. David Luban, *Legal Modernism: Law, Meaning and Violence* 77 (1994) ("eight hundred years"); Boyle, *Critical Legal Studies,* at xli ("At least since"); Tushnet, "Critical Legal Studies: Political History," at 1536 ("movement for"); Allan Hutchinson, "Introduction," in *Critical Legal Studies,* ed. Hutchinson, 1, 3 (1989) ("anachronism"); David Kennedy, "Introduction," in *Knowledges: Historical and Critical Studies in Disciplinarity,* ed. Ellen Messer-Davidow, David Shumway, and David Sylvan, 422, 424 (1993) ("good father"); Calvin Trillin, "A Reporter at Large: Harvard Law," *The New Yorker,* March 26, 1984, 53, 83 ("really wasn't").

63. See Richard Matasar, *"Brown's* Legacy in Legal Education," 7 *Harvard Blackletter Journal* 127, 132 (1990).

64. *Bakke* v. *Regents of the University of California,* 18 Cal. 3d 34, 91, 53 (1976); *De Funis* v. *Odegard,* 416 U.S. 312, 336–37 (1974). Alexander Bickel correctly observed: "*De Funis . . .* was not, I think, really a defeat. The whole performance exudes a smell of victory for next time." Bickel to Daniel Kornstein, May 29, 1974, Box 11, Folder 242, Bickel Papers.

65. *University of California Regents* v. *Bakke,* 438 U.S. 265, 366 (1978); Frank Michelman, "Super Liberal: Romance, Community and Tradition in William J. Brennan, Jr.'s Constitutional Thought," 77 *Virginia Law Review* 1261, 1290–91, 1297 (1991) (for disagreement see, e.g., id., where Michelman disputed Charles Fried's "collectivist gloss" on Brennan's affirmative action doctrine); Alexander Bickel and Philip Kurland, Brief of Anti-Defamation League of B'Nai Brith as Amicus Curiae, at 22–24 (no. 73–225) (U.S. 1973) (in *De Funis*). Since Douglas had resigned from the Court by the time it heard *Bakke,* we cannot be certain what he would have done in the case. For an example of Douglas's earlier solicitude toward groups see, e.g., *Harper* v. *Virginia Board of Elections,* 383 U.S. 663 (1966).

66. John Hart Ely, *Democracy and Distrust: A Theory of Judicial Review* 170 (1980) ("trouble"); James Fleming, "A Critique of John Hart Ely's Quest for the Ultimate Constitutional Interpretivism of Representative Democracy," 90 *Michigan Law Review* 634, 654 (1982) ("may well be"). The struggle within the Carter administration over *Bakke* is recounted in Lincoln Caplan, *The Tenth Justice: The Solicitor General and the Rules of Law* 39–47 (1987); Griffin Bell with Ronald Ostrow, *Taking Care of the Law* 28–32 (1982); Joseph Califano, *Governing America: An Insider's Report from the White House and the Cabinet* 231–43 (1981). For an example of indignation see the special issue on *Bakke* entitled "Meritocracy and Its Discontents," *New Republic,* October 15, 1977.

67. See Dallin H. Oaks, "Judicial Activism," 7 *Harvard Journal of Law and Public Policy* 1, 9 (1984) (characterizing books as "twins" and noting that Ely's book received more attention); Jesse Choper, *Judicial Review and the National Political Process: A Functional Reconsideration of the Role of the Supreme Court* 128 (1969). Choper

had first issued this warning in 1967. See Choper, "On the Warren Court and Judicial Review," 17 *Catholic University Law Review* 20, 43 (1967).

68. Ely, *Democracy and Distrust,*" at 58–59.

69. John Hart Ely, "The Supreme Court, 1977 Term—Foreword: On Discovering Fundamental Values," 92 *Harvard Law Review* 5, 5–6, 10, 21 n.77 (1978); Ely, *Democracy and Distrust,* at 74–75, 87 (emphasis in the original).

70. Ely, *Democracy and Distrust,* at 87–89, 65, 72 (emphasis in the original) (for a critique of Ely's "interpretivism," arguing that he nonetheless lay "the basis for a workable interpretivism," textualism, see Douglas Laycock, "Taking Constitutions Seriously: A Theory of Judicial Review," 59 *Texas Law Review* 343, 393, 360 [1981]); "apotheosis" is from William Eskridge and Gary Peller, "The New Public Law Movement: Moderation as a Postmodern Cultural Form," 89 *Michigan Law Review* 707, 736 (1991). Cf. id. at 772 (which presented Ely as "a transitional figure ... [who] opened the process discourse to the critical questioning of the democratic legitimacy of the legislature").

71. Saphire, "Search for Legitimacy," at 369 ("moral notions"); Archibald Cox, Book Review, 94 *Harvard Law Review* 700, 703–4 (1981) ("I lack"); Boudin, Book Review, at 1254–55 ("comport with" and "distinct"). Ely observed that one "general form of response" to *Democracy and Distrust* was: "Ely's theory is indeterminate to the point of uselessness because *Carolene Products* premises could be used, in a way I am about to demonstrate, to generate conclusion X (which conclusion is either absurd or one that on other grounds we know or assume Ely would reject)." John Hart Ely, "Democracy and the Right to Be Different," 56 *New York University Law Review* 397, 397 (1981). For an example of the "brilliant but misguided" critique of *Democracy and Distrust* see Richard Posner, "Democracy and Distrust Revisited," 77 *Virginia Law Review* 641, 650 (1991), classifying the book as a "(magnificent) failure." The professions of admiration for Ely's work did sound sincere. One can feel reviewers' gratitude to Ely for giving them so much to fight. *Democracy and Distrust* is to law professors what Hofstadter's *Age of Reform* is to twentieth-century American political historians. See, e.g., Daniel Ortiz, "Pursuing a Perfect Politics: The Allure and Failure of Process Theory," 77 *Virginia Law Review* 721, 744 (1991): "Despite its failure to describe how the Court actually reaches its decisions and its failure to deliver on its own promises for judicial review, *Democracy and Distrust* is justly celebrated. Its project may be futile, but its continuing allure tells us much about ourselves. We still hope against experience to find a way to reconcile two political institutions, simple majoritarianism and expansive judicial review, which are plainly irreconcilable."

72. Dworkin, "Forum of Principle," at 517–18, 539; Lawrence Tribe, "The Puzzling Persistence of Process-Based Constitutional Theories," 89 *Yale Law Journal* 1063, 1064–65, 1071 (1980); Fiss, "Foreword," at 2, 16–17. For scholarly treatments of rights foundationalism as distinct from process theory see, e.g., Ackerman, *We the People,* at 7–16. Gary Minda also treated them as distinct, while acknowledging their similarities: "Despite ... important differences, each side believed in the possibility of grounding law's objectivity in a Rule of Law defined by either process or rights, or a combination of both." It seems to me that the combination approach predominated. Minda, *Postmodern,* at 57. For an example of critical legal scholars' response to *Democracy and Distrust* see Mark Tushnet, "Darkness on the Edge of Town: The

Contributions of John Hart Ely to Constitutional Theory," 89 *Yale Law Journal* 1037 (1980).

73. "[L]iving off the remains" is from Mark Tushnet, "Constitutional Scholarship: What Next?" 5 *Constitutional Commentary* 28, 28 (1988). "[M]y generation" appeal is from Richard Parker, "The Past of Constitutional Theory and Its Future," 42 *Ohio State Law Journal* 223, 223, 257–58 (1981). Citing this article, Parker said in 1994: "Though a while back I wrote an article criticizing John Ely's book, which I claimed had 'perfected' (a specific kind of) process-oriented argument, I (unlike many other critics) didn't reject process-orientation as such. To the contrary, I looked forward to a revised process-orientation proceeding from open confrontation of controversial issues of value and from a revised imagination of democracy." Richard Parker, *"Here, the People Rule": A Constitutional Populist Manifesto* 130–31 n.90, 106 (1994). As the text accompanying this note suggests, I read his 1981 article more broadly. The "proliferation" quotation and point is from Eskridge and Peller, "New Public Law Movement," at 736 (for "public values" theories see, e.g., Fiss, "Foreword," at 13–14; Arthur Miller, "Toward a Definition of 'The' Constitution," 8 *University of Dayton Law Review* 633, 708 [1983] [describing Fiss's "Foreword" as "a variation on the theme struck by Professor Wechsler's call for 'neutral principles' "]). "In the more cynical" is from Eskridge and Frickey, "Making of *The Legal Process,*" at 2051. Eskridge and Peller emphasized continuity in constitutional theory in "New Public Law Movement," at 708, 736–37, 762, but one of the strengths of that article is that the authors also told an alternative version of the story, which emphasized instead "the rupture between the legal process generation and our generation." Id. at 737. According to this version: "Just as legal process theory had achieved hegemonic status at many law schools, it fell under the fierce analytic assault of law and economics and CLS. Despite their great differences, these two movements had in common a thoroughgoing intellectual critique of the legal process hegemony they confronted. . . . Once the discussion shifted from process to substance, legal process had little to offer." Id. at 742–43. As I have indicated, I think process jurisprudence always possessed a strong substantive and normative element—that is one reason the reaction against Ely was so strong. Therefore I remain in the continuity camp and would not agree "that Ely successfully integrated legal process with the activism of the Warren Court." Id. at 774.

74. Arthur Leff, "Unspeakable Ethics, Unnatural Law," 1979 *Duke Law Journal* 1229, 1229–30, 1249 (1979).

CHAPTER 3. INTERLUDE: THINKING ABOUT THINKING

1. Leff, "Unspeakable Ethics, Unnatural Law," at 1230 n. 2; "Symposia like this" is from Mark Tushnet, "Legal Scholarship: Its Causes and Cure," 90 *Yale Law Journal* 1205, 1205 (1981); "drifting" from Christopher Stone, "From a Language Perspective," 90 *Yale Law Journal* 1149, 1149 (1981). See generally Jean Stefanic, "The Law Review Symposium Issue: Community of Meaning or Re-Inscription of Hierarchy?" 63 *University of Colorado Law Review* 651, 651 (1992) (noting that "there has been approximately a two-fold increase in the number of symposium-type issues in the last decade alone" and arguing that "law review symposia have become a form of search for meaning").

2. "[H]alcyon" and "Halcion" are from Richard Fischl, "The Question That Killed Critical Legal Studies," 17 *Law and Social Inquiry* 779, 784 (1992). Estrich talked about her criminal law course in Miske Isbell, "Profs Debate Merits of 'Toughness,'" *Harvard Law Record,* November 4, 1983, 2. The statistics about women law professors are from Herma Hill Kay, "The Future of Women Law Professors," 77 *Iowa Law Review* 5, 15 (1991); "racial tokenism" is from Richard Chused, "The Hiring and Retention of Minorities and Women on American Law School Faculties," 137 *University of Pennsylvania Law Review* 537, 539 (1988); see also Richard Delgado, "Minority Law Professors' Lives: The Bell-Delgado Survey," 24 *Harvard Civil Rights–Civil Liberties Law Review* 349, 352–53 (1989). Old assumptions were being challenged in other disciplines, of course, and for the same reasons. We need only substitute law for poetry in the following account: "One way to describe the conflict in the faculty lounge, then, is to say that theory has broken out. 'Theory,' by my definition anyway, is what erupts when what was once silently agreed to in a community becomes disputed, forcing its members to formulate and defend assumptions that they previously did not even have to be aware of. As soon as OMP [Older Male Professor] and YFP [Young Female Professor] discover they hold conflicting assumptions about poetry in general, they have no choice but to have a dispute about theoretical questions: What is poetry? Should students study it and why, and how should it be taught?" Gerald Graff, *Beyond the Culture Wars: How Teaching the Conflicts Can Revitalize American Education* 52–53 (1992).

3. Samuelson, "Convergence of the Law School and the University," at 266; "With the Editors," 80 *Harvard Law Review* vii (no. 7, 1967). The information on length of articles is taken from Charles Collier, "The Use and Abuse of Humanistic Theory: Reexamining the Assumption of Interdisciplinary Scholarship," 41 *Duke Law Journal* 191, 198, 201 (1991). I thank John Schlegel for suggesting that university-wide tenure review boards did begin to impinge more directly on law professors' lives and caused an increase in law professors' publication in the 1970s. Cf. Tushnet, "Truth, Justice, and the American Way," at 1336: "[L]aw schools found that they wished (or were forced) to have ties with other departments. These ties could not be maintained if law school scholarship remained as flimsy as it had been; the sociologists, economists, and political scientists would have resented collaboration with, or promotion of professors who did not write." Of course, it may be that in reality, a few law professors were publishing more, and that most were not, or if they were, it was still not all that much (see Michael Sygert and Nathaniel Gozansky, "Senior Law Faculty Publication Study: Comparisons of Law School Productivity," 35 *Journal of Legal Education* 373, 381 [1985]). It could also be that with the growing interest in *articles* by law professors in the 1970s and 1980s, many pages of older law professors' treatises were simply overlooked. In his paper at the 1981 Yale conference on legal scholarship, Christopher Stone observed: "Treatises, some of them splendid, are still being written, but the prestige of the undertaking has tarnished." Stone, "From a Language Perspective," at 1150. See generally A. W. B. Simpson, "The Rise and Fall of the Legal Treatise: Legal Principles and the Forms of Legal Literature," 48 *University of Chicago Law Review* 632 (1981); Glendon, *Nation,* at 204–6.

4. "[O]verconfident intellectualism" is from Robert Nagel, "Meeting the Enemy," 57 *University of Chicago Law Review* 633, 653 (1990) (Nagel has expanded on these observations in his book, *Judicial Power and American Character: Censoring Our-*

selves in an Anxious Age 27–43 [1994]). Ira Lupu decried "a trend in which scholars write to, for, about, or against one another." Lupu, "Constitutional Theory and the Search for the Workable Premise," 8 *University of Dayton Law Review* 579, 586 (1983).

5. "[D]ragged in" is from Mark Tushnet, "Anti-Formalism in Recent Constitutional Cases," 83 *Michigan Law Review* 1502, 1544 (1985); "problems of internal specialization" from Lee Bollinger, "The Mind in the Major American Law School," 91 *Michigan Law Review* 2167, 2171 (1993). I do not recall that anyone made exactly Bollinger's point at the 1981 Yale conference itself, but it seems to reflect the direction in which many participants were headed. See also George Priest, "Social Science Theory and Legal Education: The Law School as University," 33 *Journal of Legal Education* 437 (1983).

6. "[O]nly resemble each other" is from Richard Posner, *The Problems of Jurisprudence* 442 (1990); "only apparent route" is from G. Edward White, "Reflections on the 'Republican Revival,' " 6 *Yale Journal of Law and the Humanities* 1, 14 (1994).

7. Wellington is quoted in Getman, *Company of Scholars,* at 268; Posner, "Present Situation in Legal Scholarship," at 1129, 1119. Compare Robert Gordon, "Lawyers, Scholars, and the 'Middle Ground,' " 91 *Michigan Law Review* 2075, 2099–2100 (1993) (Gordon cited evidence pointing toward an increase in doctrinal scholarship in major law reviews in the 1980s) with Glendon, *Nation,* at 204: "The ratio of 'practical' to 'theoretical' essays in leading law journals dropped from 4.5:1 in 1960 to 1:1 in 1985."

8. Paul Rabinow, "For Hire: Resolutely Late Modern," in *Recapturing Anthropology: Working in the Present,* ed. Richard Fox, 59, 64 (1991). I believe that in most disciplines, the comment applied with even greater force to the 1980s than the 1990s.

9. Fredric Jameson, "Postmodernism and Consumer Society," in *Postmodernism and Its Discontents: Theories, Practices,* ed. Ann Kaplan, 13, 14 (1990). The essay combines two Jameson wrote in 1983 and 1984. Id. at 29 n.1. See also Quentin Skinner, *The Return of Grand Theory in the Human Sciences* (1985). For a discussion of the marginalization of French theorists, such as Foucault and Derrida, within the French university system see Pierre Bourdieu, *Homo Academicus* (trans. Peter Collier) xviii (1988). According to one of Foucault's biographers, "In Paris, he could not venture out at night without being mobbed by fans. And even in America, he had become a star of sorts, particularly on many college campuses. Students weaned on the Talking Heads and David Lynch flocked to his public appearances, cherishing the bald savant as a kind of postmodernist sphinx, a metaphysical Eraserhead, whose demeanor was weird, whose utterances were cryptic—and whose philosophy, mirabile dictu, could nevertheless be summed in a simple mantra, consisting of two words: 'power' and 'knowledge.' " James Miller, *The Passion of Michel Foucault* 320–21 (1993).

10. "[M]ediatization" and "spectaclization" are from Dana Polan, "The Spectacle of Intellect in a Media Age: Cultural Representations and the David Abraham, Paul de Man, and Victor Farias Cases," in *Intellectuals: Aesthetics, Politics, Academics,* ed. Bruce Robbins, 343, 343 (1990); "no 'outside' " from Brenda Marshall, *Teaching the Postmodern: Fiction and Theory* 3 (1992); Fredric Jameson, *Postmodernism, or, the Cultural Logic of Late Capitalism* xiii (1992). See, e.g., Christopher Norris, "Deconstruction, Postmodernism and Philosophy: Habermas on Derrida," in *Derrida: A*

Critical Reader, ed. David Wood, 167 (1992) (arguing that deconstruction is not an offshoot of postmodernism).

11. The "definition" of "postmodern moment" is from Marshall, *Teaching the Postmodern,* at 3–4; Jean François Lyotard, *The Postmodern Condition: A Report on Knowledge* xxiv, 10, 15 (1984) (see, e.g., Jameson's own skepticism about the notion of "incredulity towards metanarratives" in *Postmodernism,* at xi–xii); Richard Rorty, ed., *The Linguistic Turn: Essays in Philosophical Method* 9 n.10 (1992 ed.); "It is not as though" is from Eagleton, *Literary Theory,* at 60.

12. Clifford Geertz, "Blurred Genres: The Refiguration of Social Thought," in *Local Knowledge: Further Essays in Interpretive Anthropology* 20 (1983). Emphasis in the original. As one scholar said, " 'blurred genres' became a metaphor of the times." Julie Klein, "Blurring, Cracking, and Crossing: Permeation and the Fracturing of Discipline," in Kennedy, *Knowledges,* at 185, 187.

13. Thomas Kuhn, *The Structure of Scientific Revolutions* (2d ed., 1970). The citation information is derived from a September 1995 Westlaw search. The cases are *Merrell Dow Pharmaceuticals, Inc.* v. *Oxendine,* 649 A. 2d. 825 (1994); *Securities Industry Association* v. *Connolly,* 883 F. 2d 1114, 1116 (1989); *Brock* v. *Merrell Dow Pharmaceuticals, Inc.,* 874 F. 2d 307, 309 n.6 (1989); *Ethyl Corporation* v. *Environmental Protection Agency,* 541 F. 2d 1, 25 n.52 (1976); *Mercado* v. *Ahmed,* 756 F. Supp. 1057, 1100 n.6 (1991). It was chic to speak of "paradigm shifts" in other fields too.

14. Kuhn, *Scientific Revolutions,* at 150, 3, 208. See David Hollinger, "T. S. Kuhn's Theory of Science and Its Implications for History," in *In the American Province: Studies in the History and Historiography of Ideas* 110–11 (1989): "Once this sense of historical development is abstracted [by historians] from *The Structure of Scientific Revolutions* it sounds like a sense of truisms. This fact only serves to illustrate a point Kuhn has insisted upon: concrete examples like Kuhn's achievement in the history of science have a staying power distinct from that of the general principles they embody." On historians' development of a sense of historicism, as we use the term today, and its impact on the relationship between history and political science see Dorothy Ross, *The Origins of American Social Science* (1991).

15. Mark Tushnet, "The Dialectics of Legal History," 57 *Texas Law Review* 1295, 1302 n.33 (1979).

CHAPTER 4. CRISIS

1. Thomas Kuhn, *The Essential Tension: Selected Studies in Scientific Tradition and Change* xiii (1977); David Harlan, "Intellectual History and the Return of Literature," 94 *American Historical Review* 581, 587 (1989) ("It required").

2. Joyce Appleby, "One Good Turn Deserves Another: Moving beyond the Linguistic; A Response to David Harlan," 94 *American Historical Review* 1326, 1328 (1989) ("are embedded"); Hans-Georg Gadamer, *Truth and Method* 324, 328 (trans. revised by Joel Weinsheimer and Donald Marshall) (1993).

3. Thomas Grey, "Hear the Other Side: Wallace Stevens and Pragmatist Legal Theory," 63 *Southern California Law Review* 1569, 1576 (1990).

4. Clifford Geertz, " 'From the Native's Point of View': On the Nature of Anthropological Understanding," in *Local Knowledge,* at 56; Bronislaw Malinowski, *A Diary in the Strict Sense of the Term* (1967).

5. Geertz, "Introduction," in *Local Knowledge,* at 5 ("cultural hermeneutics"); Geertz, "Thick Description: Toward an Interpretive Theory of Culture," in *The Interpretation of Cultures* 14, 29 (1973); Sherry Ortner, "Theory in Anthropology since the 1960s," 26 *Comparative Studies in Society and History* 126, 129 (1984); Geertz, "Ideology as a Cultural System," in *Interpretation of Cultures,* at 216 ("Culture patterns"; "provide a template"). On the basis of several definitions of ideology, Terry Eagleton said, "nobody would claim that their own thinking was ideological, just as nobody would habitually refer to themselves as Fatso." Eagleton, *Ideology: An Introduction* 2 (1991).

6. All quotations are from Geertz, "Thick Description," at 14–15, except for "the systematic study of meaning," from Geertz, *After the Fact: Two Countries, Four Decades, One Anthropologist* 114 (1995).

7. Geertz, "Thick Description," at 29–30, 14–16.

8. Id. at 16, 29. As Ortner said, Geertz was "primarily concerned with what might be called Meaning, with a capital M—the purpose, or point, or larger significance of things. Thus he quotes Northrop Frye: 'You wouldn't go to *Macbeth* to learn about the history of Scotland—you go learn what a man feels like after he's gained a kingdom and lost his soul.' " Ortner, "Theory in Anthropology," at 131 n.4.

9. Rorty, *Linguistic Turn,* at 3, 371–72. Emphasis in the original.

10. Id. at 373 ("notion of representation"); Richard Rorty, "Introduction: Antirepresentationalism, Ethnocentrism and Liberalism," in *Objectivity, Relativism, and Truth* 1 (1991) ("antirepresentationalist account"); Rorty, *Philosophy and the Mirror of Nature* 7, 9 (1979).

11. Rorty, *Mirror of Nature,* at 382, 10, 324–25.

12. Id. at 392, 315, 372; "Truth cannot be out there" is from Richard Rorty, *Contingency, Irony, and Solidarity* 5 (1989).

13. Joan Williams, "Rorty, Radicalism, Romanticism: The Politics of the Gaze," 1992 *Wisconsin Law Review* 131, 131 n.1 (1992) ("without absolutes"); Alan Megill, "Recounting the Past," 94 *American Historical Review* 627, 637 (1989) ("hermeneutic insight"); Rorty, *Mirror of Nature,* at 317–18. Emphasis in the original. Williams provides an excellent examination of the development of Rorty's thought, as does Thomas McCarthy in "Private Irony and Public Decency: Richard Rorty's New Pragmatism," 16 *Critical Inguiry* 355 (1990). See also Allan Hutchinson, "The Three 'Rs': Reading/Rorty/Radically," 103 *Harvard Law Review* 555 (1989).

   The evolution of Rorty's politics toward a moderate political liberalism has dismayed some of the scholars on the left who most admired his critique of epistemology in *Philosophy and the Mirror of Nature.* For example, in the mid-1980s, Joseph Singer declared, "My own ability to express my dissatisfaction with traditional legal theory crystallized after reading Rorty." Singer, "The Player and the Cards," at 7 n.13. But see John Stick, "Can Nihilism Be Pragmatic?" 100 *Harvard Law Review* 332, 342–43 (1986) (charging that Singer misused Rorty). More recently Singer said, "Rorty brought us to the right floor in the elevator, and then told us not to get off." Singer, "Should Lawyers Care about Philosophy?" 1989 *Duke Law Journal* 1752, 1782 (1989). See also William Weaver, "Richard Rorty and the Radical Left," 78 *Virginia Law Review* 729 (1992). According to Rorty, "the gist" of the critique from the left is "that my anti-foundationalist views produce 'a way of protecting a dominant ideology and its professionally successful practitioners from the scrutiny of argument, by deeming that critique can have no leverage against everyday beliefs and that theoretical arguments have no consequences.' " Rorty, "What Can You Expect from Anti-Foundationalist Philosophers?: A Reply to Lynn Baker," Id, at 719, 722 n.12 (quoting Jonathan Culler). Rorty complained, "I am constantly told that I seem unaware of the existence of power." Id. at 723.

As Richard Bernstein, Rorty's friend of over forty years, pointed out recently, the left is not Rorty's only problem spot: "By now Rorty has offended and antagonized just about everyone—the political left and right, traditional liberals, feminists, and both analytic and Continental philosophers. His 'strong' readings of key figures strike many as idiosyncratic creations of his own fantasies. He has been accused of being 'smug,' 'shallow,' 'elitist,' 'priggish,' 'voyeuristic,' 'insensitive,' and 'irresponsible.' 'Rorty-bashing' is rapidly becoming a new culture industry." Bernstein, "Rorty's Liberal Utopia," in *The New Constellation: The Ethical-Political Horizons of Modernity/Postmodernity* 12–13, 260 (1992).

14. Rorty, *Mirror of Nature*, at 315–18, 377. Rorty admitted that his "use of the terms epistemology and hermeneutics to stand for these ideal opposites may seem forced." Id. at 318.

15. Id. at 393–94.

16. Paul Rabinow and William Sullivan, "The Interpretive Turn: Emergence of an Approach," in *Interpretive Social Science: A Reader,* ed. Paul Rabinow and William Sullivan, 1, 5 (1979) ("denies and overcomes"); Rosemary Coombe, " 'Same as It Ever Was': Rethinking the Politics of Legal Interpretation," 34 *McGill Law Journal* 603, 609 (1989) ("If we accept"); Charles Taylor, "Interpretation and the Sciences of Man," in Rabinow and Sullivan, *Interpretive Social Science,* at 25, 48 ("not just in the minds"); Rabinow and Sullivan, "Interpretive Turn," at 6 ("These meanings are intersubjective"); Edward Rubin, "On beyond Truth: A Theory for Evaluating Legal Scholarship," 80 *California Law Review* 889, 908 n.55 (1992) ("not just a fancy term").

17. "[N]o absolutist foundation" and "shared ground" are from Gregory Leyh, "Dworkin's Hermeneutics," 39 *Mercer Law Review* 851, 855 (1988); "Relativism" and "we shall be able" from Richard Rorty, *Consequences of Pragmatism* 166, 203 (1982). Emphasis in the original.

18. Rorty, *Consequences of Pragmatism,* at 203–4, 208. According to Rorty, "the new pragmatism differs from the old in just two respects, only one of which is of much interest to people who are not philosophy professors. The first is that new pragmatists talk about language instead of experience or mind or consciousness, as the old pragmatists did. The second respect is that we have all read Kuhn, Hanson, Toulmin, and Feyerabend, and have thereby become suspicious of the term 'scientific method.' New pragmatists wish that Dewey, Sidney Hook, and Ernest Nagel had not insisted on using this term as a catchphrase, since we are unable to provide anything distinctive for it to denote. As far as I can determine, it is only these doubts about scientific method, and thus about method in general, that might matter for legal theory. The first respect in which the new pragmatism is new—its switch from experience to language—has offered philosophy professors some fruitful new ways to pose old issues. . . . But these issues are pretty remote from the concerns of non-philosophers." Richard Rorty, "The Banality of Pragmatism and the Poetry of Justice," 63 *Southern California Law Review* 1811, 1813–14 (1990). In one of the accompanying foot-

notes, Rorty continued: "Insofar as concern with language as such has entered into legal theory, it has done so in the form of the 'deconstructionist' wing of the CLS movement." Here Rorty agreed with Joan Williams: "[I]f you have Wittgenstein, you do not need Derrida." Id. at 1814 n.17.

19. Williams, "Critical Legal Studies," at 430–31 ("new epistemology" and "traditional epistemology"); Williams, "Abortion, Incommensurability, and Jurisprudence," 63 *Tulane Law Review* 1651, 1669–70 ("hard lessons" and "Once I offer").

20. David Millon, "Objectivity and Democracy," 67 *New York University Law Review* 1, 5 n.10 (1992).

21. See Coombe, "Same as It Ever Was," at 611 ("meanings reside"); Sanford Levinson and Steven Mailloux, Preface, *Interpreting Law and Literature: A Hermeneutic Reader* ix, x (1988) ("not even the simplest"). But see, e.g., Frederick Schauer, "Easy Cases," 58 *Southern California Law Review* 399, 422–23 (1985) (pointing to large number of cases "in which we can answer questions by consulting the articulated norm" and condemning "linguistic nihilism"). For Levinson's reply, see Sanford Levinson, "What Do Lawyers Know (and What Do They Do with Their Knowledge)? Comments on Schauer and Moore," id. at 441.

22. Brest, "Misconceived Quest for Original Understanding," at 205, 221–22, 231–34, 226; Gregory Leyh, "Legal Education and the Public Life," in *Legal Hermeneutics: History, Theory, and Practice,* ed. Gregory Leyh, 269, 285 (1992) ("hermeneutical howler"). See generally David Hoy, "A Hermeneutical Critique of the Originalism/ Nonoriginalism Distinction," 15 *Northern Kentucky Law Review* 479 (1988). Earl Maltz provided an assessment of the "seminal" role Brest played in transforming the originalism debate in "Foreword: The Appeal of Originalism," 1987 *Utah Law Review* 772, 772, 795–97 (1987).

23. "[V]irtually alone" is from Monaghan, "Our Perfect Constitution," at 381; Tushnet, "Legal Scholarship," at 1210.

24. Brest, "Fundamental Rights," at 1063, 1096, 1109.

25. The commentator was Geoffrey Hazard. See Hazard, "Commentary on the 'Fundamental Values' Controversy," 90 *Yale Law Journal* 1110, 1111 (1981). See, e.g., Hilary Putnam, "A Reconsideration of Deweyan Democracy," 63 *Southern California Law Review* 1671 (1991); Putnam, *The Many Faces of Realism* (1987); W. V. O. Quine, *From a Logical Point of View: 9 Logico-Philosophical Essays* 20 (1953). I am grateful to Gregory Alexander and John Schlegel for help with this paragraph. Robin West provided an excellent discussion and refutation of "the misperception" the interpretive turn led to "judicial lawlessness." But as she observed, laying that misperception to rest was not necessarily good, since interpretive constraints were likely to lead judicial interpreters away from progressive interpretations of the Constitution. Indeed instead of increasing anxiety over normative value, she would argue the interpretive turn has focused scholars' attention on "the Constitution's meaning" and has prevented them from addressing questions "about the value, wisdom, decency, or sensibility of constitutional guarantees." See West, *Progressive and Conservative Constitutionalism: Reconstructing the Fourteenth Amendment* 156–57, 74–101, 160–77 (1994).

26. George Marcus, "Past, Present and Emergent Identities: Requirements for Ethnographies of Late Twentieth-Century Modernity Worldwide," in *Modernity and Identity,* ed. Scott Lash and Jonathan Friedman, 309, 329 n.3 (Marcus protested these

attributions were unfair). For another refutation, see Graham Watson, "Rewriting Culture," in Fox, *Recapturing Anthropology,* at 73.

27. Barthes is quoted in James Clifford, "Introduction: Partial Truths," in *Writing Culture: The Poetics and Politics of Ethnography,* ed. James Clifford and George Marcus, 1, 1 (1986). "They consider it" is from C. G. Prado, quoted in Alan Malachowski, "On Teaching Rorty," in *Reading Rorty: Critical Responses to Philosophy and the Mirror of Nature (and Beyond),* ed. Alan Malachowski, 365, 366 (1990). MacIntyre is quoted in Mark Lilla, "On Goodman, Putnam, and Rorty: The Return to the 'Given,' " 52 *Partisan Review* 220, 231 (1984). See also Martha Nussbaum, "The Use and Abuse of Philosophy in Legal Education," 45 *Stanford Law Review* 1627, 1644 (1993). Compare, e.g., John Higham's characterization of Geertz as "virtually the patron saint" of a recent conference on the future of intellectual history in Higham, *New Directions in Intellectual History* xi, xvi (1979), with Paul Rabinow's more skeptical discussion of Geertz in "Representations Are Social Facts," in Clifford and Marcus, *Writing Culture,* at 234, 241–43. "[O]ld hat" is from Fish, "Milton, Thou Shouldst Be Living at This Hour," in *No Such Thing as Free Speech,* at 271. Perhaps the winners and losers of intradisciplinary disputes should be irrelevant to interdisciplinary borrowers. "[N]eed we import all the special reservations that anthropologists have about each other's work or all their infighting, any more than they need to import ours?" historian Natalie Davis asked. Davis, "Anthropology and History in the 1980s," 12 *Journal of Interdisciplinary History* 267, 273 (1981).

28. Edward S. Corwin, "Reorganization of the Federal Judiciary," testimony reprinted in *Corwin on the Constitution* ed. Richard Loss, 2: 218, 230 (1987); Alexander, "Modern Equal Protection Theories," at 5 ("Not a single" and "even a rudimentary theory"; emphasis in the original); John Valuri, "Constitutional Hermeneutics," in *The Interpretive Turn: Philosophy, Science, Culture,* ed. David Hiley, James Bohman, and Richard Shusterman, 245, 246 (1991) ("ought to do" and "will do"); Mark Tushnet, "A Note on the Revival of Textualism in Constitutional Theory," 58 *Southern California Law Review* 683, 683 n.1 (1985) ("fancy"). See James Farr, "The Americanization of Hermeneutics: Francis Lieber's Legal and Political Hermeneutics," in Leyh, *Legal Hermeneutics,* at 83; Symposium on Legal and Political Hermeneutics, 16 *Cardozo Law Review* 1879 (1995); Frances Mootz, "The New Legal Hermeneutics," 47 *Vanderbilt Law Review* 115 (1994).

29. Grant Gilmore, *The Ages of American Law* 110–11 (1977).

30. Geertz, "Local Knowledge: Fact and Law in Comparative Perspective," in *Local Knowledge,* at 232–33.

31. Grey, "Constitution as Scripture," at 1. (Perry, too, now said that he was engaged in interpretation. Michael Perry, "The Authority of Text, Tradition and Reason: A Theory of Constitutional 'Interpretation,' " 58 *Southern California Law Review* 551, 572 n.68.) For an amusing description of the impact of the interpretive turn on law professors, see Pierre Schlag, "Cannibal Moves: An Essay on the Metamorphoses of the Legal Distinction," 40 *Stanford Law Review* 927, 937–38 (1988). For an interesting discussion of interpretive turn as being interpretivist itself and a logical outgrowth of the interpretivism and "the apparent indeterminacy of all [constitutional] theories" see Stephen Feldman, "Republican Revival/Interpretive Turn," 1992 *Wisconsin Law Review* 681, 704–5). The Bobbitt quotations are from Bobbitt, *Constitutional Fate,* at 245, 237 ("the notion" and "needs no"); Bobbitt, "Reflections

Inspired by My Critics," 72 *Texas Law Review* 1869, 1872 (1994) ("legitimation") Bobbitt, *Constitutional Interpretation* ix (1992) ("solved"). (See also Bobbitt, *Constitutional Fate,* at x, 5, 237–48; but see, e.g., Owen Fiss, "Conventionalism," 58 *Southern California Law Review* 177, 181–82 [1985]: "I will concede that recovering the idea of interpretation and characterizing a decision such as *Brown* as an instance of interpretation will not solve that [counter-majoritarian] dilemma. On the other hand, a proper conception of interpretation will help us understand the pervasiveness of the countermajoritarian dilemma and thus, in my judgement, reduce its significance.")

32. Paul Brest, "Who Decides?" 58 *Southern California Law Review* 661, 661 (1985) (quoting David Hoy); "objective standard" is from Alan Brudner, "The Ideality of Difference: Toward Objectivity in Legal Interpretation," 11 *Cardozo Law Review* 1133, 1133 (1990). See generally Levinson and Mailloux, *Interpreting Law;* Leyh, *Legal Hermeneutics;* Brook Thomas, "Reflections on the Law and Literature Revival," 17 *Critical Inquiry* 510, 513–15, 523–24 (1991).

33. Stanley Fish, "Normal Circumstances, Literal Language, Direct Speech Acts, the Ordinary, the Everyday, the Obvious, What Goes without Saying, and Other Special Cases," in Rabinow and Sullivan, *Interpretive Social Science,* at 243, 246, 248–51.

34. Stanley Fish, "Introduction: Going Down the Anti-Formalist Road," in *Doing What Comes Naturally: Change, Rhetoric, and the Practice of Theory in Literary and Legal Studies* 10 (1989). Unless otherwise indicated, all of Fish's articles cited in this book are reprinted in *Doing What Comes Naturally.*

35. Id. at 10–11; Peter Brooks, "Bouillabaisse," 99 *Yale Law Journal* 1147 (1990) ("Since there are no") (restating Fish's point).

36. Fish, "Anti-Formalist Road," at 14, 27 ("constraints" and "On the one hand"); Fish, "Dennis Martinez and the Uses of Theory," at 383 ("are not using"). See also Fish, "Consequences," at 338–40.

37. Fish, "Dennis Martinez," at 584 n.60 ("anti-foundationalist theory hope").

38. "[P]rivileging is from Fish, "Change," at 142; "paean" is from Coombe, "Same as It Ever Was," at 645; Richard Posner, *Law and Literature: A Misunderstood Relation* 263, 353 (1988). For caustic readings of Fish from the left see, e.g., Pierre Schlag, "Fish v. Zapp: The Case of the Relatively Autonomous Self," 76 *Georgetown Law Journal* 37 (1987); Allan Hutchinson, *Dwelling on the Threshold: Critical Essays on Modern Legal Thought* 142–63 (1988); Steven Winter, "Bull Durham and the Uses of Theory," 42 *Stanford Law Review* 639 (1990). The theorist who condemned Fish's "antimetaphysical fetish" was Michael Moore, in Moore, "The Interpretive Turn in Modern Theory: A Turn for the Worse?" 41 *Stanford Law Review* 871, 908 (1989). But see, e.g., Stephen Feldman, "The New Metaphysics: The Interpretive Turn in Jurisprudence," 76 *Iowa Law Review* 661, 663 (1991) (contending that we should "rescue hermeneutics from Moore's . . . trash heap"); Rorty, "Banality of Pragmatism," at 1813 (dismissing Moore as one of the two people "who still think[s] pragmatism is dangerous to the moral health of our society" (according to Rorty, the other was Allan Bloom. Id.). "[T]ransforming reality" is from James Bohman, David Hisley, and Richard Shusterman, "Introduction," in *Interpretive Turn,* at 1, 13; "Fishy" from Kathryn Abrams, "The Unbearable Lightness of Being Stanley Fish," 47 *Stanford Law Review* 595, 605 (1995).

39. "[P]roperty of the right" is from Owen Fiss, "The Challenge Ahead," 1 *Yale Journal*

of Law and Humanities viii, ix–x (1988); "objectivity does not depend" is from Millon, "Objectivity and Democracy," at 9. The interpretation in this paragraph is at variance with that of Coombe in "Same as It Ever Was," at 605, n.2, who suggested that treating the interpretive turn as a liberal reaction against critical legal scholars' allegations of indeterminacy might be "revisionist intellectual history. It would seem that mainstream legal scholars were contending with some of the implications of linguistic philosophy and literary criticism before they recognized the relevance of this work to the emerging Critical Legal Studies scholarship on legal indeterminacy. For quite some time (roughly 1979–1985, to judge by publishing dates) these simultaneous initiatives developed autonomously and without explicit reference to each other." As my account indicates, I believe law professors were influenced by developments in the humanities and the social sciences, but the fact that they could use the interpretive turn to fight legal indeterminacy may have made the interpretive turn even more attractive to liberal legal scholars. Though proponents of the two initiatives—the turn to interpretation and the cls work on indeterminacy—may not have made explicit reference to each other until the mid-1980s, it certainly seems as if they were aware of each other.

40. Ronald Dworkin, "Law as Interpretation," 60 *Texas Law Review* 527, 543 (1982) ("must regard"; emphasis in the original); all other quotations from Dworkin, *Law's Empire* 214, 228–40, 255 (1986).

41. Fiss, "Objectivity and Interpretation," 34 *Stanford Law Review* 739, 745, 762, 740–41, 750 (1982) (emphasis added).

42. Sanford Levinson, "Law as Literature," 60 *Texas Law Review* 373, 391 (1982) ("meaning is created"; "There are as many"); Levinson, "On Dworkin, Kennedy, and Ely: Decoding the Legal Past," 51 *Partisan Review* 248, 259 (1984) ("Building on"); Levinson, "Conversing about Justice," 100 *Yale Law Journal* 1855, 1858 (1991) ("for better or worse"). On Iredell see James Iredell, "To the Public," August 17, 1786, and Iredell to Richard Spaight, August 26, 1787, from Griffith McRee, *Life and Correspondence of James Iredell* 2: 148, 174 (1857–58) (emphasis in the original). For the suggestion Iredell's arguments provided the impetus for Hamilton's own anticipation of judicial review in *Federalist 78,* see Snowiss, *Judicial Review,* at 45–80.

43. Stanley Fish, "Interpretation and the Pluralist Vision," 60 *Texas Law Review* 495, 495 (1982) (quoting Gerald Graff, " 'Keep Off the Grass,' 'Drop Dead,' and Other Indeterminacies: A Response to Sanford Levinson," 60 *Texas Law Review* 405, 406 [1982]; see also Fish, "Working on the Chain Gang: Interpretation in Law and Literature," id. at, 551; and Fish, "Fish v. Fiss," at 120, 126, 138); Fiss, "Conventionalism," at 182–83 ("stand united").

44. "[P]ioneering . . . special issue on interpretation" is from Fish, "Don't Know Much about the Middle Ages," at 308; Editors, "Introduction," 60 *Texas Law Review* i, iv (1982); "our own creations" is from James Boyd White, "Judicial Criticism," 20 *Georgia Law Review* 835, 860 (1986). See generally Michael Richmond, "The Cultural Milieu of Law," 13 *Nova Law Review* 89, 96 (1988); Richard Weisberg, "Text into Theory: A Literary Approach to the Constitution," 20 *Georgia Law Review* 939 (1986). I have limited my discussion of law and literature to its "law as literature" subset, which focuses on the relationship between legal and literary interpretation and the relevance of literary theory to law. For a survey of "law in literature" work,

which tends to concentrate on how law and legal themes are portrayed in literature, see, e.g., Minda, *Postmodern,* at 150–55. For a history of the law and literature movement, see David Papke, "Neo-Marxists, Nietzscheans, and New Critics: The Voices of the Contemporary Law and Literature Discourse," 1986 *American Bar Foundation Research Journal* 883 (1986).

45. Brest, "Who Decides?" at 661–62; Michael Moore, "A Natural Law Theory of Interpretation," 58 *Southern California Law Review* 277, 277 n.2 (1985) ("concern with objectivity").

46. Robert Cover, "Violence and the Word," 95 *Yale Law Journal* 1601, 1628, 1611 n.24 (1986) (see also Robert Cover, "The Supreme Court 1982 Term—Foreword: Nomos and Narrative," 97 *Harvard Law Review* 4, 40 [1983]); Wellington, "Challenges to Legal Education," at 329; Minow, "Law Turning Outward," at 89 ("to clarify"). Martha Minow, "Interpreting Rights: An Essay for Robert Cover," 96 *Yale Law Journal* 1860, 1894–95 (1987).

47. Daniel Farber, "Legal Pragmatism and the Constitution," 72 *Minnesota Law Review* 1331, 1337, 1332, 1376, 1340–41, 1347–48 (1988). Emphasis in the original. (Farber notwithstanding, some neopragmatists fell prey to the republican revival, which is discussed in the next three chapters, and which surely qualifies as a "grand theory"; see, e.g. Sunstein, *Partial Constitution,* at 141); Grey, "Hear the Other Side," at 1594; Martha Minow and Elizabeth Spelman, "In Context," 63 *Southern California Law Review* 1597, 1646–47, 1651 (1990); Minow, "The Supreme Court, 1986 Term— Foreword: Justice Engendered," 101 *Harvard Law Review* 10, 15–16, 71 (1987) (maintaining that instead of ignoring "traits of difference," "all who judge" should seek "the perspective of individuals and groups unlike themselves" and that "trying to take seriously the point of view of people labeled 'different' is a way to move beyond the current difficulties in the treatment of difference in our society"); Joseph Singer, "Property and Coercion in Federal Indian Law: The Conflict between Critical and Complacent Pragmatism," 63 *Southern California Law Review* 1821, 1838 (1990); Posner, *Problems of Jurisprudence,* at 130, 387 ("reasonableness," "judicial lodestar," and caution; see id. at 459–69 for a "pragmatist manifesto"); Posner, "What Has Pragmatism to Offer Law?" 63 *Southern California Law Review* 1653, 1654 (1990) ("ideological diversity"; see id. at 1660 for his emphasis that the "differences among current advocates of pragmatism are even more profound" than "those between a Peirce and a James, or between a James and a Dewey"; and id. at 1667–68 for his discussion of the relationship between law and economics and pragmatism); Dworkin, *Law's Empire,* at 95, 151–75, 378; Stanley Fish, "Almost Pragmatism: Richard Posner's Jurisprudence," 57 *University of Chicago Law Review* 1447, 1457–75 (1990); Minow, "Law Turning Outward," at 89; Dworkin, "Pragmatism, Right Answers, and True Banality," in *Pragmatism in Law and Society,* ed. Michael Brint and William Weaver, 359 (1991); Steven Smith, "The Pursuit of Pragmatism," 100 *Yale Law Journal* 409, 411, 445–46 (1990) (describing Dworkin as a pragmatist in disguise, challenging Posner's characterization of himself as a pragmatist, and criticizing pragmatism as "platitudinous," but concluding it does possess a valuable "exhortatory function"); Rorty, "Banality of Pragmatism," at 1811.

48. John Leubsdorf, "Deconstructing the Constitution," 40 *Stanford Law Review* 181, 189 (1987) ("immense system"); Hutchinson, "Inessentially Speaking," at 1552

("one more construction"); J. M. Balkin, "What Is a Postmodern Constitutionalism?" 90 *Michigan Law Review* 1966, 1967 (1992); Robert Lipkin, "Can American Constitutional Law Be Postmodern?" 42 *Buffalo Law Review* 317, 401 (1994). On postmodernism in legal scholarship see generally Minda, *Postmodern.*

49. Fish, "Don't Know Much about the Middle Ages," at 307. See Richard Posner, "Law and Literature: A Relation Reargued," 72 *Virginia Law Review* 1351, 1360 (1986); Posner, *Law and Literature,* at 216, 243–49, 264, 314, 352–58 (registering doubts about the "law as literature" movement).

50. "[I]nstantaneous practicality" is quoted in Francis Allen, "The New Anti-Intellectualism in American Legal Education," 28 *Mercer Law Review* 447, 450 (1977). For Carrington on law and economics, see "Discussion by Seminar Participants," 9 *Journal of Legal Studies* 323, 332–39 (1979); Carrington, Book Review, 1974 *University of Illinois Law Forum* 187 (1974) (reviewing Posner, *Economic Analysis of Law*). Carrington's 1983 speech was reprinted in the *Journal of Legal Education;* see Paul Carrington, "Of Law and the River," 34 *Journal of Legal Education* 222, 227 (1984). The only critical legal scholar Carrington specifically named in this indictment was Roberto Unger. Id. at 227. The irony here, as Neil Duxbury observed, was that Unger was "the most obvious visionary" within cls. Duxbury, *Patterns,* at 500. Elsewhere Carrington characterized cls adherents "collectively as nihilists." Quoted in Ted Fineman, "Critical Legal Studies, Professionalism, and Academic Freedom: Exploring the Tributaries of Carrington's River," 35 *Journal of Legal Education* 180, 193 n.40 (1985). I would argue that Carrington's argument was ahistorical because law students have always been dispirited.

51. The *Washington Post,* the cartoon, and Bate are quoted in Deborah Esch, "Deconstruction," in *Redrawing the Boundaries: The Transformation of English and American Literary Studies,* ed. Stephen Greenblatt and Giles Gunn, 374, 380–82 (1992). Norris is quoted in Bernard Bergonzi, *Exploding English: Criticism, Theory, Culture* 131 (1990); Bergonzi discusses the addition of the "ism" at 388. Paul Lauter noted "the privileging of theorists" in *Canons and Contexts,* at 141. Other academics questioned the idea that theory had triumphed, noting theorists could be treated better than others only if they got hired "in the first place." J. Hillis Miller, "Presidential Address 1986: The Triumph of Theory, the Resistance to Reading, and the Question of the Material Base," 102 *PMLA* 281, 286 (1987).

It is difficult to pinpoint when the culture wars within the university began, but I would guess around 1981. But see Christopher Newfield, "What Was Political Correctness? Race, the Right, and Managerial Democracy in the Humanities," 19 *Critical Inquiry* 308 (1993). According to him, the culture wars of the 1980s did not polarize the academy: "The eighties Right had all the earmarks of an outraged but doomed rear guard. Nonacademics were deeply unimpressed." It was only in 1990, with the furor over multiculturalism, that "the media start[ed] to care about this." Even if this point is true of the academy as a whole, certainly the polarization within law schools had been made public by the mid-1980s. Id. at 316–17.

52. Gary Peller, "The Politics of Reconstruction," 98 *Harvard Law Review* 863, 863 (1985) ("American legal thought" and "Although divisions"); Binder, "Critical Legal Studies as Guerilla Warfare," at 8 n.34, 2 ("Despite," "oppressed campesinos," "spoiled yuppies," and "goat cheese"). The argument that cls failed in its political

radicalism is most energetically made in Peter Goodrich, "Sleeping with the Enemy: An Essay on the Politics of Critical Legal Studies in America," in *Legal Studies as Cultural Studies: A Reader in (Post) Modern Critical Theory*, ed. Jerry Leonard, 299 (1995). Robert Nagel spoke of the stripping away of the intellectual and sociological veneer in "Meeting the Enemy," at 638, 650–51. Bator described cls as "guerilla warfare" in his remarks at "A Discussion on Critical Legal Studies at the Harvard Law School," presented by the Harvard Society for Law and Public Policy and by the Federalist Society, Harvard Club, New York City, May 13, 1985, 14. For the "counterhegemonic enclave" proposal, see Kennedy, *Legal Education,* at 121–23. For sympathetic discussions of the tenure battles of some critical legal scholars see, e.g., Jerry Frug, "McCarthyism and Critical Legal Studies," 22 *Harvard Civil Rights–Civil Liberties Law Review* 668, 676–88 (1987); Jay Feinman and Marc Feldman, "Pedagogy and Politics," 73 *Georgetown Law Journal* 875, 925, 929 n.131 (1985).

53. Horwitz's remark is mentioned in Editorial, "The Missing Questions," *Harvard Law Record,* September 23, 1983, 10; Ralph Nader, "Harvard Law: Not What It Used to Be . . ." id., April 27, 1984, 22. "Rome" and "Beirut" are from Vicki Quase, "Are Lawyers Really Necessary?: *Barrister* Interview with Duncan Kennedy," 14 *Barrister* 10, 36 (fall 1987) (quoting David Trubek); "Throughout its history" from Miguel Rodriguez, " 'Politicized' Faculty Affects Tenure, Teaching, Research," *Harvard Law Record,* March 9, 1984, 1; "most unhappy place" and "only prominent law school" from Trillin, "Reporter at Large," at 53, 73. The *Post* article is Al Kamen, "War between Professors Pervades Harvard Law," *Washington Post,* December 21, 1985, A5. Robert Clark, who later succeeded Vorenberg as Harvard Law School dean, is quoted in "Discussion on Critical Legal Studies at the Harvard Law School," at 22. See also David Margolick, "The Split at Harvard Law Goes Down to Its Foundations," *New York Times,* October 6, 1986, section 4, at 7. The candidate was Clare Dalton. Vincent Chang, "Appointments Committee Balks at Dalton Tenure," *Harvard Law Record,* April 19, 1985, 1. For further discussion of the difficulty of making appointments and the lack of confidentiality in the process, see "Discussion on Critical Legal Studies at the Harvard Law School," at 7, 22, 29. The Trillin article was a brilliant portrayal of how cls had polarized Harvard Law School faculty in the mid-1980s. (Another divisive debate among Harvard Law School professors in the early and mid-1980s, which Trillin did not discuss, related to the absence of tenured scholars of color on the faculty. See Derrick Bell, *Confronting Authority: Reflections of an Ardent Protester* [1994]; Randall Kennedy, "Racial Critiques of Legal Academia," 102 *Harvard Law Review* 1745, 1756–58 [1989].) Relations among faculty members were somewhat better at Yale, which had few or no critical legal scholars, though when Julius Getman told his colleague Geoffrey Hazard that "a union caucus that I had witnessed was far more intellectually impressive than a Yale Law School faculty meeting," Hazard replied "with some feeling. . . . 'So is a sandbox.' " Getman, *Company of Scholars,* at 92. Trillin noted that "Stanford is sometimes spoken of as the one other major law school that has on its faculty the full array of political and legal positions, but Stanford is apparently much more peaceful. Harvard professors who are asked to speculate on what causes the atmosphere are likely to say 'The weather, maybe,' or 'Personalities.' " Trillin, "Reporter at Large," at 76. The most important personality in the cls debate at Harvard, Trillin implied, was Duncan Ken-

nedy. Kennedy's more conservative colleagues, while professing their admiration for his brilliance, blamed the relatively large number of critical legal scholars at Harvard on him. To quote Paul Bator, "It's Duncan as a recruiting agency that's the problem, not Duncan as a professor." "Discussion on Critical Legal Studies at the Harvard Law School," at 32.

54. The accusations of red-baiting came from, e.g., Robert Gordon to Paul Carrington, "Of 'Law and the River,' and of Nihilism and Academic Freedom," in 35 *Journal of Legal Education* 1, 9 (1985); see generally Frug, "McCarthyism," at 681–86. "There is a deep fear" is from James Elkins, "Does Teaching Matter?" 31 *Saint Louis University Law Journal* 35, 39 (1986). For discussion of the rights-based tenor of critical legal scholars' response to Carrington see, e.g., Gunter Frankenberg, "Down by Law: Irony, Seriousness, and Reason," 83 *Northwestern Law Review* 360, 387–88 (1988).

55. Sanford Levinson, "Professing Law: Commitment of Faith or Detached Analysis?" 31 *Saint Louis University Law Journal* 3, 5, 10–11 (1986); Owen Fiss to Paul Carrington, "Of 'Law and the River' and of Nihilism and Academic Freedom," 35 *Journal of Legal Education* 26, 26 (1985); Paul Brest to Paul Carrington, id. at 16, 16.

56. Henry Louis Gates, Jr., *Loose Canons: Notes on the Culture Wars* 113 (1992). Emphasis in the original.

57. "[C]iting Rorty" is from Jules Coleman and Brian Leiter, "Determinacy, Objectivity, and Authority," 142 *University of Pennsylvania Law Review* 549, 551 (1993). Collier compared citation practices in law and philosophy in "Humanistic Theory," at 219–20, as did Nussbaum in "Philosophy in Legal Education," at 1632–33. See also Charles Collier, "Precedent and Legal Authority: A Critical History," 1988 *Wisconsin Law Review* 771, 811–12 (1988). Sanford Levinson addressed the problematic nature of footnoting practices in legal scholarship when, in a footnote to a discussion of Fish's work, he wrote: "It occurs to me, as I dutifully footnote Fish's statement that the act of footnoting is itself a bow toward the notion of objective knowledge, for I am purporting, even as I describe Fish's . . . theories, to be giving you (the reader) an 'accurate' rendition of those theories. Indeed, the point of footnotes, especially if 'cite-checked' by law review editors, is to suggest that the proof of my accuracy is that you would arrive at the same conclusions by reading the same material. This generates an obvious, albeit important, paradox, one only made worse because I of course also expect you to grasp 'my' argument and to be able to state it correctly . . . even if you . . . reject it. I suppose, therefore, that I can be accused of being one of those 'newreaders' who introduce their 'own interpretive strategy when reading someone else's text, but tacitly rely . . . on communal norms when undertaking to communicate the methods and results of [their] interpretation to [their] own readers.' " Levinson, "Law as Literature," at 382 n.33. In a recent article, two legal scholars have advocated resisting "the tyranny of paraphrase." Elizabeth Fajans and Mary Falk, "Against the Tyranny of Paraphrase: Talking Back to Texts," 78 *Cornell Law Review* 163, 165 (1993). Yet the very act of selecting which parts of a text to quote presupposes a certain interpretive stance.

58. Appleby, "One Good Turn," at 1329; Luban, *Legal Modernism,* at 67 ("old acid heads"); Peter Gabel and Duncan Kennedy, "Roll over Beethoven," 36 *Stanford Law Review* 1, 15 (1984). For a discussion of importance of this piece in the cls move toward postmodernism see Allan Hunt, "The Big Fear: Law Confronts Postmodern-

ism," 35 *McGill Law Journal* 509, 521 (1990). First-generation critical legal scholar David Kennedy discussed some of the contributions poststructuralism could make to law in his 1986 article, "Critical Theory, Structuralism and Contemporary Legal Scholars," at 276–89.

Guyora Binder persuasively argued "that post-structuralism had no influence on the first wave of critical legal scholarship, published in the 1970s. The people who introduced post-structuralism into legal scholarship were the second-generation crits—those of us who encountered post-structuralism as undergraduates in the 1970s, and then in law school read first-generation crits through the prism of our post-structuralist educations. The post-structuralism of the second generation then had a feedback influence on some of the first-generation scholars." Binder, "What's Left," 69 *Texas Law Review* 1985, 2000 n.77 (1991). According to Robert Gordon, "law schools tend to pick up mainstream intellectual opinion ten to fifteen years late." Gordon, "Critical Legal Histories," at 68. Perhaps that is because, as Binder implied, it is often carried by young law professors who bring what they have studied as undergraduates to bear on legal scholarship.

59. "[T]ext and its reading" is from Vincent Leitch, *American Literary Criticism from the Thirties to the Eighties* 288 (1988); play of signifers from Jacques Derrida, *Of Grammatology* 50, 73 (trans. Gayatri Spivak, 1976); "expands the idea" from Fiss, "Objectivity and Interpretation," at 741 (but see Jonathan Culler, *On Deconstruction: Theory and Criticism after Structuralism* 132 [1982]; J. M. Balkin, "Deconstructive Practice and Legal Theory," 96 *Yale Law Journal* 743, 785 [1987]; Balkin, "Nested Oppositions," 99 *Yale Law Journal* 1669, 1703 [1990]); "bullshit" from Paul Carrington to Robert Gordon, "Of 'Law and the River,' and of Nihilism and Academic Freedom," 35 *Journal of Legal Education* 9, 12 (1985).

60. Rorty discussed the replacement of philosophy by literary theory in *Mirror of Nature,* at 168 n. 6; "transfer point" is from Joan Vincent, "Engaging Historicism," in Fox, *Recapturing Anthropology,* at 44, 44; the discussion of the Geertzean text from Richard Fox, "For a Nearly New Culture History," id. at 93, 93–94 (emphasis added); "Ethnographic truths" and "inherently" from Clifford, "Introduction," in *Writing Culture,* at 7 (emphasis in the original); "dialogue," "cooperative," and "ideology" from Stephen Tyler, "Post-Modern Ethnography: From Document of the Occult to Occult Document," id. at 122, 126. For a parodic examination of the prestige of literary theory see George Marcus, "A Broad(er) side to the Canon: Being a Partial Account of a Year of Travel among Textual Communities in the Realm of Humanities Centers, and Including a Collection of Artificial Curiosities," in *Rereading Cultural Anthropology* ed. George Marcus, 103 (1992).

61. Clifford Geertz, "I-Witnessing: Malinowski's Children," in *The Anthropologist as Author* 90, 97 (1988). Geertz's younger colleague was Richard Fox, in "Introduction: Working in the Present," in Fox, *Recapturing Anthropology,* at 1, 6.

62. "[E]thnographic approach" is from George Marcus and Michael Fischer, *Anthropology as Cultural Critique: An Experimental Moment in the Human Sciences* 154 (1986) (Marcus and Fischer associated this approach with critical legal scholars at id.); "knee-deep" from James Elkins, "From the Symposium Editor," 39 *Journal of Legal Education* 1, 1 (1989). On the pleasure writing book reviews and obituaries provided law professors see, e.g., Francis Allen, "In Praise of Book Reviews," 79 *Michigan Law Review* 557, 558–59 (1981); J. Nicholas McGrath and David Kilgour,

"Scholarship Admired: Responses to Professor Lasson," 103 *Harvard Law Review* 2085, 2086 (1990): "How come scholars can write readable obituaries but can't write readable articles on matters of true substance?" For a discussion of the incompleteness of obituaries, see Paul Gewirtz, "A Lawyer's Death," 100 *Harvard Law Review* 2053 (1987) (noting that all the memorial tributes to Judge Henry Friendly neglected to mention that he had committed suicide). "Spaceship Me" is from Patricia Williams, "A Brief Comment with Footnotes on the Civil Rights Chronicle," 3 *Harvard Blackletter Journal* 79 (1986); "Eleven years ago" from Susan Estrich, "Rape," 95 *Yale Law Journal* 1087, 1087 (1986); David Kennedy discussed his "Spring Break" article in the introduction to *Knowledges,* at 422. Law professors seem to be more narcissistic than other scholars, by which I mean that they are more likely to draw on their own experiences and talk about themselves in their teaching. Compare virtually any law review issue in 1990, for example, with a collection of intellectual autobiographies of twenty sociologists published that same year. Bennett Berger, ed. *Authors of Their Own Lives: Intellectual Autobiographies by Twenty American Sociologists,* (1990). In the introduction, Berger, a professor at the University of California, San Diego, predicted he would be blamed for "an effort to encourage narcissistic self-indulgence and 'letting it all hang out' " and anticipated that he would be accused of practicing "California sociology." Id. at xiii, xxi. Scholars in other disciplines seem to be more self-conscious about writing about themselves than are law professors, though many scholars in other disciplines often do so today.

63. Julius Getman, "Voices," 66 *Texas Law Review* 577, 584–85 (1988). For skeptical reactions, see Patricia Wald, "Disembodied Voices—An Appellate Judge's Response," id. at 623, 628. Williams recounted her difficulties with law review editors in Patricia Williams, *The Alchemy of Race and Rights* 47–48 (1991).

64. "[M]ost precious property" is from Patricia Williams, "The Obliging Shell: An Informal Essay on Formal Equal Opportunity," 87 *Michigan Law Review* 2128, 2150 (1989) (see generally the symposium on "legal storytelling" in that issue and the symposium on "pedagogy of narrative" in 40 *Journal of Legal Education* [1990]). "[M]oi criticism" is from Adam Begley, "The I's Have It: Duke's 'Moi' Critics Expose Themselves," *Lingua Franca* 54, 57 (March/April 1994). For a discussion of her daughter and television, see Suzanna Sherry, "The Forgotten Victims," 63 *University of Colorado Law Review* 375, 378 (1992); for mention of his daughter's S.S.D.D. poster, see John Schlegel, "A Certain Narcissism: A Slight Unseemliness," 63 *University of Colorado Law Review* 595, 608 (1992). Some would say the vertical pronoun constituted nothing new. For example, according to Richard Posner, Wechsler's famous "neutral principles" argument had taken "the form of personal statement" and reflected the "patronizing" and "self-conscious performance of a master craftsman of the guild of lawyers." Posner, *Overcoming Law,* at 70–71. I disagree with Posner's assessment of Wechsler. In any event, law professors who used the first person in the 1980s did not generally portray themselves as master craftsmen.

65. Owen Fiss, "The Death of the Law?" 72 *Cornell Law Review* 1, 16, 14, 2, 9–10 (1986). Ackerman called for lawyers to abandon "a shallow Realism that has outlived its time" for a "Contructivism" that combined a politically neutral stance toward economics with the insights of Rawls. Ackerman, *Reconstructing American Law,* at 110, 44–45, 89–104. Ackerman made some similar arguments in "Law, Economics, and the Problem of Legal Culture," 1986 *Duke Law Journal* 929 (1986). At least

since the publication of *Reconstructing American Law,* critics have suggested Ackerman's work exemplified the "intellectual and moral bankruptcy of modern liberalism." Peter Teachout, "The Burden of the Liberal Song," 62 *Indiana Law Journal* 1283, 1312 (1987) (where Teachout argued instead that Ackerman had betrayed modern liberalism). I have focused on Fiss in the text because his tone, like Carrington's, was even more despairing than Ackerman's. Further, Fiss has been labeled "[p]erhaps the most eloquent and thoughtful spokesman and defender of the mainstream position of liberal legal scholars. . . . Fiss has offered honest criticism of the new movements without embracing the tainted position now attributable to Carrington." Gary Minda, "The Jurisprudential Movements of the 1980s," 50 *Ohio State Law Journal* 599, 652 (1989).

66. Fiss, "Death of the Law" at 9–11, 14–15.
67. Hutchinson, "Inessentially Speaking," at 1569 ("time and place"); Pierre Schlag, "The Problem of the Subject," 69 *Texas Law Review* 1627, 1677 (1991) ("authoritarian strategy," emphasis in the original); Clare Dalton, "The Faithful Liberal and the Question of Diversity," 12 *Harvard Women's Law Journal* 1, 3, 7 (1989) ("start to finish").
68. I am very grateful to Christine Desan for giving me a tape of the AALS meeting. Owen Fiss discussed the incident in "Robert M. Cover," 96 *Yale Law Journal* 1717, 1720 (1987).
69. Robert Cover, Owen Fiss, and Judith Resnik, *Procedure* 730 (1988).

CHAPTER 5. THE TURN TO HISTORY

1. Ackerman, *We the People,* at 25.
2. Edwin Meese, "Construing the Constitution," 19 *University of California, Davis Law Review* 22, 26 (1985); Nichol, "The Left, the Right, and Certainty," at 1183 ("avoid the change"). On Reagan's transformation of the judiciary see, e.g., Christopher Smith and Avis Jones, "The Rehnquist Court's Activism and the Risk of Injustice," 26 *Connecticut Law Review* 53 (1993); but see Timothy Tomasi and Jess Velona, "All the President's Men? A Study of Ronald Reagan's Appointments to the U.S. Court of Appeals," 87 *Columbia Law Review* 766, 792 (1987): "[W]hile Republican judges are much more conservative than their Democratic colleagues, Reagan appointees are not significantly more conservative than other Republican judges. Public focus upon a few controversial nominations . . . may have led to an incorrect generalization that all of President Reagan's appointees are rigid ideologues."
3. Lino Graglia, "Constitution, Community, and Liberty," 8 *Harvard Journal of Law and Public Policy* 291, 294–95 (1984). Insisting that "the Framers founded representative government rather than government by judiciary," Walter Berns also blamed liberal judicial activism on "prestigious law schools" in *Taking the Constitution Seriously* 228 (1987), as did Bork in *Tempting of America,* at 135–38, 343.
4. William Bradford Reynolds, "Renewing the American Constitutional Heritage," 8 *Harvard Journal of Law and Public Policy* 225, 237, 229, 234 (1984); Rehnquist, "Notion of a Living Constitution," at 699; see also Owen Fiss and Charles Krauthammer, "The Rehnquist Court," *New Republic,* March 10, 1982, 14, 18–20.
5. Jack Rakove, "Parchment Barriers and the Politics of Rights," in *A Culture of Rights*

98, 100–101 (see also Rakove, "The Madisonian Moment," 55 *University of Chicago Law Review* 473 [1988]; Rakove, "Comment," 47 *Maryland Law Review* 226 [1988]); Levy, *Original Intent,* at 398. Mark Tushnet made the same point about another form of interpretivism, textualism, in "Revival of Textualism," at 685: "I argue that textualism fails the 'laissez faire v. socialism': every version of textualism licenses a judge to require anything from laissez faire to socialism." According to William Eskridge, the same point also holds true for "the new textualism" in statutory interpretation. See Eskridge, *Dynamic Statutory Interpretation,* at 133, 230; Richard Bernstein, "Charting the Bicentennial," 87 *Columbia Law Review* 1565, 1604, 1597–98 (1987) ("cottage industry" and "widening gap"). The best early demonstration that originalism was not the original understanding came in H. Jefferson Powell, "The Original Understanding of Original Intent," 98 *Harvard Law Review* 885 (1985).

In a chapter entitled "Madison and the Origins of Originalism," Jack Rakove provides a fascinating discussion of how the politics of the early 1790s shaped the development of theories of constitutional interpretation. The legitimacy of originalist interpretation was established in 1796 when, during a debate over the Jay Treaty, Madison "delivered a speech which can be cited as a definitive early statement of the theory that the original understanding of the ratifiers of the Constitution can indeed provide an essential guide to its interpretation." Realizing its potential for radicalism, the Federalists had tried to cabin the concept of popular sovereignty in 1787–88 by insisting that the ratifers could vote only to accept or reject the Constitution and could not amend it. In his 1796 speech, however, Madison made popular sovereignty the cornerstone of originalism, saying that as the Constitution came from the Convention's Framers, "it was nothing more than the draught of a plan, nothing but a dead letter, until life and validity were breathed into it, by the voice of the people, speaking through the several state conventions. If we were to look therefore, for the meaning of the instrument, beyond the face of the instrument, we must look for it not in the general contention, which proposed, but in the state conventions, which accepted and ratified the constitution." As Rakove shows, Madison's "speech was less an affirmation of the possibilities of using the understandings of the ratifiers to fix the meaning of the Constitution than an attempt to nullify any appeal to the authority and intentions of the framers." Rakove concludes that though originalism could "be defended as a neutral mode of interpretation, the temptation to resort to it was manifestly political." See also Rakove, *Original Meanings,* at 342, 362, 365. See also id. at 96, 106–8, 116. For a discussion of the fragmentary nature of the surviving record see James Hutson, "The Creation of the Constitution: The Integrity of the Documentary Record," 65 *Texas Law Review* 12 (1986).

6. Richard Epstein, *Takings: Private Property and the Power of Eminent Domain* 31, 95, 281 (1985); Epstein, "An Outline of *Takings*," 41 *University of Miami Law Review* 3, 17 (1986) ("implacable stand"); and see Epstein, *Simple Rules for a Complex World* 128–48 (1995).

7. Thomas Grey, "The Malthusian Constitution," 41 *University of Miami Law Review* 21 (1986). The relatively sympathetic reader was Ellen Paul, who is quoted in "Proceedings of the Conference on Takings of Property and the Constitution," id. at 49, 88. Ackerman charged Epstein misused history, id. at 61; Epstein answered, "I don't cite history in my defense," id. at 66. That reply seems disingenuous. Epstein did rely

on his reading of the Founders as liberal Lockeans, though he showed little interest in the original understanding of the takings clause, which, as he observed, had no impact on takings clause jurisprudence. Epstein, *Takings,* at 9–18, 29; William Treanor, "The Original Understanding of the Takings Clause and the Political Process," 95 *Columbia Law Review* 782, 804 (1995). For attacks on Epstein's use of history, see id. at 815–55; Flaherty, "History 'Lite,' " at 556–67. For Epstein's reply to Flaherty, see Epstein, "History Lean: The Reconciliation of Private Property and Representative Government," 95 *Columbia Law Review* 591 (1995).

8. Richard Posner, "What Am I? A Potted Plant?" *New Republic,* September 28, 1987, 23. Posner noted that though some interpreted this article as an expression of opposition to the Bork nomination, it was not intended that way. Posner, *Overcoming Law,* at 230 n.2. Another prominent political conservative who opposed Bork's originalism was Harvard Law School professor Charles Fried, who became Reagan's solicitor general. See Fried, *Order and Law: Arguing the Reagan Revolution* 61–68, 81–82 (1991).

9. William Brennan, "Construing the Constitution," 19 *University of California, Davis Law Review* 2, 7, 4–5 (1985); John Paul Stevens, "Construing the Constitution," id. at 15, 20.

10. Mark Tushnet, "The U.S. Constitution and the Intent of the Framers," 36 *Buffalo Law Review* 217, 218 (1987) (reprinted from *Tikkun*); Daniel Farber, "The Originalism Debate: A Guide for the Perplexed," 49 *Ohio State Law Journal* 1085, 1098 ("Reduced to its essence"); Cass Sunstein, "The Beard Thesis and Franklin Roosevelt," 56 *George Washington Law Review* 114, 118 (1987) ("forerunners"); Larry Alexander, "A Tribute to Bernard H. Siegan," 27 *San Diego Law Review* 275, 275 (1990) ("skills as a legal historian"). In 1984, Erwin Chemerinsky observed that "the key error in much of [interpretive and noninterpretive] constitutional scholarship is that it begins with a definition of democracy that does not correspond to the American Constitution. The Constitution is based neither on a concept of democratic rule that is purely majoritarian nor on an assumption that all policies must be chosen by electorally accountable officials." Chemerinsky, "The Price of Asking the Wrong Question: An Essay on Constitutional Scholarship and Judicial Review," 62 *Texas Law Review* 1207, 1232–33 (1984). Earl Maltz, who sympathized with originalism, agreed on this point: "Although it is probably the most popular defense of originalism, the appeal to democratic theory is also the easiest to dismiss. The Constitution itself plainly establishes rights which are inconsistent with the basic concept of majoritarian rule. The existence of these rights cannot be reconciled with 'democracy' by pointing out that the Constitution itself was adopted through a democratic process; clearly, the principle of majority rule must refer to contemporary majorities, not those which existed in 1787. Thus, the appeal to democratic theory is best understood as 'a conceptually muddled groping for judicial restraint." Maltz, "The Failure of Attacks on Constitutional Originalism," 4 *Constitutional Commentary* 43, 52 (1987). Perhaps because law professors thought that questioning the equation between majoritarianism and democracy led down the path toward an "open-ended modernism" celebrating judicial discretion even Chemerinsky acknowledged would seem "heretical," few listened. Chemerinsky, *Interpreting,* at 130. For an indictment of the "New Right's appropriation of *The Federalist*" and its successful campaign to

make democracy synonymous with majoritarianism, see Sotirios Barber, *The Constitution of Judicial Power* 26–68 (1993).

11. Robert Gordon, "The Past as Authority and Social Critic: Stabilizing and Destabilizing Functions of History in Legal Argument," in *The Historic Turn in the Human Sciences,* ed. Terence McDonald (forthcoming) (see Justice Department Office of Legal Policy, *Original Meaning Jurisprudence: A Sourcebook* [March 12, 1987]); Levinson and Mailloux, "Introduction," in Levinson and Mailloux, *Interpreting Law,* at 3, 4.

12. See, e. g., Powell, "Original Understanding," at 943–44, 948; Brest, "Misconceived Quest," at 205–22, and "Fundamental Rights," at 1090–92; Tushnet, "Following the Rules," at 798–804; Dworkin, "Forum of Principle," at 482–97; and "The Bork Nomination," *New York Review of Books,* August 13, 1987, 3. Cf. Edward Rubin, "The Practice and Discourse of Legal Scholarship," 86 *Michigan Law Review* 1835, 1858–59 (1988) (suggesting that originalism could survive the hermeneutic challenge).

13. The quotations in this paragraph are from Farber, "Originalism Debate," at 1089–99; "The Senate, the Courts and the Constitution: A Debate," 12 (Center for National Policy, 1986) (McConnell) ("If historians," "No principled alternative") and Bork, *Tempting of America,* at 149 ("In dealing with such provisions" and "compelled by"). For a thoughtful defense of originalism see Richard Kay, "Adherence to the Original Intentions in Constitutional Adjudication: Three Objections and Responses," 82 *Northwestern University Law Review* 226 (1988). For originalist defenses of *Brown* in addition to Bork's, see, e.g., Meese, "Construing the Constitution," at 27–28; Harry Jaffa, "Judicial Conscience and Natural Rights: A Reply to Professor Ledewitz," Harry Jaffa, with Bruce Ledewitz, Robert Stone, and George Anastopolo, *Original Intent and the Framers of the Constitution: A Disputed Question* 237, 258–60 (1994) (justifying *Brown* on the grounds that the Constitution incorporated philosophy of natural rights, natural law, and "universal human equality" expressed in the Declaration of Independence, and made applicable to African Americans and women by the Fourteenth Amendment); Bernard Siegan, *The Supreme Court's Constitution: An Inquiry into Judicial Review and Its Impact on Society* 106 (1987) (defending *Brown* on the grounds that it furthered the right to travel). Though I have suggested originalists worked to fit *Brown* in their constitutional scheme, not all would agree. See McConnell, "Originalism and Desegregation," at 952: "In the fractured discipline of constitutional law, there is something very close to a consensus that *Brown* was inconsistent with the original understanding of the Fourteenth Amendment, except perhaps at an extremely high level of abstraction."

14. Horwitz, "Foreword: The Constitution of Change," at 40, 44, 51" (dominant tradition," "static originalism," and "historically changing"); Frederick Schauer, "An Essay on Constitutional Language," in Levinson and Mailloux, *Interpreting Law,* at 133, 138 ("most vehement critics"); Michael Perry, "The Legitimacy of Particular Conceptions of Constitutional Interpretation," 77 *Virginia Law Review* 669, 687 (1991) ("It seems difficult" and "That difficulty"). Cf. Antonin Scalia, "Originalism: The Lesser Evil," 57 *University of Cincinnati Law Review* 849, 853 (1989): "Those who have not delved into the scholarly writing on constitutional law for several years may be unaware of the explicitness with which many prominent and respected commentators reject the original meaning of the Constitution as an authoritative guide."

Elsewhere, however, Scalia conceded that "most nonoriginalists are moderate." Id. at 862. Scalia's article title indicates where he stood though he admitted "that in a crunch I may prove a faint-hearted originalist." Id. at 864.

15. See, e.g., Gordon Wood, "The Fundamentalists and the Constitution," *New York Review of Books,* February 18, 1988, 33; Rebecca Brown, "Tradition and Insight," 103 *Yale Law Journal* 177, 184 (1993).

16. Bronner, *Battle for Justice,* at 269, 298; L. A. Powe, "Making the Hard Choices Easy," 1986 *American Bar Foundation Research Journal* 57, 59 (1986) ("a white paper"); Lawrence Tribe, *Constitutional Choices* 267 (1985). On the Bork nomination as a victory for Warren Court decisions and the Ninth Amendment, see Bobbitt, *Constitutional Interpretation,* at 107–8; Sanford Levinson, "Constitutional Rhetoric and the Ninth Amendment," 64 *Chicago-Kent Law Review* 131, 134–35 (1988) Cf. Ronald Dworkin, "From Bork to Kennedy," *New York Review of Books,* December 17, 1987, 36 (arguing that in rejecting Bork, the Senate rejected originalism).

17. Lawrence Tribe, *God Save This Honorable Court: How the Choice of Supreme Court Justices Shapes Our History* ix, xv, 106–7 (1985) (for a critique of Tribe's use of history see Richard Friedman, "Tribal Myths: Ideology and the Confirmation of Supreme Court Nominations," 95 *Yale Law Journal* 1283 [1986]); Cover, "Foreword: Nomos and Narrative," at 4–10. In an elegant essay reflecting Cover's influence, David Luban maintained that Holmes was "wrong: The life of the logic is neither logic nor experience, but narrative and the only partially civilized struggle for the power it conveys. To put the point in slightly different terms, legal argument is at bottom neither analytic nor empirical but rather historical. The life of the law is not a vision of the future but a vision of the past; its passions are unleashed, to use Benjamin's words, 'by the image of enslaved ancestors rather than that of liberated grandchildren.' " Luban, *Legal Modernism,* at 211.

18. C. Vann Woodward, "The Future of the Past," 75 *American Historical Review* 711 (1970). Dworkin is quoted in Leedes, "Supreme Court Mess," at 1385; Derrida in David Simpson, "Literary Critics and the Return to History," 14 *Critical Inquiry* 721, 726–28 (1988).

19. Cheney is quoted in Harvey Kaye, *The Powers of the Past* 116–17 (1991). For other discussions of history in the 1980s, see id. at 18–21; David Lowenthal, *The Past Is a Foreign Country* 4–7, 12, 365 (1990); Michael Kammen, *Mystic Chords of Memory* 657 (1991). This love affair with the past extended to the Constitution. For a study of how Americans' attitude toward the Constitution has changed since the Founding, see Michael Kammen, *A Machine That Would Go of Itself: The Constitution in American Culture* (1986). In a fascinating essay written toward the end of the 1980s, Michael Frisch showed that fabrications of American history, such as the "mythic Betsy Ross" who sewed the flag for Washington, are more memorable for college students than American history itself. He concluded that "the consistency and extraordinary uniformity in the images offered up by these students indicates that the President, Secretary Bennett, and their followers have little cause for concern: the structure of myth and heroes, martyrs and mothers, is firmly in place." Frisch, "American History and the Structures of Collective Memory: A Modest Exercise in Empirical Iconography," 75 *Journal of American History* 1130, 1143–50, 1154 (1989).

20. Jonathan Macey, "Allan Bloom and the American Law Schools," 73 *Cornell Law Review* 1038, 1039 (1988). See Allan Bloom, *The Closing of the American Mind*

(1987). The 1988 debate about which "great books" Stanford undergraduates would be required to read may have inaugurated the new phase of the culture wars. See Mary Louise Pratt, "Humanities for the Future: Reflections on the Western Culture Debate at Stanford," in *The Politics of Liberal Education,* ed. Darryl Gless and Barbara Herrnstein Smith, 13 (1992). The editors of Harvard's 1991 English Institute chose *English Inside and Out: The Places of Literary Criticism* as the title for their volume "because it captures our sense that the current debates are in part the result of blurring the boundaries between inside (the classroom, the department, the academy, the field of specialization, the institute) and out (our various constituencies or communities)." Susan Gubar and Jonathan Kamholtz, "Introduction," in *English Inside and Out,* 1, 7.

21. "Rehistoricization" is from Vincent, "Engaging Historicism," at 52. Historians had also become interested in anthropology (see, e.g., Robert Darnton, *The Great Cat Massacre* [1984]), leading the anthropologist Emiko Ohnuky-Tierny to speak of the beginning of a new era, which featured "the historicization of anthropology and the anthropologization of history." Ohnuki-Tierney, "Introduction: The Historicization of Anthropology," in *Culture through Time: Anthropological Approaches,* ed. Ohnuki-Tierney, 1, 22 (1990). For a discussion of the "historicity of understanding" and the relationship between history and hermeneutics see Gadamer, *Truth and Method,* at 265, 299, 335–39. On the revival of historical sociology, see Peter Burke, *History and Social Theory* 145 (1992).

22. The description of the new historicism quoted in this paragraph is from Louis Montrose, "New Historicisms," in *Redrawing the Boundaries,* at 392, 410, 394; Gayatri Spivak, "The New Historicism: Political Commitment and the Postmodern Critic," in *The New Historicism,* ed. H. Aram Veeser, 277, 280 (1989); Miller, "Triumph. of Theory," at 283, 286; Miller, "The Disputed Ground: Deconstruction and Literary Studies," in *Deconstruction Is/in America: A New Sense of the Political,* ed. Anselm Haverkamp, 79 (1995). On the emergence of the new historicism see, e.g., the essays in Veeser's *New Historicism;* Jeffrey Cox and Larry Reynolds, "The Historicist Enterprise," in *New Historical Literary Study: Essays on Reproducing Texts, Representing History,* ed. Jeffrey Cox and Larry Reynolds, (1993). I do not imply the new historicism swept literary theory. For an excellent discussion of fashions in literary theory, see generally Murray Krieger, "Literary Invention, Critical Fashion, and the Impulse to Theoretical Change: 'Or Whether Revolution Be the Same,' " in *Studies in Historical Change,* ed. Ralph Cohen, 179 (1992).

Because the discussion of the relationship between theory and politics in the text is brief, several caveats are necessary. I am not saying that the 1987 news of Paul de Man's wartime writings for a Nazi newspaper actually delegitimated deconstruction, though David Lehman, a critic of deconstruction, implied it should have and did, in *Signs of the Times: Deconstruction and the Fall of Paul de Man* 253–61 (1992). But I do agree with Jameson that "it seems unquestionable that the twin Heidegger and de Man 'scandals' have been carefully orchestrated to delegitimate Derridean deconstruction." Jameson, *Postmodernism,* at 257. (On the 1988 exposure of Heidegger's enthusiastic Nazism, see Victor Farias, *Heidegger and Nazism,* ed. Joseph Margolis and Tom Rockmore [1989].) Nor am I attributing any political stance to new historicists, though I would agree with Louis Montrose: "Right-wing critics in the academy, the popular press, and the federal government have yoked new historicism with

Marxism and feminism in an unholy trinity bent on sullying, with its political credo of race, class, and gender, the enduring and universal concerns of the great authors and works." Montrose, "New Historicisms," at 408. And I am not suggesting, as Lentricchia and other Marxists have done, that radical political critique is incompatible with deconstruction in America. See, e.g., Frank Lentricchia, *After the New Criticism* 169–77 (1980). I also am not siding with critics such as Bryan Palmer, Steven Watts, and Frederick Crews, who suggest that all poststructuralism makes radical action outside the university's walls impossible: "Much writing that appears under the designer label of poststructuralism/postmodernism is, quite bluntly, *crap,* a kind of academic wordplaying with no possible link to anything but the pseudo-intellectualized ghettoes of the most self-promotionally avant-garde enclaves of that bastion of protectionism, the University." Bryan Palmer, *Descent into Discourse: The Reification of Language and the Writing of Social History* 199 (1990). (See also Steven Watts, "The Idiocy of American Studies: Poststructuralism, Language, and Politics in the Age of Self-Fulfillment," 43 *American Quarterly* 625, 649–57 [1991]; Frederick Crews, *The Critics Bear It Away* xviii–xx [1992].) Rather, as an outsider to literary theory, I would think that deconstruction and radical political critique could be compatible (see, e.g., Michael Ryan, *Marxism and Deconstruction: A Critical Articulation* [1992]; Gayatri Spivak, *The Post-Colonial Critic: Interviews, Strategies, Dialogues,* ed. Sarah Harasym [1990]). As Lentricchia himself said, they were for Derrida himself as a French intellectual. The debate over whether postmodernism is consistent with radical politics has erupted only recently in legal scholarship. See Joel Handler, "Postmodernism, Protest and the New Social Movements," 26 *Law and Society Review* 697 (1992); Comments on [Handler's] Presidential Address, id. at 773–819.

23. Richard Ohmann, "Teaching Historically," in *Pedagogy Is Politics: Literary Theory and Critical Teaching,* ed. Maria-Regina Kecht, 173, 179 (1992).

24. Robert Gordon, "Historicism in Legal Scholarship," 90 *Yale Law Journal* 1017, 1017 (1981). But see "Summary of Discussion of Historicism in Legal Scholarship," 90 *Yale Law Journal* 1060, 1060 (1981). There some conference participants denied that Gordon's insight frightened most legal scholars. I disagree. I think in part because he advocated historicism, and in part because of his own association with critical legal studies, Gordon did scare legal scholars. As the legal anthropologist Carol Greenhouse wrote, "Law has a mythic dimension in its self-totalization, its quality of being in time (in that it is a human product) but also out of time (where did it or does it begin or end?) and in its promise of systematic yet permutable meaning. The myth is essentially a temporal one. Specifically, the law's implicit claim is to invoke the total system of its own distinctions simultaneously in a way that both individualizes subjects/citizens and orients them toward particular forms of action. That such symbolism has been effective only since the late Middle Ages reveals the continued capacity of modern society to generate myth." Greenhouse, "Just in Time: Temporality and the Cultural Legitimation of Law," 98 *Yale Law Journal* 1631, 1640 (1989).

Historicism probably frightened scholars in other disciplines too. According to Rorty, "The ferocity [in reaction to Kuhn's *Structure of Scientific Revolutions*] was found . . . mainly among professional philosophers. Kuhn's description of how science works was no shock to the scientists whose rationality the philosophers were concerned to protect." Rorty, *Mirror of Nature,* at 333 n.16. Kuhn thought he scared the scientists. "The group of students who come to them [historians of science] from the sciences is very often the most rewarding group they teach. But it also usually the most frustrating at the start. Because science students 'know the right answers,' it is particularly difficult to make them analyze an older science in its own terms." Kuhn, *Scientific Revolutions,* at 167 n.3.

25. See, e.g., Elizabeth Fox-Genovese, "Literary Criticism and the Politics of the New Historicism," in Veeser, *New Historicism,* at 213. Lynn Hunt described historians' dislike of theory in Hunt, "History as Gesture, or, The Scandal of History," in *Consequences of Theory,* ed. Jonathan Arac and Barbara Johnson, 91, 98 (1991).

26. Bernard Bailyn, "The Challenge of Modern Historiography," 87 *American Historical Review* 1, 6–8 (1982). See, e.g., James Davidson, "The New Narrative History: How New, How Narrative?" 12 *Reviews in American History* 322 (1984); Thomas Bender, "Wholes and Parts: The Need for Synthesis in American History," 73 *Journal of American History* 120 (1986); Eric Monkkonen, "The Dangers of Synthesis," 91 *American Historical Review* 1146 (1986), and "A Round Table: Synthesis in American History," 74 *Journal of American History* 107 (1987). Peter Novick adopted a good news–bad news approach toward the condition of history as a discipline in the 1980s: "The bad news was that the American historical profession was fragmented beyond any hope of unification. The good news was that the fragments were doing very well indeed." Novick, *That Noble Dream,* at 592. A recent survey of American historians suggested that they are "[s]tudying little pieces, yet yearning for ways to hold the pieces together." David Thelen, "The Practice of American History," 81 *Journal of American History* 933, 938 (1994).

27. See generally Daniel Rodgers, "Republicanism: The Career of a Concept," 79 *Journal of American History* 11, 25–34 (1992). Rodgers attributes the popularity of republicanism to the problems of social history. I also attribute the popularity of republicanism to the problems of history as a discipline.

28. Richard Rorty, "The Historiography of Philosophy: Four Genres," in *Philosophy in History,* ed. Rorty, J. B. Schneewind, and Quentin Skinner, 49, 49 (1984).

29. Gregory Alexander, "Time and Property in the American Republican Legal Culture," 66 *New York University Law Review* 273, 279 (1991) (Alexander observed at 279 n.17: "In practicing 'presentist' history, I am affirming the Jeffersonian idea . . . that each generation, or in my terms, each culture, is primarily responsible to itself, rather than to the past. To impose our vocabulary and our dilemmas on past discourses is to act upon that responsibility. It is also an act of self-expression and self-creation. In that sense this article itself constitutes a republican act"); Ackerman, *We the People,* at 23, 165.

30. Michael Sandel, "Introduction," in *Liberalism and Its Critics,* ed. Michael Sandel, 1, 5 (1984) ("But in"; "Even as"); Sandel, *Liberalism and the Limits of Justice* 1 (1982). Sandel provided a valuable overview of the liberalism-communitarian debate in *Liberalism and Its Critics,* as did Stephen Miullhall and Adam Swift in *Liberals and Communitarians* (1992). According to Mullhall and Swift, "any attempt to understand the communitarian critique of liberalism as a whole must begin with an assessment of the work of Michael Sandel. . . . [I]t was Sandel's book that first elicited the label 'communitarian' and brought about the retrospective recruitment of other

writers to that flag. Moreover, Sandel's book is explicitly structured as a critique of John Rawls's work." Id. at 40.

31. Sandel, *Limits of Justice,* at 177, 165, 178; Sandel, "Introduction," in *Liberalism and Its Critics,* at 3 ("vision of the good life").

32. Alasdair MacIntyre, *After Virtue: A Study in Moral Theory* 221 (1981) (as MacIntyre put it, "I am someone's son or daughter, someone else's cousin or uncle; I am a citizen of this or that city, a member of this or that guild or profession; I belong to this clan, that tribe, this nation. As such, I inherit from the past of my family, my city, my tribe, my nation, a variety of debts, inheritances, rightful expectations and obligations. These constitute the given of my life, my moral starting point. This is in part what gives my life its own moral philosophy." Id. at 220); Sandel, *Limits of Justice,* at 179, 181. In formulating her own condemnation of "rights talk" and its glorification of the "lone rights-bearer," Mary Ann Glendon drew on Sandel's critique that liberalism had overlooked the situated nature of the self. Glendon, *Rights Talk: The Impoverishment of Political Discourse* 48, 191 n.4 (1991). Most now believe Sandel mischaracterized Rawls's theory of self. See the sources cited in Lawrence Solum, "Situating Political Liberalism," 69 *Chicago-Kent Law Review* 549, 557 (1994).

33. Sandel, "Introduction," in *Liberalism and Its Critics,* at 6–7.

34. The quotations in this paragraph are from Michael Sandel, "Democrats and Community," *New Republic,* February 22, 1988, 20, 22–23, except the definition of a "procedural republic" and discussion of "the modern American welfare state," which are from Sandel, "The Political Theory of the Procedural Republic," in *The Power of Public Ideas,* ed. Robert Reich, 109, 110 (1988). See also Sandel, "The Procedural Republic and the Unencumbered Self," 12 *Political Theory* 81 (1984); Sandel, "After the Nation-State: Reinventing Democracy," 9 *New Perspectives Quarterly* 4 (fall 1992).

35. Thomas Grey, Book Review, 25 *Stanford Law Review* 286, 302-5 (1973). In exploring the impact of the work of Sandel and others on law professors, I found the following especially useful: Stephen Gardbaum, "Law, Politics, and the Claims of Community," 90 *Michigan Law Review* 685 (1992); William Powers, "On the Priority of Justice," 63 *Texas Law Review* 1569 (1985); Jordan Steiker, "Creating a Community of Liberals," 69 *Texas Law Review* 795 (1991); Shiffrin, "Liberalism, Radicalism."

36. Vincent Blasi, "Introduction," in *Law and Liberalism in the 1980s,* ed. Vincent Blasi, ix, xiii (1991) ("invited cynicism"); Thomas Nagel, *The View from Nowhere* 1, 141 (1986) ("[W]e begin from our position inside the world and try to transcend it").

37. Robert Bellah, Richard Madsen, William Sullivan, Ann Swidler, and Stephen Tipton, *Habits of the Heart: Individualism and Commitment in American Life* 144, 284–85 (1986 ed.).

38. Steiker, "Community of Liberals," at 798. At least, few academic lawyers expressed their concern in print. Steven Gey would argue that law professors still do not use the term "community" with any clarity and that for them, the concept remains problematic. See Gey, "The Unfortunate Revival of Civic Republicanism," 141 *University of Pennsylvania Law Review* 801, 814–22 (1993). Stephen Gardbaum rightly pointed to "the complete confusion associated with communitarianism in moral and political philosophy, a confusion that was imported into legal theory as part of the total

package." Gardbaum, "Law, Politics, and the Claims of Community," at 691. Like Gardbaum, I believe that law professors have suffered from that confusion. I think historians have as well. Despite the term's problematic nature, I have therefore freely used the adjective *communitarian* in describing the vision behind academic lawyers' and historians' republican revival. For my purposes, it is significant that this confusion existed, that it has only begun to be unraveled recently, and that historians and some academic lawyers perceived liberalism as being in conflict with neorepublicanism. For a compelling case that legal liberals such as Fiss and Dworkin could advocate community nonaberrationally and that the neorepublican vision may be compatible with liberalism, see, e.g., Gardbaum, "Law, Politics, and the Claims of Community," at 689–95, 732, 749, 752.

39. Joan Williams, "Virtue and Oppression," in *Nomos XXXIV: Virtue,* ed. John Chapman and William Galston, 309, 309 (1992); William Galston, "Introduction," id. at 1, 1; Gordon Wood, "The Virtues and the Interests," *New Republic,* February 11, 1991, 32, 33.

40. Isaac Kramnick, "The 'Great National Discussion': The Discourse of Politics in 1787," 45 *William and Mary Quarterly* 3d ser., 3, 4 (1988) ("forever ridding"); Steven Dworetz, *The Unvarnished Doctrine: Locke, Liberalism, and the American Revolution* 12, 7 (1990) ("most stunning," "Locke et" ["Locke and nothing more"] "omnia praeter" ["all things except Locke"]); Bernard Bailyn, *The Ideological Origins of the American Revolution* (1967); Gordon Wood, *The Creation of the American Republic, 1776–1787* (1969); J. G. A. Pocock, *The Machiavellian Moment: Florentine Political Thought and the Atlantic Republican Tradition* (1975). The shift away from Locke and Hartz in historiography began even before publication of Bailyn's and Wood's books, with the appearance of Caroline Robbins's *The Eighteenth-Century Commonwealthman* (1959). Robert Shalhope assessed the importance of her work in "Toward a Republican Synthesis: The Emergence of an Understanding of Republicanism in American Historiography," 29 *William and Mary Quarterly* 3d ser., 49, 57–59 (1972).

41. Bailyn, *Ideological Origins,* at viii–xi, 161, 26–28, 34–36, 43–46. Joyce Appleby credited Bailyn with replacing "the tired old notion of intellectual influence with the exciting concept of ideology." Appleby, "Republicanism and Ideology," in *Liberalism and Republicanism in the Historical Imagination,* ed. Joyce Appleby, 277, 281 (1992). Bailyn described his approach as "anthropological" in "The Central Themes of the American Revolution: An Interpretation," in *Essays on the American Revolution,* ed. Stephen Kurtz and James Hutson, 3, 23 (1973). Though Bailyn did speak of Geertz in his 1973 essay (id. at 11) he mentioned the anthropologist nowhere in *Ideological Origins.* Nevertheless, most historians have stressed Geertz's emphasis on Bailyn (see, e.g., Appleby, *Liberalism and Republicanism,* at 284, 328–29; but see Colin Gordon, "Crafting a Usable Past: Consensus, Ideology, and Historians of the American Revolution," 46 *William and Mary Quarterly* 3d ser., 671, 679 n.17 [1989], for the suggestion that *Ideological Origins* did not reflect Geertz's influence). Bailyn is frequently credited with launching the republican revival, even though as Appleby observed, "curiously the word *republicanism* does not figure prominently in his text." Appleby, *Liberalism and Republicanism,* at 280.

42. Wood, *Creation of the American Republic,* at 49–55, 29, 418, 606.

43. Bickel, *Least Dangerous Branch,* at 16; Wood, *Creation of the American Republic,*

at 383, 388, 462, 562; John Murrin, "Gordon S. Wood and the Search for Liberal America," 44 *William and Mary Quarterly* 597, 599 (1987) ("Although early critics were slow to grasp the point, *Creation of the American Republic* was an intellectual approach to the Revolution that made social conflict more, not less, relevant to the larger story. The threat of aristocracy, the palpable reality of gentility, and the clash of interests all became central components of Wood's analysis." Id.). Wood, however, was never as negative about Founding Fathers as Beard, and over the years, his compassion and appreciation for them has grown. See, e.g., Wood, "Interests and Disinterestedness," in *Beyond Confederation: Origins of the Constitution and American National Identity,* ed. Richard Beeman, Stephen Botein, and Edward Carter, 69, 109 (1987); Wood, *The Radicalism of the American Revolution* 230, 253–59, 368–69 (1991).

44. Rakove, *Original Meanings,* at 330, 336 (see also Rakove, "Parchment Barriers," at 124–42).

45. Wood, *Creation of the American Republic,* at 542–43, 563.

46. Pocock, *Machiavellian Moment,* at 545, vii–viii, 462, 509 (see also id. at 217–18, 543); Pocock, "Authority and Property: The Question of Liberal Origins," in *Virtue, Commerce, and History: Essays on Political Thought and History, Chiefly in the Eighteenth Century* 51, 66 (1985) ("Age of Reason"); Pocock, "Virtue and Commerce in the Eighteenth Century," 3 *Journal of Interdisciplinary History* 119, 120 (1972) ("culminating generation").

47. Pocock, *Machiavellian Moment,* at 551 ("quarrel"); "Virtue and Commerce," at 120 ("an ideology" and "a tradition"). The extent to which the classics influenced the Founders has remained controversial among historians ever since Wood challenged Bailyn's view that they were " 'window dressing' " and argued that "Americans' compulsive interest in the ancient republics was in fact crucial to their attempt to understand the moral and social basis of politics" Compare *Bailyn's Ideological Origins,* at 24, with Wood, *Creation of the American Republic,* at 50). Paul Rahe has argued that the republicanism of the Founding Fathers bore very little resemblance to that of the ancients. In referring to the "ancients," Rahe focused almost exclusively on Athenians. Rahe, *Republicanism: Ancient and Modern: Classical Republicanism and the American Revolution* (1991); see especially x, 170, 192, 199–200, 250–56, 351, 421–22, 568, 581–86, 601–5, 615–16, 650, 733, 742–47, 777, 1113, n.20. M. N. S. Sellers insisted that "American republican sensibilities derived from Roman models," in Sellers, *American Republicanism: Roman Ideology in the United States Constitution* 20 (1994) (see also id. at 7, 61–63, 99, 105, 214, 218–20, 244). Carl J. Richard tried to steer a middle way through the debate, contending that "the classics exerted a formative influence upon the founders, both directly, and through the mediation of Whig and American perspectives." Richard, *The Founders and the Classics* 7–8 (1994). See also id. at 31–32, 55, 83, 123, 159–60, 183, 196, 232–33. I am not sure a middle way exists, and I side with Bailyn. It may also be that the Founding Fathers' concept of virtue bore little resemblance to that held by English adherents of "Country" ideology. Jack Greene, "The Concept of Virtue in Late Colonial British America," in *Imperatives, Behaviors, and Identities: Essays in Early American Cultural History,* ed. Jack Greene, 214 (1992).

48. Pocock, "Virtue and Commerce," at 128–29, 134.

49. Id. at 122–24. For a provocative discussion of Pocock's conception of "the force of

an existing view" as "epistemological" and the implications of his "partisan" tilting against Locke see Appleby, *Liberalism and Republicanism,* at 132–33.

50. Pocock, "Virtues, Rights, and Manners: A Model for Historians of Political Thought," in *Virtue, Commerce, and History,* at 41–47. Pocock did not equate Court ideology with liberalism. According to him, "The pluralist consensus, now subject to criticism under the none-too-appropriate name of 'liberalism,' was, in its origins as a doctrine, English rather than American, Court rather than Country. There is not, at present, sufficient evidence that it was significantly Lockean. Locke was simply not a central figure in the Court-Country debates, though an ingenious analyst would no doubt have little difficulty in interpreting him so that he would rank on the Court side." Pocock, "Virtue and Commerce," at 128–29.

51. Gordon Wood, "Hellfire Politics," *New York Review of Books,* February 28, 1985, 29, 29 ("If Pocock") (see generally Appleby, *Liberalism and Republicanism,* at 23); Pocock, *Machiavellian Moment,* at 526–27. Later, Pocock objected to Gordon Wood's statement that "it was my strategy 'to eliminate Locke as the patron saint of American culture and replace him with Machiavelli.' Really, I had no such intention; it would be nearer the mark to say that in displacing Locke as 'patron saint' I was suggesting that American politics had no patron saints, or rather no scribes of the covenant, at all, and that this has been the nature of my blasphemy." Pocock, "Between Gog and Magog: The Republican Thesis and the *Ideologica Americana,*" 68 *Journal of the History of Ideas* 325, 342 (1987).

52. All quotations are from Pocock, *Machiavellian Moment,* at 543–44, except "American psyche," from Pocock, "Virtue and Commerce," at 134.

53. Rodgers, "Republicanism," at 19 ("Virtue"); Michael Zuckert, *Natural Rights and the New Republicanism* 160 (1994) ("Participation"). "[T]he Revolution was paradigmatically determined and an essay in Kuhnian 'normal science.' " Pocock, *Machiavellian Moment,* at 508.

54. "[P]rescriptive authority" is from Gardbaum, "Law, Politics, and the Claims of Community," at 690 n.14; Richard Fallon, "What Is Republicanism and Is It Worth Reviving?" 102 *Harvard Law Review* 1695, 1695 (1989) ("day seems"). The information in this paragraph was taken from a September 1995 Westlaw search. The case was *Strahler* v. *St. Luke's Hospital,* 706 S.W. 2d 7, 16 n.2 (dissent of Judge Warren Welliver) (1986). For Welliver's use of Rawls see his dissent in *Jensen* v. *ARA Servs., Inc.,* 736 S.W. 2d 374, 381–82 (1987), which is discussed in Leslie Francis, "Law and Philosophy: From Skepticism to Value Theory," 27 *Loyola of Los Angeles Law Review* 65, 83 (1993). Certainly not all academic lawyers adored Pocock. See, e.g., John Reid, "The Jurisprudence of Liberty: The Ancient Constitution in the Legal Historiography of the Seventeenth and Eighteenth Centuries," in *The Roots of Liberty: Magna Carta, Ancient Constitution, and the Anglo-American Tradition of Rule of Law,* ed. Ellis Sandoz, 147 (1992).

55. Joyce Appleby pointed out that their focus made republicanism more appealing to law professors than it was to historians in her comment on Michelman's and Sunstein's work, which I discuss later. "[A] deliberative" is from Michael Perry, *Morality, Politics, and Law* 151 (1988); see also Perry, *Love and Power: The Role of Religion and Morality in American Politics* 138 (1991). More recently, Perry has made a move toward enlisting history on his side by developing a normative argument for originalism. See Perry, *The Constitution in the Courts: Law or Politics* 9–10, 50, 201–4

(1994). At times earlier in his career, Perry also seemed to be headed toward advocacy of originalism for normative reasons. See Lawrence Solum, "Originalism as Transformative Politics," 63 *Tulane Law Review* 1599, 1629 (1989). For constitutional law casebooks highlighting the republican synthesis see Geoffrey Stone, Cass Sunstein, Louis Seidman, and Mark Tushnet, *Constitutional Law* (1986); Daniel Farber and Suzanna Sherry, *A History of the American Constitution* (1989). "[T]he constitution provides" and "most self-interested" are from Gey, "Unfortunate Revival," at 806, 821. See also id. at 865.

56. W. Burlette Carter, "Robert Gordon Gives Twenty Fifth Holmes Lecture: Traces the Tradition of American Lawyers to Present," *Harvard Law Record,* March 1, 1985, 4. Suzanna Sherry, "Without Virtue There Can Be No Liberty," 78 *Minnesota Law Review* 61, 69, 73, 77 (1993) ("Responsibility"). Of course historians produce jeremiads too; see, e.g., Michael Zuckerman, "Charles Beard and the Constitution: The Uses of Enchantment," 56 *George Washington Law Review* 81, 86–94 (1987). For some especially negative reactions to the republican revival see, e.g., Fallon, "What Is Republicanism" (concluding that it was not worth reviving); Gey, "Unfortunate Revival"; Michael Fitts, "The Vices of Virtue: A Political Party Perspective on Civic Virtue Reforms of the Legal Process," 136 *University of Pennsylvania Law Review* 1567 (1989) (arguing that an emphasis on civic virtue leads to ideological politics, which in turn heightens the possibility of deadlock and political conservatism, and lessens the possibility of popular understanding and helping the poor); Martin Redish and Gary Lippman, "Freedom of Expression and the Civic Republican Revival in Constitutional Theory: The Ominous Implications," 89 *California Law Review* 267, 295 (1991) ("All branches of civic republican theory threaten the key principles underlying free speech theory, because of their near-universal dismissal of the individual's value—other than as a political spoke in the communitarian wheel"); Robert Post, *Constitutional Domains: Democracy, Community, Management* 289, 268 (1995) ("[I]n the absence of a convincing alternative normative account of democracy . . . [t]he collectivist theory of freedom of speech [which "subordinates individual rights of expression to collective processes of public deliberation"] clearly has its uses, but the case has not yet been made for its displacement of traditional First Amendment jurisprudence").

57. Cass Sunstein, "Interest Groups in American Public Law," 38 *Stanford Law Review* 29 (1985).

58. "[R]epublican thought" is from Cass Sunstein, "Beyond the Republican Revival," 97 *Yale Law Journal* 1539, 1540 (1988); "emphasized the capacity" from Transcript, "Republicanism in Legal Culture" (Association of American Law Schools, January 1987) (see also, e.g., Sunstein, "Interest Groups," at 39–43, 81). With the passage of time, Sunstein railed against the "court-centeredness" of American constitutional theory ever more boldly. See, e.g., Sunstein, *Partial Constitution,* at 9, 139. As Bruce Ackerman has reminded us, *The Federalist* has "not yet lost its hold on the legal mind." Ackerman, "The Storrs Lectures: Discovering the Constitution," 93 *Yale Law Journal* 1013, 1016 (1984). This is an understatement. For an especially vigorous defense of the sincerity of *The Federalist* see Ahkil Amar, "Of Sovereignty and Federalism," 96 *Yale Law Journal* 1425, 1498 (1987). Cf., e.g., Bernard Bailyn, *Faces of Revolution: Personalities and Themes in the Struggle for American Independence* 271 n.12 (1990) (describing the "enormous importance accorded the *Federalist* pa-

pers" as "largely a twentieth century phenomenon," and noting that the "exquisite refinement of analysis" in recent studies of *The Federalist* "would have amazed the harried authors, who wrote polemically, to help win a major battle"). Little attention was paid to *Federalist 10* in the 125 years between 1787 and Charles Beard's "discovery" of it in *An Economic Interpretation of the United States.* Douglas Adair, "The Tenth Federalist Revisited," 8 *William and Mary Quarterly* 3d ser., 48 (1951). Paul Bourke traced the pluralist reading of *Federalist 10* back to the World War I writings of Harold Laski, in "The Pluralist Reading of James Madison's Tenth Federalist," 9 *Perspectives in American History* 271 (1975).

59. Frank Michelman, "The Supreme Court 1985 Term—Foreword: Traces of Self-Government," 100 *Harvard Law Review* 4, 17 n.69, 65–66, 55 (1986); "problematic relationship" is from Michelman, "Law's Republic," 97 *Yale Law Journal* 1493, 1500–1501 (1988). Michelman's approach in "Traces of Self-Government" was consistent with his earlier work in that in his discussion of local government law and takings jurisprudence, for example, he had emphasized conflict between two competing visions of government. Indeed it might be said that Michelman's approach to law, generally, is a binary one, in which two visions of government, which correspond roughly to the public choice and public interest models, compete with each other through two judicial models. See, e.g., Michelman, "Political Markets and Community Self-Determination: Competing Judicial Models of Local Government Legitimacy"; Michelman, "Possession v. Distribution in the Constitutional Idea of Property," 72 *Iowa Law Review* 1319 (1987); Michelman, "Conceptions of Democracy in American Constitutional Argument: The Case of Pornography Regulation," 56 *Tennessee Law Review* 291 (1989); Michelman, "Conceptions of Democracy in American Constitutional Argument: Voting Rights," 41 *Florida Law Review* 443 (1989).

60. Michelman, "Traces of Self-Government," at 17, 50–55, 19–20, 58–66; Michelman, "Law's Republic," at 1496–97, 1522 ("authoritarianism," "looking backward jurisprudence," and "adjudicative actions").

61. Michelman, "Traces of Self-Government," at 23, 25, 74, 55.

62. Id. at 56, 74. According to Michelman, "Judges perhaps enjoy a situational advantage over the people at large in listening for voices from the margins." Michelman, "Law's Republic," at 1537.

63. Michelman, "Traces of Self-Government," at 74.

64. Id. at 16 (see also Sunstein, "Interest Groups," at 86); Chemerinsky, "Foreword: Vanishing Constitution," at 99.

65. Michelman, "Traces of Self-Government," at 75.

66. Michelman, "Traces of Self-Government," at 24 (quoting Richard Bernstein, *Beyond Objectivism and Relativism: Science, Hermeneutics, and Praxis* 16–20 [1983]; see also Michelman, "Traces of Self-Government," at 26–31 for discussion of the parallels between republicanism and Kantianism); and both Michelman's and Sunstein's remarks in Transcript, "Republicanism in Legal Culture." Stephen Feldman traced Michelman's increasing reliance on dialogue and apparent decreasing emphasis on the objective common good in "The Persistence of Power and the Struggle for Dialogical Standards in Postmodern Constitutional Jurisprudence: Michelman, Habermas, and Civic Republicanism," 81 *Georgetown Law Journal* 2243, 2246–58 (1993). Feldman provided an excellent argument for synthesizing republicanism and the in-

terpretive turn into a theory of "republican interpretivism," which would lack the drawbacks of both republicanism and the interpretive turn, in "Republican Revival," at 714–24, especially 716.

67. Michelman, "Conceptions of Democracy: Voting Rights," at 449, 445, 445 n.6, 449, 447 n.10, 457 n.57 (quoting Morton Horwitz). Many of us who have been influenced by legal scholarship back away from our text in our footnotes.

68. "[H]aunted" is from Linda Hirshman, "The Virtue of Liberality in American Communal Life," 88 *Michigan Law Review* 983, 985 (1990); Paul Kahn, *Legitimacy and History: Self-Government in American Constitutional Theory* 2, 171 (1992); and Michelman and Sunstein in Transcript, "Republicanism in Legal Culture."

69. Sunstein, "Beyond the Republican Revival," at 1548–58, 1541, 1566–69; Sunstein, "Republicanisms, Rights: A Comment on Pangle," 66 *Chicago-Kent Law Review* 177, 179 (1990) ("republicanism of rights"). Sunstein discusses a "deliberative democracy," which includes "liberal republicanism" in *Partial Constitution,* at 133, 134–45. See James Fleming, "Constructing the Substantive Constitution," 82 *Texas Law Review* 211, 242 n.143 (1993) (noting that "[i]n effect Sunstein and Ackerman are in competition to be the new Madison"; I would add Michelman to this group). Gey located the modern civic republicans on the left and stressed their parallels to nineteenth-century utopian socialists in "Unfortunate Revival," at 817 n.48, 891. His implicit definition of a leftist as one who argues "in favor of strong wealth distribution and anti-discrimination legislation" also encompasses many of the people I would characterize as legal liberals. Id. at 851. For an excellent discussion of the relationship between neorepublicanism and political liberalism see J. David Hoeveler, Jr., "Original Intent and the Politics of Republicanism," 75 *Marquette Law Review* 863, 875–76 (1992). But see Kahn, *Supreme Court and Constitutional Theory,* at 201–2 (insisting that to dismiss Michelman and other contemporary scholars "as merely seeking to extend the New Deal's welfare state without the qualms about judicial activity is incorrect.") For discussion of the continuity between Sunstein's "liberal republicanism" and his "deliberative democracy" see James Kloppenberg, "Deliberative Democracy and Judicial Supremacy," in *Law and History* (forthcoming); Sunstein, *Partial Constitution,* at 134. For the argument that, when pressed, many "soft" antiliberals cave to liberalism see Steven Holmes, *The Anatomy of Antiliberalism* 88, 156, 181, 264 (1993).

70. "[T]olerance and deliberation" are from Sherry, "Responsible Republicanism," at 136 (Sherry herself would add an emphasis on "individual responsibility," id. at 133 n.5, 145–55); the remaining quotations are from Michelman, "Law's Republic," at 1496, 1532. See also Sunstein, "Beyond the Republican Revival," at 1539–40, 1580–81; *Bowers* v. *Hardwick,* 478 U.S. 186 (1986). For a discussion of the democratization of privacy, see Steven Schnably, "Beyond Griswold: Foucauldian and Republican Approaches to Privacy," 23 *Connecticut Law Review* 861, 903 (1991).

Libertarians joined political liberals and the left in questioning the regulation of sexual morality, while arguing that the Constitution provided more protection for property rights than the left and liberals acknowledged. See, e.g., Stephen Macedo, *The New Right v. The Constitution* 59–60, 69, 79 (1987); Posner, *Overcoming Law,* at 561–62; Richard Epstein, "Modern Republicanism: The Flight from Substance," 97 *Yale Law Journal* 1633, 1645–46 (1988); Epstein, *Simple Rules,* at 110, 141, 169,

316–17. Politically conservative originalists have shown no patience for libertarian arguments on behalf of the libertine. According to one, "Mr. Macedo's theory, if taken seriously, would render the Supreme Court not so much a continuing constitutional convention but a wildly esoteric Ivy League seminar in moral philosophy." "Postscript: A Debate on Judicial Activism," in *The New Right,* at 109 (remarks of Gary McDowell).

71. Fisher, "Modern American Legal Theory," at 311–12. See also Mark Seidenfeld, "A Civic Republican Justification for the Bureaucratic State," 105 *Harvard Law Review* 1512 (1992); (but see Note, "Civic Republican Administrative Theory: Bureaucrats as Deliberative Democrats," 107 *Harvard Law Review* 1401, 1409–10, 1417–18 [1994]); Cass Sunstein, *Democracy and the Problem of Free Speech* 163, xvii (1993). Jennifer Nedelsky's pathbreaking *Private Property and the Limits of American Constitutionalism: The Madison Framework and Its Legacy* (1990) was one of the most impressive demonstrations of the obvious and specific implications a shift from an interpretation stressing the triumph of liberalism in 1787 to one pointing to the predominance of republicanism would have for contemporary constitutional law. Nedelsky, however, was skeptical of the republican revival, arguing, "Most of what is most important about the 1787 Constitution seems to me to be liberal rather than republican." Id. at 175.

72. White, "Reflections," at 21.

73. "Critique is all there is" is the famous sentence with which Mark Tushnet ended *Red, White, and Blue,* at 318 (where Tushnet treated republicanism more kindly than liberalism, although he concluded that "[n]either the liberal tradition nor the republican one can accommodate the aspects of experience that the other takes as central"). See Unger, "Critical Legal Studies Movement," at 668–70, 602; Unger, *Knowledge and Politics,* at 261 ("community" as "political equivalent of love"). As Unger explained in a 1984 postscript to his 1975 book *Knowledge and Politics,* "superliberalism" represented an abandonment of the "antiliberalism" he originally advocated in *Knowledge and Politics.* Id. at 340; see also Unger, *False Necessity: Anti-Necessitarian Social Theory in the Service of Radical Democracy* (1987).

74. Morton Horwitz, "History and Theory," 96 *Yale Law Journal* 1825, 1834 (1987); see also Horwitz, "Republicanism and Liberalism in American Constitutional Thought," 29 *William and Mary Law Review* 57 (1987). Sunstein distinguished his views from Horwitz's in his review of Horwitz's recent book. See Sunstein, "Where Politics Ends," *New Republic,* August 3, 1992, 38.

75. Owen Fiss, "The Law Regained," 75 *Cornell Law Review* 245, 246–47 (1989). Fiss also now believed that as critical legal studies was becoming more constructive, so law and economics was in decline.

76. The critic is James Pope, in "Republican Moments: The Role of Direct Popular Power in the American Constitutional Order," 139 *University of Pennsylyania Law Review* 287, 302 (quoting Michelman, "Foreword: On Protecting the Poor," at 9–16). On the connection between republicanism and Rawls, see Lawrence Sager, "The Incorrigible Constitution," 65 *New York University Law Review* 893, 923 (1990). See also Christopher Edley, "The Governance Crisis, Legal Theory, and Political Ideology," 1991 *Duke Law Journal* 561, 594 (1991) (applying a similar critique to Sunstein). For Sunstein's response, see Sunstein, "Administrative Substance," id. at 607, 612 n.18. In Sunstein's case, it might also be said he was developing republicanism

for John Hart Ely. Fleming, "Constructing the Substantive Constitution," at 280. Ely had little use for the republican revival (see Ely, "Another Such Victory: Constitutional Theory and Practice in a World Where Courts Are No Different from Legislatures," 77 *Virginia Law Review* 833, 840 n.4). On Michelman's and Sunstein's continued search for objective foundations of justice and common good, see Feldman, "The Persistence of Power," at 2258 (concluding that Michelman's "neo-transcendental arguments ultimately reduce to sophisticated attempts to resurrect modernist objectivism. Michelman thus inadvertently reintroduces problems that he had attempted to avoid by developing civic republicanism into a strong form of dialogic politics"). See also Stephen Feldman, "Exposing Sunstein's Naked Preferences," 1989 *Duke Law Journal* 1335, 1343 (1990). Deconstructing Sunstein's enthusiasm for judicial enforcement of public values, or common goods, as opposed to private values, or "naked preferences," Feldman demonstrated that preferences are never "naked." Like public values, or the common good, they are socially, politically and judicially constructed. One generation's public values may be another's naked preferences. "Consequently, in constitutional adjudication, the question whether a legislative action is based on either a naked preference or a public value does not have a neutral, objective, and preexisting answer. Instead, the Court, as well as the rest of the culture and community, constantly is defining and redefining the meanings of naked and public preferences. And because naked preferences are not preexisting—exogenous to social influences and autonomously chosen by individuals—Sunstein's theory of judicial review, lacking the support of its foundation, shudders, groans, and ultimately collapses." Gey documented Michelman's and Sunstein's denials "that their theory posits the existence of a predefined and objective set of ethical principles, which all proper civic republican communities will endorse," in "Unfortunate Revival," at 829 n.87.

CHAPTER 6. LAWYERS V. HISTORIANS

1. Stanley Katz, quoted in David Margolick, "Justice Holmes's 1935 Bequest Remains Unfulfilled," in the *New York Times,* May 3, 1983, D26 ("Lawyers are arrogant"); Tushnet, "Constitutional Scholarship: What Next" at 31; Philip Frickey, "Constitutional Scholarship: What Next?" 5 *Constitutional Commentary* 67, 68 (1988) ("any lawyer can read").
2. The characterization of Summers is from Julius Getman, "The Internal Scholarly Jury," 39 *Journal of Legal Education* 337, 339 n.2 (1989). See Clyde Summers, "The Supreme Court and Industrial Democracy," in *German and American Constitutional Thought: Contexts, Interaction, and Historical Realities,* ed. Hermann Wellenreuther, 415, 443 (1990).
3. Laura Kalman, "The American Labor Movement and the Rule of Law," in Wellenreuther, *German and American Constitutional Thought,* at 484, 486–87. In making this argument, I was drawing on the work of David M. Rabban; see Rabban, "Has the NLRA Hurt Labor?" 54 *University of Chicago Law Review* 426 (1987).
4. "Discussion," in Wellenreuther, *German and American Constitutional Thought,* at 490, 498–99.
5. See Bernstein, "Charting the Constitution," at 1578 (quoting Nelson); "Law and Society in American History: Essays in Honor of J. Willard Hurst," 10 *Law and*

Society Review 5, 187 (1975). Martin Flaherty has made an intriguing argument that abiding by historical standards is "hard and time-consuming work, often too hard and time-consuming to meet the imperatives of legal scholarship," in "History 'Lite,' " at 554. See also 526–27 n.16. I disagree.

6. David M. Rabban, "The Emergence of Modern First Amendment Doctrine," 50 *University of Chicago Law Review* 1205, 1208–11, 1283–1317 (1983); Rabban, "The First Amendment in Its Forgotten Years," 90 *Yale Law Journal* 514, 586–91 (1981). *Schenck* v. *United States,* 249 U.S. 47, 52 (1919); Zechariah Chafee, Jr., "Freedom of Speech in War Time," 32 *Harvard Law Review* 932 (1919).

7. Rabban, "Emergence," at 1211, 1311–17; *Abrams* v. *United States,* 250 U.S. 616, 630 (1919). "In the *Republic,* Hesiod's myth of the gold, silver, bronze, and iron races is described as a 'noble lie' designed to make citizens believe that the different occupational classes they occupy are the work of 'the earth, which is their mother' rather than of their rearing and education, which they must believe 'were like dreams.' The purpose of this is to make them defend their city 'as though the land they are in was a mother.' " Luban, *Legal Modernism,* at 327.

8. Rabban, "First Amendment Forgotten Years," at 590–91.

9. Letter from William E. Nelson to Robert Gordon, reprinted in "An Exchange on Critical Legal Studies between Robert W. Gordon and William E. Nelson," 6 *Law and History Review* 139, 161 (1988); see also Nelson, "1981–1984," in *The Literature of American Legal History,* ed. William E. Nelson and John Reid, 261, 270–74 (1985). The quotation about omelettes is taken from Burke, *History and Social Theory,* at 147 (quoting Ronald Dore). A more positive way of putting it might be to say that legal omelettes may demand greater attention to political theory than historical ones. See David A. J. Richards, *Conscience and the Constitution: History, Theory and Law of the Reconstruction Amendments* 9, 16, 145–47, 252–53 (1994).

10. Wood, "Rhetoric and Reality," at 9, 19 ("movement of class" and "cooked up pieces"); Hartz, *Liberal Tradition,* at 252, 10; Wood, "The Significance of the Early Republic," 8 *Journal of the Early Republic* 1, 8 (1988) ("revolutionary Americans"); Bailyn, "Central Themes of the American Revolution," at 11 ("Both views are wrong") (see also Bailyn, "Political Experience and Enlightenment Ideas in Eighteenth-Century America," 67 *American Historical Review* 339 [1962]). Historians challenged Bailyn's assessment of the significance of his work. On the one hand, Bailyn was accused of not going far enough in acknowledging that language created meaning. With his famous statement that "[m]en cannot do what they have no means of saying they have done; and what they do must in part be what they can and say and conceive that it is," Pocock suggested that Bailyn had stopped short in *The Ideological Origins of the American Revolution.* According to Pocock, "Bailyn flung a most refreshing challenge at that historians' orthodoxy which insists that ideologies and concepts are purely epiphenomenal to other social phenomena—that they are always effect and never cause. But, looked at more narrowly, the argument of the Bailyn school appears far less causal than structural. A reevaluation of the historiography of political thought has been going on for a long time, and it seems less useful to consider conceptual systems as theories (which here includes 'ideologies') and to mediate them back to 'practice' than to treat them as elaborations, explorations, and unpackings of the conceptual languages used within society. If language is not epiphenomenal but part of the structure of both personality and world, it is

legitimate once more to study the languages men have used and to ask how far they could have done other, or been other, than their languages indicate." Pocock thought Bailyn treated "'language' as a dependent variable." Pocock, "Virtue and Commerce," at 122. On the other hand, Bailyn and Wood were charged with going too far with language, with ignoring social and economic explanations for the American Revolution, and with confusing ideas with action, cause with effect, motives with tactics, attitude with behavior. See, e.g., Jesse Lemisch, "Bailyn Besieged in His Bunker," 4 *Radical History Review* 72 (1977); Gordon, "Usable Past," at 679–81; Jackson Turner Main, Book Review, 26 *William and Mary Quarterly* 3d ser., 604, 606 (1969) (leveling charge at Wood). Gordon Wood denied the charge in "Rhetoric and Reality," at 23, as did Bailyn himself in "Central Themes of the American Revolution," at 14–15. Jack Rakove has suggested that Bailyn, in denying the charge could be fairly applied to his own work in "Central Themes," leveled it at Wood's writing. Rakove himself believed that "Wood's emphases have inadvertently spurred an overly intellectual approach to the study of American politics after 1776." Rakove, "Gordon S. Wood, the 'Republican Synthesis,' and the Path Not Taken," 44 *William and Mary Quarterly* 3d ser., 617, 618, 621–22 (1987). Meanwhile Wood denied the charge could be applied to his own work and discussed the impact of "historiographical polemics . . . [on] Bailyn's unwillingness to entertain social explanations of the Revolution." Gordon Wood, "Ideology and the Origins of Liberal America," 44 *William and Mary Quarterly* 3d ser., 628, 629–30 (1987); Wood, "The Creative Imagination of Bernard Bailyn," in *The Transformation of Early American History: Society, Authority, and Ideology,* ed. James Henretta, Michael Kammen, and Stanley Katz, 16, 28–39 (1991). In the case of Wood's *Creation of the American Republic,* I think the text clearly indicates the relevance of social conflict to the Revolution.

11. Rodgers, "Republicanism," at 21–22; McDonald, *Novus Ordo Seclorum,* at viii; Appleby, "A Different Kind of Independence: The Postwar Structuring of the Historical Study of Early America," 50 *William and Mary Quarterly* 3d ser., 54, 245, 261 (1993). Appleby stressed the dangers of the ideological approach in *Liberalism and Republicanism in the Historical Imagination,* warning that it remained a "borrowing" from anthropologists, who tended to focus on how ideology melded together "small, cohesive, and frequently nonliterate societies. . . . By insisting upon the hegemony of a particular political tradition on theoretical grounds, the republican revisionists have resisted seeing that in pluralistic, uncensored, literate societies, the ideological predispositions of human beings have an opposite effect. Instead of insuring social solidarity, competing ideologies thwart it and embarrass the efforts of government to secure order." Id. at 286–87. See also id. at 134–35, 332.

12. Rodgers, "Republicanism," at 16; J. H. Hexter, "Republic, Virtue, Liberty, and the Political Universe of J. G. A. Pocock," in *On Historians: Reappraisals of Some of the Makers of Modern History* 255, 261, 256 (1978). Appleby made the point that historians paid less attention to the normative vision and vocabulary of republicanism than did law professors in her comment on Michelman's and Sunstein's work at the AALS. Transcript, "Republicanism in Legal Culture."

13. Lance Banning, *The Jeffersonion Persuasion: Evolution of a Party Ideology* 13 (1978) (see also Banning, "Jeffersonian Ideology Revisited: Liberal and Classical Ideas in the New American Republic," 31 *William and Mary Quarterly* 3d ser., 3 [1974]); Thomas Pangle, *The Spirit of Modern Republicanism* 28–29 (1988); Thomas Pangle, "The

Classical Challenge to the American Constitution," 66 *Chicago-Kent Law Review* 145, 175 (1990); Appleby, *Liberalism and Republicanism,* at 23 ("magnet"); Appleby, "Different Kind of Independence," at 264 ("like so many").

14. Adams is quoted, for example, in Linda Kerber, "Making Republicanism Useful," 97 *Yale Law Journal* 1663, 1663 (1988). According to Wood, however, when Adams made that observation, "his memory was playing him badly. These repeated statements of his later years that a republic 'may signify any thing, every thing, or nothing' represented the bewilderment of a man whom ideas had passed by. Back in 1776 republicanism was not such a confused conception in the minds of Americans." Wood, *Creation of the American Republic,* at 48. Like Kerber, Appleby would disagree. Appleby, *Liberalism and Republicanism,* at 321. For an overview of the historical scholarship on republicanism see the excellent essay by Rodgers, "Republicanism."

15. Wood, "Ideology and Origins," at 634; Pocock, "Republicanism and the *Ideologia Americana,*" at 344. Wood focused on the dangers of paradigms in "The Virtues and the Interests," at 34, suggesting, "Perhaps this is in part because the leading contestants were trained as political theorists and not as historians." Yet he also faulted historians for this mistake (id.), and he himself committed it in "Significance of the Early Republic," at 11. According to Richard Sinopoli, "Wood has altogether abandoned his earlier view in stating that 'for early Americans there never was a stark dictionary of traditions, whether liberal or republican.' " Sinopoli, *The Foundations of American Citizenship: Liberalism, the Constitution and Civic Virtue* 12–13 (1992), quoting Wood, "Hellfire Politics," at 30. But "Significance of the Early Republic" appeared after "Hellfire Politics," and Sinopoli's hope of demolishing the republican paradigm surely affected the way he read Wood. Wood has continued to emphasize the importance of republicanism to early Americans and recently suggested it may have remained significant through the War of 1812. Wood, *Radicalism,* at 96, 109, 169, 189–90, 229, 327.

16. See, e.g., the essays collected in Appleby, *Liberalism and Republicanism;* Conversation with Joyce Appleby, May 1992. Gordon made the comment about "the legal avant garde" in the AALS session "Republicanism in Legal Culture."

17. Conversation with David Rabban, March 1992; Transcript, "Republicanism in Legal Culture."

18. Transcript, "Republicanism in Legal Culture"; "ransacked" is from Donald Lutz, *A Preface to American Political Theory* 140 (1992).

19. Transcript, "Republicanism in Legal Culture"; Sunstein, "Beyond the Republican Revival," at 1564. Cf. Sunstein's remarks about the limits of history's usefulness to constitutional law in *Partial Constitution,* at 121, and his more recent observation that though there was no commitment to a unitary executive at the Founding, changed circumstances demanded one in order to make sense of the Founders' design. Lawrence Lessig and Cass Sunstein, "The President and the Administration," 94 *Columbia Law Review* 1, 102–3 (1994). Sunstein did not abandon "originalism" in this article, though he and his coauthor said the term seemed "decreasingly helpful." Id. at 3 n.3. Sunstein may now be moving toward the idea of fidelity through translation. See, e.g., id. at 93: "[C]onstitional words are [not] simply bottles into which any generation simply pours its own values. The interpreter's role is to take account of changing circumstances insofar as these bear on the question how best the framers'

commitments are to be implemented. As we understand it, the interpreter is bound by the duty of fidelity; the Constitution should not be made to take the values that are not fairly traceable to founding commitments." See also Lessig, "Fidelity in Translation," 71 *Texas Law Review* 1165 (1993).

20. Wood, *Creation of the American Republic,* at viii (Wood continued to make this point in the 1980s); Mark Tushnet, "The Concept of Tradition in Constitutional Historiography," 29 *Wiliam and Mary Law Review* 93, 96 (1987); Kerber, "Making Republicanism Useful," at 1667–69 (emphasis in the original). Hendrik Hartog also pointed to the ahistorical nature of law professors' project, in Hartog, "Imposing Constitutional Traditions," 29 *William and Mary Law Review* 81–82 (1987).

21. H. Jefferson Powell, "Reviving Republicanism," 97 *Yale Law Journal* 1703, 1706, 1711 (1988) (but see Flaherty, "History 'Lite,' " at 576: "Contrary to H. Jefferson Powell, the difficulty is not that Sunstein advances a 'hybrid' liberal/republican Founding that cannot 'serve as a corrective to the concepts that it already embodied,' such as interest group pluralism, which Sunstein would like to correct. Rather, the problem is that Sunstein *speaks* of a historical 'hybrid' but *talks* only about its deliberative democratic aspects when he considers governmental institutions and the ideas underlying them"); Kerber, "Making Republicanism Useful," at 1671.

22. Paul Brest, "Further beyond the Republican Revival: Toward Radical Republicanism," 97 *Yale Law Journal* 1623, 1627 n.29, 1628 (1988). See also, e.g., Kathryn Abrams, "Law's Republicanism," 97 *Yale Law Journal* 1591, 1603 (1988); Powell, *Moral Tradition,* at 209–10; West, *Progressive Constitutionalism,* at 283, 352 n.124 (for Paul Brest's own declaration of interest in the republican revival see "Further Beyond" and Brest, "The Thirty-First Cleveland-Marshall Fund Lecture, Constitutional Citizenship," 34 *Cleveland State Law Review* 175 [1986]); Kahn, *Legitimacy and History,* at 136, 172, 220.

23. Hartog, "Imposing Constitutional Traditions," at 78. It does seem, however, that "the signal importance of liberal notions of rights and liberty in the 19th century women's rights movement" should not blind us to the notion of "a plurality of conceptions of rights . . . including affirmative republican and communitarian conceptions which figured prominently in African-American, agrarian, and labor movement history." William Forbath, "Why Is This Rights Talk Different from All Other Rights Talk? Demoting the Court and Reimagining the Constitution," 46 *Stanford Law Review* 1717, 1793 n.91 (1994).

24. "[P]ossessed," "manly," and "Christian Sparta" are from Wood, *Creation of the American Republic,* at 59, 53, 118; Gregory Alexander, " 'Fragmented Survival': Republicanism as Rhetoric," *CLS: Newsletter of the Conference on Critical Legal Studies* 76, 80 (November 1989); Kerber, "Making Republicanism Useful," at 1672; Kathleen Sullivan, "Rainbow Republicanism," 97 *Yale Law Journal* 1713, 1722 (1988) ("valiant but"). See Jan Lewis, "The Republican Wife: Virtue and Seduction in the Early Republic," 44 *William and Mary Quarterly* 3d ser., 689, 710–14 (1987) for an exploration of the "self-abasing virtue" and deference demanded of the republican wife; "Skepticism" from Derrick Bell and Preeta Bansal, "The Republican Revival and Racial Politics," 97 *Yale Law Journal* 1609, 1609 (1987); "egalitarianism" and "authoritativeness" from Kahn, *Legitimacy and History,* at 172. See also Richard Delgado, "Rodrigo's Fifth Chronicle: Civitas, Civil Wrongs, and the Politics of Denial," 45 *Stanford Law Review* 1581, 1594–96, 1604 (1993).

25. Mari Matsuda, "Looking to the Bottom: Critical Legal Studies and Reparations," 22 *Harvard Civil Rights–Civil Liberties Law Review* 323, 394 (1988) ("rights rhetoric"); Richard Delgado, "When a Story Is Just a Story: Does Voice Really Matter?" 76 *Virginia Law Review* 95, 95 n.1 (1990); Kimberle Crenshaw, "Race, Reform and Retrenchment: Transformation and Legitimation in Antidiscrimination Law," 101 *Harvard Law Review* 1331, 1370 (1988); Patricia Williams, "Minority Critique of CLS: Alchemical Notes: Reconstructing Ideals from Deconstructed Rights," 22 *Harvard Civil Rights–Civil Liberties Law Review* 401, 431 (1987); Gates, *Loose Canons,* at 187; Freeman, "Quest for Equality of Opportunity," at 313 ("great power" and "taking on"); Adem Addis, "Individualism, Communitarianism, and the Rights of Ethnic Minorities," 67 *Notre Dame Law Review* 615, 621 (1991) ("critical pluralism" and "difference and dialogue"). See generally Richard Delgado and Jean Stefanic, "Critical Race Theory: An Annotated Bibliography," 79 *Virginia Law Review* 461 (1993); Richard Delgado, ed., *Critical Race Theory: The Cutting Edge* (1995).

When I suggest critical race theory caused critical legal scholars to tone down their hostility to legal liberalism, I have in mind Alan Freeman's essay responding to critical race theory. As he vacillated between emphasizing the importance of rights and critiquing them there, Freeman included a footnote: "At this point, as I go back and forth in my own thoughts and feelings, I am reminded of a song of the sixties, 'Both Sides Now,' written and performed by the Canadian poet-folksinger, Joni Mitchell. The song is about the contradictions of experience, focusing on clouds, love, and life, respectively. Despite what she 'knows,' her decision in each case is to choose existential commitment over resignation. I think a similar verse could be written about 'rights.' " Freeman, "Racism, Rights," at 331 n.93. Once critical legal scholars began writing in that more ambivalent way about rights and other issues, critical legal studies may have lost some of the intellectual bite that some found attractive in critical legal scholars' earlier, more confident declarations and its "apocalyptic, Blakean view of liberal legalism." William Forbath, "Taking Lefts Seriously," 92 *Yale Law Journal* 1041, 1045 (1983).

The most glaring possible exception I have found to my generalization that critical race theorists used history sensitively is Mari Matsuda's claim that W. E. B. Du Bois "wrote of [Booker T.] Washington with respect and admiration" in "Looking to the Bottom," at 352. (Cf. W. E. B. Du Bois, "Of Mr. Booker T. Washington and Others," in *The Souls of Black Folk,* ed. Nathan Hare and Alvin Poussant, 79 (1969); Kennedy, "Racial Critiques of Legal Academia," at 1785.) Here Matsuda downplayed past intraracial conflict to make a vital point about the importance of race as an analytical category, though her interpretation did describe the early relationship between Du Bois and Washington. Louis Harlan, *Booker T. Washington: The Wizard of Tuskegee, 1901–1915* 50–51, 362–63 (1983). Du Bois's obituary for Washington was mixed. He wrote, "[I]n stern justice, we must lay on the soul of this man, a heavy responsibility for the consummation of Negro disenfranchisement, the decline of the Negro College and public school and the firmer establishment of color caste in this country." But he also described Washington as "the greatest Negro leader since Frederick Douglass, and the most distinguished man, white or black, who has come out of the Civil War." Du Bois, "Booker T. Washington," reprinted in *Writings in Periodicals Edited by W. E. B. Du Bois, Selections from the Crisis,* ed. Herbert Aptheker, 1: 113 (1983).

NOTES TO PAGES 179–180 333

26. Michelman is quoted in Stephanie Goldberg, "The Law, a New Theory Holds, Has a White Voice," *New York Times,* July 17, 1992, B8 (see also Michelman, "Law's Republic," at 1530). Richard Delgado made the marginalization accusation in "The Imperial Scholar Revisited: How to Marginalize Outsider Writing, Ten Years Later," 140 *University of Pennsylvania Law Review* 1349 (1992). On feminism see Anne Dailey, "Feminism's Return to Liberalism," 102 *Yale Law Journal* 1265 (1993). (For warnings that the reconstitution of liberalism is a misguided strategy see, e.g., Cynthia Ward, "A Kinder, Gentler Liberalism? Visions of Empathy in Feminist and Communitarian Literature," 61 *University of Chicago Law Review* 929 [1994].) Paul Brest suggested feminism and critical race theory have eclipsed critical legal studies in "Plus Ça Change," 91 *Michigan Law Review* 1945, 1946 (1993), as did Neil Duxbury in *Patterns,* at 426–28, 468, 501–9. See generally Richard Fischl, "The Question That Killed Critical Legal Studies," 17 *Law and Social Inquiry* 779, 782 (1992) (arguing that the killer question was *"What would you put in its [the rule of law's] place?"* Id. at 782. Emphasis in the original). For an overview of the debate over narrative jurisprudence and "voice" see, e.g., Daniel Farber and Suzanna Sherry, "Telling Stories Out of School: An Essay on Legal Narratives," 45 *Stanford Law Review* 807 (1993); Richard Delgado, "On Telling Stories in School: A Reply to Farber and Sherry," 46 *Vanderbilt Law Review* 665 (1993); Jane Baron, "Resistance to Stories," 67 *Southern California Law Review* 255 (1994). For an examination of the relationship between that debate and the debate over essentialism see Richard Delgado, "The Inward Turn in Outsider Jurisprudence," 34 *William and Mary Law Review* 741 (1993). See also Angela Harris, "Race and Essentialism in Feminist Legal Theory," 42 *Stanford Law Review* 581 (1990); Joan Williams, "Dissolving the Sameness/Difference Debate: A Post-Modern Path beyond Essentialism in Feminist and Critical Race Theory," 1991 *Duke Law Journal* 296 (1991).
27. Morton Horwitz, "Republican Origins of Constitutionalism," in *Toward a Usable Past: Liberty under State Constitutions,* ed. Paul Finkelman and Stephen Gottlieb, 148, 149, 152 (1991).
28. Linda Kerber, "The Republican Ideology of the Revolutionary Generation," 37 *American Quarterly* 474, 480–81 (1985); Rodgers, "Republicanism," at 38: "At its worst, employed for too many ends and distended too far, it ran the danger of explaining everything, even that most Hartzian of categories, to which it stuck with a tenacity inexplicable except in terms of rivalry for the same explanatory space: the 'American mind.' " Rodgers's obituary may be premature. Cf. the essays in *The Republican Synthesis Revisited: Essays in Honor of George Athan Bilias,* ed. Milton Klein, Richard Brown, and John Hench (1992). Nor has Rodgers's attempt to bury Progressivism been wholly successful. See Daniel Rodgers, "In Search of Progressivism," 10 *Reviews in American History* 113 (1982). In his 1972 essay, Robert Shalhope had also cautioned historians against using the concept of republicanism as "a catchall to be superimposed upon everything and everybody." Shalhope, "Toward a Republican Synthesis," at 73.
29. Tushnet, "Constitutional Scholarship: What Next" at 29–30; Burke, *History and Social Theory,* at 3 ("dialogue of the deaf"). I suspect that efforts at communication between historians and law professors have proved a "dialogue of the deaf" for many of the same reasons that efforts at communication between sociologists and historians

have proved disappointing. As Charles Tilly said, sociologists "have long supposed they could rake up historical facts from historians' fields in order to incorporate them into sociological analyses." Tilly, Book Review, 91 *Contemporary Sociology* 535 (1990). So have lawyers. For their part, historians cast as skeptical an eye on sociologists' normativity as they do on that of lawyers.

30. It may be, as Daniel Scott Smith has argued, that the emphasis on context has pushed "questions of change . . . to the background of what historians actually do." See Smith, "Context, Time, History," in *Theory, Method, and Practice in Social and Cultural History,* ed. Peter Karsten and John Modell, 13, 29 (1992). It may also be, as Samuel Hays said, that continuity "is more subtle, more difficult to identify, and easy to forget amid the more powerful elements of change. Just because the fact of change is so obvious in our minds, the search for continuity is more challenging and intriguing." Hays, "On the Meaning and Analysis of Change in History," id. at 33, 47.

31. See, e.g., Robert Cover, *Justice Accused* xi (1975). He is quoted in Tanina Rostain, "Robert M. Cover," 96 *Yale Law Journal* 1713, 1715 (1987).

32. See Ernest May, *"Lessons" of the Past: The Use and Misuse of History in American Foreign Policy* (1973). Perhaps we historians take our denial of the authority of the past to extremes. As Otis Graham observes, "The more we learn about the use of history lessons in policymaking, the less we are inclined to welcome their influence. The generals of policy continue to fight the last war, plunging into misjudgment by failing to understand what historian C. Vann Woodward calls 'the built-in obsolescence of the lessons taught by historians.' . . . Can this skepticism of [historical] analogies be carried too far? Not long ago, hearing my exposition on the dangers of analogies . . . Nelson Polsby thundered: 'No land wars in Asia! Don't invade Russia in the wintertime!' " Graham, *Losing Time: The Industrial Policy Debate* 247–48 (1992). On the "volley of analogies unleashed across America's public discourse" by the Bosnian crisis, see Graham, "Editors' Corner: The History Watch," 15 *Public Historian* 7, 11–14 (1993).

33. Kerber "Making Republicanism Useful," at 1672.

34. Fischer, *Historians' Fallacies,* at 132–33, 135.

35. Gadamer, *Truth and Method,* at 299. "Every encounter with tradition that takes place within historical consciousness involves the experience of a tension between the text and the present. The hermeneutic task consists in not covering up this tension by attempting a naive assimilation of the two but in consciously bringing it out." Id. at 306. Karl Popper, *The Poverty of Historicism* 94–95, 143–49 (1986 ed.). For Popper, historicism was synonymous with determinism and associated with totalitarianism. He dedicated his book to the "memory of the countless men, women and children of all creeds or nations or races who fell victims to the fascist and communist belief in Inexorable Laws of Historical Destiny."

36. Novick, *That Noble Dream,* at 594, 598. Novick summarized the "objectivist creed": "The assumptions on which it rests include a commitment to the reality of the past, and to truth as correspondence to that reality; a sharp separation between knower and known, between fact and value, and above all, between history and fiction. Historical facts are seen as prior to and independent of interpretation: the value of an interpretation is judged by how well it accounts for the facts; if contradicted by the facts, it must be abandoned. Truth is one, not perspectival. Whatever patterns

exist in history are 'found,' not 'made.' Though successive generations of historians might, as their perspectives shifted, attribute different significance to events in the past, the meaning of those events was unchanging. . . . Objectivity is held to be at grave risk when history is written for utilitarian purposes. One corollary of all this is that historians, as historians, must purge themselves of external loyalties: the historian's primary allegiance is to 'the objective historical truth,' and to professional colleagues who share a commitment to cooperative, cumulative efforts to advance toward that goal." Id. at 1–2. Jane Larson and Clyde Spillenger wrote recently: "Today, when scholars use the words 'objectivity' or 'neutrality' in describing the ideal point of view for the scholar, they are more likely to be expressing an aspiration for something a bit more humble—such as fairness and credibility." Larson and Spillenger, " 'That's Not History': The Boundaries of Advocacy and Scholarship," 12 *Public Historian* 33, 38 (1990). Whether law professors realize the objectivist creed is in decline among historians is unclear. See Kay, "Adherence to Original Intentions," at 252: "[T]he fact that history is a well-established discipline to which thousands of sensible people have devoted and continue to devote their energy and intelligence" strengthens "the force" of the position that "objectively correct historical conclusions" are possible.

37. FitzGerald, *America Revised,* at 47, 27. Curiously, FitzGerald did not seem wholly aware of how often academic history changed.

38. Simon Schama, *Dead Certainties (Unwarranted Speculations)* (1991); Gordon Wood, "Novel History," *New York Review of Books,* June 27, 1991, 12, 12; Joyce Appleby, Lynn Hunt, and Margaret Jacob, *Telling the Truth about History* 207, 251 (1994).

39. James Kloppenberg, "The Theory and Practice of American Legal History," 106 *Harvard Law Review* 1332, 1335–37 (1993); Kloppenberg, "Objectivity and Historicism: A Century of American Historical Writing," 94 *American Historical Review* 1011, 1026–29 (1989) ("This approach acknowledges both the indispensability of the scientific method of verifying facts and the equally indispensable hermeneutic method of interpreting the meanings of the past we seek to explain"); Kloppenberg, "Deconstructive and Hermeneutic Strategies for Intellectual History: The Recent Work of Dominick LaCapra and David Hollinger," 9 *Intellectual History Newsletter* 3 (April 1987).

40. Kloppenberg, "Objectivity and Historicism," at 1029; Ackerman, *We the People,* at 219. In applauding Rorty's historicism in *Philosophy and the Mirror of Nature,* David Hollinger observed that historians "are among the last people to fear that the entire enterprise of justification will be undermined by the more widespread recognition of its historicity. This fear on the part of some philosophers is a matter of genuine puzzlement to many historians. A note for the *Newsletter of the Intellectual History Group,* therefore, can simply report that Rorty takes up the good old cause where Thomas S. Kuhn left off." Hollinger, "The Voice of Intellectual History in the Conversation of Mankind: A Note on Richard Rorty," in Hollinger, *American Province,* at 171–72.

41. Buhle, *History and the New Left,* at 29 ("all the virtues"); Williams, "Culture and Certainty," at 720. According to Collingwood, "the true historian never prophesies." R. G. Collingwood, *The Idea of History* 68 (1956). See Wood, "Bernard Bailyn," at 41–42; Fischer, *Historians' Fallacies,* at 135–40, 314. David Hackett Fischer has said, "There are some very strict tautological rules of historical scholarship, which are

rather like the rules of chess. When a chess player sits down to play a game, he must respect a rule which requires him to move his bishops on the diagonal. Nobody will arrest him if he doesn't. But if he refuses to play that way, then he isn't exactly playing chess." Id. at xix.

42. Woodward, "The Future of the Past," at 724. Questioned about the difference between his work as a historian and a lawyer, Staughton Lynd explained: "Law is like history with dessert. For instance, I'm working on a case that involves a company moving away from Youngstown after allegedly promising to the union, during collective bargaining negotiations five years ago, that it would stay. Maybe it's called law instead of history, but I'm doing exactly what I used to do as a historian. I'm ferreting out documents. I'm talking to people. I'm trying to understand why the policy changed from one point in time to another. But as a historian when you get to the last chapter, that's it; whereas a lawyer has the chance of going a little further. . . . [T]here's the satisfaction that after you get done analyzing the situation, you can have a shot at trying to do something about it." Lynd, *Visions of History,* ed. Henry Abelove, 149, 154 (1983).

43. See David Dow, "When Words Mean What We Believe They Say: The Case of Article V," 76 *Iowa Law Review* 1, 9 n.35 (1990) (noting that while Sunstein leaned toward Pocock, Ahkil Amar relied on Wood). "[T]he Framers of the Constitution expected" is from Monaghan, "Our Perfect Constitution," at 371 n.112 (citing Bernard Bailyn, David Davis, David Donald, John Thomas, Robert Wiebe, and Gordon Wood, *The Great Republic* 338 [1977]). For an example of the use of historian as talking head that bothers me as a twentieth-century Americanist, see the reference to Richard Hofstadter's *Age of Reform* as the "definitive" history of the Progressive movement and era. Douglas Hsiao, "Invisible Cities: The Constitutional Status of Direct Democracy in a Democratic Republic," 41 *Duke Law Journal* 1267, 1274 (1991); Hofstadter, *The Age of Reform: From Bryan to F.D.R.* (1955). I believe the greatness of *The Age of Reform* lies precisely in the fact that it sparked a generation of revisionist work on Progressivism. Americanists in the field generally consider it the most influential book on recent American history published in the second half of the twentieth century, but they do not agree with it. When I assign this book to undergraduates or graduate students, I generally say: "This is the greatest book on twentieth-century American history. And it's all wrong." See also Alan Brinkley, "In Retrospect: Richard Hofstadter's *The Age of Reform*: A Reconsideration," 13 *Reviews in American History* 462 (1985).

44. Kerber, "Making Republicanism Useful," at 1664–65.

45. Joan Williams, "Clio Meets Portia: Objectivity in the Courtroom and the Classroom," in *Ethics and Public History: An Anthology,* ed. Theodore Karamanski, 45, 47 (1990); William E. Leuchtenburg, "The Historian in the Public Realm," 97 *American Historical Review* 1, 11 (1992).

46. Edmund S. Morgan to Frankfurter, October 13, 1954, Folder 186, Box 19, Frankfurter Papers.

47. Winifred Rothenberg, "Explanation in History: In Defense of Operationalism," in *Theory, Method, and Practice,* at 134, 145–46. Emphasis in the original.

48. Carl Degler, "The Sociologist as Historian: Riesman's *The Lonely Crowd*," 15 *American Quarterly* 483 (1963). See, e.g., Degler, *Out of Our Past: The Forces That Shaped Modern America* (1959). The phrase "historians' machismo" is one I heard

Gordon use in a lecture at Northwestern Law School. I switch from the third-person plural to the first-person plural here because while I have never before written about republicanism, I have delighted in displays of "historians' machismo." I remember, for example, my satisfaction at thinking I had been the first historian to consult the Homer Bone Papers at the University of Puget Sound. I have now surmised that William E. Leuchtenburg was there before me.

49. Henry Hart, untitled article, n.d., Box 24, Folder 11, Hart Papers; Herbert Gutman, Interview, in Abelove, *Visions of History,* at 187, 203; Rorty, *Contingency,* at 97. "As late as the nineteenth century, history remained for many a seamless whole scarcely distinguishable from the present, human nature the same in all epochs. . . . [T]he past's alien character came to be widely recognized and accepted only near the turn of this century when a 'Chinese wall between past and present' was definitely erected. . . . Recognizing the past as a foreign country cost historians dear. Distanced and differentiated, it ceased to be a source of useful lessons and became a heap of quaint anachronisms. . . . Against the irrelevance of so alien a past, certain benefits also emerged. . . . With the loss of its exemplary role, the past ceased to exert an influence over the present." Lowenthal, *Foreign Country,* at 232–33. See also Ross, *Origins of American Social Science,* at 285–86, 312–15.

50. Novick, *That Noble Dream,* at 2 ("objective historian's role"); Appleby, Hunt, and Jacob, *Telling the Truth,* at 259, 284 ("qualified objectivity" and "measured relativism"); David Sokolow, "From Kurosawa to (Duncan) Kennedy: The Lessons of *Rashomon* for Current Legal Education," 1991 *Wisconsin Law Review* 969, 983–84 (1991) (observing that witnesses are sworn to tell the truth, but attorneys are not); Monroe Friedman, "Judge Frankel's Search for Truth," 123 *University of Pennsylvania Law Review* 1060, 1060 (1975) ("process of historical research"); Fischer, *Historians' Fallacies,* at 280 ("historical processes").

51. Rakove, "Comment," at 232; "in a society" is from Rakove, *Original Meanings,* at 366–67. He also quotes Judith Shklar: "Jefferson's heirs were torn irresolutely between his contempt for tradition and Madison's prudent fondness for it." According to Rakove, "It was Jefferson who better grasped the habits of democracy, Madison who better understood its perils. But perhaps Jefferson also saw more clearly than his friend what the experience of founding a republic finally meant, perhaps even to the conservative framers themselves. Having learned so much from the experience of a mere decade of self-government, and having celebrated their own ability to act from 'reflection and choice,' would they not find the idea that later generations could not improve upon their discoveries incredible?" Yet he recognizes that "language, or at least the language constitutive of a polity, cannot be infinitely malleable. If nothing in the text of the Constitution literally constrains or even instructs us to read it as its framers and ratifiers might have done, we may still have soundly Madisonian reasons for attempting to recover its original meanings. But then we also have to ask why we are doing so. Is it because we truly believe that language can only mean now what it meant then? Or is it because the meditations about popular government that we encounter there remain more profound than those that the ordinary politics of our endless democratic present usually sustains?" Id. at 367–68.

52. Transcript, "Republicanism in Legal Culture." At the time Jefferson wrote those words in 1816, Americans' attitude toward their history and the Founding was itself ambivalent and in a state of flux. See Lowenthal, *Foreign Country,* at 105–24.

53. Robert Burt, *The Constitution in Conflict* 36 (1992). John Schlegel has asked whether anyone builds a "scheme of social organization from ground zero." Personal communication.

54. Amar, "Sovereignty and Federalism," at 1426 n.9 (emphasis in the original); Frederick Schauer, "Judicial Self-Understanding and the Internalization of Constitutional Rules," 61 *University of Colorado Law Review* 749, 754 (1990) ("why someone"); John Reid, *Constitutional History of the American Revolution: Authority to Tax*, at 135 (danger of confusing history with precedent). See Collier, "Precedent and Legal Authority," for a brilliant exposition of the different—and contrasting—conceptions of precedential authority.

55. Tushnet, "Concept of Tradition," at 96. Emphasis in the original.

CHAPTER 7. TRADING PLACES

1. Gordon, "Historicism," at 1055.

2. Barber, *Constitution of Judicial Power*, at 119–20, 68.

3. Kelly, "Clio and the Court," at 119 ("love affair"). I question the vitality of legal liberalism in the Epilogue, and Mark Tushnet has queried whether historians should help lawyers ground decisions in "historians' history," in Tushnet, "Should Historians Accept the Supreme Court's Invitation?" 15 *Organization of American Historians Newsletter* 12 (1987).

4. Horwitz, "Foreword: The Constitution of Change," at 36–37, 39–40; Brown, "Tradition and Insight," at 183 ("It seems so comfortingly"). *Planned Parenthood* v. *Casey,* 112 S. Ct. 2791, 2812 (1992). For an interesting discussion of the relationship between originalism and stare decisis, which suggests that much constitutional law is "unconstitutional" in that it departs from the original understanding, and that originalism generally does—and often should—yield to stare decisis, see Henry Monaghan, "Stare Decisis and Constitutional Adjudication," 88 *Columbia Law Review* 723, 739, 744, 760 (1988).

5. *Michael H.* v. *Gerald D.,* 491 U.S. 110, 127 n.6 (1989) (emphasis added); Brown, "Tradition and Insight," at 179–80, 202, 216; L. Benjamin Young, "Justice Scalia's History and Tradition: The Chief Nightmare in Professor Tribe's Anxiety Closet," 78 *Virginia Law Review* 581, 587–88 (1992) ("liberals must now"). See also Lawrence Tribe and Michael Dorf, *On Reading the Constitution* 104 (1991): "Justice Scalia is aware that his tradition-bound approach to constitutional interpretation would severely curtail the Supreme Court's role in protecting individual liberties. Indeed, since he regards judicial protection of unenumerated rights as illegitimate, such a curtailment would seem to be the purpose of his method." For the argument that Scalia's approach is unworkable, see id. at 98–114. For an excellent discussion of the difference between history and tradition see Soifer, *Company We Keep,* at 104, 125, 138–39, 242 n.10. For an overview of the function of tradition in Supreme Court cases, the feminist reaction against Scalia's traditionalism, and a new proposed approach to tradition and change, see Katharine Bartlett, "Tradition, Change, and the Idea of Progress in Feminist Legal Thought," 1995 *Wisconsin Law Review* 303 (1995).

6. Gordon, "Historicism," at 1055 (Morton Horwitz tried to open the dialogue when he wrote: "We must become more self-conscious about legal historiography and the

ways in which controversies over political and legal theory influence legal historical inquiry. It is time for us to bridge the chasm between legal theory and legal history." Horwitz, "History and Theory," at 1835. See also Morton Horwitz, "Republicanism in American Constitutional Thought," 29 *William and Mary Law Review* 57, 74 [1987]); Karl Llewellyn, *The Common Law Tradition: Deciding Appeals* 122 (1960) (for a critique suggesting that Llewellyn's concept of "situation sense" was unclear and ambiguous see William Twining, *Karl Llewellyn and the Realist Movement* 216–27 [1973]; for a defense of "situation sense," which nevertheless conceded its untidiness, see Steven Smith, "Reductionism in Legal Thought," 91 *Columbia Law Review* 68, 98–103 [1991]). "We have to learn" and "Historical adjudication" are from Reid, "Law and History," at 204–5.

7. De Voto is quoted in Michael Kammen, *Mystic Chords of Memory: The Transformation of Tradition in American Culture* 498 (1991); historians' perpetuation of myths is discussed in Arthur Schlesinger, Jr., *The Disuniting of America: Reflections on a Multicultural Society* 53–54 (1992); American Historical Association president Conyers Read is quoted in Novick, *That Noble Dream,* at 318. See Michael Zuckerman, "Myth and Method: The Current Crises in American Historical Writing," 17 *History Teacher* 219, 221 (1984): "American historians have rarely been less consequential than they have been in this past decade, when they devoted themselves so unswervingly to the dispassionate, professional pursuit of truth. For contemporary historians have given up more than just the shibboleths of the Cold War, dispensed with more than just the dogmas of modernization, and grown wary of more than just the claims of corporate liberalism. They have nearly divested themselves of every energizing construct." Zuckerman made an important point, though I believe his statement came closer to describing the historical profession in the 1970s than the 1980s. I would also emphasize that it is unclear whether professional historians have ever exercised a real influence over society. Theodore Roosevelt did, of course, but he was not a professional historian.

8. William McNeill, *Mythistory and Other Essays* 3, 25 (1986).

9. Id. at 37; Kammen, *Mystic Chords of Memory,* at 481–82; Macaulay is quoted in Miller, *Supreme Court and History,* at 196. For another discussion of the complementary nature of myth and history see J. G. A. Pocock, "The Origins of the Study of the Past: A Comparative Approach," 4 *Comparative Studies in Society and History* 209 (1962). According to C. Vann Woodward, "We have never faced up to the relationship between myth and history. Without tackling the semantic difficulties involved, we know that *myth* has more than pejorative uses and that it can be used to denote more than what one deems false about the other man's beliefs. In the nonpejorative sense myths are images, or collections of them, charged with values, aspirations, ideals and meanings. In the words of Mark Schorer, they are 'the instruments by which we continually struggle to make our experience intelligible to ourselves.' Myths *can* be, in short, 'a good thing.' No man in his right mind, and surely not a responsible historian, will knowingly and wantonly destroy a precious thing. . . . Serious history is the critique of myths, however, not the embodiment of them. Neither is it the destruction of myths." C. Vann Woodward, "Behind the Myths," in *The Future of the Past* 278 (1989). Carl Becker observed: "Myths often serve a useful purpose because even if not true they symbolize something that is true and worth remembering. The story of George Washington and the cherry tree is a myth,

but it has served to impress on the minds of people a fact of first rate importance—namely that George Washington happened to be a man of absolute integrity." *"What Is the Good of History?" Selected Letters of Carl L. Becker, 1900–1945,* ed. Michael Kammen, 316 (1973). Lowenthal notes that "some newly minted reproductions convey historical immediacy better than originals do. . . . The sheer ingenuity of replication can help bring history to life." Lowenthal, *Foreign Country,* at 293.

10. Schlesinger, *Disuniting of America,* at 137; see Kammen, *Mystic Chords of Memory,* at 537. Cf. Sanford Levinson, *Constitutional Faith* 4, 12 (1988). Martha Minow has asked: "What about a sense of continuity with the past is important to the creation of meaning, identity, and legitimacy? Is this something special to American culture, given the absence of other unifying possibilities? The debate over multiculturalism in history curriculae seems very much premised on that idea; having so little else in common, the teaching of a shared history (however constructed) seems to many to be central to the teaching of a shared culture. This idea bears an odd resemblance to the claim by others that the one thing we share in this country is law. . . . Maybe this is why the relationship between law and history here is important to address, more so than law and economics, say; the contest for meaning, identity, and national legitimacy as well as professional standards and civility appears in the debates between law professors and historians." Personal communication.

11. Kammen, *Mystic Chords of Memory,* at 482, 657.

12. Hofstadter is quoted in Bernard Sternsher, *Consensus, Conflict, and American Historians* 285 (1975). The constitutional historian Herman Belz has observed "growing professional acceptance" of "the trend toward explicitly normative historiography." Belz, "History and Theory," 11 *Constitutional Commentary* 45 (1994). See Kent Greenwalt, " 'Truth' or Consequences," in *Nomos XXXVII: Theory and Practice,* ed. Lan Shapiro and Judith DeCew, 386, 394 (1995) (hypothesizing that "believers in objective value judgments will be somewhat more likely than others to opt for truth rather than practical effects").

13. Elizabeth Koed, "A Symbol Transformed: How 'Liberty Enlightening the World' Became 'The Mother of Exiles,' " 2 *Social Contract* 137 (1992); John Higham, "The Transformation of the Statue of Liberty," in *Send These to Me: Immigrants in Urban America* 71, 75 (1984); for the argument that the United States should take those words more seriously in formulating its immigration policy see Mark Gibney, "United States Immigration Policy and the 'Huddled Masses' Myth," 3 *Georgetown Immigration Law Journal* 361, 386 (1989) (claiming that the United States has not proved "a haven for the 'huddled masses,' " but rather one for those who "have been well educated and from the elite strata of their societies. Still, the imagery of the 'huddled masses' continues to exert a very strong influence on how we view immigrants, . . . [and] also how we view ourselves").

14. See, e.g., Barbara Howe and Emory Kemp, eds., *Public History: An Introduction* (1986); David Trask and Robert Pomeroy, eds., *The Craft of Public History: An Annotated Select Bibliography* (1983); W. Andrew Achenbaum, "Public History's Past, Present and Prospects," 92 *American Historical Review* 1162 (1987); Robert Kelley, "Public History: Its Origin, Nature and Prospects," 1 *Public Historian* 16 (1978). Examples of history for policymakers include Richard Neustadt and Ernest May, *Thinking in Time: The Uses of History for Decision-Makers* (1986), and Richard Neustadt and Harvey Fineberg, *The Epidemic That Never Was* (1983).

15. "[P]aid liars" is from Albert Hurtado, "Historians and Their Employers: A Perspective on Professional Ethics," 8 *Public Historian* 47, 51 (1986). Hurtado himself did not subscribe to this indictment. "[W]hores" is from Harold Green, who is quoted in J. Morgan Kousser, "Are Expert Witnesses Whores? Reflections on Objectivity in Scholarship and Expert Witnessing," 6 *Public Historian* 5, 5 (1984). For the suggestion that lawyers neglect countervailing evidence see James Mohr, "Historically Based Legal Briefs: Observations of a Participant in the *Webster* Case," 12 *Public Historian* 19, 20 (1990). For the remarks of the two law professors, see Larson and Spillenger, "That's Not History," at 40 n.17.

16. Thomas Haskell and Sanford Levinson, "Academic Freedom and Expert Witnessing: Historians and the *Sears* Case," 66 *Texas Law Review* 1629, 1654 n.122 (1988). See *Equal Employment Opportunity Commission v. Sears, Roebuck & Co.* 625 F. Supp. 1264 (N.D. Ill. 1986), aff'd. 839 F. 2d 302 (7th Cir. 1988); Katherine Jellison, "History in the Courtroom: The *Sears* Case in Perspective," 9 *Public Historian* 9, 12 (1987); Ruth Milkman, "Women's History and the Sears Case," 12 *Feminist Studies* 375 (1986); Novick, *That Noble Dream*, at 502–10; Jon Wiener, "The *Sears* case: Women's History on Trial," *Nation*, September 7, 1985, 1. Historians have acted as if the *Sears* case turned on historical interpretations, but as Haskell and Levinson pointed out, "the historians were playing small roles in a legal drama of epic proportions. The Sears trial was first and foremost a pitched battle over the meaning of statistical data." Haskell and Levinson, "Academic Freedom," at 1636.

17. Joan Williams, "Deconstructing Gender," 87 *Michigan Law Review* 797, 830 (1989) ("many women's historians"); Alice Kessler-Harris, "Equal Employment Opportunity v. Sears, Roebuck and Company: A Personal Account," 35 *Radical History Review* 57, 73 (1986). As Joan Scott said, Kessler-Harris "had trouble finding a simple and singular model that would at once acknowledge difference *and* refuse it as an acceptable explanation for the Sears employment pattern. So she fell into great difficulty maintaining consistency in the face of hostile questioning." Scott, "The *Sears* Case," in *Gender and the Politics of History*, ed. Joan Scott, 171 (1988) (emphasis in the original). See also Alice Kessler-Harris, "Academic Freedom and Expert Witnessing: A Response to Haskell and Levinson," 67 *Texas Law Review* 429 (1988).

18. Horwitz, "Republican Origins," at 148. Kousser suggested expert witnessing allowed him to be objective and do good, in "Are Expert Witnesses Whores," at 7.

19. S. Charles Bolton, "The Historian as Expert Witness: Creationism in Arkansas," 4 *Public Historian* 59, 66 (1982). "One intuits the difference between working in a library and participating in a court room drama, but until one has experienced it, the disjunction between the two remains abstract. Accustomed to developing the subtle distinctions of an argument, to negotiating about fine points of interpretation, the historian quickly discovers that these skills must be abandoned in testifying. Maintaining a position is as important as the position taken. Consistency is not merely a virtue but evidence of one's expertise. Yet the temptation to overgeneralize or to state a case in its sharpest form must also be resisted. I discovered to my sorrow that either one can be quickly penetrated in a cross-examination." Kessler-Harris, "Equal Employment Opportunity," at 72.

20. Mohr, "Legal Briefs," at 24. The cases are *Patterson v. McLean Credit Union*, 491 U.S. 164 (1989); *Planned Parenthood v. Casey*, 112 S. Ct. 2791 (1992); *Webster v. Reproductive Health Services*, 492 U.S. 490 (1989). On the value of amicus briefs

over expert testimony see Ronald Roesch, Stephen Golding, Valerie Hans, and N. Dickson Reppucci, "Social Science and the Courts: The Role of Amicus Curiae Briefs," 15 *Law and Human Behavior* 1, 3–4 (1991). Naturally, sometimes well-done history offers no support for the political results the historian wishes to reach. See Charles Lofgren, "A Comment on William Wiecek, 'Clio as Hostage . . . ,' " 24 *California Western Law Review* 269, 272 (1987–88).

21. James Mohr, *Abortion in America: The Origins and Evolution of National Policy, 1800–1900* (1978); "Brief for the United States as Amicus Curiae Supporting Appellants," *Webster* v. *Reproductive Health Services,* October Term 1989, U.S. Supreme Court (No. 88–605), 13, 16–17. Mohr, "Legal Briefs," at 24. Mohr summarized the argument of his book as a "dispassionate analysis of the history of abortion policy and practice in the United States confirms to fair-minded observers that the Republic's dominant response, regardless of changing positions on specific details and alterations in legislative fiat, has consistently been one of tolerance toward the women actually affected by the reproductive decisions involved." Mohr, "Legal Briefs," at 23. Not all historians agree with Mohr. See the sources cited in Michael McConnell, "How to Promote Serious Deliberation about Abortion," 58 *University of Chicago Law Review* 1181, 1183 n.4 (1991). Mohr's book is nevertheless regarded as a classic.

22. Sylvia Law, "Conversations between Historians and the Constitution," 12 *Public Historian* 11, 15 (1990).

23. "Brief of 281 American Historians as Amici Curiae Supporting Appellees," 12 *Public Historian* 57 (1990); other historians added their names as signatories after the brief was filed. On the influence of the brief see, e.g., the sources cited in Law, "Conversations," at 16 n.9. Law also adapted a portion of the brief for an article that was featured prominently in a Sunday issue of the *Atlanta Journal and Constitution.* Law, "Abortion in America: A Tangled History," *Atlanta Journal and Constitution,* May 7, 1989, D1.

24. Law, "Conversations," at 14. See "Court Transcript: Justices Hear Argument on Missouri Case, Argument by Frank Susman, Lawyer for Missouri Abortion Clinics," *New York Times,* April 27, 1989, B12, B13: "I think it is somewhat ironic that the sole historical source cited by the Solicitor General in his brief in an effort to dispute this fact is work by Mr. James Moore [*sic*], 'Abortion in America.' And yet Mr. Moore, along with 280 other eminent historians in this country, have filed a brief supporting the position of the appellees when it comes to the historical history." The argument did not convince Justice Scalia, who apparently did not believe historians spoke with any added authority. "You mentioned the historical brief," he told Susman. "There is more than one historical brief here and one filed by the Association for Public Justice simply contradicts your history." Id.

25. See "Brief of 250 American Historians as Amici Curiae in Support of Planned Parenthood of Southeastern Pennsylvania," *Planned Parenthood of Southeastern Pennsylvania* v. *Robert P. Casey,* October Term 1991, U.S. Supreme Court (Nos. 91–744 and 91–902); *Planned Parenthood* v. *Casey,* at 2859.

26. Mohr, "Legal Briefs," at 19, 26. Mohr later reiterated this point. According to law professor Gerard Bradley, who telephoned Mohr to ask him to explain inconsistencies between the book and the brief, Mohr said that "where inconsistencies exist he stood by the book rather than the brief, and he confessed that he was uncomfortable with

the way his work was cited for some of the brief's claims. But he went on to express the view that the belief was a 'political document,' the work of a 'citizen' not a 'scholar.' " Bradley, "Academic Integrity Betrayed," 1 *First Things* 10, 11 (1990).

27. Prominent historians besides Mohr have studied the movement led by professional doctors to criminalize abortion in the nineteenth century and the refusal of feminists of that era to endorse abortion. Reva Siegel summarized their work in "Reasoning from the Body," 44 *Stanford Law Review* 261, 280–324 (1992).

28. Estelle Freedman, "Historical Interpretation and Legal Advocacy: Rethinking the *Webster* Amicus Brief," 12 *Public Historian* 27, 30–31 (1990).

29. Id. at 28, 31 (Emphasis in the original). Siegel provided such a legal argument in "Reasoning from the Body," at 348–81, although it is unclear whether she would use it in a courtroom.

30. See Ahkil Amar, "A Neo-Federalist View of Article III: Separating the Two Tiers of Federal Jurisdiction," 63 *Boston University Law Review* 205, 207 n.7 (1985) ("[A]lthough I believe that there is more to constitutional law than interpretivism, narrowly understood, I recognize that many other actors in our legal culture—Congressmen, judges, scholars, and practitioners—subscribe to a narrower brand of interpretivism. Because I seek to convert them to my vision of federal jurisdiction, I must speak their language"); Amar, "Our Forgotten Constitution," at 293 ("Mine is not an invitation to noninterpretivism based on a vague theory of changed circumstances"); Freedman, "Historical Interpretation," at 31.

31. H. Jefferson Powell, "Rules for Originalists," 73 *Virginia Law Review* 659, 660 (1987). Powell himself, however, maintained that "our tendency to search for the constitutional views founding-era Americans generally shared has led us to ignore what was perhaps their greatest achievement—the creation of a shared political and legal language that made reasoned debate possible." He criticized constitutional theorists for their "failure to recognize that American constitutionalism is a linguistic tradition of political debate rather than a determinate set of political outcomes." Powell, "The Political Grammar of Early Constitutional Law," 71 *North Carolina Law Review* 949, 950, 1008 (1993).

32. Powell, "Rules for Originalists," at 662–68.

33. Id. at 668–78; Ahkil Amar, "The Bill of Rights and the Fourteenth Amendment," 101 *Yale Law Journal* 1192, 1260 (1992); Amar, "The Bill of Rights as a Constitution," 100 *Yale Law Journal* 1131 (1991); Amar, "The Creation and Reconstruction of the Bill of Rights," 16 *Southern Illinois University Law Journal* 337 (1992). For a historian's critique of Amar's interpretation see, e.g., Paul Finkelman, "The Ten Amendments as a Declaration of Rights," 16 *Southern Illinois University Law Journal* 351, 352 n.16, 370–74 (1992).

34. Powell, "Rules for Originalists," at 678–90.

35. Id. at 691.

36. Quotations are from Peter Huber, *Galileo's Revenge: Junk Science in the Courtroom* 2, 209 (1993). See *Daubert* v. *Merrell Dow*, 113 S.Ct. 2786 (1993) (holding that the Federal Rules of Evidence superseded *Frye* v. *United States*, 293 F. 2d 1013 [1923]). *Frye* had held scientific expert testimony admissible only if it were gathered through a methodology " 'generally accepted as a reliable technique' . . . by recognized authorities in the field." Id. at 1130. For the contention that *Frye* had been dead since

the 1970s, long before Justice Blackmun's opinion in *Daubert* officially buried it, see Huber, *Galileo's Revenge,* at 15–17.

37. William Eskridge, "A Social Constructionist Critique of Posner's *Sex and Reason:* Steps toward a Gay Legal Agenda," 103 *Yale Law Journal* 333, 345, 346 n.34 (hypothesizing that Posner's "coyness" in his discussion of *Bowers v. Hardwick* in *Sex and Reason* [1992] may have been due to his position as a federal judge: "Academic work ought to be bold [as Posner's usually is]." Id. at 346). The cases of both Lani Guinier and Robert Bork suggest that provocative scholarship may haunt the academic tapped for public service—but that is a different matter.

38. Ruth Colker, "Feminist Litigation: An Oxymoron—A Study of the Briefs Filed in *William L. Webster* v. *Reproductive Health Services,*" 13 *Harvard Women's Law Journal* 137, 156 (1990).

39. Sarah Burns, "Notes from the Field: A Reply to Professor Colker," 13 *Harvard Women's Law Journal* 189, 194 (1990) ("Feminist litigation"); R. L. Bard, "Advocacy Masquerading as Scholarship: or, Why Legal Scholars Cannot Be Trusted," 55 *Brooklyn Law Review* 853 (1989). In rare instances, briefs become scholarship. For example, because of their significance for the "takings" issue, Richard Epstein's and Joseph Sax's briefs in *Lucas* v. *South Carolina Coastal Council* were published in 26 *Loyola of Los Angeles Law Review* 943, 995 (1993).

40. *Runyon* v. *McCrary,* 427 U.S. 160 (1976); *Jones* v. *Alfred H. Mayer Co.,* 392 U.S. 409 (1968); Eric Foner, *Reconstruction: America's Unfinished Revolution, 1863–1877* 243–45 (1988); Randall Kennedy, "The Politics of Scholarship," 98 *Yale Law Journal* 521, 537–39 (1989).

41. Foner, *Reconstruction,* at 256.

42. Robert Kaczorowski, "The Enforcement Provisions of the Civil Rights Act of 1866: A Legislative History in Light of *Runyon* v. *McCrary,*" 98 *Yale Law Journal* 565, 566 (1989).

43. John Hope Franklin, "The Historian and the Public Policy," in *Race and History: Selected Essays, 1938–1988* 310 (1989).

44. *Planned Parenthood* v. *Casey,* at 2815–16; Nagel, *Judicial Power,* at 61; Glendon, *Nation,* at 4 (see also 113–17, 158); Horwitz, "Foreword: The Constitution of Change," at 35, 92.

45. Such criteria for evaluating "good public history" would force me to rethink my treatment of Clyde Summers in Germany. If I had another opportunity to comment on his work, I would not so vehemently say his treatment of the NLRA as a charter of industrial democracy was ahistorical. An activist by temperament, Summers thought in terms of the courtroom rather than the classroom. Further, historians have located a nineteenth-century "labor republicanism," which included a vision of industrial democracy (see, e.g., Leon Fink, *Workingmen's Democracy: The Knights of Labor and American Politics* [1983]; Sean Wilentz, *Chants Democratic: New York City and the Rise of the American Working Class, 1788–1850* [1984]). The legislative history of the NLRA also indicated its drafters' concern with industrial democracy. Mark Barenberg has placed the act in the context of Wagner's progressive thought. "In Wagner's vision, achieving workers' democratic consent and substantive freedom through collective empowerment took absolute precedence over the goals of macroeconomic stabilization and growth" (Barenberg, "The Political Economy of the Wagner Act," at 1390 n.31). And the goal of industrial democracy may sometimes be

consistent with that of industrial peace, which I consider to be the principal purpose of Congress in passing the Wagner Act. I could in good faith write an article pointing to the NLRA's roots in a longstanding dream of industrial democracy, though I would not tie that vision to the legislative history of the act as closely as Summers did. Given another chance, I would hope I would make a more nuanced response, which might have helped him to historicize his point of view more carefully.

46. Gordon, "Historicism," at 1021.

47. G. Edward White, *The Marshall Court and Cultural Change, 1815–1835* 195, 787–88 (see also id. at 70–72) (abridged ed. 1991).

48. Id. at 782, 788; Powell, "Reviving Republicanism," at 1707.

49. "[P]resent depiction" and "overcome by dialogue" are from Daniel Reimer, "The Role of 'Community' in the Pacific Northwest Logging Debate," 66 *University of Colorado Law Review* 223, 244 (1995); Benjamin Barber, *Strong Democracy* 160 (1984); Jeremy Waldron, *Liberal Rights: Collected Papers, 1981–1991* 379–85 (1993) (rights as fallbacks: "The Veronan equivalent of marriage by a judge in a civil ceremony, which ought to have been available to Romeo and Juliet when their families failed to provide the necessary support, would seem a cold and arid setting for a wedding compared to the lavish ceremony which a loving community might have offered. That the liberal can concede. The point is that the civil ceremony would have been better than nothing"); Michelman, "Law's Republic," at 1495; James Madison, "Vices of the Political System of the United States," April 1787, reprinted in *The Founder's Constitution,* ed. Philip Kurland and Ralph Lerner, 166–69 (1987). See also Madison, id. at 129, and *Federalist 51* (James Madison), id. at 330–31. Gordon Wood explained why few Americans worried about individual rights and the "tyranny of the majority" in the era of the American Revolution in *Creation of the American Republic,* at 61–63. (In thinking about the history of American rights-consciousness, I have found two books especially helpful: the essays collected in David Thelen, *The Constitution in American Life* [1988] and Lawrence Friedman, *The Republic of Choice: Law, Authority, and Culture* [1990].) According to Gey, "Professors Sunstein and Michelman might take a very different view of political power if they adopted the perspective of political losers instead of political winners. . . . Losers' principles guarantee that a political system governed by popular consent in the first year of its existence will continue to be governed by popular consent in perpetuity. In other words, losers' principles ensure that a democracy remains democratic." Gey, "Unfortunate Revival," at 873–74, 882 (See also Gey, "Is Moral Relativism a Constitutional Command?" 70 *Indiana Law Journal* 331, 367–72 [1995]). The Wiebe quotation is from *Self-Rule,* at 265; see also id. at 39–111, 185–88. Likewise Pangle noted that "it is worth underlining—as Machiavelli and Montesquieu both do—the importance of chastity as a civic as well as a private virtue in the classical republican tradition." Pangle, "Comments on Cass Sunstein's 'Republicanism and the Preference Problem,' " 66 *Chicago-Kent Law Review* 205, 209 n.17 (1990). For an examination of the compatibility of the republican revival with political conservatism see Hoeveler, "Original Intent," at 892–98 (noting, however, that "conservatives have not seized on the republican theme for their cause in the way that liberal scholars have." Id. at 893).

50. Galston, *Liberal Purposes,* at 42, 213, 89, 290, 222–25; Holmes, *Anatomy of An-*

tiliberalism, at 177, 198 (emphasis in the original); Joseph Raz, *The Morality of Freedom* 183 (1986).

51. "[A]round diversity" is from James Gardner, "The Ambiguity of Legal Dreams: A Communitarian Defense of Judicial Restraint," 71 *North Carolina Law Review* 805, 835 (1993); Gey, "Unfortunate Revival" at 838 ("oxymoronic"). For an examination of the value of personal autonomy in contemporary life see Raz, *Morality of Freedom.* For a shrill critique of Sandel's communitarianism, see Brian Barry, Book Review, 94 *Ethics* 523, 525 (1984) (at the end of Sandel's "road stand Torquemada, Stalin, Hitler, and Begin").

52. Cass Sunstein, "The Idea of a Useable Past," 95 *Columbia Law Review* 601, 606 (1995); Wood, "The Virtues and the Interests" ("stakes"); Wood, "Ideology and Origins," at 632–33 ("it may be"). Wood also made this point in "Fundamentalists," at 40. Elsewhere Wood wrote that as a historian, he saw the issues "differently from the political philosophers and legal theorists. All of them seem to speak and write as if we had more freedom and choice in the matter than we do. They seem to suggest that people can actually be talked into restoring classical politics or even aspects of classical politics to American political life. I suppose intellectuals and scholars have to believe that such things can happen, that their ideas can matter in this way; or else they could never muster the energy to think and write as they do. But historians are blessed with a different obligation: they do not have as their primary purpose the changing of our present minds on behalf of a cause; instead their principal purpose is to describe and explain what happened in the past. If their written history should have the effect of changing our minds about the present and future, all well and good, but that is not, or at least should not, be the main goal of writing history." Wood, "Comment on Galston Paper," 66 *Chicago-Kent Law Review* 69, 70–71 (1990).

53. Frank Easterbrook, "Abstraction and Authority," 59 *University of Chicago Law Review* 348, 380 (1992); Wood, "Bernard Bailyn," at 41 ("connect the past"); Wood, "Comment on Galston," at 72 ("obviously meaningful").

54. Kerber, "Making Republicanism Useful," at 1672. Law professors have recently focused greater attention on the Antifederalists, as well as the Federalists. See, e.g., Suzette Hemberger, "Dead Stepfathers," 84 *Northwestern University Law Review* 220 (1989).

55. Ackerman, *We the People,* at 317–18 ("opposition" and "engaged"); Ackerman, "Liberating Abstraction," 59 *University of Chicago Law Review* 341 (1992) ("liberal Democrat"); "Proceedings of the Conference on Takings," at 154 ("liberal republican"). Sanford Levinson has described Ackerman's enterprise as "the most important and imaginative work now being done in the area of constitutional theory." Levinson, "Accounting for Constitutional Change (Or, How Many Times Has the United States Constitution Been Amended? [A] <26; [B] 26; [C] >26; [D] All of the Above)," 8 *Constitutional Commentary* 409, 429 (1991). According to the Galstons, "*We the People* represents Ackerman's effort to mediate between liberal democratic theorists and their civic republican critics," and "tension between liberalism and civic republicanism . . . pervades *We the People.*" Miriam and William Galston, "Reason, Consent, and the U.S. Constitution: Bruce Ackerman's *We the People,*" 104 *Ethics* 446, 447, 449 (1994). Ackerman would be more likely to describe the book as neoliberal. See Bruce Ackerman, "Rooted Cosmopolitanism," id. at 516, 534–35. Sunstein

would dispute the suggestion *We the People* subscribes to the republican revival; according to him, "Ackerman understates the extent to which the Framers intended to produce public-spirited deliberation by the representatives. His conception of normal politics sells the Framers a bit short." Sunstein, "New Deals," *New Republic,* January 20, 1992, 32, 36.

56. Ackerman, *We the People,* at 178, 193–94, 217–21, 6, 250, 29, 243, 287 (emphasis in the original).

57. Id. at 34, 43–49 (emphasis in the original); Ackerman, "Transformative Appointments," 101 *Harvard Law Review* 1164, 1181, 1178 (1987) ("If the American people" and Bork nomination as failed constitutional moment).

58. Ackerman, *We the People,* at 262–65, 7–16, 303–5 (emphasis added). "American government is losing" and "power of historical memory" are from Ackerman, "Rooted Cosmopolitanism," at 526.

59. Ackerman, *We the People,* at 137, 141. As a golfer and a historian of the United States in the twentieth century who has never considered the public school integral to the New Deal, I would ask Frank Michelman's question here: "why education and not golf?" Michelman, "Foreword: On Protecting the Poor," at 59. I think Ackerman can come up with a better justification for *Brown.* According to H. Jefferson Powell "While Ackerman carefully avoids comment on *Roe,* his defense of *Griswold* seems equally applicable to the question of abortion rights." Powell, *Moral Tradition,* at 196 n.51.

60. Ackerman, *We the People,* at 139–40.

61. Suzanna Sherry, "The Ghost of Liberalism Past," 105 *Harvard Law Review* 918, 933–34 (1992); Edmund S. Morgan, "The Fiction of 'The People,' " *New York Review of Books,* April 23, 1992, 46, 48.

62. Raoul Berger to David Donald, March 29, 1976, Box 1, Folder 11, Berger Papers. My friend does not want to be identified. Flaherty has "personally noted informal skepticism about the *We the People* project voiced by some at various legal history conferences and colloquia. Often, however, the doubts expressed go not to any discrete point Ackerman has made, but instead voice a general concern about keeping legal theorists off historians' turf." Flaherty, "History 'Lite,' " at 584 n.292.

63. Compare Arthur Link, *Woodrow Wilson and the Progressive Era: 1910–1917* 2, 34 (1954), with John Morton Blum, *The Republican Roosevelt.* See Mark Tushnet, "Dia-Tribe," 78 *Michigan Law Review* 694 (1980); Matthew Finkin, "Revisionism in Labor Law," 43 *Maryland Law Review* 23 (1984); Steven Stowe, "Thinking about Reviews," 78 *Journal of American History* 591 (1993). It is possible that "intradisciplinary polemics" simply strike outsiders as overheated. For example, from my perspective, Tushnet has engaged in his share of polemics within legal discourse; but consider his review of Himmelfarb's *The New History and the Old:* "The essays are filled with apocalyptic imagery, which leads a reader not engaged as Himmelfarb is in intradisciplinary polemics to want to say, 'Lighten up.' It is, after all, one thing to see a world in a grain of sand and rather another to see the decline of Western civilization in the *Journal of Social History.*" Tushnet, "Constitutional Law and Himmelfarb on Social History," 82 *Northwestern University Law Review* 864, 864 (1988).

64. Robert Fogel, " 'Scientific' History and Traditional History," in *Which Road to the Past? Two Views of History,* ed. Robert Fogel and G. R. Elton, 7, 54 (1983).

65. Further, historians might prove reluctant to attack someone senior. Like the generative semanticists who condemned Noam Chomsky, law professors seem to take pleasure in "killing the fathers" (see Harris, *Linguistics Wars,* at 198–213). They also seem ready to reward those who do so, though there are some notable exceptions (Tushnet discusses one in "Critical Legal Studies: Political History," at 1532). Law professors and linguists might dismiss historians as toadies, but I would prefer to think that ours is a tradition of deference, which is, as Pocock observes, "not a hierarchical but a republican characteristic." Pocock, *Machiavellian Moment,* at 515.

66. Edmund S. Morgan, Book Review, 24 *William and Mary Quarterly* 3d ser., 454 (1967) (reviewing Alan Heimert, *Religion and the American Mind from the Great Awakening to the Revolution* [1966]). See also Novick, *That Noble Dream,* at 612–21 (discussing the David Abraham "case," an instance in which the intensity of reaction against David Abraham's work forced that scholar out of the historical profession). Generally speaking, I think historians often evaluate scholarship that supports their own as "good," without giving their reasons for doing so. Law professors are more candid, being more likely to say that a work is "good" or "bad" because it supports or undercuts their own. See Rubin, "On Beyond Truth," at 889.

67. Edmund S. Morgan, *Inventing the People: The Rise of Popular Sovereignity in England and America* 14, 275, 267 (1988); Morgan, "Fiction of 'The People,' " at 48.

68. Bruce Ackerman, "The Marketplace of Ideas," 90 *Yale Law Journal* 1131, 1134–35 (1981) (emphasis in the original). For a similar complaint about a University of Chicago law professor's failure to consult with the social workers and public administration, and finance experts whose offices were within a block of his, see Posner, *Overcoming Law,* at 209.

69. Ackerman, *We the People,* at 28, ix.

70. Compare Jack Rakove, Book Review, 79 *Journal of American History* 226, 227 (1992) (emphasis in the original; "the legal reconstructionist" is from a personal communication from Rakove) and Bernstein, "Charting the Constitution," at 1600–1602, with Eben Moglen's elegantly ironic critique, "The Incompleat Burkean: Bruce Ackerman's Foundation for Constitutional History," 5 *Yale Journal of Law and Humanities* 531 (1993); Sherry, "Ghost of Liberalism"; William Fisher, "The Defects of Dualism," 59 *University of Chicago Law Review* 955 (1992); Michael Klarman, "Constitutional Fact/Constitutional Fiction: A Critique of Bruce Ackerman's Theory of Constitutional Moments," 44 *Stanford Law Review* 759 (1992); Frederick Schauer, "Deliberating about Deliberation," 90 *Michigan Law Review* 1187 (1992); Dow, "When Words Mean," at 46–51.

   As a twentieth-century historian, I take a more positive view of Ackerman's account of what went on during "my" period, the New Deal, than do Klarman, Dow, or Schauer. True, handed Ackerman's manuscript, another historian or I might have picked apart his story of the New Deal. Recall that he stressed the 1936 presidential election as the moment of triumph for "we the people" over the Supreme Court. How could he present the 1936 election as a referendum on the Court's interpretation of New Deal legislation? The New Deal's popularity had been apparent well before the 1936 election. The Democrats' victory in the congressional elections of 1934 represented even more of a triumph for FDR than his own stunning victory in 1936. Arthur Krock concluded in 1934 that the New Deal had won "the most overwhelming victory in the history of American politics." William Allen White wrote after the midterm elections that FDR had been "all but crowned by the people" (Krock and White are quoted in Arthur Schlesinger, Jr., *The Politics of Upheaval* 1 [1960]). Yet soon after Americans had affirmed their commitment to Roosevelt in 1934, a majority of the Court began invalidating New Deal legislation. Why would FDR's win in 1936 affect the Court?

In fact, the Republicans showed more hostility to the Supreme Court in 1936 than did the Democrats. Their platform promised to seek a constitutional amendment to overturn the Court's decision in *Morehead* v. *New York* ex rel. *Tipaldo,* 298 U.S. 587 (1936), in which Justice Roberts had voted with the conservative "Four Horsemen" to overturn New York's minimum wage law. The attorney general cautioned Roosevelt that "if the Democrats sought to outbid the Republicans they ran the risk of going so far as to shift the whole emphasis of the campaign to the constitutional question." As a result the Democratic platform only talked vaguely of seeking a "clarifying amendment . . . if . . . [such] problems cannot be effectively solved by legislation." And FDR deliberately avoided mentioning the Supreme Court in the 1936 campaign. William E. Leuchtenburg, "The Origin of Franklin D. Roosevelt's Court-Packing Plan," 1966 *Supreme Court Review* 347, 378–79 (1966).

That was sensible. As Ackerman himself recognized elsewhere, the Senate despised FDR's Court Packing proposal (Ackerman, "Transformative Appointments," at 1175–76). According to Leuchtenburg, "The President's [1937] message [on Court Packing] generated an intensity of response unmatched by any legislative controversy of this century, save perhaps for the League of Nations episode. . . . So intensely did opponents object to the plan that a number of Democratic senators searched desperately for some device that would free them of the need to commit themselves." Nevertheless, but for a heat wave and the death of the Senate majority leader, the Senate might have accepted Court Packing (William E. Leuchtenburg, "Franklin D. Roosevelt's Supreme Court 'Packing' Plan," in *Essays on the New Deal,* ed. Harold Hollingsworth and William Holmes, 69, 76, 88 [1969]; Leuchtenburg, "FDR's Court-Packing Plan: A Second Life, a Second Death," 1985 *Duke Law Journal* 673, 682–87 [1985]). Yet FDR's plan failed, taking down with it both his New Deal coalition in the Senate and the "myth of Rooseveltian invincibility" (James Patterson, *Congressional Conservatism and the New Deal* 126–27 [1967]).

The thesis of the "switch in time" also remains controversial. Justice Roberts later prepared a memorandum for Felix Frankfurter, which Frankfurter published in 1955, "proving" that Roberts had decided to vote with four other justices to reverse *Morehead* in December 1936, before FDR announced his Court Packing proposal (Felix Frankfurter, "Mr. Justice Roberts," 104 *University of Pennsylvania Law Review* 311 [1955]). So, too, Court Packing did not cow the conservative Four Horsemen—after FDR proposed it, they still voted against New Deal legislation. To Dow and Klarman, Ackerman's history was therefore "bad history" (Klarman, "Constitutional Fact/Fiction," at 774–75 n.98; Dow, "When Words Mean," at 51).

While Ackerman might have marshaled his evidence more convincingly, I suspect he correctly concluded that the Court did "switch" under political pressure. (For a recent argument that the Court did not switch under political pressure see Barry Cushman, "Rethinking the New Deal Court," 80 *Virginia Law Review* 201 [1994]. I follow Leuchtenburg in finding Cushman's argument unpersuasive. Leuchtenburg, *Supreme Court Reborn,* at 317–18 n.95, 310–11 n.17, 231–34 [1995].) Though FDR remained silent about the Court while he sought reelection, the condemnation of *Morehead* in both party platforms showed widespread dissatisfaction with the Court. Roberts's protestation, in a later memorandum, that he changed his position on minimum wage laws before FDR announced Court Packing never rang true. Further, the justice's memorandum did not explain why he voted to sustain the taxing provisions of the Social Security Act in the spring of 1937, repudiating his own interpretation of the taxing power the prior year. Richard Friedman recently suggested that political pressures did not affect Hughes's votes. "As to Roberts, it is more difficult to be confident." Friedman does, however, also speculate Roberts and Hughes could have changed their minds independent of political pressure. (Friedman, "Switching Time and Other Thought Experiments: The Hughes Court and Constitutional Transformation," 142 *University of Pennsylvania Law Review* 1891, 1935, 1955–60 [1994]. Compare *Steward Machine Company* v. *Davis,* 301 U.S. 548 [1937], with *U.S.* v. *Butler.*) A recent article in the *Harvard Law Review* comes close to suggesting that Frankfurter himself may have made up the Roberts memorandum to justify the Court's legitimacy at a time when *Brown* was under attack for undermining the rule of law. (Michael Ariens, "A Thrice-Told Tale, or Felix the Cat," 107 *Harvard Law Review* 620, 645–51, 664, 669–75 [1994]. But see Richard Friedman, "A Reaffirmation: The Authenticity of the Roberts Memorandum, or Felix the Non-Forger," 142 *University of Pennsylvania Law Review* 1985 [1994], contending that the possibility Frankfurter forged the Roberts memorandum was "baseless" and that the original Roberts memorandum, which Ariens was unable to find, was almost certainly stolen from the Frankfurter Papers. Id.)

Other clues also point to the "switch in time" under pressure thesis. One of the Four Horsemen, Willis Van Devanter, did resign on May 18, 1937, the day the Senate Judiciary Committee was scheduled to vote on FDR's Court Packing Bill. "It was so perfectly timed as a strategic move that it seems unlikely to have been accidental," Robert Jackson remarked (Jackson is quoted in Alpheus Mason, *Harlan Fisk Stone: Pillar of the Law* 461 [1957]). According to Leuchtenburg, "Van Devanter's action was widely believed to have been the result of counsel from Senators Borah and Wheeler [two of the most vociferous opponents of Court Packing]. Borah lived in the same apartment house on Connecticut Avenue [as Van Devanter]; the two were on 'Hello, Bill' and 'Hello, Willis' terms." Though Borah specifically denied that accusation, I believe that Roberts switched sides under pressure from Chief Justice Hughes, and/or that Van Devanter did resign in the hope that FDR would drop Court Packing. What Van Devanter could not know was that FDR had promised the next vacancy on the Court to Sen. Joe Robinson, "a 65-year-old conservative. If appointing Robinson was to be the climax of his campaign to bring young, liberal men to the Court, the enterprise would turn out to be a fiasco. It seemed more necessary than ever to balance the expected Robinson appointment by creating vacancies for liberal justices" (Leuchtenburg, "Franklin D. Roosevelt's Supreme Count 'Packing' Plan," at 96–101). So FDR persevered, and as Leuchtenburg has pointed out, we too often forget that he was almost successful (Leuchtenburg, "FDR's Plan," at 673). Perhaps Hughes decided that continual 5–4 decisions would damage the Court's reputation, so he, with some help from Roberts, engineered the switch. Leuchtenburg quoted one columnist who said, "No insider doubts that the whole change of trend represented in the decisions was solely the work of Mr. Hughes. Everyone gives Mr.

Hughes credit for arguing Associate Justice Roberts into position" (Leuchtenburg, "Franklin D. Roosevelt's Supreme Court 'Packing' Plan," at 94).

As Ackerman has said, "considering its importance," the constitutional dimensions of the New Deal are "incredibly underresearched," and I am only guessing when I postulate that the Court switched under pressure and that 1937 might be considered a constitutional moment. (Ackerman, *We the People,* at 337 n.3.) The definitive answer, if a document ever existed which provided one and that document has not been stolen, lies in the archives. Surely Ackerman would benefit from asking William E. Leuchtenburg, who is writing a two-volume book about Court Packing based on extensive archival work, to read the relevant portions of the next installment of *We the People* in manuscript. (Leuchtenburg discussed his work in progress in *Supreme Court Reborn,* at ix.)

Though I am sympathetic to Ackerman's view of the New Deal, I am less persuaded by his account of the election of 1944 as triggering the triumph of a "new internationalism," which, as another exercise in "higher lawmaking," constituted an amendment to the treaty clause of the Constitution. According to Ackerman, between 1943 and 1947 the treaty clause—requiring approval of treaties by two-thirds of the Senate—became optional, and the Senate's "treaty-making monopoly" crumbled. Here it is the Senate, which made the "switch in time," acquiescing to the "birth of the congressional-executive agreement" without a formal constitutional amendment. "During and after the War, the President won the constitutional authority to substitute the agreement of [simple majorities of] both Houses for the traditional advice and consent of the Senate. . . . [T]he President and Congress modernized the treaty-making system by adapting the techniques they had used to transform domestic constitutional law in the 1930s. After all, it was these New Deal techniques that allowed the country to weather the economic storms that had destroyed democracy in Europe. It was therefore entirely appropriate to rely on them once again to express the will of the people rather than place undue pressure upon the peculiarly dysfunctional formalisms of Article V. Efficacy, democracy, legitimacy: who can ask for anything more?" (Bruce Ackerman and David Golove, "Is NAFTA Constitutional?" 108 *Harvard Law Review* 801, 883–88, 908–913, 897, 803, 916 [1995].) Without subscribing to Lawrence Tribe's sharp challenge to Ackerman and Golove's account, I would simply follow John Blum in suggesting that the 1944 election, and the subsequent events, expressed the "limits" of an internationalism that was too frequently reluctant, bland, and superficial (Blum, *V Was for Victory,* at 299, 302–23; Lawrence Tribe, "Taking Text and Structure Seriously: Reflections on Free-Form Method in Constitutional Interpretation," 108 *Harvard Law Review* 1223, 1249–78 [1995]).

71. Thomas Landry, "*Ackermania!*: Who *Are* We the People?" 47 *University of Miami Law Review* 267, 288 (1992); Powell, *Moral Tradition,* at 200; Terrance Sandalow, "Abstract Democracy," 9 *Constitutional Commentary* 309, 335 (1992); Pope, "Republican Moments," at 313 (quoting Avi Soifer; for Soifer's skepticism about the republican revival, see Soifer, *Company We Keep,* at 31, 55, 71, 198–99 n.3); Robert Lipkin, "Can American Constitutional Law Be Postmodern?" 42 *Buffalo Law Review* 318, 361, 369 (1994); Lawrence Lessig, "Understanding Changed Readings: Fidelity and Theory," 47 *Stanford Law Review* 395, 453–72 (1995); Michelman, "Law's Republic," at 1521. See also "Symposium on Bruce Ackerman's *We the People,*" 104 *Ethics* 445 (1994).

72. Ackerman, *We the People,* at 41; Ackerman, "Discovering the Constitution," at 1017–18 n.6.
73. Flaherty, "History 'Lite,' " at 585.
74. Wood, *Creation of the American Republic,* at 389 ("deliberately or evenly") (see also Rosemarie Zagarri, *A Woman's Dilemma: Mercy Otis Warren* 119–23 [1995]; Murray Dry, "The Debate over Ratification of the Constitution," in *The Blackwell Encyclopedia of the American Revolution,* ed. Jack Greene and J. R. Pole, 471, 479 [1991]; Peter Onuf, "Sovereignty," id. at 661, 665–67; Herbert Storing, *What the Anti-Federalists Were For* 13–14 [1981]; Stanley Elkins and Eric McKitrick, *The Age of Federalism: The Early American Republic, 1788–1800* 31–34 (1993). Richard Kay recognized Elkins and McKitrick's point in an article unfortunately entitled "The Illegality of the Constitution," 4 *Constitutional Commentary* 57 (1987).
75. Bruce Ackerman and Neal Katyal, "Our Unconventional Founding," 62 *University of Chicago Law Review* 475 (1995). One historian who might not feel that way is Jack Rakove, who builds on Ackerman's work to argue the Founders attempted "to establish new standards of constitutional legality as well as constitutional legitimacy." Rakove, *Original Meanings,* at 128–29.
76. Ahkil Amar, "Philadelphia Revisited: Amending the Constitution Outside Article V," 55 *University of Chicago Law Review* 1043, 1092, 1096 (1988) ("betrays" and "tinkers"); Amar, "The Consent of the Governed: Constitutional Amendment Outside the New Deal," 94 *Columbia Law Review* 457, 463 n.14 (1994) ("If James Madison's").
77. "[S]ophisticated theorists," "We the People," "about the People's," "The People retain," and "popular sovereignty amendment path" are from Amar, "Consent of the Governed," at 496, 462–63, 499–500 (emphasis in the original); the remaining quotations are from Amar, "Philadelphia Revisited," at 1048, 1076–77 (quoting Ely, *Democracy and Distrust,* at 11), 1085–86. Unlike Ackerman, Amar does not see Reconstruction as a constitutional convention. He believes that Congress made the best possible effort under the circumstances to conform with Article V. See Amar, "The Central Meaning of Republican Government: Popular Sovereignty, Majority Rule, and the Denominator Problem," 65 *University of Colorado Law Review* 749, 780–86 (1994). Amar there makes a lawyerly argument on behalf of the decision by the Reconstruction Congress to exclude from readmission to the Union those southern states that refused to ratify the Fifteenth Amendment, even though most northern states excluded blacks from political participation at the time. He argues it was consistent with the promise that the United States "shall guarantee to every State in this Union a Republican Form of Government" in Article IV, Section IV of the Constitution. According to Amar, "the subtle invocation of the people in the Republican Government Clause of Article IV reaffirms basic principles of popular sovereignty— of the right of the people to ordain and establish government, of their right to alter or abolish it, and of the centrality of popular majority rule, in these exercises of popular sovereignty." Id. at 762. For a sharp dissent, see G. Edward White, "Reading the Guarantee Clause," id. at 787, 801–2.
78. Amar, "Philadelphia Revisited," at 1096, 1102.
79. Tribe, "Text and Structure," at 1289–90, 1246; see also id. at 1286.
80. Id. at 1302–3, 1224–25, 1227 (emphasis in the original).

81. Rakove, *Original Meanings,* at 9–10. I draw my beliefs about Founders' intent from id. I have also benefited from Barber, *Constitution of Judicial Power,* who reads *Federalist 78* "to say that judicial review is not an instrument of judicial supremacy; it is rather an instrument of constitutional supremacy, and constitutional supremacy in turn means the supremacy of the people over their representatives." Barber suggests this reading is the "correct kind of originalism . . . what I call the classical theory of judicial review," and that the classical theory can be used "to defend Warren-style judicial activism." Id. at 249 n.22, x. I like Barber's thesis, though as the text suggests, I lack his certitude. (For an alternative reading of *Federalist 78,* grounding it in the contemporary context of the Federalists' need to reassure Antifederalists that the Constitution would protect states' rights, for example, see Sosin, *Aristocracy of the Long Robe,* at 257–69.) I do not, however, agree with Barber that modernism "choked off" classical theory or that a resurgent moral realism in philosophy should be enlisted in the service of reviving and defending the classical theory. Barber, *Constitution of Judicial Power,* at 108, 174–236. I have also admired Erwin Chemerinsky's sustained critique of the "majoritarian paradigm," though I would follow Barber in challenging "Chemerinsky's view . . . that after decades of powerful scholarly criticism of New Right originalism, critics of the New Right cannot avail themselves of originalist arguments." Id. at 251 n.40. See Chemerinsky, "Foreword: Vanishing Constitution," at 103. Also useful were Snowiss, *Judicial Review,* and Leslie Goldstein, *In Defense of the Text: Democracy and Constitutional Theory* (1991). Though her understanding of the permissible scope of judicial review at the time of *Federalist 78* is more limited than mine, Snowiss provides further support for the idea that in the late eighteenth century, it was "clearly understood" that no "effort . . . to eliminate judicial review's policy component" could succeed. Snowiss's own account of the origins of judicial review "supports the widely made criticism of interpretivism that text and intent cannot function for constitutional law as they do for ordinary law." Id. at 204–5, 214. Though I do not share her textualism, I also found Goldstein's discussion of popular sovereignty helpful. Goldstein, *In Defense of the Text,* at 67–84. For a discussion of the relationship between history and constitutional theory, see Kahn, *Legitimacy and History,* at 32, 189, 218–20.

82. Rakove, Book Review, at 227; Rakove, *Original Meanings,* at 346.

83. Elizabeth Mensch and Alan Freeman, "A Republican Agenda for Hobbesian America?" 41 *Florida Law Review* 581, 599 (1989).

84. Bruce Ackerman, "Higher Lawmaking," in *Responding to Imperfection: The Theory and Practice of Constitutional Amendment,* ed. Sanford Levinson, 63, 69 n.3, 72–73 n.4 (1995) (emphasis added). *Responding to Imperfection* is a valuable collection of essays on the idea of constitutional amendment. Another useful source is John Vile, *Contemporary Questions Surrounding the Constitutional Amending Process* (1993).

85. At times in the past, Ackerman also seemed to point to the difference between legality and legitimacy, though not as clearly as he and Katyal do in "Unconventional Founding." See Ackerman, "Discovering the Constitution," at 1061.

86. The book dedicated to Bickel was Bruce Ackerman, *Private Property and the Constitution* (1977); Ackerman, *We the People,* at 66.

87. Bruce Ackerman, "Robert Bork's Grand Inquisition," 99 *Yale Law Journal* 1419, 1437–38 (1990) (emphasis in the original).

EPILOGUE

1. Tom Wolfe, *Radical Chic and Mau-Mauing the Flak Catchers* 79 (1970).

2. Malcolm Feeley, "Hollow Hopes, Flypaper, and Metaphors," 17 *Law and Social Inquiry* 745, 758 (1992).

3. Nagel, *Judicial Power,* at 144; Kenneth Karst, *Law's Promise, Law's Expression: Visions of Power in the Politics of Race, Gender, and Religion* 9, 90–94, 202, 210–11 (1993).

4. For the argument that legislatures are not necessarily bastions of majoritarianism see, e.g., Chemerinsky, "Foreword: Vanishing Constitution," at 78–81. For the argument the Supreme Court has practiced majoritarianism see, e.g., Barry Friedman, "Dialogue and Judicial Review," 91 *Michigan Law Review* 577, 607 650, 678 (1993). But see Michael Solimine and James Walker, "The Supreme Court, Judicial Review, and the Public: Leadership versus Dialogue," 11 *Constitutional Commentary* 1, 2–5 (1994) (criticizing Friedman's use and interpretation of public opinion data).

5. Powell, *Moral Tradition,* at 7, 254.

6. Giradeau Spann, *Race against the Court: The Supreme Court and Minorities in Contemporary America* 4, 169 (1993); Elizabeth Mensch and Alan Freeman, *The Politics of Virtue: Is Abortion Debatable?* 126, 66 (1993) (as I indicated in the Prologue, I believe Garrow's book shows that the legalization of abortion would not have happened anyway; see Kalman, "The Promise and Peril of Privacy," 22 *Reviews in American History* 725, 728 [1994]); West, *Progressive Constitutionalism,* at 3–4, 286, 289; Linda Greenhouse, "Farewell to the Old Order in the Court: The Right Goes Activist and the Center Is a Void," *New York Times,* July 2, 1995, section 4, 1, 4; Collins and Skover, "Future of Liberal Legal Scholarship," at 212–37.

7. Harvard Sitkoff, *The Struggle for Black Equality 1954–1980* 24 (1981); Derrick Bell, "Racial Realism—After We're Gone: Prudent Speculations on America in a Post-Racial Age," in *Critical Race Theory,* at 2, 2–3 (Bickel's prediction).

8. David Garrow, "On Race, It's Thomas v. an Old Ideal," *New York Times,* July 2, 1995, section 4, 1, 5 (quoting Thomas, *Missouri v. Jenkins,* 115 S.Ct. 2038, 2065 [1995]).

9. Alex M. Johnson, "Bid Whist, Tonk, and *United States* v. *Fordice:* Why Intergrationism Fails African-Americans Again," 81 *California Law Review* 1401, 1409 (1993); Michael Klarman, "*Brown,* Racial Change, and the Civil Rights Movement," 80 *Virginia Law Review* 7, 85 (1994). The work of political scientist Del Dickson lends some support to the backlash hypothesis. Dickson, "State Court Defiance," at 1426. See also Mary Dudziak, "Desegregation as a Cold War Imperative," 41 *Stanford Law Review* 61 (1988); Stephan Lesher, *George Wallace: American Populist* 154–56, 169, 241 (1994).

10. Michael Klarman, "*Brown* v. *Board of Education:* Facts and Political Correctness," 80 *Virginia Law Review* 185, 186, 199 (1994). Charles McCurdy has described Klarman as an "indefatigable advocate" of process theory. McCurdy, "Foreword," id. at 1, 3.

11. Perhaps it will turn out that the decisive moment was the 1986 case of *Bowers* v. *Hardwick,* which many scholars say does not even "come out right," as at least they think *Roe* did.

12. Gerald Rosenberg, "*Brown* is Dead! Long Live *Brown!* The Endless Attempt to Canonize a Case," 80 *Virginia Law Review* 161 (1994); William Eskridge and Philip Frickey, "Foreword: Law as Equilibrium," 108 *Harvard Law Review* 26, 27–28, 87–88 (1994). But see Ely, "Another Such Victory," at 854 (suggesting that the legal process school has virtually disappeared). According to him, "in the writing of emerging academics, the position that judges should not invariably enforce their policy choices in the name of the Constitution has become not simply wrongheaded but essentially inconceivable." Further, they wrap their position "in gobbledygook—generally stressing how democratic it is to have an unelected judiciary superimposing 'our values' on the decisions of our elected representatives." Id. at 844 n.26, 865.

13. Levy, *Original Intent,* at 284–85.

14. McConnell, "Originalism and the Desegregation Decisions" at 1100. On the basis of his study of the congressional debate around statutory enforcement of the Fourteenth Amendment between 1868 and 1875, McConnell argued that the Fourteenth Amendment "was understood to outlaw public school segregation" during Reconstruction. Id. The McConnell article is cited by Justice Thomas in *Missouri* v. *Jenkins,* at 2065, and is challenged by Michael Klarman in "A Response to Professor McConnell," 81 *University of Virginia Law Review* 1881 (1995). But see Michael McConnell, "A Reply to Profesor Klarman," id. at 1937. (For other originalist scholarship by McConnell, see, e.g., McConnell, "The Origins and Historical Understanding of Free Exercise of Religion," 103 *Harvard Law Review* 1409 [1990]). The picture of the costumed justices accompanies Greenhouse, "Blowing the Dust off the Constitution," at 1.

Compare William Treanor, Note, "The Origins and Original Significance of the Just Compensation of the Fifth Amendment," 94 *Yale Law Journal* 695, 709 (1985) ("Madison was a liberal"), with Treanor, "Original Understanding of the Takings Clause." As Treanor explained, because he had originally seen liberalism and republicanism as "polar opposites" and understood the rise of the just compensation requirement "in revolutionary America and in the early republic as a product of the rise of liberalism" ("Original Understanding," at 826), he had explained the narrow scope of the takings clause on the grounds that Madison "intended it only to apply to direct physical takings of property by the federal government ("Origins," at 711). By 1995, historical scholarship stressing the interdependence of liberalism and republicanism and the persistence of republicanism pointed Treanor in a different direction in explaining the takings clauses in the Constitution and state constitutions. Now he asked, "why the takings clauses were limited to physical possession" and contended that "those limitations can best be understood as reflecting the republican idea that in a certain sphere the state should continue to control the definition of property interests." By Treanor's account, the takings principle reflected Madison's attempt to mediate between his liberal desire to protect property he believed vulnerable in the political process (such as property interests in land and slaves) and his republican realization government had to be empowered to promote the public good, even when the value of property was diminished in the process. ("Original Understanding," at 826, 854.)

Treanor used this conclusion to argue for the continued relevance of the original understanding of the takings clause. Noting that the Supreme Court, including its leading originalist Justice Scalia, had "essentially ignored" the original understanding, Treanor argued "that the framers' requirement of compensation for physical seizures but not for regulations might be based on a principle relevant to modern constitutional discourse." The Founders' rationale could be preserved. "[T]ranslating the original understanding into a contemporary takings jurisprudence means that courts today should protect those whose property interests are, given modern political realities, particularly unlikely to receive fair compensation from majoritarian decisionmakers"—those individuals threatened with confiscation of property by the military and minority communities "likely to receive more than their share of hazardous waste siting" because they "are not full participants in the political process." Thus instead of Epstein's version of takings jurisprudence, which would hold the New Deal unconstitutional, we would have a *Carolene Products* footnote 4 takings jurisprudence in the spirit of John Hart Ely. (Id. at 803, 810, 856, 865, 873.)

15. Smith, "Pursuit of Pragmatism," at 435 ("its counsel").

16. See Stephen Holmes, *Passions and Constraint: On the Theory of Liberal Democracy* 12, 236–66 (1995); Dvoretz, *Unvarnished Doctrine,* at 11–12, 31–32, 174, 26–27, 101–15; Sinopoli, *American Citizenship,* at 126; Michael Zuckert, *Natural Rights and the New Republicanism* xix, 151, 298–319 (1994). On Berlin, compare John Gray, *Isaiah Berlin* (1995) with Steven Lukes, "Liberalism Is Not Enough," *Times Literary Supplement,* February 20, 1995, 5, 10. One recent intellectual biography written by a historian that also insists on the continued validity of "liberal republicanism" is Lance Banning, *The Sacred Fire of Liberty: James Madison and the Founding of the Federal Republic* 9–10, 77, 368, 406 n. 2, 428 n. 3 (1995).

17. Powell, "Rules for Originalists," at 695.

18. Farber, "Legal Pragmatism," at 1339. I avoid here the question of whether continuity with the past is independently valuable in ensuring law's integrity. See Smith, "Pursuit of Pragmatism," at 413–20. As Smith says, "Pragmatists dislike and distrust theory. Pragmatists also like and need theory." Id. at 429. Substitute the word *history* for *theory.*

19. Bartlett, "Idea of Progress in Feminist Legal Thought," at 330.

20. Many friends have emphasized how much they hate the sound of the word *interdisciplinarity.* "[S]tory of the mutual enlightenment" is from Andrew Abbott, "History and Sociology: The Lost Synthesis," in *Engaging the Past: The Uses of History across the Social Sciences,* ed. Eric Monkkonen, 77, 104 (1994). On the lenders' reaction to interdisciplinary boundaries see, e.g., Flaherty, "History 'Lite,' " at 526 (law professors' history "at times falls below even the standards of undergraduate history writing"; see also id. at 551–52); Carolyn Heilbrun and Judith Resnik, "Convergences: Law, Literature, and Feminism," 99 *Yale Law Journal* 1913, 1926 (1990) (a tactful expression of concern from an English professor about the way law professors in the law and literature movement use literature); John Adams, "Anthropology and History in the 1980s," 12 *Journal of Interdisciplinary History* 253 (1981) (a complaint by an anthropologist that historians have thoughtlessly misused anthropology); and Barrett Rutman, "History and Anthropology: Clio's Dalliances," 19 *Historical Methods* 120, 121 (summer 1986) (a blunt reminder by a historian that "when Clio goes to bed with you it is for her own satisfaction, not yours").

21. William Twining, *Blackstone's Tower: The English Law School* 2, 37, 54, 57, 178 (1994). Neil Duxbury observes that a "distinctive style of academic soul-seeking al-

most seems to run in . . . [the] blood" of American law professors. Duxbury, *Patterns,* at 322. On the influence of German law professors and law professors on the Continent generally, see, e.g., R. C. Van Caenegem, *Judges, Legislators and Law Professors* 53–54, 62–65, 84–109 (1987).

22. Corwin is quoted in Richard Loss, "Introduction," in *Corwin on the Constitution: The Judiciary* 2: 19 (1987); Robert Gordon, "Introduction: J. Willard Hurst and the Common Law Tradition in American Legal Historiography," 10 *Law and Society Review* 9, 32 (1975).

23. Quoted in Gary Minda, "Jurisprudence at Century's End," 43 *Journal of Legal Education* 27, 28 (1993).

24. Alexander, "What We Do," at 1885; Winter, "Bull Durham," at 679; Getman, *Company of Scholars,* at 54; Richard Posner, "Goodbye to the Bluebook," 53 *University of Chicago Law Review* 1343, 1351 (1986); Pierre Schlag, "The Brilliant, the Curious and the Wrong," 39 *Stanford Law Review* 917, 925–26 (1987); Robert Post, "Legal Scholarship and the Practice of Law," 63 *University of Colorado Law Review* 615, 624 (1992) (see also Robert Post, "Lani Guinier, Joseph Biden, and the Vocation of Legal Scholarship," 11 *Constitutional Commentary* 185, 192 [1994]: "There is an ever-growing predominance of utopian scholarship in the law reviews; within elite schools utopian accents have almost become *de rigueur*"). Glendon is quoted in Sanford Levinson, "Judge Edwards' Indictment of 'Impractical' Scholars: The Need for a Bill of Particulars," 91 *Michigan Law Review* 2010, 2017 n.27 (1993).

25. Rubin, "Practice and Discourse," at 1853 ("irreducible normativity;"); Campos, "Advocacy and Scholarship," at 851 ("How does"); Richard Delgado, "Norms and Normal Science: Toward a Critique of Normativity in Legal Thought," 139 *University of Pennsylvania Law Review* 933, 960 (1991) ("all those *normativos*"); Elyce Zenoff, "I Have Seen the Enemy and They Are Us," 35 *Journal of Legal Education* 21, 21 (1986) (repeating complaints about law reviews); John Kester, Preliminary President's Report, April 23, 1963, Box 34, Folder 2, Hart Papers ("Hemingways"). For an especially vigorous denunciation of student-edited law reviews see Lloyd Cohen, "On Judging Whether to Publish Articles That Claim to Refute the Coase Theorem: Analogies to Bayesian Methods," 38 *Wayne Law Review* 18 (1991). For discussion of the normativity of legal scholarship see Symposium, "The Critique of Normativity," 139 *University of Pennsylvania Law Review* 801 (1991).

26. Pierre Schlag, "Normativity and the Politics of Form," 139 *University of Pennsylvania Law Review* 801, 870 (1991); Max Stier, Kelly Klaus, Dan Bagatell, and Jeffrey Rachlinski, "Law Review Usage and Suggestions for Improvement: A Survey of Attorneys, Professors and Judges," 44 *Stanford Law Review* 1467, 1483–85 (1992); Mark Tushnet, "An Essay on Rights," 62 *Texas Law Review* 1363, 1386 n.71 (1984). For the argument that legal scholarship still has an important impact on the profession see, e.g., Robert Gordon, "Lawyers, Scholars, and the 'Middle Ground,' " 91 *Michigan Law Review* 2075, 2084 (1993).

27. Erwin Griswold, Introduction, "Essays Commemorating the One Hundredth Anniversary of the *Harvard Law Review,*" 100 *Harvard Law Review* 728, 728 (1987) ("pithy comments" is from an unnumbered note the editors of the review apparently appended to Dean Griswold's introduction); Review, "Twenty Years with the Editors," 79 *Yale Law Journal* 1198, 1201 (1970) ("drumming his fingers"). It is possible that law reviews were never useful to most practitioners, but at least the first

issue of the *Harvard Law Review* expressed the hope "that the Review may be serviceable to the profession at large." Quoted in Kenneth Lasson, "Scholarship Amok: Excesses in the Pursuit of Truth and Tenure," 103 *Harvard Law Review* 926, 929 (1990). Further, compare the state of affairs now to that thirty-five years ago. "The philosophic distance travelled since I was a law student in the late 1950's may best be indicated by the fact that, among editors of the *Harvard Law Review* at that time, it was almost universally considered a publication blunder to have published the Hart-Fuller debate in a now classic issue of that review. I recall editors buttressing their views with letters from practitioners who threatened to terminate their subscriptions if the Review continued to waste its pages on jurisprudential nonsense instead of on articles designed to aid practitioner research on hot subjects of large law firm litigation." Anthony D'Amato, "Whither Jurisprudence?" 6 *Cardozo Law Review* 971, 982–83 (1985). Law review articles were expected to be useful to practitioners. When they were not, attorneys complained, and editors of law reviews took the complaints seriously. See "With the Editors," 71 *Harvard Law Review* vii (no. 6, 1958). Today law review articles are not expected to be useful to practitioners, who complain in vain. Two rave reviews of Lasson's article by practitioners appear in "Scholarship Admired: Responses to Professor Lasson," 103 *Harvard Law Review* 2085, 2085–86 (1991). Lasson has discussed some of the other favorable reviews he received in "On Letters and Law Reviews: A Jaded Rejoinder," 24 *Connecticut Law Review* 201, 203–4 (1991). See Harry Edwards, "The Growing Disjunction between Legal Education and the Legal Profession," 91 *Michigan Law Review* 34, 34, 37 (1992); Symposium on Legal Education, id. at 1921 (1993).

28. J. Cunyon Gordon, "A Response from the Visitor from Another Planet," 91 *Michigan Law Review* 1953, 1960 (1993) ("brain dead"); Stephen Griffin, "What Is Constitutional Theory? The Newer Theory and the Decline of the Learned Tradition," 62 *Southern California Law Review* 493, 496 (1989) ("esoteric"); Fisher, "Modern American Legal Theory," at 319, 364. But see Kahn *The Supreme Court and Constitutional Theory*, at 97, 101, 207, 211, 262 (making a strong case that Supreme Court justices do and should rely on scholars' constitutional theory. Kahn however, is skeptical about the value of the republican revival to the Court. Id. at 212, 247, 265. See also John S. Elson, "The Case against Legal Scholarship or, If the Professor Must Publish, Must the Profession Perish?" 39 *Journal of Legal Education* 343, 350 (1989) ("Few legal educators . . . seem disturbed by the growing gap between the world of practice and scholarship"). For discussion of whether law professors influence judges see, e.g., Patricia Wald, "Teaching the Trade: An Appellate Judge's View of Practice-Oriented Legal Education," 36 *Journal of Legal Education* 35, 42 (1986); Lea Brilmayer, "Do We Really All Believe That Judges Should Be Influenced by Political Pressure?" 61 *University of Colorado Law Review* 703, 704 (1990); Frank Easterbrook, "What's So Special about Judges?" id. at 773, 779; Frederick Schauer, "The Authority of Legal Scholarship," 139 *University of Pennsylvania Law Review* 1003, 1022 (1991); Sanford Levinson, "The Audience for Constitutional Meta-Theory (or Why, and to Whom, Do I Write the Things I Do?)" 63 *University of Colorado Law Review* 389 (1992); David Ebel, "Why and to Whom Do Constitutional Meta-Theorists Write?—A Response to Professor Levinson," id. at 409; Pierre Schlag, "Writing for Judges," id. at 419, 421. For a measurement of reputation by citation see, e.g., Richard Posner, *Cardozo: A Study in Reputation* (1990).

29. Hirshman, "Virtue of Liberality," at 1034 ("legalarboraphobia"); Collier, "Humanistic Theory," at 205. While she observes "a persistent undercurrent [of] . . . concern" among legal academics about the influence of their work on "the development of the law" today, Judge Judith Kaye reminds us "that scholarly law review articles going back more than half a century have been devoted to measuring the impact of scholarly law review articles." Kaye, "One Judge's View of Academic Law Review Writing," 39 *Journal of Legal Education* 313, 314–15 (1989).

30. Collier, "Humanistic Theory," at 205. For discussion of Prince Charles, the pope, and postmodernity, see Harvey, *Condition of Postmodernity,* at 41.

31. Brest, "Plus Ça Change," at 1950; Schlegel, *American Legal Realism,* at 257; Pierre Schlag, " 'Le Hors de Texte, C'est Moi': The Politics of Form and the Domestication of Deconstruction," 11 *Cardozo Law Review* 1631, 1656 (1990); Fish, "Almost Pragmatism," at 1470. Charles Collier would also argue that law professors have not yet really confronted other disciplines and that they will not be able to find the intellectual authority they seek in them. See Collier, "Interdisciplinary Legal Scholarship in Search of a Paradigm," 42 *Duke Law Journal* 840, 842, 848 (1993); Collier, "Intellectual Authority and Institutional Authority," 42 *Journal of Legal Education* 151 (1992).

32. Rorty is quoted in Levinson, "Law as Literature," at 401 n.117, 115; Lyotard in Harvey, *Condition of Postmodernity,* at 52. For a similar reading of Derrida as committed to "a transcendental norm of justice" see J. M. Balkin, "Transcendental Deconstruction, Transcendent Justice," 92 *Michigan Law Review* 1131, 1174, 1185–86 (1994). At a colloquium at Cardozo Law School on "deconstruction and the possibility of justice" at which Derrida gave the keynote address he said, "I tried to demonstrate that justice, in the most unheard-of-sense of this word, was the undeconstructible itself, thus another name of deconstruction (deconstruction? deconstruction *is* justice). This supposed a decisive distinction and one of incalculable scope between law and justice." Jacques Derrida, "The Time Is Out of Joint," in *Deconstruction Is/in America,* 14, 31. See Derrida, "Force of Law: The Mystical Foundation of Authority," 11 *Cardozo Law Review* 919, 945 (1990).

33. Jennifer Wicke, "Postmodern Identity and the Legal Subject," 62 *University of Colorado Law Review* 455, 455–56, 458, 463 (1991). For an eloquent appeal for modernism in law and against postmodernism by a law professor see Luban, *Legal Modernism,* at 8–13, 80, 380.

34. Jerome Frank, *Law and the Modern Mind* 60 (1930) ("Word-Magic"); Thomas Bergin, "The Law Teacher: A Man Divided against Himself," 54 *Virginia Law Review* 637, 638 (1968). For a discussion of the gap between law professors and students, see Kronman, *Lost Lawyer,* at 265–68.

35. Paul Carrington, "Butterfly Effects: The Possibilities of Law Teaching in a Democracy," 41 *Duke Law Journal* 741, 789 (1992) ("colonial outpost"). For a discussion of the reception of doctrinal scholarship see, e.g., Posner, *Overcoming Law,* at 84–95.

36. Pauline Rosenau, *Post-Modernism and the Social Sciences: Insight, Inroads, and Intrusions* 124 (1992) ("Legal theory"); Drucilla Cornell, "Toward a Modern/Postmodern Reconstruction of Ethics," 133 *University of Pennsylvania Law Review* 291, 351 n.330 (1985) ("there is much"). Cornell has high hopes for Barthian readings: "Lawyers and law professors would no longer be able to justify running away from

their moral responsibilities in the name of some unjustifiable technical mumbo-jumbo. Moral debate would find its way back into the law schools. Idealistic lawyers committed to social change would benefit, because they would see that they were not trapped under the leaden weight of a tradition they believed to perpetuate injustice. It would become possible to see lawyering as a romantic profession in which the lawyer can play a significant role in shaping our moral discourse." See also David Kennedy, "Some Comments on Law and Postmodernism: A Symposium Response to Professor Jennifer Wicke," 62 *University of Colorado Law Review* 475, 481 (1991): "I think the idea here is a division of labor in which the lawyers would be responsible for holding it all together against all odds while the culture people took it apart. I think that it is a bad job, and I do not think we can do it. Not only that, I think it is too late. It is the lawyers, after all, who have come over to postmodernism, joined contemporary culture, only to encounter strange exhortations to keep the machinery of modernity well oiled. . . . [Law] does not have the qualities of fixity, order, meaning, or identity we might hope for. We lawyers have been in vertigo about the loss for some time, but so far no one has been able to put things back together."

INDEX

Abel, Richard, 289n51
Abortion, 6–7, 86, 198–201, 205, 207, 232
Abrams v. *United States (1919)*, 170
Ackerman, Bruce, 40, 135, 155, 183, 235, 249n15, 310n65, 346n55, 348n70; influenced by republican revival, 8, 132; law school background of, 50, 61; on housing codes, 65, 78; as Rawls enthusiast, 66–68; *Reconstructing American Law,* 127; on study of history, 143, 229; *We the People,* 212–221; "Our Unconventional Founding," 222; on legality and legitimacy, 222–228
Activism. *See* Judicial activism
Adams, John, 174, 177, 211, 261n42
Adams, Samuel, 177
Affirmative action, 87–88
African Americans, 177; and segregation, 27–29, 34, 73, 233–234;

application of Fourteenth Amendment, 27, 34, 73, 314n13; deprived of legal equality, 205–206; leaders, 332n25
Albert, Lee, 289n51
Alexander, Gregory, 9, 143, 177
Alexander, Larry, 241
Amar, Ahkil, 8, 189, 202, 203, 221–229, 235
Amendments, constitutional, 212–213, 220, 222–224, 226–227
American Civil Liberties Union, 133
American Historical Association, 60, 139, 142, 185–186, 194
American Journal of Legal History, 68
American Revolution. *See* Revolutionary War
American Society for Legal History, 75
Anglicans, 9, 186
Anthropology, 102–104, 110, 125–126, 139–140